50% OFF
PSAT Test Prep Course!

By Mometrix

Dear Customer,

We consider it an honor and a privilege that you chose our PSAT Study Guide. As a way of showing our appreciation and to help us better serve you, we are offering **50% off our online PSAT Prep Course.** Many PSAT courses are needlessly expensive and don't deliver enough value. With our course, you get access to the best PSAT prep material, and you only pay half price.

We have structured our online course to perfectly complement your printed study guide. The PSAT Test Prep Course contains **in-depth lessons** that cover all the most important topics, over **1100+ practice questions** to ensure you feel prepared, more than **600+ flashcards** for studying on the go, and over **200 instructional videos.**

Online PSAT Prep Course

Topics Covered:

- Reading
  - Information and Ideas
  - Making and Evaluating Predictions
  - Drawing Conclusions and Summarizing
- Writing
  - Writing Essays
  - Parts of Speech
  - Common Sentence Errors
- Mathematics
  - Foundational Math Concepts
  - Problem Solving and Data Analysis
  - Algebra and Advanced Math
- And More!

Course Features:

- PSAT Study Guide
  - Get access to content from the best reviewed study guide available.
- Track Your Progress
  - Our customized course allows you to check off content you have studied or feel confident with.
- 10 Full-Length Practice Tests
  - With 1400+ practice questions and lesson reviews, you can test yourself again and again to build confidence.
- PSAT Flashcards
  - Our course includes a flashcard mode consisting of over 450 content cards to help you study.

To receive this discount, visit us at mometrix.com/university/psat or simply scan this QR code with your smartphone. At the checkout page, enter the discount code: **PSAT50OFF**

If you have any questions or concerns, please contact us at support@mometrix.com.

FREE Study Skills Videos/DVD Offer

Dear Customer,

Thank you for your purchase from Mometrix! We consider it an honor and a privilege that you have purchased our product and we want to ensure your satisfaction.

As part of our ongoing effort to meet the needs of test takers, we have developed a set of Study Skills Videos that we would like to give you for FREE. These videos cover our *best practices* for getting ready for your exam, from how to use our study materials to how to best prepare for the day of the test.

All that we ask is that you email us with feedback that would describe your experience so far with our product. Good, bad, or indifferent, we want to know what you think!

To get your FREE Study Skills Videos, you can use the **QR code** below, or send us an **email** at studyvideos@mometrix.com with *FREE VIDEOS* in the subject line and the following information in the body of the email:

- The name of the product you purchased.
- Your product rating on a scale of 1-5, with 5 being the highest rating.
- Your feedback. It can be long, short, or anything in between. We just want to know your impressions and experience so far with our product. (Good feedback might include how our study material met your needs and ways we might be able to make it even better. You could highlight features that you found helpful or features that you think we should add.)

If you have any questions or concerns, please don't hesitate to contact me directly.

Thanks again!

Sincerely,

Jay Willis
Vice President
jay.willis@mometrix.com
1-800-673-8175

PSAT

Prep Book 2022 and 2023

2 Full-Length Practice Tests

Secrets Study Guide for the College Board PSAT, Step-by-Step Video Tutorials

5th Edition

Written and edited by the Mometrix College Admissions Test Team

Printed in the United States of America

This paper meets the requirements of ANSI/NISO Z39.48-1992 (Permanence of Paper).

Paperback
ISBN 13: 978-1-5167-2110-8
ISBN 10: 1-5167-2110-1

Dear Future Exam Success Story

First of all, **THANK YOU** for purchasing Mometrix study materials!

Second, congratulations! You are one of the few determined test-takers who are committed to doing whatever it takes to excel on your exam. **You have come to the right place.** We developed these study materials with one goal in mind: to deliver you the information you need in a format that's concise and easy to use.

In addition to optimizing your guide for the content of the test, we've outlined our recommended steps for breaking down the preparation process into small, attainable goals so you can make sure you stay on track.

We've also analyzed the entire test-taking process, identifying the most common pitfalls and showing how you can overcome them and be ready for any curveball the test throws you.

Standardized testing is one of the biggest obstacles on your road to success, which only increases the importance of doing well in the high-pressure, high-stakes environment of test day. Your results on this test could have a significant impact on your future, and this guide provides the information and practical advice to help you achieve your full potential on test day.

Your success is our success

We would love to hear from you! If you would like to share the story of your exam success or if you have any questions or comments in regard to our products, please contact us at **800-673-8175** or **support@mometrix.com**.

Thanks again for your business and we wish you continued success!

Sincerely,
The Mometrix Test Preparation Team

Need more help? Check out our flashcards at:
http://mometrixflashcards.com/PSAT

TABLE OF CONTENTS

Introduction

Thank you for purchasing this resource! You have made the choice to prepare yourself for a test that could have a huge impact on your future, and this guide is designed to help you be fully ready for test day. Obviously, it's important to have a solid understanding of the test material, but you also need to be prepared for the unique environment and stressors of the test, so that you can perform to the best of your abilities.

For this purpose, the first section that appears in this guide is the **Secret Keys**. We've devoted countless hours to meticulously researching what works and what doesn't, and we've boiled down our findings to the five most impactful steps you can take to improve your performance on the test. We start at the beginning with study planning and move through the preparation process, all the way to the testing strategies that will help you get the most out of what you know when you're finally sitting in front of the test.

We recommend that you start preparing for your test as far in advance as possible. However, if you've bought this guide as a last-minute study resource and only have a few days before your test, we recommend that you skip over the first two Secret Keys since they address a long-term study plan.

If you struggle with **test anxiety**, we strongly encourage you to check out our recommendations for how you can overcome it. Test anxiety is a formidable foe, but it can be beaten, and we want to make sure you have the tools you need to defeat it.

Secret Key #1 – Plan Big, Study Small

There's a lot riding on your performance. If you want to ace this test, you're going to need to keep your skills sharp and the material fresh in your mind. You need a plan that lets you review everything you need to know while still fitting in your schedule. We'll break this strategy down into three categories.

Information Organization

Start with the information you already have: the official test outline. From this, you can make a complete list of all the concepts you need to cover before the test. Organize these concepts into groups that can be studied together, and create a list of any related vocabulary you need to learn so you can brush up on any difficult terms. You'll want to keep this vocabulary list handy once you actually start studying since you may need to add to it along the way.

Time Management

Once you have your set of study concepts, decide how to spread them out over the time you have left before the test. Break your study plan into small, clear goals so you have a manageable task for each day and know exactly what you're doing. Then just focus on one small step at a time. When you manage your time this way, you don't need to spend hours at a time studying. Studying a small block of content for a short period each day helps you retain information better and avoid stressing over how much you have left to do. You can relax knowing that you have a plan to cover everything in time. In order for this strategy to be effective though, you have to start studying early and stick to your schedule. Avoid the exhaustion and futility that comes from last-minute cramming!

Study Environment

The environment you study in has a big impact on your learning. Studying in a coffee shop, while probably more enjoyable, is not likely to be as fruitful as studying in a quiet room. It's important to keep distractions to a minimum. You're only planning to study for a short block of time, so make the most of it. Don't pause to check your phone or get up to find a snack. It's also important to **avoid multitasking**. Research has consistently shown that multitasking will make your studying dramatically less effective. Your study area should also be comfortable and well-lit so you don't have the distraction of straining your eyes or sitting on an uncomfortable chair.

The time of day you study is also important. You want to be rested and alert. Don't wait until just before bedtime. Study when you'll be most likely to comprehend and remember. Even better, if you know what time of day your test will be, set that time aside for study. That way your brain will be used to working on that subject at that specific time and you'll have a better chance of recalling information.

Finally, it can be helpful to team up with others who are studying for the same test. Your actual studying should be done in as isolated an environment as possible, but the work of organizing the information and setting up the study plan can be divided up. In between study sessions, you can discuss with your teammates the concepts that you're all studying and quiz each other on the details. Just be sure that your teammates are as serious about the test as you are. If you find that your study time is being replaced with social time, you might need to find a new team.

Secret Key #2 – Make Your Studying Count

You're devoting a lot of time and effort to preparing for this test, so you want to be absolutely certain it will pay off. This means doing more than just reading the content and hoping you can remember it on test day. It's important to make every minute of study count. There are two main areas you can focus on to make your studying count.

Retention

It doesn't matter how much time you study if you can't remember the material. You need to make sure you are retaining the concepts. To check your retention of the information you're learning, try recalling it at later times with minimal prompting. Try carrying around flashcards and glance at one or two from time to time or ask a friend who's also studying for the test to quiz you.

To enhance your retention, look for ways to put the information into practice so that you can apply it rather than simply recalling it. If you're using the information in practical ways, it will be much easier to remember. Similarly, it helps to solidify a concept in your mind if you're not only reading it to yourself but also explaining it to someone else. Ask a friend to let you teach them about a concept you're a little shaky on (or speak aloud to an imaginary audience if necessary). As you try to summarize, define, give examples, and answer your friend's questions, you'll understand the concepts better and they will stay with you longer. Finally, step back for a big picture view and ask yourself how each piece of information fits with the whole subject. When you link the different concepts together and see them working together as a whole, it's easier to remember the individual components.

Finally, practice showing your work on any multi-step problems, even if you're just studying. Writing out each step you take to solve a problem will help solidify the process in your mind, and you'll be more likely to remember it during the test.

Modality

Modality simply refers to the means or method by which you study. Choosing a study modality that fits your own individual learning style is crucial. No two people learn best in exactly the same way, so it's important to know your strengths and use them to your advantage.

For example, if you learn best by visualization, focus on visualizing a concept in your mind and draw an image or a diagram. Try color-coding your notes, illustrating them, or creating symbols that will trigger your mind to recall a learned concept. If you learn best by hearing or discussing information, find a study partner who learns the same way or read aloud to yourself. Think about how to put the information in your own words. Imagine that you are giving a lecture on the topic and record yourself so you can listen to it later.

For any learning style, flashcards can be helpful. Organize the information so you can take advantage of spare moments to review. Underline key words or phrases. Use different colors for different categories. Mnemonic devices (such as creating a short list in which every item starts with the same letter) can also help with retention. Find what works best for you and use it to store the information in your mind most effectively and easily.

Secret Key #3 – Practice the Right Way

Your success on test day depends not only on how many hours you put into preparing, but also on whether you prepared the right way. It's good to check along the way to see if your studying is paying off. One of the most effective ways to do this is by taking practice tests to evaluate your progress. Practice tests are useful because they show exactly where you need to improve. Every time you take a practice test, pay special attention to these three groups of questions:

- The questions you got wrong
- The questions you had to guess on, even if you guessed right
- The questions you found difficult or slow to work through

This will show you exactly what your weak areas are, and where you need to devote more study time. Ask yourself why each of these questions gave you trouble. Was it because you didn't understand the material? Was it because you didn't remember the vocabulary? Do you need more repetitions on this type of question to build speed and confidence? Dig into those questions and figure out how you can strengthen your weak areas as you go back to review the material.

Additionally, many practice tests have a section explaining the answer choices. It can be tempting to read the explanation and think that you now have a good understanding of the concept. However, an explanation likely only covers part of the question's broader context. Even if the explanation makes perfect sense, **go back and investigate** every concept related to the question until you're positive you have a thorough understanding.

As you go along, keep in mind that the practice test is just that: practice. Memorizing these questions and answers will not be very helpful on the actual test because it is unlikely to have any of the same exact questions. If you only know the right answers to the sample questions, you won't be prepared for the real thing. **Study the concepts** until you understand them fully, and then you'll be able to answer any question that shows up on the test.

It's important to wait on the practice tests until you're ready. If you take a test on your first day of study, you may be overwhelmed by the amount of material covered and how much you need to learn. Work up to it gradually.

On test day, you'll need to be prepared for answering questions, managing your time, and using the test-taking strategies you've learned. It's a lot to balance, like a mental marathon that will have a big impact on your future. Like training for a marathon, you'll need to start slowly and work your way up. When test day arrives, you'll be ready.

Start with the strategies you've read in the first two Secret Keys—plan your course and study in the way that works best for you. If you have time, consider using multiple study resources to get different approaches to the same concepts. It can be helpful to see difficult concepts from more than one angle. Then find a good source for practice tests. Many times, the test website will suggest potential study resources or provide sample tests.

Practice Test Strategy

If you're able to find at least three practice tests, we recommend this strategy:

UNTIMED AND OPEN-BOOK PRACTICE

Take the first test with no time constraints and with your notes and study guide handy. Take your time and focus on applying the strategies you've learned.

TIMED AND OPEN-BOOK PRACTICE

Take the second practice test open-book as well, but set a timer and practice pacing yourself to finish in time.

TIMED AND CLOSED-BOOK PRACTICE

Take any other practice tests as if it were test day. Set a timer and put away your study materials. Sit at a table or desk in a quiet room, imagine yourself at the testing center, and answer questions as quickly and accurately as possible.

Keep repeating timed and closed-book tests on a regular basis until you run out of practice tests or it's time for the actual test. Your mind will be ready for the schedule and stress of test day, and you'll be able to focus on recalling the material you've learned.

Secret Key #4 – Pace Yourself

Once you're fully prepared for the material on the test, your biggest challenge on test day will be managing your time. Just knowing that the clock is ticking can make you panic even if you have plenty of time left. Work on pacing yourself so you can build confidence against the time constraints of the exam. Pacing is a difficult skill to master, especially in a high-pressure environment, so **practice is vital**.

Set time expectations for your pace based on how much time is available. For example, if a section has 60 questions and the time limit is 30 minutes, you know you have to average 30 seconds or less per question in order to answer them all. Although 30 seconds is the hard limit, set 25 seconds per question as your goal, so you reserve extra time to spend on harder questions. When you budget extra time for the harder questions, you no longer have any reason to stress when those questions take longer to answer.

Don't let this time expectation distract you from working through the test at a calm, steady pace, but keep it in mind so you don't spend too much time on any one question. Recognize that taking extra time on one question you don't understand may keep you from answering two that you do understand later in the test. If your time limit for a question is up and you're still not sure of the answer, mark it and move on, and come back to it later if the time and the test format allow. If the testing format doesn't allow you to return to earlier questions, just make an educated guess; then put it out of your mind and move on.

On the easier questions, be careful not to rush. It may seem wise to hurry through them so you have more time for the challenging ones, but it's not worth missing one if you know the concept and just didn't take the time to read the question fully. Work efficiently but make sure you understand the question and have looked at all of the answer choices, since more than one may seem right at first.

Even if you're paying attention to the time, you may find yourself a little behind at some point. You should speed up to get back on track, but do so wisely. Don't panic; just take a few seconds less on each question until you're caught up. Don't guess without thinking, but do look through the answer choices and eliminate any you know are wrong. If you can get down to two choices, it is often worthwhile to guess from those. Once you've chosen an answer, move on and don't dwell on any that you skipped or had to hurry through. If a question was taking too long, chances are it was one of the harder ones, so you weren't as likely to get it right anyway.

On the other hand, if you find yourself getting ahead of schedule, it may be beneficial to slow down a little. The more quickly you work, the more likely you are to make a careless mistake that will affect your score. You've budgeted time for each question, so don't be afraid to spend that time. Practice an efficient but careful pace to get the most out of the time you have.

Secret Key #5 – Have a Plan for Guessing

When you're taking the test, you may find yourself stuck on a question. Some of the answer choices seem better than others, but you don't see the one answer choice that is obviously correct. What do you do?

The scenario described above is very common, yet most test takers have not effectively prepared for it. Developing and practicing a plan for guessing may be one of the single most effective uses of your time as you get ready for the exam.

In developing your plan for guessing, there are three questions to address:

- When should you start the guessing process?
- How should you narrow down the choices?
- Which answer should you choose?

When to Start the Guessing Process

Unless your plan for guessing is to select C every time (which, despite its merits, is not what we recommend), you need to leave yourself enough time to apply your answer elimination strategies. Since you have a limited amount of time for each question, that means that if you're going to give yourself the best shot at guessing correctly, you have to decide quickly whether or not you will guess.

Of course, the best-case scenario is that you don't have to guess at all, so first, see if you can answer the question based on your knowledge of the subject and basic reasoning skills. Focus on the key words in the question and try to jog your memory of related topics. Give yourself a chance to bring the knowledge to mind, but once you realize that you don't have (or you can't access) the knowledge you need to answer the question, it's time to start the guessing process.

It's almost always better to start the guessing process too early than too late. It only takes a few seconds to remember something and answer the question from knowledge. Carefully eliminating wrong answer choices takes longer. Plus, going through the process of eliminating answer choices can actually help jog your memory.

Summary: Start the guessing process as soon as you decide that you can't answer the question based on your knowledge.

How to Narrow Down the Choices

The next chapter in this book (**Test-Taking Strategies**) includes a wide range of strategies for how to approach questions and how to look for answer choices to eliminate. You will definitely want to read those carefully, practice them, and figure out which ones work best for you. Here though, we're going to address a mindset rather than a particular strategy.

Your odds of guessing an answer correctly depend on how many options you are choosing from.

Number of options left	5	4	3	2	1
Odds of guessing correctly	20%	25%	33%	50%	100%

You can see from this chart just how valuable it is to be able to eliminate incorrect answers and make an educated guess, but there are two things that many test takers do that cause them to miss out on the benefits of guessing:

- Accidentally eliminating the correct answer
- Selecting an answer based on an impression

We'll look at the first one here, and the second one in the next section.

To avoid accidentally eliminating the correct answer, we recommend a thought exercise called **the $5 challenge**. In this challenge, you only eliminate an answer choice from contention if you are willing to bet $5 on it being wrong. Why $5? Five dollars is a small but not insignificant amount of money. It's an amount you could afford to lose but wouldn't want to throw away. And while losing $5 once might not hurt too much, doing it twenty times will set you back $100. In the same way, each small decision you make—eliminating a choice here, guessing on a question there—won't by itself impact your score very much, but when you put them all together, they can make a big difference. By holding each answer choice elimination decision to a higher standard, you can reduce the risk of accidentally eliminating the correct answer.

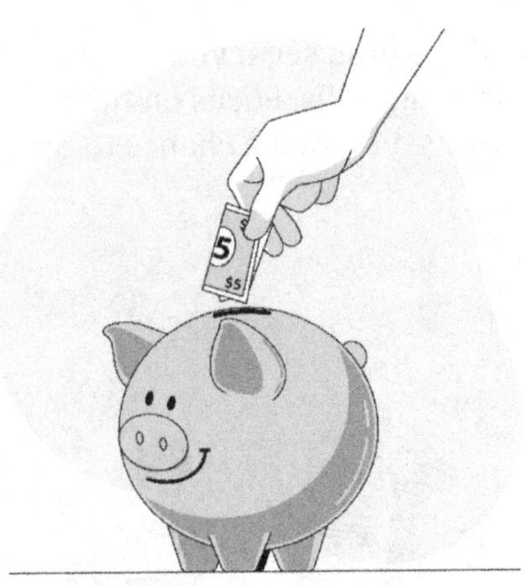

The $5 challenge can also be applied in a positive sense: If you are willing to bet $5 that an answer choice *is* correct, go ahead and mark it as correct.

Summary: Only eliminate an answer choice if you are willing to bet $5 that it is wrong.

Which Answer to Choose

You're taking the test. You've run into a hard question and decided you'll have to guess. You've eliminated all the answer choices you're willing to bet $5 on. Now you have to pick an answer. Why do we even need to talk about this? Why can't you just pick whichever one you feel like when the time comes?

The answer to these questions is that if you don't come into the test with a plan, you'll rely on your impression to select an answer choice, and if you do that, you risk falling into a trap. The test writers know that everyone who takes their test will be guessing on some of the questions, so they intentionally write wrong answer choices to seem plausible. You still have to pick an answer though, and if the wrong answer choices are designed to look right, how can you ever be sure that you're not falling for their trap? The best solution we've found to this dilemma is to take the decision out of your hands entirely. Here is the process we recommend:

Once you've eliminated any choices that you are confident (willing to bet $5) are wrong, select the first remaining choice as your answer.

Whether you choose to select the first remaining choice, the second, or the last, the important thing is that you use some preselected standard. Using this approach guarantees that you will not be enticed into selecting an answer choice that looks right, because you are not basing your decision on how the answer choices look.

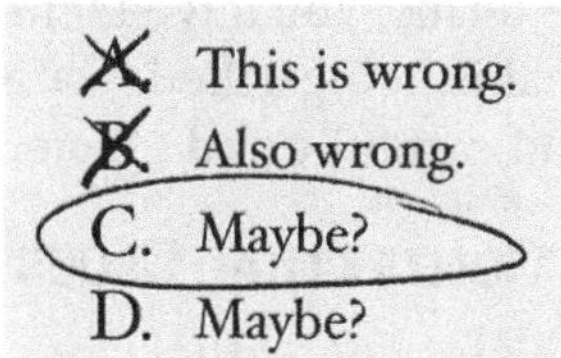

This is not meant to make you question your knowledge. Instead, it is to help you recognize the difference between your knowledge and your impressions. There's a huge difference between thinking an answer is right because of what you know, and thinking an answer is right because it looks or sounds like it should be right.

Summary: To ensure that your selection is appropriately random, make a predetermined selection from among all answer choices you have not eliminated.

Test-Taking Strategies

This section contains a list of test-taking strategies that you may find helpful as you work through the test. By taking what you know and applying logical thought, you can maximize your chances of answering any question correctly!

It is very important to realize that every question is different and every person is different: no single strategy will work on every question, and no single strategy will work for every person. That's why we've included all of them here, so you can try them out and determine which ones work best for different types of questions and which ones work best for you.

Question Strategies

⊘ Read Carefully

Read the question and the answer choices carefully. Don't miss the question because you misread the terms. You have plenty of time to read each question thoroughly and make sure you understand what is being asked. Yet a happy medium must be attained, so don't waste too much time. You must read carefully and efficiently.

⊘ Contextual Clues

Look for contextual clues. If the question includes a word you are not familiar with, look at the immediate context for some indication of what the word might mean. Contextual clues can often give you all the information you need to decipher the meaning of an unfamiliar word. Even if you can't determine the meaning, you may be able to narrow down the possibilities enough to make a solid guess at the answer to the question.

⊘ Prefixes

If you're having trouble with a word in the question or answer choices, try dissecting it. Take advantage of every clue that the word might include. Prefixes can be a huge help. Usually, they allow you to determine a basic meaning. *Pre-* means before, *post-* means after, *pro-* is positive, *de-* is negative. From prefixes, you can get an idea of the general meaning of the word and try to put it into context.

⊘ Hedge Words

Watch out for critical hedge words, such as *likely, may, can, sometimes, often, almost, mostly, usually, generally, rarely,* and *sometimes.* Question writers insert these hedge phrases to cover every possibility. Often an answer choice will be wrong simply because it leaves no room for exception. Be on guard for answer choices that have definitive words such as *exactly* and *always.*

⊘ Switchback Words

Stay alert for *switchbacks.* These are the words and phrases frequently used to alert you to shifts in thought. The most common switchback words are *but, although,* and *however.* Others include *nevertheless, on the other hand, even though, while, in spite of, despite,* and *regardless of.* Switchback words are important to catch because they can change the direction of the question or an answer choice.

☑ Face Value

When in doubt, use common sense. Accept the situation in the problem at face value. Don't read too much into it. These problems will not require you to make wild assumptions. If you have to go beyond creativity and warp time or space in order to have an answer choice fit the question, then you should move on and consider the other answer choices. These are normal problems rooted in reality. The applicable relationship or explanation may not be readily apparent, but it is there for you to figure out. Use your common sense to interpret anything that isn't clear.

Answer Choice Strategies

☑ Answer Selection

The most thorough way to pick an answer choice is to identify and eliminate wrong answers until only one is left, then confirm it is the correct answer. Sometimes an answer choice may immediately seem right, but be careful. The test writers will usually put more than one reasonable answer choice on each question, so take a second to read all of them and make sure that the other choices are not equally obvious. As long as you have time left, it is better to read every answer choice than to pick the first one that looks right without checking the others.

☑ Answer Choice Families

An answer choice family consists of two (in rare cases, three) answer choices that are very similar in construction and cannot all be true at the same time. If you see two answer choices that are direct opposites or parallels, one of them is usually the correct answer. For instance, if one answer choice says that quantity *x* increases and another either says that quantity *x* decreases (opposite) or says that quantity *y* increases (parallel), then those answer choices would fall into the same family. An answer choice that doesn't match the construction of the answer choice family is more likely to be incorrect. Most questions will not have answer choice families, but when they do appear, you should be prepared to recognize them.

☑ Eliminate Answers

Eliminate answer choices as soon as you realize they are wrong, but make sure you consider all possibilities. If you are eliminating answer choices and realize that the last one you are left with is also wrong, don't panic. Start over and consider each choice again. There may be something you missed the first time that you will realize on the second pass.

☑ Avoid Fact Traps

Don't be distracted by an answer choice that is factually true but doesn't answer the question. You are looking for the choice that answers the question. Stay focused on what the question is asking for so you don't accidentally pick an answer that is true but incorrect. Always go back to the question and make sure the answer choice you've selected actually answers the question and is not merely a true statement.

☑ Extreme Statements

In general, you should avoid answers that put forth extreme actions as standard practice or proclaim controversial ideas as established fact. An answer choice that states the "process should be used in certain situations, if..." is much more likely to be correct than one that states the "process should be discontinued completely." The first is a calm rational statement and doesn't even make a definitive, uncompromising stance, using a hedge word *if* to provide wiggle room, whereas the second choice is far more extreme.

☑ Benchmark

As you read through the answer choices and you come across one that seems to answer the question well, mentally select that answer choice. This is not your final answer, but it's the one that will help you evaluate the other answer choices. The one that you selected is your benchmark or standard for judging each of the other answer choices. Every other answer choice must be compared to your benchmark. That choice is correct until proven otherwise by another answer choice beating it. If you find a better answer, then that one becomes your new benchmark. Once you've decided that no other choice answers the question as well as your benchmark, you have your final answer.

☑ Predict the Answer

Before you even start looking at the answer choices, it is often best to try to predict the answer. When you come up with the answer on your own, it is easier to avoid distractions and traps because you will know exactly what to look for. The right answer choice is unlikely to be word-for-word what you came up with, but it should be a close match. Even if you are confident that you have the right answer, you should still take the time to read each option before moving on.

General Strategies

☑ Tough Questions

If you are stumped on a problem or it appears too hard or too difficult, don't waste time. Move on! Remember though, if you can quickly check for obviously incorrect answer choices, your chances of guessing correctly are greatly improved. Before you completely give up, at least try to knock out a couple of possible answers. Eliminate what you can and then guess at the remaining answer choices before moving on.

☑ Check Your Work

Since you will probably not know every term listed and the answer to every question, it is important that you get credit for the ones that you do know. Don't miss any questions through careless mistakes. If at all possible, try to take a second to look back over your answer selection and make sure you've selected the correct answer choice and haven't made a costly careless mistake (such as marking an answer choice that you didn't mean to mark). This quick double check should more than pay for itself in caught mistakes for the time it costs.

☑ Pace Yourself

It's easy to be overwhelmed when you're looking at a page full of questions; your mind is confused and full of random thoughts, and the clock is ticking down faster than you would like. Calm down and maintain the pace that you have set for yourself. Especially as you get down to the last few minutes of the test, don't let the small numbers on the clock make you panic. As long as you are on track by monitoring your pace, you are guaranteed to have time for each question.

☑ Don't Rush

It is very easy to make errors when you are in a hurry. Maintaining a fast pace in answering questions is pointless if it makes you miss questions that you would have gotten right otherwise. Test writers like to include distracting information and wrong answers that seem right. Taking a little extra time to avoid careless mistakes can make all the difference in your test score. Find a pace that allows you to be confident in the answers that you select.

⊘ Keep Moving

Panicking will not help you pass the test, so do your best to stay calm and keep moving. Taking deep breaths and going through the answer elimination steps you practiced can help to break through a stress barrier and keep your pace.

Final Notes

The combination of a solid foundation of content knowledge and the confidence that comes from practicing your plan for applying that knowledge is the key to maximizing your performance on test day. As your foundation of content knowledge is built up and strengthened, you'll find that the strategies included in this chapter become more and more effective in helping you quickly sift through the distractions and traps of the test to isolate the correct answer.

Now that you're preparing to move forward into the test content chapters of this book, be sure to keep your goal in mind. As you read, think about how you will be able to apply this information on the test. If you've already seen sample questions for the test and you have an idea of the question format and style, try to come up with questions of your own that you can answer based on what you're reading. This will give you valuable practice applying your knowledge in the same ways you can expect to on test day.

Good luck and good studying!

Three-Week PSAT Study Plan

On the next few pages, we've provided an optional study plan to help you use this study guide to its fullest potential over the course of three weeks. If you have six weeks available and want to spread it out more, spend two weeks on each section of the plan.

Below is a quick summary of the subjects covered in each week of the plan.

- Week 1: Reading Test
- Week 2: Writing and Language Test
- Week 3: Mathematics Test

Please note that not all subjects will take the same amount of time to work through.

Two full-length practice tests are included in this study guide. We recommend saving any additional practice tests until after you've completed the study plan. Take this practice test timed and without any reference materials a day or two before the real thing as one last practice run to get you in the mode of answering questions at a good pace.

Week 1: Reading Test

Instructional Content

First, read carefully through the Reading Test chapter in this book, checking off your progress as you go:

❑ Information and Ideas
❑ Rhetoric
❑ Synthesis
❑ Reading Passages
❑ Final Warnings

As you read, do the following:

- Highlight any sections, terms, or concepts you think are important
- Draw an asterisk (*) next to any areas you are struggling with
- Watch the review videos to gain more understanding of a particular topic
- Take notes in your notebook or in the margins of this book

After you've read through everything, go back and review any sections that you highlighted or that you drew an asterisk next to, referencing your notes along the way.

Practice Test #1

Now that you've read over the instructional content, it's time to take a practice test. Complete the Reading Test section of Practice Test #1. Take this test with **no time constraints**, and feel free to reference the applicable sections of this guide as you go. Once you've finished, check your answers against the provided answer key. For any questions you answered incorrectly, review the answer rationale, and then **go back and review** the applicable sections of the book. The goal in this stage is to understand why you answered the question incorrectly, and make sure that the next time you see a similar question, you will get it right.

Practice Test #2

Next, take the Reading Test section of Practice Test #2. This time, give yourself **60 minutes** (the amount of time you will have on the real PSAT) to complete all of the questions. You should again feel free to reference the guide and your notes, but be mindful of the clock. If you run out of time before you finish all of the questions, mark where you were when time expired, but go ahead and finish taking the practice test. Once you've finished, check your answers against the provided answer key and as before, review the answer rationale for any that you answered incorrectly and go back and review the associated instructional content. Your goal is still to increase understanding of the content but also to get used to the time constraints you will face on the test.

Week 2: Writing and Language Test

Instructional Content

First, read carefully through the Writing and Language Test chapter in this book, checking off your progress as you go:

- ❏ Expression of Ideas
- ❏ Standard English Conventions
- ❏ Agreement and Sentence Structure
- ❏ Punctuation
- ❏ Common Errors

As you read, do the following:

- Highlight any sections, terms, or concepts you think are important
- Draw an asterisk (*) next to any areas you are struggling with
- Watch the review videos to gain more understanding of a particular topic
- Take notes in your notebook or in the margins of this book

After you've read through everything, go back and review any sections that you highlighted or that you drew an asterisk next to, referencing your notes along the way.

Practice Test #1

Now that you've read over the instructional content, it's time to take a practice test. Complete the Writing and Language Test section of Practice Test #1. Take this test with **no time constraints**, and feel free to reference the applicable sections of this guide as you go. Once you've finished, check your answers against the provided answer key. For any questions you answered incorrectly, review the answer rationale, and then **go back and review** the applicable sections of the book. The goal in this stage is to understand why you answered the question incorrectly, and make sure that the next time you see a similar question, you will get it right.

Practice Test #2

Next, take the Writing and Language Test section of Practice Test #2. This time, give yourself **35 minutes** (the amount of time you will have on the real PSAT) to complete all of the questions. You should again feel free to reference the guide and your notes, but be mindful of the clock. If you run out of time before you finish all of the questions, mark where you were when time expired, but go ahead and finish taking the practice test. Once you've finished, check your answers against the provided answer key, and as before, review the answer rationale for any that you answered incorrectly and then go back and review the associated instructional content. Your goal is still to increase understanding of the content but also to get used to the time constraints you will face on the test.

Week 3: Mathematics Test

INSTRUCTIONAL CONTENT

First, read carefully through the Mathematics Test chapter in this book, checking off your progress as you go:

- ❑ How to Approach the Math Questions
- ❑ Foundational Math Concepts
- ❑ Heart of Algebra
- ❑ Problem Solving and Data Analysis
- ❑ Passport to Advanced Math
- ❑ Additional Topics in Math
- ❑ Student Produced Response

As you read, do the following:

- Highlight any sections, terms, or concepts you think are important
- Draw an asterisk (*) next to any areas you are struggling with
- Watch the review videos to gain more understanding of a particular topic
- Take notes in your notebook or in the margins of this book

After you've read through everything, go back and review any sections that you highlighted or that you drew an asterisk next to, referencing your notes along the way.

PRACTICE TEST #1

Now that you've read over the instructional content, it's time to take a practice test. Complete the Mathematics Test section of Practice Test #1. Take this test with **no time constraints**, and feel free to reference the applicable sections of this guide as you go. Once you've finished, check your answers against the provided answer key. For any questions you answered incorrectly, review the answer rationale, and then **go back and review** the applicable sections of the book. The goal in this stage is to understand why you answered the question incorrectly, and make sure that the next time you see a similar question, you will get it right.

PRACTICE TEST #2

Next, take the Mathematics Test section of Practice Test #2. This time, give yourself **25 minutes** to complete the No-Calculator questions and **45 minutes** to complete the Calculator questions. You should again feel free to reference the guide and your notes, but be mindful of the clock. If you run out of time before you finish all of the questions, mark where you were when time expired, but go ahead and finish taking the practice test. Once you've finished, check your answers against the provided answer key, and as before, review the answer rationale for any that you answered incorrectly and then go back and review the associated instructional content. Your goal is still to increase understanding of the content but also to get used to the time constraints you will face on the test.

Reading Test

Reading Test Overview

READING TEST OVERVIEW

The reading portion of the PSAT consists of one 60-minute section. It will contain 5 single passages or passage pairs. There will be a total of 47 questions relating to these passages. The breakdown of passages and questions is in the table below.

U.S and World Literature	1 passage; 9 questions	20%
History/Social Studies	2 passages, or 1 passage and 1 pair; 9-10 questions each	40%
Science	2 passages, or 1 passage and 1 pair; 9-10 questions each	40%

The PSAT Reading Test will contain a range of text complexities from grades 9-10 and post-secondary entry. The passages will cover U.S. and World Literature, History/Social Studies, and Science. The test will also contain 1-2 graphical representations. These may include tables, graphs, and charts. They will vary in level of difficulty as well as data density, and number of variables.

QUESTION TYPES IN THE READING SECTION

INFORMATION AND IDEAS

The questions tested in this section will focus on the informational content contained in the text.

- **Reading Closely** - These questions will focus on the student's ability to read a passage and extrapolate beyond the information presented. They will look at both the explicit and implicit meanings of the text.
- **Determining Explicit Meanings** - These questions will require the student to identify information explicitly stated in the text.
- **Determining Implicit Meanings** - The questions in this section will require the student to read the text and then draw inferences from the text and form logical conclusions.
- **Using Analogical Reasoning** - The student will be required to extrapolate information and ideas from the text to answer these questions. They will also need to be able to apply this information and ideas to new, analogous situations.
- **Citing Textual Evidence** - These questions will ask the student to support their answer with evidence from the text. The student should be able to specifically identify the information in the text and properly cite it.
- **Determining Central Ideas and Themes** - For these questions, the student should be able to identify central ideas and themes that are explicitly stated in the text. They will also need to be able to determine implicit central ideas and themes from the text.
- **Summarizing** - These questions will test the student's ability to identify a summary of a text after reading the text. The student should be able to identify a reasonable summary of the text or of key information presented in the text.
- **Understanding Relationships** - Texts will contain many different relationships between individuals, events, and ideas. These questions will test the student's ability to identify explicitly stated relationships as well as determine implicit ones.

- **Interpreting Words and Phrases in Context** - These questions will ask the student to determine the meaning of words and phrases from the text. The student must use context clues to help determine the meaning of these words and phrases.

Rhetoric

The questions in this section will focus on the rhetorical analysis of a text.

- **Analyzing Word Choice** - Authors use specific words, phrases, and patterns of words in their writing. The student will be asked to determine how these help shape the meaning and tone in the text.
- **Analyzing Text Structure** - For these questions, students will be asked to answer questions about why the author structured the text a certain way. They will also be asked about the relationship between a part of the text and the whole text.
- **Analyzing Point of View** - These questions will ask the student to determine the author's point of view. They will also need to determine the influence that this point of view has on the content and style of the text.
- **Analyzing Purpose** - These questions will ask the student to determine the purpose of a text or a piece of a text. The pieces of text are typically one paragraph of the text.
- **Analyzing Arguments** - Students will need to be able to analyze arguments in a text for their structure and content.
- **Analyzing Claims and Counterclaims** - These questions will ask the student to identify explicitly stated claims and counterclaims made in a text. They will also need to be able to determine implicit claims and counterclaims made in a text.
- **Assessing Reasoning** - These questions will require students to assess the soundness of an author's reasoning in text.
- **Analyzing Evidence** - For these questions, the student will be asked to determine how the author uses evidence to support his claims and counterclaims.

Synthesis

The questions in this section will focus on synthesizing across multiple sources of information.

- **Analyzing Multiple Texts** - The student will be required to synthesize information and ideas across multiple texts. This means that they will need to apply all the other aforementioned skills to analyze paired passages.
- **Analyzing Quantitative Information** - These questions will test the student's ability to analyze quantitative information. This information may be presented in graphs, tables, and charts and may relate to other information presented in the text.

Command of Evidence

Understanding a Passage

One of the most important skills in reading comprehension is the identification of **topics** and **main ideas**. There is a subtle difference between these two features. The topic is the subject of a text (i.e., what the text is all about). The main idea, on the other hand, is the most important point being made by the author. The topic is usually expressed in a few words at the most while the main idea often needs a full sentence to be completely defined. As an example, a short passage might be written on the topic of penguins, and the main idea could be written as *Penguins are different from other birds in many ways*. In most nonfiction writing, the topic and the main idea will be **stated directly** and often appear in a sentence at the very beginning or end of the text. When being tested on an understanding of the author's topic, you may be able to skim the passage for the general idea by reading only the first sentence of each paragraph. A body paragraph's first sentence is often—but not always—the main **topic sentence** which gives you a summary of the content in the paragraph.

However, there are cases in which the reader must figure out an **unstated** topic or main idea. In these instances, you must read every sentence of the text and try to come up with an overarching idea that is supported by each of those sentences.

Note: The main idea should not be confused with the thesis statement. While the main idea gives a brief, general summary of a text, the thesis statement provides a **specific perspective** on an issue that the author supports with evidence.

Review Video: Topics and Main Ideas
Visit mometrix.com/academy and enter code: 407801

Supporting details are smaller pieces of evidence that provide backing for the main point. In order to show that a main idea is correct or valid, an author must add details that prove their point. All texts contain details, but they are only classified as supporting details when they serve to reinforce some larger point. Supporting details are most commonly found in informative and persuasive texts. In some cases, they will be clearly indicated with terms like *for example* or *for instance*, or they will be enumerated with terms like *first*, *second*, and *last*. However, you need to be prepared for texts that do not contain those indicators. As a reader, you should consider whether the author's supporting details really back up his or her main point. Details can be factual and correct, yet they may not be **relevant** to the author's point. Conversely, details can be relevant, but be ineffective because they are based on opinion or assertions that cannot be proven.

Review Video: Supporting Details
Visit mometrix.com/academy and enter code: 396297

An example of a main idea is: *Giraffes live in the Serengeti of Africa*. A supporting detail about giraffes could be: *A giraffe in this region benefits from a long neck by reaching twigs and leaves on tall trees.* The main idea gives the general idea that the text is about giraffes. The supporting detail gives a specific fact about how the giraffes eat.

Organization of the Text

The way a text is organized can help readers understand the author's intent and his or her conclusions. There are various ways to organize a text, and each one has a purpose and use. Usually, authors will organize information logically in a passage so the reader can follow and locate the information within the text. However, since not all passages are written with the same logical structure, you need to be familiar with several different types of passage structure.

Review Video: Organizational Methods to Structure Text
Visit mometrix.com/academy and enter code: 606263

Review Video: Sequence of Events in a Story
Visit mometrix.com/academy and enter code: 807512

Chronological

When using **chronological** order, the author presents information in the order that it happened. For example, biographies are typically written in chronological order. The subject's birth and childhood are presented first, followed by their adult life, and lastly the events leading up to the person's death.

Cause and Effect

One of the most common text structures is **cause and effect**. A **cause** is an act or event that makes something happen, and an **effect** is the thing that happens as a result of the cause. A cause-and-effect relationship is not always explicit, but there are some terms in English that signal causes, such as *since, because*, and *due to*. Furthermore, terms that signal effects include *consequently, therefore, this leads to*. As an example, consider the sentence *Because the sky was clear, Ron did not bring an umbrella*. The cause is the clear sky, and the effect is that Ron did not bring an umbrella. However, readers may find that sometimes the cause-and-effect relationship will not be clearly noted. For instance, the sentence *He was late and missed the meeting* does not contain any signaling words, but the sentence still contains a cause (he was late) and an effect (he missed the meeting).

Review Video: Cause and Effect
Visit mometrix.com/academy and enter code: 868099

Multiple Effects

Be aware of the possibility for a single cause to have **multiple effects.** (e.g., *Single cause*: Because you left your homework on the table, your dog engulfed the assignment. *Multiple effects*: As a result, you receive a failing grade, your parents do not allow you to go out with your friends, you miss out on the new movie, and one of your classmates spoils it for you before you have another chance to watch it).

Multiple Causes

Also, there is the possibility for a single effect to have **multiple causes.** (e.g., *Single effect*: Alan has a fever. *Multiple causes*: An unexpected cold front came through the area, and Alan forgot to take his multi-vitamin to avoid getting sick.) Additionally, an effect can in turn be the cause of another effect, in what is known as a cause-and-effect chain. (e.g., As a result of her disdain for procrastination, Lynn prepared for her exam. This led to her passing her test with high marks. Hence, her resume was accepted and her application was approved.)

Cause and Effect in Persuasive Essays

Persuasive essays, in which an author tries to make a convincing argument and change the minds of readers, usually include cause-and-effect relationships. However, these relationships should not always be taken at face value. Frequently, an author will assume a cause or take an effect for granted. To read a persuasive essay effectively, readers need to judge the cause-and-effect relationships that the author is presenting. For instance, imagine an author wrote the following: *The parking deck has been unprofitable because people would prefer to ride their bikes.* The relationship is clear: the cause is that people prefer to ride their bikes, and the effect is that the parking deck has been unprofitable. However, readers should consider whether this argument is conclusive. Perhaps there are other reasons for the failure of the parking deck: a down economy, excessive fees, etc. Too often, authors present causal relationships as if they are fact rather than opinion. Readers should be on the alert for these dubious claims.

Problem-Solution

Some nonfiction texts are organized to **present a problem** followed by a solution. For this type of text, the problem is often explained before the solution is offered. In some cases, as when the problem is well known, the solution may be introduced briefly at the beginning. Other passages may focus on the solution, and the problem will be referenced only occasionally. Some texts will outline multiple solutions to a problem, leaving readers to choose among them. If the author has an interest or an allegiance to one solution, he or she may fail to mention or describe accurately some of the other solutions. Readers should be careful of the author's agenda when reading a problem-solution text. Only by understanding the author's perspective and interests can one develop a proper judgment of the proposed solution.

Compare and Contrast

Many texts follow the **compare-and-contrast** model in which the similarities and differences between two ideas or things are explored. Analysis of the similarities between ideas is called **comparison**. In an ideal comparison, the author places ideas or things in an equivalent structure, i.e., the author presents the ideas in the same way. If an author wants to show the similarities between cricket and baseball, then he or she may do so by summarizing the equipment and rules for each game. Be mindful of the similarities as they appear in the passage and take note of any differences that are mentioned. Often, these small differences will only reinforce the more general similarity.

Review Video: Compare and Contrast
Visit mometrix.com/academy and enter code: 798319

Thinking critically about ideas and conclusions can seem like a daunting task. One way to ease this task is to understand the basic elements of ideas and writing techniques. Looking at the ways different ideas relate to each other can be a good way for readers to begin their analysis. For instance, sometimes authors will write about two ideas that are in opposition to each other. Or, one author will provide his or her ideas on a topic, and another author may respond in opposition. The analysis of these opposing ideas is known as **contrast**. Contrast is often marred by the author's obvious partiality to one of the ideas. A discerning reader will be put off by an author who does not engage in a fair fight. In an analysis of opposing ideas, both ideas should be presented in clear and reasonable terms. If the author does prefer a side, you need to read carefully to determine the areas where the author shows or avoids this preference. In an analysis of opposing ideas, you should proceed through the passage by marking the major differences point by point with an eye that is looking for an explanation of each side's view. For instance, in an analysis of capitalism and communism, there is an importance in outlining each side's view on labor, markets, prices, personal responsibility, etc. Additionally, as you read through the passages, you should note whether the opposing views present each side in a similar manner.

Sequence

Readers must be able to identify a text's **sequence**, or the order in which things happen. Often, when the sequence is very important to the author, the text is indicated with signal words like *first*, *then*, *next*, and *last*. However, a sequence can be merely implied and must be noted by the reader. Consider the sentence *He walked through the garden and gave water and fertilizer to the plants*. Clearly, the man did not walk through the garden before he collected water and fertilizer for the plants. So, the implied sequence is that he first collected water, then he collected fertilizer, next he walked through the garden, and last he gave water or fertilizer as necessary to the plants. Texts do not always proceed in an orderly sequence from first to last. Sometimes they begin at the end and start over at the beginning. As a reader, you can enhance your understanding of the passage by taking brief notes to clarify the sequence.

Making Connections to Enhance Comprehension

Reading involves thinking. For good comprehension, readers make **text-to-self**, **text-to-text**, and **text-to-world connections**. Making connections helps readers understand text better and predict what might occur next based on what they already know, such as how characters in the story feel or what happened in another text. Text-to-self connections with the reader's life and experiences make literature more personally relevant and meaningful to readers. Readers can make connections before, during, and after reading—including whenever the text reminds them of something similar they have encountered in life or other texts. The genre, setting, characters, plot elements, literary structure and devices, and themes an author uses allow a reader to make connections to other works of literature or to people and events in their own lives. Venn diagrams and other graphic organizers help visualize connections. Readers can also make double-entry notes: key content, ideas, events, words, and quotations on one side, and the connections with these on the other.

Summarizing Literature to Support Comprehension

When reading literature, especially demanding works, **summarizing** helps readers identify important information and organize it in their minds. They can also identify themes, problems, and solutions, and can sequence the story. Readers can summarize before, during, and after they read. They should use their own words, as they do when describing a personal event or giving directions. Previewing a text's organization before reading by examining the book cover, table of contents, and illustrations also aids summarizing. Making notes of key words and ideas in a graphic organizer while reading can benefit readers in the same way. Graphic organizers are another useful method; readers skim the text to determine main ideas and then narrow the list with the aid of the organizer. Unimportant details should be omitted in summaries. Summaries can be organized using description, problem-solution, comparison-contrast, sequence, main ideas, or cause-and-effect.

Review Video: Summarizing Text
Visit mometrix.com/academy and enter code: 172903

Paraphrasing

Paraphrasing is another method that the reader can use to aid in comprehension. When paraphrasing, one puts what they have read into their own words by rephrasing what the author has written, or one "translates" all of what the author shared into their own words by including as many details as they can.

Chapter Quiz

1. All of the following are used for good comprehension, EXCEPT:

a. Text-to-self connections.
b. Text-to-others connections.
c. Text-to-text connections.
d. Text-to-world connections.

2. All of the following are terms in English that signal causes, EXCEPT:

a. Because.
b. Due to.
c. Since.
d. Therefore.

Chapter Quiz Answer Key

1. B: Reading involves thinking. For good comprehension, readers make text-to-self, text-to-text, and text-to-world connections. Making connections helps readers understand text better and predict what might occur next based on what they already know, such as how characters in the story feel or what happened in another text. Text-to-self connections with the reader's life and experiences make literature more personally relevant and meaningful to readers. Readers can make connections before, during, and after reading—including whenever the text reminds them of something similar they have encountered in life or other texts. The genre, setting, characters, plot elements, themes, and literary structure and devices an author uses allow a reader to make connections to other works of literature or to people and events in their own lives. Venn diagrams and other graphic organizers help visualize connections. Readers can also make double-entry notes: key content, ideas, events, words, and quotations on one side, and the connections with these on the other.

2. D: One of the most common text structures is cause and effect. A cause is an act or event that makes something happen, and an effect is the thing that happens as a result of the cause. A cause-and-effect relationship is not always explicit, but there are some terms in English that signal causes, such as *since*, *because*, and *due to*. Furthermore, terms that signal effects include *consequently, therefore,* and *this leads to*. As an example, consider the sentence, "Because the sky was clear, Ron did not bring an umbrella." The cause is the clear sky, and the effect is that Ron did not bring an umbrella. However, readers may find that sometimes the cause-and-effect relationship will not be clearly noted. For instance, the sentence, "He was late and missed the meeting," does not contain any signaling words, but the sentence still contains a cause ("he was late") and an effect ("he missed the meeting").

Making Predictions

When we read literature, **making predictions** about what will happen in the writing reinforces our purpose for reading and prepares us mentally. A **prediction** is a guess about what will happen next. Readers constantly make predictions based on what they have read and what they already know. We can make predictions before we begin reading and during our reading. Consider the following sentence: *Staring at the computer screen in shock, Kim blindly reached over for the brimming glass of water on the shelf to her side.* The sentence suggests that Kim is distracted, and that she is not looking at the glass that she is going to pick up. So, a reader might predict that Kim is going to knock over the glass. Of course, not every prediction will be accurate: perhaps Kim will pick the glass up cleanly. Nevertheless, the author has certainly created the expectation that the water might be spilled.

As we read on, we can test the accuracy of our predictions, revise them in light of additional reading, and confirm or refute our predictions. Predictions are always subject to revision as the reader acquires more information. A reader can make predictions by observing the title and illustrations; noting the structure, characters, and subject; drawing on existing knowledge relative to the subject; and asking "why" and "who" questions. Connecting reading to what we already know enables us to learn new information and construct meaning. For example, before third-graders read a book about Johnny Appleseed, they may start a KWL chart—a list of what they *Know*, what they *Want* to know or learn, and what they have *Learned* after reading. Activating existing background knowledge and thinking about the test before reading improves comprehension.

Review Video: Predictive Reading
Visit mometrix.com/academy and enter code: 437248

Test-taking tip: To respond to questions requiring future predictions, your answers should be based on evidence of past or present behavior and events.

Evaluating Predictions

When making predictions, readers should be able to explain how they developed their prediction. One way readers can defend their thought process is by citing textual evidence. Textual evidence to evaluate reader predictions about literature includes specific synopses of the work, paraphrases of the work or parts of it, and direct quotations from the work. These references to the text must support the prediction by indicating, clearly or unclearly, what will happen later in the story. A text may provide these indications through literary devices such as foreshadowing. Foreshadowing is anything in a text that gives the reader a hint about what is to come by emphasizing the likelihood of an event or development. Foreshadowing can occur through descriptions, exposition, and dialogue. Foreshadowing in dialogue usually occurs when a character gives a warning or expresses a strong feeling that a certain event will occur. Foreshadowing can also occur through irony. However, unlike other forms of foreshadowing, the events that seem the most likely are the opposite of what actually happens. Instances of foreshadowing and irony can be summarized, paraphrased, or quoted to defend a reader's prediction.

Review Video: Textual Evidence for Predictions
Visit mometrix.com/academy and enter code: 261070

Drawing Conclusions from Inferences

Inferences about literary text are logical conclusions that readers make based on their observations and previous knowledge. An inference is based on both what is found in a passage or a story and what is known from personal experience. For instance, a story may say that a character is frightened and can hear howling in the distance. Based on both what is in the text and personal knowledge, it is a logical conclusion that the character is frightened because he hears the sound of wolves. A good inference is supported by the information in a passage.

Implicit and Explicit Information

By inferring, readers construct meanings from text that are personally relevant. By combining their own schemas or concepts and their background information pertinent to the text with what they read, readers interpret it according to both what the author has conveyed and their own unique perspectives. Inferences are different from **explicit information**, which is clearly stated in a passage. Authors do not always explicitly spell out every meaning in what they write; many meanings are implicit. Through inference, readers can comprehend implied meanings in the text, and also derive personal significance from it, making the text meaningful and memorable to them. Inference is a natural process in everyday life. When readers infer, they can draw conclusions about what the author is saying, predict what may reasonably follow, amend these predictions as they continue to read, interpret the import of themes, and analyze the characters' feelings and motivations through their actions.

Example of Drawing Conclusions from Inferences

Read the excerpt and decide why Jana finally relaxed.

> Jana loved her job, but the work was very demanding. She had trouble relaxing. She called a friend, but she still thought about work. She ordered a pizza, but eating it did not help. Then, her kitten jumped on her lap and began to purr. Jana leaned back and began to hum a little tune. She felt better.

You can draw the conclusion that Jana relaxed because her kitten jumped on her lap. The kitten purred, and Jana leaned back and hummed a tune. Then she felt better. The excerpt does not explicitly say that this is the reason why she was able to relax. The text leaves the matter unclear, but the reader can infer or make a "best guess" that this is the reason she is relaxing. This is a logical conclusion based on the information in the passage. It is the best conclusion a reader can make based on the information he or she has read. Inferences are based on the information in a passage, but they are not directly stated in the passage.

Test-taking tip: While being tested on your ability to make correct inferences, you must look for **contextual clues**. An answer can be true, but not the best or most correct answer. The contextual clues will help you find the answer that is the **best answer** out of the given choices. Be careful in your reading to understand the context in which a phrase is stated. When asked for the implied meaning of a statement made in the passage, you should immediately locate the statement and read the **context** in which the statement was made. Also, look for an answer choice that has a similar phrase to the statement in question.

Review Video: Inference
Visit mometrix.com/academy and enter code: 379203

Review Video: How to Support a Conclusion
Visit mometrix.com/academy and enter code: 281653

CHAPTER QUIZ

1. Which of the following describes logical conclusions that readers make based on their observations and previous knowledge?

a. Imperatives
b. Interrogatives
c. Inferences
d. Predictions

CHAPTER QUIZ ANSWER KEY

1. C: Inferences about literary text are logical conclusions that readers make based on their observations and previous knowledge. An inference is based on both what is found in a passage or a story and what is known from personal experience. For instance, a story may say that a character is frightened and can hear howling in the distance. Based on both what is in the text and personal knowledge, it is a logical conclusion that the character is frightened because they hear the sound of wolves. A good inference is supported by the information in a passage.

PURPOSES FOR WRITING

In order to be an effective reader, one must pay attention to the author's **position** and **purpose**. Even those texts that seem objective and impartial, like textbooks, have a position and bias. Readers need to take these positions into account when considering the author's message. When an author uses emotional language or clearly favors one side of an argument, his or her position is clear. However, the author's position may be evident not only in what he or she writes, but also in what he or she doesn't write. In a normal setting, a reader would want to review some other texts on the same topic in order to develop a view of the author's position. If this was not possible, then you would want to at least acquire some background about the author. However, since you are in the middle of an exam and the only source of information is the text, you should look for language and argumentation that seems to indicate a particular stance on the subject.

Review Video: Author's Position
Visit mometrix.com/academy and enter code: 827954

Usually, identifying the author's **purpose** is easier than identifying his or her position. In most cases, the author has no interest in hiding his or her purpose. A text that is meant to entertain, for instance, should be written to please the reader. Most narratives, or stories, are written to entertain, though they may also inform or persuade. Informative texts are easy to identify, while the most difficult purpose of a text to identify is persuasion because the author has an interest in making this purpose hard to detect. When a reader discovers that the author is trying to persuade, he or she should be skeptical of the argument. For this reason, persuasive texts often try to establish an entertaining tone and hope to amuse the reader into agreement. On the other hand, an informative tone may be implemented to create an appearance of authority and objectivity.

An author's purpose is evident often in the organization of the text (e.g., section headings in bold font points to an informative text). However, you may not have such organization available to you in your exam. Instead, if the author makes his or her main idea clear from the beginning, then the likely purpose of the text is to inform. If the author begins by making a claim and provides various arguments to support that claim, then the purpose is probably to persuade. If the author tells a story or wants to gain the reader's attention more than to push a particular point or deliver information, then his or her purpose is most likely to entertain. As a reader, you must judge authors on how well they accomplish their purpose. In other words, you need to consider the type of passage (e.g., technical, persuasive, etc.) that the author has written and if the author has followed the requirements of the passage type.

Making Logical Conclusions about a Passage

A reader should always be drawing conclusions from the text. Sometimes conclusions are **implied** from written information, and other times the information is **stated directly** within the passage. One should always aim to draw conclusions from information stated within a passage, rather than to draw them from mere implications. At times an author may provide some information and then describe a counterargument. Readers should be alert for direct statements that are subsequently rejected or weakened by the author. Furthermore, you should always read through the entire passage before drawing conclusions. Many readers are trained to expect the author's conclusions at either the beginning or the end of the passage, but many texts do not adhere to this format.

Drawing conclusions from information implied within a passage requires confidence on the part of the reader. **Implications** are things that the author does not state directly, but readers can assume based on what the author does say. Consider the following passage: *I stepped outside and opened my umbrella. By the time I got to work, the cuffs of my pants were soaked.* The author never states that it is raining, but this fact is clearly implied. Conclusions based on implication must be well supported by the text. In order to draw a solid conclusion, readers should have **multiple pieces of evidence**. If readers have only one piece, they must be assured that there is no other possible explanation than their conclusion. A good reader will be able to draw many conclusions from information implied by the text, which will be a great help on the exam.

Drawing Conclusions

A common type of inference that a reader has to make is **drawing a conclusion**. The reader makes this conclusion based on the information provided within a text. Certain facts are included to help a reader come to a specific conclusion. For example, a story may open with a man trudging through the snow on a cold winter day, dragging a sled behind him. The reader can logically **infer** from the setting of the story that the man is wearing heavy winter clothes in order to stay warm. Information is implied based on the setting of a story, which is why **setting** is an important element of the text. If the same man in the example was trudging down a beach on a hot summer day, dragging a surf board behind him, the reader would assume that the man is not wearing heavy clothes. The reader makes inferences based on their own experiences and the information presented to them in the story.

Test-taking tip: When asked to identify a conclusion that may be drawn, look for critical "hedge" phrases, such as *likely*, *may*, *can*, and *will often*, among many others. When you are being tested on this knowledge, remember the question that writers insert into these hedge phrases to cover every possibility. Often an answer will be wrong simply because there is no room for exception. Extreme positive or negative answers (such as always or never) are usually not correct. When answering these questions, the reader **should not** use any outside knowledge that is not gathered directly or reasonably inferred from the passage. Correct answers can be derived straight from the passage.

EXAMPLE

Read the following sentence from *Little Women* by Louisa May Alcott and draw a conclusion based upon the information presented:

> *You know the reason Mother proposed not having any presents this Christmas was because it is going to be a hard winter for everyone; and she thinks we ought not to spend money for pleasure, when our men are suffering so in the army.*

Based on the information in the sentence, the reader can conclude, or **infer**, that the men are away at war while the women are still at home. The pronoun *our* gives a clue to the reader that the character is speaking about men she knows. In addition, the reader can assume that the character is speaking to a brother or sister, since the term "Mother" is used by the character while speaking to another person. The reader can also come to the conclusion that the characters celebrate Christmas, since it is mentioned in the **context** of the sentence. In the sentence, the mother is presented as an unselfish character who is opinionated and thinks about the wellbeing of other people.

COMPARING TWO STORIES

When presented with two different stories, there will be **similarities** and **differences** between the two. A reader needs to make a list, or other graphic organizer, of the points presented in each story. Once the reader has written down the main point and supporting points for each story, the two sets of ideas can be compared. The reader can then present each idea and show how it is the same or different in the other story. This is called **comparing and contrasting ideas**.

The reader can compare ideas by stating, for example: "In Story 1, the author believes that humankind will one day land on Mars, whereas in Story 2, the author believes that Mars is too far away for humans to ever step foot on." Note that the two viewpoints are different in each story that the reader is comparing. A reader may state that: "Both stories discussed the likelihood of humankind landing on Mars." This statement shows how the viewpoint presented in both stories is based on the same topic, rather than how each viewpoint is different. The reader will complete a comparison of two stories with a conclusion.

Review Video: Comparing Two Stories
Visit mometrix.com/academy and enter code: 833765

OUTLINING A PASSAGE

As an aid to drawing conclusions, **outlining** the information contained in the passage should be a familiar skill to readers. An effective outline will reveal the structure of the passage and will lead to solid conclusions. An effective outline will have a title that refers to the basic subject of the text, though the title does not need to restate the main idea. In most outlines, the main idea will be the first major section. Each major idea in the passage will be established as the head of a category. For instance, the most common outline format calls for the main ideas of the passage to be indicated with Roman numerals. In an effective outline of this kind, each of the main ideas will be represented by a Roman numeral and none of the Roman numerals will designate minor details or secondary ideas. Moreover, all supporting ideas and details should be placed in the appropriate place on the outline. An outline does not need to include every detail listed in the text, but it should feature all of those that are central to the argument or message. Each of these details should be listed under the corresponding main idea.

Review Video: Outlining
Visit mometrix.com/academy and enter code: 584445

USING GRAPHIC ORGANIZERS

Ideas from a text can also be organized using **graphic organizers**. A graphic organizer is a way to simplify information and take key points from the text. A graphic organizer such as a timeline may have an event listed for a corresponding date on the timeline, while an outline may have an event listed under a key point that occurs in the text. Each reader needs to create the type of graphic organizer that works the best for him or her in terms of being able to recall information from a story. Examples include a spider-map, which takes a main idea from the story and places it in a bubble with supporting points branching off the main idea. An outline is useful for diagramming the main and supporting points of the entire story, and a Venn diagram compares and contrasts characteristics of two or more ideas.

Review Video: Graphic Organizers
Visit mometrix.com/academy and enter code: 665513

SUMMARIZING

A helpful tool is the ability to **summarize** the information that you have read in a paragraph or passage format. This process is similar to creating an effective outline. First, a summary should accurately define the main idea of the passage, though the summary does not need to explain this main idea in exhaustive detail. The summary should continue by laying out the most important supporting details or arguments from the passage. All of the significant supporting details should be included, and none of the details included should be irrelevant or insignificant. Also, the summary should accurately report all of these details. Too often, the desire for brevity in a summary leads to the sacrifice of clarity or accuracy. Summaries are often difficult to read because they omit all of the graceful language, digressions, and asides that distinguish great writing. However, an effective summary should communicate the same overall message as the original text.

EVALUATING A PASSAGE

It is important to understand the logical conclusion of the ideas presented in an informational text. **Identifying a logical conclusion** can help you determine whether you agree with the writer or not. Coming to this conclusion is much like making an inference: the approach requires you to combine the information given by the text with what you already know and make a logical conclusion. If the author intended for the reader to draw a certain conclusion, then you can expect the author's argumentation and detail to be leading in that direction.

One way to approach the task of drawing conclusions is to make brief **notes** of all the points made by the author. When the notes are arranged on paper, they may clarify the logical conclusion. Another way to approach conclusions is to consider whether the reasoning of the author raises any pertinent questions. Sometimes you will be able to draw several conclusions from a passage. On occasion these will be conclusions that were never imagined by the author. Therefore, be aware that these conclusions must be **supported directly by the text.**

Evaluation of Summaries

A summary of a literary passage is a condensation in the reader's own words of the passage's main points. Several guidelines can be used in evaluating a summary. The summary should be complete yet concise. It should be accurate, balanced, fair, neutral, and objective, excluding the reader's own opinions or reactions. It should reflect in similar proportion how much each point summarized was covered in the original passage. Summary writers should include tags of attribution, like "Macaulay argues that" to reference the original author whose ideas are represented in the summary. Summary writers should not overuse quotations; they should only quote central concepts or phrases they cannot precisely convey in words other than those of the original author. Another aspect of evaluating a summary is considering whether it can stand alone as a coherent, unified composition. In addition, evaluation of a summary should include whether its writer has cited the original source of the passage they have summarized so that readers can find it.

Chapter Quiz

1. Which of the following is most important when drawing conclusions from a text?

a. The conclusions make sense to others.
b. The conclusions are supported directly by the text.
c. The conclusions agree with previous convictions.
d. The conclusions align with the author's purpose for writing the text.

2. All of the following are true about summaries, EXCEPT:

a. They should focus on the main point of the text rather than proportional to how much each point was covered in the passage.
b. They should be accurate, balanced, fair, neutral, and objective.
c. They should be complete and concise.
d. They should only quote central concepts or phrases that cannot be precisely conveyed in words other than those of the original author.

Chapter Quiz Answer Key

1. B: It is important to understand the logical conclusion of the ideas presented in an informational text. Identifying a logical conclusion can help readers determine whether they agree with the writer or not. Coming to this conclusion is much like making an inference: the approach requires readers to combine the information given by the text with what they already know and make a logical conclusion. If the author intended for the reader to draw a certain conclusion, then readers can expect the author's argumentation and detail to be leading in that direction. Sometimes a reader will be able to draw several conclusions from a passage. On occasion these will be conclusions that were never imagined by the author. Therefore, be aware that these conclusions must be supported directly by the text.

2. A: A summary of a literary passage is a condensation in the reader's own words of the passage's main points. Several guidelines can be used in evaluating a summary. The summary should be complete yet concise. It should be accurate, balanced, fair, neutral, and objective, excluding the reader's own opinions or reactions. It should reflect in similar proportion how much each point summarized was covered in the original passage. Summary writers should include tags of attribution, like "Macaulay argues that" to reference the original author whose ideas are represented in the summary. Summary writers should not overuse quotations, but only quote central concepts or phrases they cannot precisely convey in words other than those of the original author. Another aspect of evaluating a summary is considering whether it can stand alone as a coherent, unified composition. In addition, evaluation of a summary should include whether its writer has cited the original source of the passage they have summarized so that readers can find it.

Words in Context

Synonyms and Antonyms

When you understand how words relate to each other, you will discover more in a passage. This is explained by understanding **synonyms** (e.g., words that mean the same thing) and **antonyms** (e.g., words that mean the opposite of one another). As an example, *dry* and *arid* are synonyms, and *dry* and *wet* are antonyms.

There are many pairs of words in English that can be considered synonyms, despite having slightly different definitions. For instance, the words *friendly* and *collegial* can both be used to describe a warm interpersonal relationship, and one would be correct to call them synonyms. However, *collegial* (kin to *colleague*) is often used in reference to professional or academic relationships, and *friendly* has no such connotation.

If the difference between the two words is too great, then they should not be called synonyms. *Hot* and *warm* are not synonyms because their meanings are too distinct. A good way to determine whether two words are synonyms is to substitute one word for the other word and verify that the meaning of the sentence has not changed. Substituting *warm* for *hot* in a sentence would convey a different meaning. Although warm and hot may seem close in meaning, warm generally means that the temperature is moderate, and hot generally means that the temperature is excessively high.

Antonyms are words with opposite meanings. *Light* and *dark*, *up* and *down*, *right* and *left*, *good* and *bad*: these are all sets of antonyms. Be careful to distinguish between antonyms and pairs of words that are simply different. *Black* and *gray*, for instance, are not antonyms because gray is not the opposite of black. *Black* and *white*, on the other hand, are antonyms.

Not every word has an antonym. For instance, many nouns do not. What would be the antonym of *chair*? During your exam, the questions related to antonyms are more likely to concern adjectives. You will recall that adjectives are words that describe a noun. Some common adjectives include *purple*, *fast*, *skinny*, and *sweet*. From those four adjectives, *purple* is the item that lacks a group of obvious antonyms.

Review Video: What Are Synonyms and Antonyms?
Visit mometrix.com/academy and enter code: 105612

Affixes

Affixes in the English language are morphemes that are added to words to create related but different words. Derivational affixes form new words based on and related to the original words. For example, the affix *-ness* added to the end of the adjective *happy* forms the noun *happiness.* Inflectional affixes form different grammatical versions of words. For example, the plural affix *-s* changes the singular noun *book* to the plural noun *books*, and the past tense affix *-ed* changes the present tense verb *look* to the past tense *looked.* Prefixes are affixes placed in front of words. For example, *heat* means to make hot; *preheat* means to heat in advance. Suffixes are affixes placed at the ends of words. The *happiness* example above contains the suffix *-ness.* Circumfixes add parts both before and after words, such as how *light* becomes *enlighten* with the prefix *en-* and the suffix

-en. Interfixes create compound words via central affixes: *speed* and *meter* become *speedometer* via the interfix *-o-*.

Review Video: Affixes
Visit mometrix.com/academy and enter code: 782422

Word Roots, Prefixes, and Suffixes to Help Determine Meanings of Words

Many English words were formed from combining multiple sources. For example, the Latin *habēre* means "to have," and the prefixes *in-* and *im-* mean a lack or prevention of something, as in *insufficient* and *imperfect.* Latin combined *in-* with *habēre* to form *inhibēre,* whose past participle was *inhibitus.* This is the origin of the English word *inhibit,* meaning to prevent from having. Hence by knowing the meanings of both the prefix and the root, one can decipher the word meaning. In Greek, the root *enkephalo-* refers to the brain. Many medical terms are based on this root, such as encephalitis and hydrocephalus. Understanding the prefix and suffix meanings (*-itis* means inflammation; *hydro-* means water) allows a person to deduce that encephalitis refers to brain inflammation and hydrocephalus refers to water (or other fluid) in the brain.

Review Video: Determining Word Meanings
Visit mometrix.com/academy and enter code: 894894

Review Video: Root Words in English
Visit mometrix.com/academy and enter code: 896380

Prefixes

While knowing prefix meanings helps ESL and beginning readers learn new words, other readers take for granted the meanings of known words. However, prefix knowledge will also benefit them for determining meanings or definitions of unfamiliar words. For example, native English speakers and readers familiar with recipes know what *preheat* means. Knowing that *pre-* means in advance can also inform them that *presume* means to assume in advance, that *prejudice* means advance judgment, and that this understanding can be applied to many other words beginning with *pre-.* Knowing that the prefix *dis-* indicates opposition informs the meanings of words like *disbar, disagree, disestablish,* and many more. Knowing *dys-* means bad, impaired, abnormal, or difficult informs *dyslogistic, dysfunctional, dysphagia,* and *dysplasia.*

Suffixes

In English, certain suffixes generally indicate both that a word is a noun, and that the noun represents a state of being or quality. For example, *-ness* is commonly used to change an adjective into its noun form, as with *happy* and *happiness, nice* and *niceness,* and so on. The suffix *-tion* is commonly used to transform a verb into its noun form, as with *converse* and *conversation or move* and *motion.* Thus, if readers are unfamiliar with the second form of a word, knowing the meaning of the transforming suffix can help them determine meaning.

Prefixes for Numbers

Prefix	Definition	Examples
bi-	two	bisect, biennial
mono-	one, single	monogamy, monologue
poly-	many	polymorphous, polygamous
semi-	half, partly	semicircle, semicolon
uni-	one	uniform, unity

Prefixes for Time, Direction, and Space

Prefix	Definition	Examples
a-	in, on, of, up, to	abed, afoot
ab-	from, away, off	abdicate, abjure
ad-	to, toward	advance, adventure
ante-	before, previous	antecedent, antedate
anti-	against, opposing	antipathy, antidote
cata-	down, away, thoroughly	catastrophe, cataclysm
circum-	around	circumspect, circumference
com-	with, together, very	commotion, complicate
contra-	against, opposing	contradict, contravene
de-	from	depart
dia-	through, across, apart	diameter, diagnose
dis-	away, off, down, not	dissent, disappear
epi-	upon	epilogue
ex-	out	extract, excerpt
hypo-	under, beneath	hypodermic, hypothesis
inter-	among, between	intercede, interrupt
intra-	within	intramural, intrastate
ob-	against, opposing	objection
per-	through	perceive, permit
peri-	around	periscope, perimeter
post-	after, following	postpone, postscript
pre-	before, previous	prevent, preclude
pro-	forward, in place of	propel, pronoun
retro-	back, backward	retrospect, retrograde
sub-	under, beneath	subjugate, substitute
super-	above, extra	supersede, supernumerary
trans-	across, beyond, over	transact, transport
ultra-	beyond, excessively	ultramodern, ultrasonic

Negative Prefixes

Prefix	Definition	Examples
a-	without, lacking	atheist, agnostic
in-	not, opposing	incapable, ineligible
non-	not	nonentity, nonsense
un-	not, reverse of	unhappy, unlock

Extra Prefixes

Prefix	Definition	Examples
for-	away, off, from	forget, forswear
fore-	previous	foretell, forefathers
homo-	same, equal	homogenized, homonym
hyper-	excessive, over	hypercritical, hypertension
in-	in, into	intrude, invade
mal-	bad, poorly, not	malfunction, malpractice
mis-	bad, poorly, not	misspell, misfire
neo-	new	Neolithic, neoconservative
omni-	all, everywhere	omniscient, omnivore
ortho-	right, straight	orthogonal, orthodox
over-	above	overbearing, oversight
pan-	all, entire	panorama, pandemonium
para-	beside, beyond	parallel, paradox
re-	backward, again	revoke, recur
sym-	with, together	sympathy, symphony

Below is a list of common suffixes and their meanings:

Adjective Suffixes

Suffix	Definition	Examples
-able (-ible)	capable of being	toler*able*, ed*ible*
-esque	in the style of, like	picturesque, grotesque
-ful	filled with, marked by	thankful, zestful
-ific	make, cause	terrific, beatific
-ish	suggesting, like	churlish, childish
-less	lacking, without	hopeless, countless
-ous	marked by, given to	religious, riotous

Noun Suffixes

Suffix	Definition	Examples
-acy	state, condition	accuracy, privacy
-ance	act, condition, fact	acceptance, vigilance
-ard	one that does excessively	drunkard, sluggard
-ation	action, state, result	occupation, starvation
-dom	state, rank, condition	serfdom, wisdom
-er (-or)	office, action	teach*er*, elevat*or*, hon*or*
-ess	feminine	waitress, duchess
-hood	state, condition	manhood, statehood
-ion	action, result, state	union, fusion
-ism	act, manner, doctrine	barbarism, socialism
-ist	worker, follower	monopolist, socialist
-ity (-ty)	state, quality, condition	acid*ity*, civil*ity*, twen*ty*
-ment	result, action	Refreshment
-ness	quality, state	greatness, tallness
-ship	position	internship, statesmanship
-sion (-tion)	state, result	revi*sion*, expedi*tion*
-th	act, state, quality	warmth, width
-tude	quality, state, result	magnitude, fortitude

Verb Suffixes

Suffix	Definition	Examples
-ate	having, showing	separate, desolate
-en	cause to be, become	deepen, strengthen
-fy	make, cause to have	glorify, fortify
-ize	cause to be, treat with	sterilize, mechanize

Denotative vs. Connotative Meaning

The **denotative** meaning of a word is the literal meaning. The **connotative** meaning goes beyond the denotative meaning to include the emotional reaction that a word may invoke. The connotative meaning often takes the denotative meaning a step further due to associations the reader makes with the denotative meaning. Readers can differentiate between the denotative and connotative meanings by first recognizing how authors use each meaning. Most non-fiction, for example, is fact-based and authors do not use flowery, figurative language. The reader can assume that the writer is using the denotative meaning of words. In fiction, the author may use the connotative meaning. Readers can determine whether the author is using the denotative or connotative meaning of a word by implementing context clues.

Review Video: Connotation and Denotation
Visit mometrix.com/academy and enter code: 310092

Nuances of Word Meaning Relative to Connotation, Denotation, Diction, and Usage

A word's denotation is simply its objective dictionary definition. However, its connotation refers to the subjective associations, often emotional, that specific words evoke in listeners and readers. Two or more words can have the same dictionary meaning, but very different connotations. Writers use diction (word choice) to convey various nuances of thought and emotion by selecting synonyms for other words that best communicate the associations they want to trigger for readers. For example, a car engine is naturally greasy; in this sense, "greasy" is a neutral term. But when a person's smile, appearance, or clothing is described as "greasy," it has a negative connotation. Some words have even gained additional or different meanings over time. For example, *awful* used to be used to describe things that evoked a sense of awe. When *awful* is separated into its root word, awe, and suffix, -ful, it can be understood to mean "full of awe." However, the word is now commonly used to describe things that evoke repulsion, terror, or another intense, negative reaction.

Review Video: Word Usage in Sentences
Visit mometrix.com/academy and enter code: 197863

Context Clues

Readers of all levels will encounter words that they have either never seen or have encountered only on a limited basis. The best way to define a word in **context** is to look for nearby words that can assist in revealing the meaning of the word. For instance, unfamiliar nouns are often accompanied by examples that provide a definition. Consider the following sentence: *Dave arrived at the party in hilarious garb: a leopard-print shirt, buckskin trousers, and bright green sneakers.* If a reader was unfamiliar with the meaning of garb, he or she could read the examples (i.e., a leopard-print shirt, buckskin trousers, and high heels) and quickly determine that the word means *clothing*. Examples will not always be this obvious. Consider this sentence: *Parsley, lemon, and flowers were just a few of the items he used as garnishes.* Here, the word *garnishes* is exemplified by parsley, lemon, and flowers. Readers who have eaten in a variety of restaurants will probably be able to identify a garnish as something used to decorate a plate.

Review Video: Context Clues
Visit mometrix.com/academy and enter code: 613660

Using Contrast in Context Clues

In addition to looking at the context of a passage, readers can use contrast to define an unfamiliar word in context. In many sentences, the author will not describe the unfamiliar word directly; instead, he or she will describe the opposite of the unfamiliar word. Thus, you are provided with some information that will bring you closer to defining the word. Consider the following example: *Despite his intelligence, Hector's low brow and bad posture made him look obtuse.* The author writes that Hector's appearance does not convey intelligence. Therefore, *obtuse* must mean unintelligent. Here is another example: *Despite the horrible weather, we were beatific about our trip to Alaska*. The word *despite* indicates that the speaker's feelings were at odds with the weather. Since the weather is described as *horrible*, then *beatific* must mean something positive.

Substitution to Find Meaning

In some cases, there will be very few contextual clues to help a reader define the meaning of an unfamiliar word. When this happens, one strategy that readers may employ is **substitution**. A good reader will brainstorm some possible synonyms for the given word, and he or she will substitute these words into the sentence. If the sentence and the surrounding passage continue to make sense, then the substitution has revealed at least some information about the unfamiliar word. Consider the sentence: *Frank's admonition rang in her ears as she climbed the mountain.* A reader unfamiliar with *admonition* might come up with some substitutions like *vow, promise, advice, complaint,* or *compliment.* All of these words make general sense of the sentence, though their meanings are diverse. However, this process has suggested that an admonition is some sort of message. The substitution strategy is rarely able to pinpoint a precise definition, but this process can be effective as a last resort.

Occasionally, you will be able to define an unfamiliar word by looking at the descriptive words in the context. Consider the following sentence: *Fred dragged the recalcitrant boy kicking and screaming up the stairs.* The words *dragged*, *kicking*, and *screaming* all suggest that the boy does not want to go up the stairs. The reader may assume that *recalcitrant* means something like unwilling or protesting. In this example, an unfamiliar adjective was identified.

Additionally, using description to define an unfamiliar noun is a common practice compared to unfamiliar adjectives, as in this sentence: *Don's wrinkled frown and constantly shaking fist identified him as a curmudgeon of the first order*. Don is described as having a *wrinkled frown and constantly shaking fist*, suggesting that a *curmudgeon* must be a grumpy person. Contrasts do not always provide detailed information about the unfamiliar word, but they at least give the reader some clues.

Words with Multiple Meanings

When a word has more than one meaning, readers can have difficulty determining how the word is being used in a given sentence. For instance, the verb *cleave*, can mean either *join* or *separate*. When readers come upon this word, they will have to select the definition that makes the most sense. Consider the following sentence: *Hermione's knife cleaved the bread cleanly*. Since a knife cannot join bread together, the word must indicate separation. A slightly more difficult example would be the sentence: *The birds cleaved to one another as they flew from the oak tree.* Immediately, the presence of the words *to one another* should suggest that in this sentence *cleave* is being used to mean *join*. Discovering the intent of a word with multiple meanings requires the same tricks as defining an unknown word: look for contextual clues and evaluate the substituted words.

Context Clues to Help Determine Meanings of Words

If readers simply bypass unknown words, they can reach unclear conclusions about what they read. However, looking for the definition of every unfamiliar word in the dictionary can slow their reading progress. Moreover, the dictionary may list multiple definitions for a word, so readers must search the word's context for meaning. Hence context is important to new vocabulary regardless of reader methods. Four types of context clues are examples, definitions, descriptive words, and opposites. Authors may use a certain word, and then follow it with several different examples of what it describes. Sometimes authors actually supply a definition of a word they use, which is especially true in informational and technical texts. Authors may use descriptive words that elaborate upon a vocabulary word they just used. Authors may also use opposites with negation that help define meaning.

Examples and Definitions

An author may use a word and then give examples that illustrate its meaning. Consider this text: "Teachers who do not know how to use sign language can help students who are deaf or hard of hearing understand certain instructions by using gestures instead, like pointing their fingers to indicate which direction to look or go; holding up a hand, palm outward, to indicate stopping; holding the hands flat, palms up, curling a finger toward oneself in a beckoning motion to indicate 'come here'; or curling all fingers toward oneself repeatedly to indicate 'come on', 'more', or 'continue.'" The author of this text has used the word "gestures" and then followed it with examples, so a reader unfamiliar with the word could deduce from the examples that "gestures" means "hand motions." Readers can find examples by looking for signal words "for example," "for instance," "like," "such as," and "e.g."

While readers sometimes have to look for definitions of unfamiliar words in a dictionary or do some work to determine a word's meaning from its surrounding context, at other times an author may make it easier for readers by defining certain words. For example, an author may write, "The company did not have sufficient capital, that is, available money, to continue operations." The author defined "capital" as "available money," and heralded the definition with the phrase "that is." Another way that authors supply word definitions is with appositives. Rather than being introduced by a signal phrase like "that is," "namely," or "meaning," an appositive comes after the vocabulary word it defines and is enclosed within two commas. For example, an author may write, "The Indians introduced the Pilgrims to pemmican, cakes they made of lean meat dried and mixed with fat, which proved greatly beneficial to keep settlers from starving while trapping." In this example, the appositive phrase following "pemmican" and preceding "which" defines the word "pemmican."

Descriptions

When readers encounter a word they do not recognize in a text, the author may expand on that word to illustrate it better. While the author may do this to make the prose more picturesque and vivid, the reader can also take advantage of this description to provide context clues to the meaning of the unfamiliar word. For example, an author may write, "The man sitting next to me on the airplane was obese. His shirt stretched across his vast expanse of flesh, strained almost to bursting." The descriptive second sentence elaborates on and helps to define the previous sentence's word "obese" to mean extremely fat. A reader unfamiliar with the word "repugnant" can decipher its meaning through an author's accompanying description: "The way the child grimaced and shuddered as he swallowed the medicine showed that its taste was particularly repugnant."

Opposites

Text authors sometimes introduce a contrasting or opposing idea before or after a concept they present. They may do this to emphasize or heighten the idea they present by contrasting it with something that is the reverse. However, readers can also use these context clues to understand familiar words. For example, an author may write, "Our conversation was not cheery. We sat and talked very solemnly about his experience and a number of similar events." The reader who is not familiar with the word "solemnly" can deduce by the author's preceding use of "not cheery" that "solemn" means the opposite of cheery or happy, so it must mean serious or sad. Or if someone writes, "Don't condemn his entire project because you couldn't find anything good to say about it," readers unfamiliar with "condemn" can understand from the sentence structure that it means the opposite of saying anything good, so it must mean reject, dismiss, or disapprove. "Entire" adds another context clue, meaning total or complete rejection.

Syntax to Determine Part of Speech and Meanings of Words

Syntax refers to sentence structure and word order. Suppose that a reader encounters an unfamiliar word when reading a text. To illustrate, consider an invented word like "splunch." If this word is used in a sentence like "Please splunch that ball to me," the reader can assume from syntactic context that "splunch" is a verb. We would not use a noun, adjective, adverb, or preposition with the object "that ball," and the prepositional phrase "to me" further indicates "splunch" represents an action. However, in the sentence, "Please hand that splunch to me," the reader can assume that "splunch" is a noun. Demonstrative adjectives like "that" modify nouns. Also, we hand someone some*thing*—a thing being a noun; we do not hand someone a verb, adjective, or adverb. Some sentences contain further clues. For example, from the sentence, "The princess wore the glittering splunch on her head," the reader can deduce that it is a crown, tiara, or something similar from the syntactic context, without knowing the word.

Syntax to Indicate Different Meanings of Similar Sentences

The syntax, or structure, of a sentence affords grammatical cues that aid readers in comprehending the meanings of words, phrases, and sentences in the texts that they read. Seemingly minor differences in how the words or phrases in a sentence are ordered can make major differences in meaning. For example, two sentences can use exactly the same words but have different meanings based on the word order:

- "The man with a broken arm sat in a chair."
- "The man sat in a chair with a broken arm."

While both sentences indicate that a man sat in a chair, differing syntax indicates whether the man's or chair's arm was broken.

Determining Meaning of Phrases and Paragraphs

Like unknown words, the meanings of phrases, paragraphs, and entire works can also be difficult to discern. Each of these can be better understood with added context. However, for larger groups of words, more context is needed. Unclear phrases are similar to unclear words, and the same methods can be used to understand their meaning. However, it is also important to consider how the individual words in the phrase work together. Paragraphs are a bit more complicated. Just as words must be compared to other words in a sentence, paragraphs must be compared to other paragraphs in a composition or a section.

Determining Meaning in Various Types of Compositions

To understand the meaning of an entire composition, the type of composition must be considered. **Expository writing** is generally organized so that each paragraph focuses on explaining one idea, or part of an idea, and its relevance. **Persuasive writing** uses paragraphs for different purposes to organize the parts of the argument. **Unclear paragraphs** must be read in the context of the paragraphs around them for their meaning to be fully understood. The meaning of full texts can also be unclear at times. The purpose of composition is also important for understanding the meaning of a text. To quickly understand the broad meaning of a text, look to the introductory and concluding paragraphs. Fictional texts are different. Some fictional works have implicit meanings, but some do not. The target audience must be considered for understanding texts that do have an implicit meaning, as most children's fiction will clearly state any lessons or morals. For other fiction, the application of literary theories and criticism may be helpful for understanding the text.

Additional Resources for Determining Word Meaning and Usage

While these strategies are useful for determining the meaning of unknown words and phrases, sometimes additional resources are needed to properly use the terms in different contexts. Some words have multiple definitions, and some words are inappropriate in particular contexts or modes of writing. The following tools are helpful for understanding all meanings and proper uses for words and phrases.

- **Dictionaries** provide the meaning of a multitude of words in a language. Many dictionaries include additional information about each word, such as its etymology, its synonyms, or variations of the word.
- **Glossaries** are similar to dictionaries, as they provide the meanings of a variety of terms. However, while dictionaries typically feature an extensive list of words and comprise an entire publication, glossaries are often included at the end of a text and only include terms and definitions that are relevant to the text they follow.

- **Spell Checkers** are used to detect spelling errors in typed text. Some spell checkers may also detect the misuse of plural or singular nouns, verb tenses, or capitalization. While spell checkers are a helpful tool, they are not always reliable or attuned to the author's intent, so it is important to review the spell checker's suggestions before accepting them.
- **Style Manuals** are guidelines on the preferred punctuation, format, and grammar usage according to different fields or organizations. For example, the Associated Press Stylebook is a style guide often used for media writing. The guidelines within a style guide are not always applicable across different contexts and usages, as the guidelines often cover grammatical or formatting situations that are not objectively correct or incorrect.

Chapter Quiz

1. Which of the following affixes refers to the *-o-* in "speedometer"?

a. Prefix
b. Suffix
c. Interfix
d. Circumfix

2. Adding the suffix *-ness* to a word typically does which of the following?

a. Changes a verb to a noun
b. Changes a verb to an adjective
c. Changes an adjective to a noun
d. Changes a noun to a verb

3. Which of the following is NOT considered a common adjective suffix?

a. *-acy*
b. *-able*
c. *-ish*
d. *-less*

4. Which of the following defines the noun suffix *-ation*?

a. Act, condition, fact
b. Action, state, result
c. Quality, state, result
d. State, rank, condition

Chapter Quiz Answer Key

1. C: Prefixes are affixes placed in front of words. For example, *heat* means to make hot, while *preheat* means to heat in advance. Suffixes are affixes placed at the ends of words. The *happiness* example above contains the suffix *-ness.* Circumfixes add parts both before and after words, such as how *light* becomes *enlighten* with the prefix *en-* and the suffix *-en.* Interfixes create compound words via central affixes: *speed* and *meter* become *speedometer* via the interfix *-o-*.

2. C: In English, certain suffixes generally indicate both that a word is a noun, and that the noun represents a state of being or quality. For example, *-ness* is commonly used to change an adjective into its noun form, as with *happy* and *happiness, kind* and *kindness,* and so on.

3. A: Adjective suffixes:

Suffix	Definition	Examples
-able (-ible)	capable of being	tolerable, edible
-esque	in the style of, like	picturesque, grotesque
-ful	filled with, marked by	thankful, zestful
-ific	make, cause	terrific, beatific
-ish	suggesting, like	churlish, childish
-less	lacking, without	hopeless, countless
-ous	marked by, given to	religious, riotous

4. B: Noun suffixes:

Suffix	Definition	Examples
-acy	state, condition	accuracy, privacy
-ance	act, condition, fact	acceptance, vigilance
-ard	one that does excessively	drunkard, sluggard
-ation	action, state, result	occupation, starvation
-dom	state, rank, condition	serfdom, wisdom
-er (-or)	office, action	teacher, elevator, honor
-ess	feminine	waitress, duchess
-hood	state, condition	manhood, statehood
-ion	action, result, state	union, fusion
-ism	act, manner, doctrine	barbarism, socialism
-ist	worker, follower	monopolist, socialist
-ity (-ty)	state, quality, condition	acidity, civility, twenty
-ment	result, action	refreshment
-ness	quality, state	greatness, tallness
-ship	position	internship, statesmanship
-sion (-tion)	state, result	revision, expedition
-th	act, state, quality	warmth, width
-tude	quality, state, result	magnitude, fortitude

Literal and Figurative Meaning

When language is used **literally**, the words mean exactly what they say and nothing more. When language is used **figuratively**, the words mean something beyond their literal meaning. For example, "The weeping willow tree has long, trailing branches and leaves" is a literal description. But "The weeping willow tree looks as if it is bending over and crying" is a figurative description—specifically, a **simile** or stated comparison. Another figurative language form is **metaphor**, or an implied comparison. A good example is the metaphor of a city, state, or city-state as a ship, and its governance as sailing that ship. Ancient Greek lyrical poet Alcaeus is credited with first using this metaphor, and ancient Greek tragedian Aeschylus then used it in *Seven Against Thebes,* and then Plato used it in the *Republic.*

Figures of Speech

A **figure of speech** is a verbal expression whose meaning is figurative rather than literal. For example, the phrase "butterflies in the stomach" does not refer to actual butterflies in a person's stomach. It is a metaphor representing the fluttery feelings experienced when a person is nervous or excited—or when one "falls in love," which does not mean physically falling. "Hitting a sales target" does not mean physically hitting a target with arrows as in archery; it is a metaphor for meeting a sales quota. "Climbing the ladder of success" metaphorically likens advancing in one's career to ascending ladder rungs. Similes, such as "light as a feather" (meaning very light, not a feather's actual weight), and hyperbole, like "I'm starving/freezing/roasting," are also figures of speech. Figures of speech are often used and crafted for emphasis, freshness of expression, or clarity.

> **Review Video: Figures of Speech**
> Visit mometrix.com/academy and enter code: 111295

Figurative Language

Figurative language extends past the literal meanings of words. It offers readers new insight into the people, things, events, and subjects covered in a work of literature. Figurative language also enables readers to feel they are sharing the authors' experiences. It can stimulate the reader's senses, make comparisons that readers find intriguing or even startling, and enable readers to view the world in different ways. When looking for figurative language, it is important to consider the context of the sentence or situation. Phrases that appear out of place or make little sense when read literally are likely instances of figurative language. Once figurative language has been recognized, context is also important to determining the type of figurative language being used and its function. For example, when a comparison is being made, a metaphor or simile is likely being used. This means the comparison may emphasize or create irony through the things being compared. Seven specific types of figurative language include: alliteration, onomatopoeia, personification, imagery, similes, metaphors, and hyperbole.

> **Review Video: Figurative Language**
> Visit mometrix.com/academy and enter code: 584902

Alliteration and Onomatopoeia

Alliteration describes a series of words beginning with the same sounds. **Onomatopoeia** uses words imitating the sounds of things they name or describe. For example, in his poem "Come Down, O Maid," Alfred Tennyson writes of "The moan of doves in immemorial elms, / And murmuring of innumerable bees." The word "moan" sounds like some sounds doves make, "murmuring" represents the sounds of bees buzzing. Onomatopoeia also includes words that are simply meant to represent sounds, such as "meow," "kaboom," and "whoosh."

> **Review Video: Alliterations Are All Around**
> Visit mometrix.com/academy and enter code: 462837

Personification

Another type of figurative language is **personification**. This is describing a non-human thing, like an animal or an object, as if it were human. The general intent of personification is to describe things in a manner that will be comprehensible to readers. When an author states that a tree *groans* in the wind, he or she does not mean that the tree is emitting a low, pained sound from a mouth. Instead, the author means that the tree is making a noise similar to a human groan. Of course, this personification establishes a tone of sadness or suffering. A different tone would be established if the author said that the tree was *swaying* or *dancing*. Alfred Tennyson's poem "The Eagle" uses all of these types of figurative language: "He clasps the crag with crooked hands." Tennyson used alliteration, repeating /k/ and /kr/ sounds. These hard-sounding consonants reinforce the imagery, giving visual and tactile impressions of the eagle.

Review Video: Personification
Visit mometrix.com/academy and enter code: 260066

Similes and Metaphors

Similes are stated comparisons using "like" or "as." Similes can be used to stimulate readers' imaginations and appeal to their senses. Because a simile includes *like* or *as,* the device creates more space between the description and the thing being described than a metaphor does. If an author says that *a house was like a shoebox*, then the tone is different than the author saying that the house *was* a shoebox. Authors will choose between a metaphor and a simile depending on their intended tone.

Similes also help compare fictional characters to well-known objects or experiences, so the reader can better relate to them. William Wordsworth's poem about "Daffodils" begins, "I wandered lonely as a cloud." This simile compares his loneliness to that of a cloud. It is also personification, giving a cloud the human quality loneliness. In his novel *Lord Jim* (1900), Joseph Conrad writes in Chapter 33, "I would have given anything for the power to soothe her frail soul, tormenting itself in its invincible ignorance like a small bird beating about the cruel wires of a cage." Conrad uses the word "like" to compare the girl's soul to a small bird. His description of the bird beating at the cage shows the similar helplessness of the girl's soul to gain freedom.

Review Video: Similes
Visit mometrix.com/academy and enter code: 642949

A **metaphor** is a type of figurative language in which the writer equates something with another thing that is not particularly similar, instead of using *like* or *as*. For instance, *the bird was an arrow arcing through the sky*. In this sentence, the arrow is serving as a metaphor for the bird. The point of a metaphor is to encourage the reader to consider the item being described in a *different way*. Let's continue with this metaphor for a flying bird. You are asked to envision the bird's flight as being similar to the arc of an arrow. So, you imagine the flight to be swift and bending. Metaphors are a way for the author to describe an item *without being direct and obvious*. This literary device is a lyrical and suggestive way of providing information. Note that the reference for a metaphor will not always be mentioned explicitly by the author. Consider the following description of a forest in winter: *Swaying skeletons reached for the sky and groaned as the wind blew through them.* In this example, the author is using *skeletons* as a metaphor for leafless trees. This metaphor creates a spooky tone while inspiring the reader's imagination.

Literary Examples of Metaphor

A **metaphor** is an implied comparison, i.e., it compares something to something else without using "like", "as", or other comparative words. For example, in "The Tyger" (1794), William Blake writes, "Tyger Tyger, burning bright, / In the forests of the night." Blake compares the tiger to a flame not by saying it is like a fire, but by simply describing it as "burning." Henry Wadsworth Longfellow's poem "O Ship of State" (1850) uses an extended metaphor by referring consistently throughout the entire poem to the state, union, or republic as a seagoing vessel, referring to its keel, mast, sail, rope, anchors, and to its braving waves, rocks, gale, tempest, and "false lights on the shore." Within the extended metaphor, Wordsworth uses a specific metaphor: "the anchors of thy hope!"

Ted Hughes' Animal Metaphors

Ted Hughes frequently used animal metaphors in his poetry. In "The Thought Fox," a model of concise, structured beauty, Hughes characterizes the poet's creative process with succinct, striking imagery of an idea entering his head like a wild fox. Repeating "loneliness" in the first two stanzas emphasizes the poet's lonely work: "Something else is alive / Beside the clock's loneliness." He treats an idea's arrival as separate from himself. Three stanzas detail in vivid images a fox's approach from the outside winter forest at starless midnight—its nose, "Cold, delicately" touching twigs and leaves; "neat" paw prints in snow; "bold" body; brilliant green eyes; and self-contained, focused progress—"Till, with a sudden sharp hot stink of fox," he metaphorically depicts poetic inspiration as the fox's physical entry into "the dark hole of the head." Hughes ends by summarizing his vision of a poet as an interior, passive idea recipient, with the outside world unchanged: "The window is starless still; the clock ticks, / The page is printed."

Review Video: Metaphors in Writing
Visit mometrix.com/academy and enter code: 133295

Hyperbole

Hyperbole is excessive exaggeration used for humor or emphasis rather than for literal meaning. For example, in *To Kill a Mockingbird*, Harper Lee wrote, "People moved slowly then. There was no hurry, for there was nowhere to go, nothing to buy and no money to buy it with, nothing to see outside the boundaries of Maycomb County." This was not literally true; Lee exaggerates the scarcity of these things for emphasis. In "Old Times on the Mississippi," Mark Twain wrote, "I... could have hung my hat on my eyes, they stuck out so far." This is not literal, but makes his description vivid and funny. In his poem "As I Walked Out One Evening", W. H. Auden wrote, "I'll love you, dear, I'll love you / Till China and Africa meet, / And the river jumps over the mountain / And the salmon sing in the street." He used things not literally possible to emphasize the duration of his love.

Review Video: Hyperbole and Understatement
Visit mometrix.com/academy and enter code: 308470

Literary Irony

In literature, irony demonstrates the opposite of what is said or done. The three types of irony are **verbal irony**, **situational irony**, and **dramatic irony**. Verbal irony uses words opposite to the meaning. Sarcasm may use verbal irony. One common example is describing something that is confusing as "clear as mud." For example, in his 1986 movie *Hannah and Her Sisters,* author, director, and actor Woody Allen says to his character's date, "I had a great evening; it was like the Nuremburg Trials." Notice these employ similes. In situational irony, what happens contrasts with what was expected. O. Henry's short story *The Gift of the Magi* uses situational irony: a husband and wife each sacrifice their most prized possession to buy each other a Christmas present. The irony is that she sells her long hair to buy him a watch fob, while he sells his heirloom pocket-watch to buy her the jeweled combs for her hair she had long wanted; in the end, neither of them can use their gifts. In dramatic irony, narrative informs audiences of more than its characters know. For example, in *Romeo and Juliet,* the audience is made aware that Juliet is only asleep, while Romeo believes her to be dead, which then leads to Romeo's death.

Review Video: What is the Definition of Irony?
Visit mometrix.com/academy and enter code: 374204

Idioms

Idioms create comparisons, and often take the form of similes or metaphors. Idioms are always phrases and are understood to have a meaning that is different from its individual words' literal meaning. For example, "break a leg" is a common idiom that is used to wish someone luck or tell them to perform well. Literally, the phrase "break a leg" means to injure a person's leg, but the phrase takes on a different meaning when used as an idiom. Another example is "call it a day," which means to temporarily stop working on a task, or find a stopping point, rather than literally referring to something as "a day." Many idioms are associated with a region or group. For example, an idiom commonly used in the American South is "'til the cows come home." This phrase is often used to indicate that something will take or may last for a very long time, but not that it will literally last until the cows return to where they reside.

Chapter Quiz

1. Who is credited with first using the metaphor of a city, state, or city-state as a ship?

a. Theseus
b. Aeschylus
c. Alcaeus
d. Plato

2. How many forms of irony are there?

a. Two
b. Three
c. Four
d. Five

Chapter Quiz Answer Key

1. C: Another figurative language form is metaphor, or an implied comparison. A good example is the metaphor of a city, state, or city-state as a ship, and its governance as sailing that ship. Ancient Greek lyrical poet Alcaeus is credited with first using this metaphor, followed by ancient Greek tragedian Aeschylus using it in *Seven Against Thebes,* and then Plato using it in the *Republic.*

2. B: In literature, irony demonstrates the opposite of what is said or done. The three types of irony are verbal irony, situational irony, and dramatic irony. Verbal irony uses words opposite to the meaning. Sarcasm may use verbal irony. One common example is describing something that is confusing as "clear as mud." In his 1986 movie *Hannah and Her Sisters,* author, director, and actor Woody Allen says to his character's date, "I had a great evening; it was like the Nuremburg Trials." Notice these employ similes. In situational irony, what happens contrasts with what was expected. O. Henry's short story *The Gift of the Magi* uses situational irony: a husband and wife each sacrifice their most prized possession to buy each other a Christmas present. The irony is that she sells her long hair to buy him a watch fob, while he sells his heirloom pocket-watch to buy her the jeweled combs for her hair she had long wanted; in the end, neither of them can use their gifts. In dramatic irony, narrative informs audiences of more than its characters know. For example, in *Romeo and Juliet,* the audience is made aware that Juliet is only asleep, while Romeo believes her to be dead, which then leads to Romeo's death.

Information and Ideas

Text Features in Informational Texts

The **title of a text** gives readers some idea of its content. The **table of contents** is a list near the beginning of a text, showing the book's sections and chapters and their coinciding page numbers. This gives readers an overview of the whole text and helps them find specific chapters easily. An **appendix**, at the back of the book or document, includes important information that is not present in the main text. Also at the back, an **index** lists the book's important topics alphabetically with their page numbers to help readers find them easily. **Glossaries**, usually found at the backs of books, list technical terms alphabetically with their definitions to aid vocabulary learning and comprehension. Boldface print is used to emphasize certain words, often identifying words included in the text's glossary where readers can look up their definitions. **Headings** separate sections of text and show the topic of each. **Subheadings** divide subject headings into smaller, more specific categories to help readers organize information. **Footnotes**, at the bottom of the page, give readers more information, such as citations or links. **Bullet points** list items separately, making facts and ideas easier to see and understand. A **sidebar** is a box of information to one side of the main text giving additional information, often on a more focused or in-depth example of a topic.

Illustrations and **photographs** are pictures that visually emphasize important points in text. The captions below the illustrations explain what those images show. Charts and tables are visual forms of information that make something easier to understand quickly. Diagrams are drawings that show relationships or explain a process. Graphs visually show the relationships among multiple sets of information plotted along vertical and horizontal axes. Maps show geographical information visually to help readers understand the relative locations of places covered in the text. Timelines are visual graphics that show historical events in chronological order to help readers see their sequence.

Review Video: Informative Text
Visit mometrix.com/academy and enter code: 924964

Language Use

Literal and Figurative Language

As in fictional literature, informational text also uses both **literal language**, which means just what it says, and **figurative language**, which imparts more than literal meaning. For example, an informational text author might use a simile or direct comparison, such as writing that a racehorse "ran like the wind." Informational text authors also use metaphors or implied comparisons, such as "the cloud of the Great Depression." Imagery may also appear in informational texts to increase the reader's understanding of ideas and concepts discussed in the text.

Explicit and Implicit Information

When informational text states something explicitly, the reader is told by the author exactly what is meant, which can include the author's interpretation or perspective of events. For example, a professor writes, "I have seen students go into an absolute panic just because they weren't able to complete the exam in the time they were allotted." This explicitly tells the reader that the students were afraid, and by using the words "just because," the writer indicates their fear was exaggerated out of proportion relative to what happened. However, another professor writes, "I have had students come to me, their faces drained of all color, saying 'We weren't able to finish the exam.'" This is an example of implicit meaning: the second writer did not state explicitly that the students were panicked. Instead, he wrote a description of their faces being "drained of all color." From this description, the reader can infer that the students were so frightened that their faces paled.

Review Video: Explicit and Implicit Information
Visit mometrix.com/academy and enter code: 735771

Technical Language

Technical language is more impersonal than literary and vernacular language. Passive voice makes the tone impersonal. For example, instead of writing, "We found this a central component of protein metabolism," scientists write, "This was found a central component of protein metabolism." While science professors have traditionally instructed students to avoid active voice because it leads to first-person ("I" and "we") usage, science editors today find passive voice dull and weak. Many journal articles combine both. Tone in technical science writing should be detached, concise, and professional. While one may normally write, "This chemical has to be available for proteins to be digested," professionals write technically, "The presence of this chemical is required for the enzyme to break the covalent bonds of proteins." The use of technical language appeals to both technical and non-technical audiences by displaying the author or speaker's understanding of the subject and suggesting their credibility regarding the message they are communicating.

Technical Material for Non-Technical Readers

Writing about **technical subjects** for **non-technical readers** differs from writing for colleagues because authors place more importance on delivering a critical message than on imparting the maximum technical content possible. Technical authors also must assume that non-technical audiences do not have the expertise to comprehend extremely scientific or technical messages, concepts, and terminology. They must resist the temptation to impress audiences with their scientific knowledge and expertise and remember that their primary purpose is to communicate a message that non-technical readers will understand, feel, and respond to. Non-technical and technical styles include similarities. Both should formally cite any references or other authors' work utilized in the text. Both must follow intellectual property and copyright regulations. This includes the author's protecting his or her own rights, or a public domain statement, as he or she chooses.

Review Video: Technical Passages
Visit mometrix.com/academy and enter code: 478923

Non-Technical Audiences

Writers of technical or scientific material may need to write for many non-technical audiences. Some readers have no technical or scientific background, and those who do may not be in the same field as the authors. Government and corporate policymakers and budget managers need technical information they can understand for decision-making. Citizens affected by technology or science are a different audience. Non-governmental organizations can encompass many of the preceding groups. Elementary and secondary school programs also need non-technical language for presenting technical subject matter. Additionally, technical authors will need to use non-technical language when collecting consumer responses to surveys, presenting scientific or para-scientific material to the public, writing about the history of science, and writing about science and technology in developing countries.

Use of Everyday Language

Authors of technical information sometimes must write using non-technical language that readers outside their disciplinary fields can comprehend. They should use not only non-technical terms, but also normal, everyday language to accommodate readers whose native language is different than the language the text is written in. For example, instead of writing that "eustatic changes like thermal expansion are causing hazardous conditions in the littoral zone," an author would do better to write that "a rising sea level is threatening the coast." When technical terms cannot be avoided, authors should also define or explain them using non-technical language. Although authors must cite references and acknowledge their use of others' work, they should avoid the kinds of references or citations that they would use in scientific journals—unless they reinforce author messages. They should not use endnotes, footnotes, or any other complicated referential techniques because non-technical journal publishers usually do not accept them. Including high-resolution illustrations, photos, maps, or satellite images and incorporating multimedia into digital publications will enhance non-technical writing about technical subjects. Technical authors may publish using non-technical language in e-journals, trade journals, specialty newsletters, and daily newspapers.

MAKING INFERENCES ABOUT INFORMATIONAL TEXT

With informational text, reader comprehension depends not only on recalling important statements and details, but also on reader inferences based on examples and details. Readers add information from the text to what they already know to draw inferences about the text. These inferences help the readers to fill in the information that the text does not explicitly state, enabling them to understand the text better. When reading a nonfictional autobiography or biography, for example, the most appropriate inferences might concern the events in the book, the actions of the subject of the autobiography or biography, and the message the author means to convey. When reading a nonfictional expository (informational) text, the reader would best draw inferences about problems and their solutions, and causes and their effects. When reading a nonfictional persuasive text, the reader will want to infer ideas supporting the author's message and intent.

STRUCTURES OR ORGANIZATIONAL PATTERNS IN INFORMATIONAL TEXTS

Informational text can be **descriptive**, appealing to the five senses and answering the questions what, who, when, where, and why. Another method of structuring informational text is sequence and order. **Chronological** texts relate events in the sequence that they occurred, from start to finish, while how-to texts organize information into a series of instructions in the sequence in which the steps should be followed. **Comparison-contrast** structures of informational text describe various ideas to their readers by pointing out how things or ideas are similar and how they are different. **Cause and effect** structures of informational text describe events that occurred and identify the causes or reasons that those events occurred. **Problem and solution** structures of informational texts introduce and describe problems and offer one or more solutions for each problem described.

DETERMINING AN INFORMATIONAL AUTHOR'S PURPOSE

Informational authors' purposes are why they write texts. Readers must determine authors' motivations and goals. Readers gain greater insight into a text by considering the author's motivation. This develops critical reading skills. Readers perceive writing as a person's voice, not simply printed words. Uncovering author motivations and purposes empowers readers to know what to expect from the text, read for relevant details, evaluate authors and their work critically, and respond effectively to the motivations and persuasions of the text. The main idea of a text is what the reader is supposed to understand from reading it; the purpose of the text is why the author has written it and what the author wants readers to do with its information. Authors state some purposes clearly, while other purposes may be unstated but equally significant. When stated purposes contradict other parts of a text, the author may have a hidden agenda. Readers can better evaluate a text's effectiveness, whether they agree or disagree with it, and why they agree or disagree through identifying unstated author purposes.

IDENTIFYING AUTHOR'S POINT OF VIEW OR PURPOSE

In some informational texts, readers find it easy to identify the author's point of view and purpose, such as when the author explicitly states his or her position and reason for writing. But other texts are more difficult, either because of the content or because the authors give neutral or balanced viewpoints. This is particularly true in scientific texts, in which authors may state the purpose of their research in the report, but never state their point of view except by interpreting evidence or data.

To analyze text and identify point of view or purpose, readers should ask themselves the following four questions:

1. With what main point or idea does this author want to persuade readers to agree?
2. How does this author's word choice affect the way that readers consider this subject?
3. How do this author's choices of examples and facts affect the way that readers consider this subject?
4. What is it that this author wants to accomplish by writing this text?

Review Video: Understanding the Author's Intent
Visit mometrix.com/academy and enter code: 511819

Review Video: Author's Position
Visit mometrix.com/academy and enter code: 827954

EVALUATING ARGUMENTS MADE BY INFORMATIONAL TEXT WRITERS

When evaluating an informational text, the first step is to identify the argument's conclusion. Then identify the author's premises that support the conclusion. Try to paraphrase premises for clarification and make the conclusion and premises fit. List all premises first, sequentially numbered, then finish with the conclusion. Identify any premises or assumptions not stated by the author but required for the stated premises to support the conclusion. Read word assumptions sympathetically, as the author might. Evaluate whether premises reasonably support the conclusion. For inductive reasoning, the reader should ask if the premises are true, if they support the conclusion, and if so, how strongly. For deductive reasoning, the reader should ask if the argument is valid or invalid. If all premises are true, then the argument is valid unless the conclusion can be false. If it can, then the argument is invalid. An invalid argument can be made valid through alterations such as the addition of needed premises.

USE OF RHETORIC IN INFORMATIONAL TEXTS

There are many ways authors can support their claims, arguments, beliefs, ideas, and reasons for writing in informational texts. For example, authors can appeal to readers' sense of **logic** by communicating their reasoning through a carefully sequenced series of logical steps to help "prove" the points made. Authors can appeal to readers' **emotions** by using descriptions and words that evoke feelings of sympathy, sadness, anger, righteous indignation, hope, happiness, or any other emotion to reinforce what they express and share with their audience. Authors may appeal to the **moral** or **ethical values** of readers by using words and descriptions that can convince readers that something is right or wrong. By relating personal anecdotes, authors can supply readers with more accessible, realistic examples of points they make, as well as appealing to their emotions. They can provide supporting evidence by reporting case studies. They can also illustrate their points by making analogies to which readers can better relate.

Chapter Quiz

1. Which of the following is the first step in evaluating an informational text?

a. Read word assumptions sympathetically
b. List all premises sequentially
c. Determine if the premises are true
d. Identify the argument's conclusion

2. Which of the following is NOT considered a type of appeal for an author to use?

a. Logic
b. Ethics
c. Emotions
d. Imagination

Chapter Quiz Answer Key

1. D: When evaluating an informational text, the first step is to identify the argument's conclusion. After that comes identifying the author's premises that support the conclusion. The reader should try to paraphrase premises for clarification and make the conclusion and premises fit. List all premises first, sequentially numbered, then finish with the conclusion. Identify any premises or assumptions not stated by the author but required for the stated premises to support the conclusion. Read word assumptions sympathetically, as the author might. Evaluate whether premises reasonably support the conclusion. For inductive reasoning, the reader should ask if the premises are true, if they support the conclusion, and how strong that support is. For deductive reasoning, the reader should ask if the argument is valid or invalid. If all premises are true, then the argument is valid unless the conclusion can be false. If it can, then the argument is invalid. An invalid argument can be made valid through alterations such as the addition of needed premises.

2. D: There are many ways authors can support their claims, arguments, beliefs, ideas, and reasons for writing in informational texts. For example, authors can appeal to readers' sense of logic by communicating their reasoning through a carefully sequenced series of logical steps to support their positions. Authors can appeal to readers' emotions by using descriptions and words that evoke feelings of sympathy, sadness, anger, righteous indignation, hope, happiness, or any other emotion to reinforce what they express and share with their audience. Authors may appeal to the moral or ethical values of readers by using words and descriptions that can convince readers that something is right or wrong. By relating personal anecdotes, authors can appeal to readers' emotions and supply them with more accessible, realistic examples of points they make. They can provide supporting evidence by reporting case studies. They can also illustrate their points by making analogies to which readers can better relate.

Rhetoric

Persuasive Techniques

To **appeal using reason**, writers present logical arguments, such as using "If... then... because" statements. To **appeal to emotions**, authors may ask readers how they would feel about something or to put themselves in another's place, present their argument as one that will make the audience feel good, or tell readers how they should feel. To **appeal to character**, **morality**, or **ethics**, authors present their points to readers as the right or most moral choices. Authors cite expert opinions to show readers that someone very knowledgeable about the subject or viewpoint agrees with the author's claims. **Testimonials**, usually via anecdotes or quotations regarding the author's subject, help build the audience's trust in an author's message through positive support from ordinary people. **Bandwagon appeals** claim that everybody else agrees with the author's argument and persuade readers to conform and agree, also. Authors **appeal to greed** by presenting their choice as cheaper, free, or more valuable for less cost. They **appeal to laziness** by presenting their views as more convenient, easy, or relaxing. Authors also anticipate potential objections and argue against them before audiences think of them, thereby depicting those objections as weak.

Authors can use **comparisons** like analogies, similes, and metaphors to persuade audiences. For example, a writer might represent excessive expenses as "hemorrhaging" money, which the author's recommended solution will stop. Authors can use negative word connotations to make some choices unappealing to readers, and positive word connotations to make others more appealing. Using **humor** can relax readers and garner their agreement. However, writers must take care: ridiculing opponents can be a successful strategy for appealing to readers who already agree with the author, but can backfire by angering other readers. **Rhetorical questions** need no answer, but create effect that can force agreement, such as asking the question, "Wouldn't you rather be paid more than less?" **Generalizations** persuade readers by being impossible to disagree with. Writers can easily make generalizations that appear to support their viewpoints, like saying, "We all want peace, not war" regarding more specific political arguments. **Transfer** and **association** persuade by example: if advertisements show attractive actors enjoying their products, audiences imagine they will experience the same. **Repetition** can also sometimes effectively persuade audiences.

Review Video: Using Rhetorical Strategies for Persuasion
Visit mometrix.com/academy and enter code: 302658

Classical Author Appeals

In his *On Rhetoric,* ancient Greek philosopher Aristotle defined three basic types of appeal used in writing, which he called *pathos*, *ethos*, and *logos*. ***Pathos*** means suffering or experience and refers to appeals to the emotions (the English word *pathetic* comes from this root). Writing that is meant to entertain audiences, by making them either happy, as with comedy, or sad, as with tragedy, uses *pathos*. Aristotle's *Poetics* states that evoking the emotions of terror and pity is one of the criteria for writing tragedy. ***Ethos*** means character and connotes ideology (the English word *ethics* comes from this root). Writing that appeals to credibility, based on academic, professional, or personal merit, uses *ethos*. ***Logos*** means "I say" and refers to a plea, opinion, expectation, word or speech, account, opinion, or reason (the English word *logic* comes from this root.) Aristotle used it to mean persuasion that appeals to the audience through reasoning and logic to influence their opinions.

Critical Evaluation of Effectiveness of Persuasive Methods

First, readers should identify the author's **thesis**—what he or she argues for or against. They should consider the argument's content and the author's reason for presenting it. Does the author offer **solutions** to problems raised? If so, are they realistic? Note all central ideas and evidence supporting the author's thesis. Research any unfamiliar subjects or vocabulary. Readers should then outline or summarize the work in their own words. Identify which types of appeals the author uses. Readers should evaluate how well the author communicated meaning from the reader's perspective: Did they respond to emotional appeals with anger, concern, happiness, etc.? If so, why? Decide if the author's reasoning sufficed for changing the reader's mind. Determine whether the content and presentation were accurate, cohesive, and clear. Readers should also ask themselves whether they found the author believable or not, and why or why not.

EVALUATING AN ARGUMENT

Argumentative and persuasive passages take a stand on a debatable issue, seek to explore all sides of the issue, and find the best possible solution. Argumentative and persuasive passages should not be combative or abusive. The word *argument* may remind you of two or more people shouting at each other and walking away in anger. However, an argumentative or persuasive passage should be a calm and reasonable presentation of an author's ideas for others to consider. When an author writes reasonable arguments, his or her goal is not to win or have the last word. Instead, authors want to reveal current understanding of the question at hand and suggest a solution to a problem. The purpose of argument and persuasion in a free society is to reach the best solution.

EVIDENCE

The term **text evidence** refers to information that supports a main point or minor points and can help lead the reader to a conclusion about the text's credibility. Information used as text evidence is precise, descriptive, and factual. A main point is often followed by supporting details that provide evidence to back up a claim. For example, a passage may include the claim that winter occurs during opposite months in the Northern and Southern hemispheres. Text evidence for this claim may include examples of countries where winter occurs in opposite months. Stating that the tilt of the Earth as it rotates around the sun causes winter to occur at different times in separate hemispheres is another example of text evidence. Text evidence can come from common knowledge, but it is also valuable to include text evidence from credible, relevant outside sources.

Review Video: Textual Evidence
Visit mometrix.com/academy and enter code: 486236

Evidence that supports the thesis and additional arguments needs to be provided. Most arguments must be supported by facts or statistics. A fact is something that is known with certainty, has been verified by several independent individuals, and can be proven to be true. In addition to facts, examples and illustrations can support an argument by adding an emotional component. With this component, you persuade readers in ways that facts and statistics cannot. The emotional component is effective when used alongside objective information that can be confirmed.

CREDIBILITY

The text used to support an argument can be the argument's downfall if the text is not credible. A text is **credible**, or believable, when its author is knowledgeable and objective, or unbiased. The author's motivations for writing the text play a critical role in determining the credibility of the text and must be evaluated when assessing that credibility. Reports written about the ozone layer by an environmental scientist and a hairdresser will have a different level of credibility.

Review Video: Author Credibility
Visit mometrix.com/academy and enter code: 827257

APPEAL TO EMOTION

Sometimes, authors will appeal to the reader's emotion in an attempt to persuade or to distract the reader from the weakness of the argument. For instance, the author may try to inspire the pity of the reader by delivering a heart-rending story. An author also might use the bandwagon approach, in which he suggests that his opinion is correct because it is held by the majority. Some authors resort to name-calling, in which insults and harsh words are delivered to the opponent in an attempt to distract. In advertising, a common appeal is the celebrity testimonial, in which a famous person endorses a product. Of course, the fact that a famous person likes something should not really mean anything to the reader. These and other emotional appeals are usually evidence of poor reasoning and a weak argument.

Review Video: Emotional Language in Literature
Visit mometrix.com/academy and enter code: 759390

Counter Arguments

When authors give both sides to the argument, they build trust with their readers. As a reader, you should start with an undecided or neutral position. If an author presents only his or her side to the argument, then they are not exhibiting credibility and are weakening their argument.

Building common ground with readers can be effective for persuading neutral, skeptical, or opposed readers. Sharing values with undecided readers can allow people to switch positions without giving up what they feel is important. People who may oppose a position need to feel that they can change their minds without betraying who they are as a person. This appeal to having an open mind can be a powerful tool in arguing a position without antagonizing other views. Objections can be countered on a point-by-point basis or in a summary paragraph. Be mindful of how an author points out flaws in counter arguments. If they are unfair to the other side of the argument, then you should lose trust with the author.

Rhetorical Devices

- An **anecdote** is a brief story authors may relate to their argument, which can illustrate their points in a more real and relatable way.
- **Aphorisms** concisely state common beliefs and may rhyme. For example, Benjamin Franklin's "Early to bed and early to rise / Makes a man healthy, wealthy, and wise" is an aphorism.
- **Allusions** refer to literary or historical figures to impart symbolism to a thing or person and to create reader resonance. In John Steinbeck's *Of Mice and Men,* protagonist George's last name is Milton. This alludes to John Milton, who wrote *Paradise Lost*, and symbolizes George's eventual loss of his dream.
- **Satire** exaggerates, ridicules, or pokes fun at human flaws or ideas, as in the works of Jonathan Swift and Mark Twain.
- A **parody** is a form of satire that imitates another work to ridicule its topic or style.
- A **paradox** is a statement that is true despite appearing contradictory.
- **Hyperbole** is overstatement using exaggerated language.
- An **oxymoron** combines seeming contradictions, such as "deafening silence."
- **Analogies** compare two things that share common elements.
- **Similes** (stated comparisons using the words *like* or *as*) and **metaphors** (stated comparisons that do not use *like* or *as*) are considered forms of analogy.
- When using logic to reason with audiences, **syllogism** refers either to deductive reasoning or a deceptive, very sophisticated, or subtle argument.
- **Deductive reasoning** moves from general to specific, **inductive reasoning** from specific to general.
- **Diction** is author word choice that establishes tone and effect.
- **Understatement** achieves effects like contrast or irony by downplaying or describing something more subtly than warranted.

- **Chiasmus** uses parallel clauses, the second reversing the order of the first. Examples include T. S. Eliot's "Has the Church failed mankind, or has mankind failed the Church?" and John F. Kennedy's "Ask not what your country can do for you; ask what you can do for your country."
- **Anaphora** regularly repeats a word or phrase at the beginnings of consecutive clauses or phrases to add emphasis to an idea. A classic example of anaphora was Winston Churchill's emphasis of determination: "[W]e shall fight on the beaches, we shall fight on the landing grounds, we shall fight in the fields and in the streets, we shall fight in the hills; we shall never surrender..."

Chapter Quiz

1. Which of the following rhetorical devices exaggerates, ridicules, or pokes fun at human flaws or ideas?

a. Allusions
b. Satire
c. Parody
d. Hyperbole

2. An author arguing that his point is correct because everybody else already agrees with it is an example of which persuasive technique?

a. Appeal to laziness
b. Bandwagon appeal
c. Testimonials
d. Generalizations

Chapter Quiz Answer Key

1. B: Rhetorical devices:

- An anecdote is a brief story authors may relate to their argument, which can illustrate their points in a more real and relatable way.
- Aphorisms concisely state common beliefs and may rhyme. For example, Benjamin Franklin's "Early to bed and early to rise / Makes a man healthy, wealthy, and wise" is an aphorism.
- Allusions refer to literary or historical figures to impart symbolism to a thing or person and to create reader resonance. In John Steinbeck's *Of Mice and Men,* protagonist George's last name is Milton. This alludes to John Milton, who wrote *Paradise Lost*, and symbolizes George's eventual loss of his dream.
- Satire exaggerates, ridicules, or pokes fun at human flaws or ideas, as in the works of Jonathan Swift and Mark Twain.
- A parody is a form of satire that imitates another work to ridicule its topic or style.
- A paradox is a statement that is true despite appearing contradictory.
- Hyperbole is overstatement using exaggerated language.
- An oxymoron combines seeming contradictions, such as "deafening silence."
- Analogies compare two things that share common elements.
- Similes (stated comparisons using the words *like* or *as*) and metaphors (stated comparisons that do not use *like* or *as*) are considered forms of analogy.
- When using logic to reason with audiences, syllogism refers either to deductive reasoning or a deceptive, very sophisticated, or subtle argument.

- Deductive reasoning moves from general to specific, while inductive reasoning moves from specific to general.
- Diction is author word choice that establishes tone and effect.
- Understatement achieves effects like contrast or irony by downplaying or describing something more subtly than warranted.
- Chiasmus uses parallel clauses, with the second clause reversing the order of the first. Examples include T. S. Eliot's "Has the Church failed mankind, or has mankind failed the Church?" and John F. Kennedy's "Ask not what your country can do for you—ask what you can do for your country."
- Anaphora regularly repeats a word or phrase at the beginnings of consecutive clauses or phrases to add emphasis to an idea. A classic example of anaphora was Winston Churchill's emphasis of determination: "[W]e shall fight on the beaches, we shall fight on the landing grounds, we shall fight in the fields and in the streets, we shall fight in the hills; we shall never surrender..."

2. B: Bandwagon appeals claim that everybody else agrees with the author's argument and thus try to persuade readers to conform and agree as well.

Author's Argument in Argumentative Writing

In argumentative writing, the argument is a belief, position, or opinion that the author wants to convince readers to believe as well. For the first step, readers should identify the **issue**. Some issues are controversial, meaning people disagree about them. Gun control, foreign policy, and the death penalty are all controversial issues. The next step is to determine the **author's position** on the issue. That position or viewpoint constitutes the author's argument. Readers should then identify the **author's assumptions**: things he or she accepts, believes, or takes for granted without needing proof. Inaccurate or illogical assumptions produce flawed arguments and can mislead readers. Readers should identify what kinds of **supporting evidence** the author offers, such as research results, personal observations or experiences, case studies, facts, examples, expert testimony and opinions, and comparisons. Readers should decide how relevant this support is to the argument.

Review Video: Argumentative Writing
Visit mometrix.com/academy and enter code: 561544

Evaluating an Author's Argument

The first three reader steps to **evaluate an author's argument** are to identify the **author's assumptions**, identify the **supporting evidence**, and decide **whether the evidence is relevant**. For example, if an author is not an expert on a particular topic, then that author's personal experience or opinion might not be relevant. The fourth step is to assess the **author's objectivity**. For example, consider whether the author introduces clear, understandable supporting evidence and facts to support the argument. The fifth step is evaluating whether the author's **argument is complete**. When authors give sufficient support for their arguments and also anticipate and respond effectively to opposing arguments or objections to their points, their arguments are complete. However, some authors omit information that could detract from their arguments. If instead they stated this information and refuted it, it would strengthen their arguments. The sixth step in evaluating an author's argumentative writing is to assess whether the **argument is valid**. Providing clear, logical reasoning makes an author's argument valid. Readers should ask themselves whether the author's points follow a sequence that makes sense, and whether each point leads to the next. The seventh step is to determine whether the author's **argument is credible**, meaning that it is convincing and believable. Arguments that are not valid are not credible, so step seven depends on step six. Readers should be mindful of their own biases as they evaluate and should not expect authors to conclusively prove their arguments, but rather to provide effective support and reason.

Evaluating an Author's Method of Appeal

To evaluate the effectiveness of an appeal, it is important to consider the author's purpose for writing. Any appeals an author uses in their argument must be relevant to the argument's goal. For example, a writer that argues for the reclassification of Pluto, but primarily uses appeals to emotion, will not have an effective argument. This writer should focus on using appeals to logic and support their argument with provable facts. While most arguments should include appeals to logic, emotion, and credibility, some arguments only call for one or two of these types of appeal. Evidence can support an appeal, but the evidence must be relevant to truly strengthen the appeal's effectiveness. If the writer arguing for Pluto's reclassification uses the reasons for Jupiter's classification as evidence, their argument would be weak. This information may seem relevant because it is related to the classification of planets. However, this classification is highly dependent on the size of the celestial object, and Jupiter is significantly bigger than Pluto. This use of evidence is illogical and does not support the appeal. Even when appropriate evidence and appeals are used, appeals and arguments lose their effectiveness when they create logical fallacies.

Opinions, Facts, and Fallacies

Critical thinking skills are mastered through understanding various types of writing and the different purposes of authors can have for writing different passages. Every author writes for a purpose. When you understand their purpose and how they accomplish their goal, you will be able to analyze their writing and determine whether or not you agree with their conclusions.

Readers must always be aware of the difference between fact and opinion. A **fact** can be subjected to analysis and proven to be true. An **opinion**, on the other hand, is the author's personal thoughts or feelings and may not be altered by research or evidence. If the author writes that the distance from New York City to Boston is about two hundred miles, then he or she is stating a fact. If the author writes that New York City is too crowded, then he or she is giving an opinion because there is no objective standard for overpopulation. Opinions are often supported by facts. For instance, an author might use a comparison between the population density of New York City and that of other major American cities as evidence of an overcrowded population. An opinion supported by facts tends to be more convincing. On the other hand, when authors support their opinions with other opinions, readers should employ critical thinking and approach the argument with skepticism.

Review Video: Fact or Opinion
Visit mometrix.com/academy and enter code: 870899

Reliable Sources

When you have an argumentative passage, you need to be sure that facts are presented to the reader from **reliable sources**. An opinion is what the author thinks about a given topic. An opinion is not common knowledge or proven by expert sources, instead the information is the personal beliefs and thoughts of the author. To distinguish between fact and opinion, a reader needs to consider the type of source that is presenting information, the information that backs-up a claim, and the author's motivation to have a certain point-of-view on a given topic. For example, if a panel of scientists has conducted multiple studies on the effectiveness of taking a certain vitamin, then the results are more likely to be factual than those of a company that is selling a vitamin and simply claims that taking the vitamin can produce positive effects. The company is motivated to sell their product, and the scientists are using the scientific method to prove a theory. Remember, if you find sentences that contain phrases such as "I think...", then the statement is an opinion.

Biases

In their attempts to persuade, writers often make mistakes in their thought processes and writing choices. These processes and choices are important to understand so you can make an informed decision about the author's credibility. Every author has a point of view, but authors demonstrate a **bias** when they ignore reasonable counterarguments or distort opposing viewpoints. A bias is evident whenever the author's claims are presented in a way that is unfair or inaccurate. Bias can be intentional or unintentional, but readers should be skeptical of the author's argument in either case. Remember that a biased author may still be correct. However, the author will be correct in spite of, not because of, his or her bias.

A **stereotype** is a bias applied specifically to a group of people or a place. Stereotyping is considered to be particularly abhorrent because it promotes negative, misleading generalizations about people. Readers should be very cautious of authors who use stereotypes in their writing. These faulty assumptions typically reveal the author's ignorance and lack of curiosity.

Review Video: Bias and Stereotype
Visit mometrix.com/academy and enter code: 644829

Chapter Quiz

1. Which of the following is NOT one of the first three steps of evaluating an author's argument?

a. Identify the author's assumptions
b. Identify the supporting evidence
c. Evaluate if the author's argument is complete
d. Decide if the supporting evidence is relevant

Chapter Quiz Answer Key

1. C: The first three reader steps to evaluate an author's argument are to identify the author's assumptions, identify the supporting evidence, and decide whether the evidence is relevant. For example, if an author is not an expert on a particular topic, then that author's personal experience or opinion might not be relevant. The fourth step is to assess the author's objectivity. For example, consider whether the author introduces clear, understandable supporting evidence and facts to support the argument. The fifth step is evaluating whether the author's argument is complete. When authors give sufficient support for their arguments and also anticipate and respond effectively to opposing arguments or objections to their points, their arguments are complete. However, some authors omit information that could detract from their arguments. If instead they stated this information and refuted it, it would likely strengthen their arguments. The sixth step in evaluating an author's argumentative writing is to assess whether the argument is valid. Providing clear, logical reasoning makes an author's argument valid. Readers should ask themselves whether the author's points follow a sequence that makes sense, and whether each point leads to the next. The seventh step is to determine whether the author's argument is credible, meaning that it is convincing and believable. Arguments that are not valid are not credible, so step seven depends on step six. Readers should be mindful of their own biases as they evaluate and should not expect authors to conclusively prove their arguments, but rather to provide effective support and reason.

Writing and Language Test

Writing and Language Test Overview

Writing and Language Test Overview

The writing and language portion of the PSAT consists of one 35-minute section. It will contain 4 passages and there will be a total of 44 questions relating to these passages. The breakdown of passages and questions is shown in the table below.

Careers	1 passage; 11 questions	25%
History/Social Studies	1 passage; 11 questions	25%
Humanities	1 passage; 11 questions	25%
Science	1 passage; 11 questions	25%

The PSAT Writing and Language Test will contain a range of text complexities from grades 9-10 to post-secondary entry. The passages will cover the subjects from the table above. The test will also contain one or more graphics in one or more sets of questions. These may include tables, graphs, and charts. They will vary in level of difficulty as well as data density, and number of variables.

The questions on the Writing and Language portion of the test are divided into two categories. The first category, called **Expression of Ideas**, is essentially testing whether students understand how to effectively communicate ideas in writing. The second category, called **Standard English Conventions**, is essentially testing whether students are able to practically apply their knowledge of the conventions of standard written English. Both types of questions are set in the context of revising a sample written passage. Students are asked to modify specific portions of the passage by selecting the best words, phrases, concepts, order, and structure to ensure that the final version of the passage adheres to the conventions of writing, is consistent with the author's style and purpose, and effectively conveys the message the author intends.

Question Types in the Writing and Language Section

The questions in this section will focus on the revision of a text. They will ask the student to revise for topic development, accuracy, logic, cohesion, and rhetorically effective use of language. Many of the skills needed for these questions are the same skills as are needed for the Reading Test or are built upon those skills.

Proposition and Support

Proposition questions will require the student to add, retain, or revise central ideas, main claims, counterclaims, and topic sentences. These revisions should be made to convey arguments, information, and ideas more clearly and effectively. *Support* questions will ask the student to add, revise, or retain information and ideas with the intention of supporting claims in the text.

Focus

For these questions, students will be asked to add, revise, retain, or delete information for the sake of relevance. These revisions should make the text more relevant and focused.

These questions are generally straightforward and do not require any special skills to answer. The correct answer will be the one that best stays on topic and coherently contributes to the author's main point in the paragraph or passage.

Quantitative Information

These questions will ask the student to relate information presented quantitatively to information presented in the text. The quantitative information may be in the form of graphs, charts, and tables.

The only particular skill needed for these questions is the ability to read and understand the information contained within a graphic. Questions will typically require you to select the choice that accurately reflects the quantitative information conveyed by the graphic. Answer choices for this type of question are often long, so reading through them can be time-consuming. However, you should be able to scan the answer choices for numbers and quickly determine which ones match the quantities with their correct values. In general, there should be only one choice that uses the correct values (i.e., a single question won't ask you to both determine the correct quantitative information and decide how to state it in the most concise way).

Organization

For these questions, the student should revise the text with the intention of improving the logical order that the information is presented in.

These questions generally come at the end of a paragraph (or the whole passage) and ask you to decide whether a sentence (or a paragraph) should be moved to a different location. Since these questions come at the end of the paragraph, you will already have read the paragraph when you get to them, so start by mentally relocating the sentence into each of the suggested positions to see what makes the most sense. In some cases, the sentence may fit into a logical progression within the paragraph that will give you a clue about where it ought to go. Does the sentence refer back to anything that has already been said? At other times, there may be grammatical clues within the sentence that offer hints. Do the verb tenses transition from past to present or present to future over the course of the paragraph? Even if you can't determine exactly which choice would be considered the best, you can usually use these techniques to rule out some of them.

Introductions, Conclusions, and Transitions

These questions require the student to revise the beginning or ending of passages, paragraphs, and sentences. Students will ensure that transition words, phrases, or sentences are used effectively to connect the information and ideas being presented in the passage.

This is often the largest single category of questions on the Writing and Language test. There will usually be 5-7 of these questions on each test.

Precision

For these questions, students will revise the text to improve the exactness or context-appropriateness of word choice.

This is as close as the Writing and Language test gets to testing your vocabulary directly. As with everything on the test, these questions are asked within the context of the passage, but you will have to select the word from among the answer choices that most closely means what the author intends. Connotation and tone will play some role here, but rarely will you be presented with more than one choice whose dictionary definition fits the situation.

Concision

For these questions, students will revise the text to improve the economy of word choice. This means they should cut out wordiness and redundancy.

In general, these questions can be solved by feel. The incorrect choices on these questions tend to be rambling or awkward. If you pick the answer that uses a simple construction, does not repeat itself, and carries a reasonable meaning, you'll get it right just about every time.

Style and Tone

These questions require the student to revise the style and tone of the text. These revisions are made primarily to ensure consistency of style and tone throughout the passage but also to improve the appropriateness of the style and tone to the author's purpose.

Syntax

These questions will require the student to use varied sentence structure to achieve the desired rhetorical purpose.

Expression of Ideas

Brainstorming

Brainstorming is a technique that is used to find a creative approach to a subject. This can be accomplished by simple **free-association** with a topic. For example, with paper and pen, write every thought that you have about the topic in a word or phrase. This is done without critical thinking. You should put everything that comes to your mind about the topic on your scratch paper. Then, you need to read the list over a few times. Next, look for patterns, repetitions, and clusters of ideas. This allows a variety of fresh ideas to come as you think about the topic.

Free Writing

Free writing is a more structured form of brainstorming. The method involves taking a limited amount of time (e.g., 2 to 3 minutes) to write everything that comes to mind about the topic in complete sentences. When time expires, review everything that has been written down. Many of your sentences may make little or no sense, but the insights and observations that can come from free writing make this method a valuable approach. Usually, free writing results in a fuller expression of ideas than brainstorming because thoughts and associations are written in complete sentences. However, both techniques can be used to complement each other.

Planning

Planning is the process of organizing a piece of writing before composing a draft. Planning can include creating an outline or a graphic organizer, such as a Venn diagram, a spider-map, or a flowchart. These methods should help the writer identify their topic, main ideas, and the general organization of the composition. Preliminary research can also take place during this stage. Planning helps writers organize all of their ideas and decide if they have enough material to begin their first draft. However, writers should remember that the decisions they make during this step will likely change later in the process, so their plan does not have to be perfect.

Drafting

Writers may then use their plan, outline, or graphic organizer to compose their first draft. They may write subsequent drafts to improve their writing. Writing multiple drafts can help writers consider different ways to communicate their ideas and address errors that may be difficult to correct without rewriting a section or the whole composition. Most writers will vary in how many drafts they choose to write, as there is no "right" number of drafts. Writing drafts also takes away the pressure to write perfectly on the first try, as writers can improve with each draft they write.

Revising, Editing, and Proofreading

Once a writer completes a draft, they can move on to the revising, editing, and proofreading steps to improve their draft. These steps begin with making broad changes that may apply to large sections of a composition and then making small, specific corrections. **Revising** is the first and broadest of these steps. Revising involves ensuring that the composition addresses an appropriate audience, includes all necessary material, maintains focus throughout, and is organized logically. Revising may occur after the first draft to ensure that the following drafts improve upon errors from the first draft. Some revision should occur between each draft to avoid repeating these errors. The **editing** phase of writing is narrower than the revising phase. Editing a composition should include steps such as improving transitions between paragraphs, ensuring each paragraph is on topic, and improving the flow of the text. The editing phase may also include correcting grammatical errors that cannot be fixed without significantly altering the text. **Proofreading** involves fixing misspelled words, typos, other grammatical errors, and any remaining surface-level flaws in the composition.

Recursive Writing Process

However you approach writing, you may find comfort in knowing that the revision process can occur in any order. The **recursive writing process** is not as difficult as the phrase may make it seem. Simply put, the recursive writing process means that you may need to revisit steps after completing other steps. It also implies that the steps are not required to take place in any certain order. Indeed, you may find that planning, drafting, and revising can all take place at about the same time. The writing process involves moving back and forth between planning, drafting, and revising, followed by more planning, more drafting, and more revising until the writing is satisfactory.

Review Video: Recursive Writing Process
Visit mometrix.com/academy and enter code: 951611

Technology in the Writing Process

Modern technology has yielded several tools that can be used to make the writing process more convenient and organized. Word processors and online tools, such as databases and plagiarism detectors, allow much of the writing process to be completed in one place, using one device.

Technology for Planning and Drafting

For the planning and drafting stages of the writing process, word processors are a helpful tool. These programs also feature formatting tools, allowing users to create their own planning tools or create digital outlines that can be easily converted into sentences, paragraphs, or an entire essay draft. Online databases and references also complement the planning process by providing convenient access to information and sources for research. Word processors also allow users to keep up with their work and update it more easily than if they wrote their work by hand. Online word processors often allow users to collaborate, making group assignments more convenient. These programs also allow users to include illustrations or other supplemental media in their compositions.

Technology for Revising, Editing, and Proofreading

Word processors also benefit the revising, editing, and proofreading stages of the writing process. Most of these programs indicate errors in spelling and grammar, allowing users to catch minor errors and correct them quickly. There are also websites designed to help writers by analyzing text for deeper errors, such as poor sentence structure, inappropriate complexity, lack of sentence variety, and style issues. These websites can help users fix errors they may not know to look for or may have simply missed. As writers finish these steps, they may benefit from checking their work for any plagiarism. There are several websites and programs that compare text to other documents and publications across the internet and detect any similarities within the text. These websites show the source of the similar information, so users know whether or not they referenced the source and unintentionally plagiarized its contents.

Technology for Publishing

Technology also makes managing written work more convenient. Digitally storing documents keeps everything in one place and is easy to reference. Digital storage also makes sharing work easier, as documents can be attached to an email or stored online. This also allows writers to publish their work easily, as they can electronically submit it to other publications or freely post it to a personal blog, profile, or website.

Chapter Quiz

1. Which of the following is a more structured form of brainstorming?

a. Free writing
b. Planning
c. Drafting
d. Proofreading

Chapter Quiz Answer Key

1. A: Free writing is a more structured form of brainstorming. The method involves taking a limited amount of time (e.g., two to three minutes) to write everything that comes to mind about the topic in complete sentences. When time expires, review everything that has been written down. Many of the sentences may make little or no sense, but the insights and observations that can come from free writing make this method a valuable approach. Usually, free writing results in a fuller expression of ideas than brainstorming because thoughts and associations are written in complete sentences. However, both techniques can be used to complement each other.

Main Ideas, Supporting Details, and Outlining a Topic

A writer often begins the first paragraph of a paper by stating the **main idea** or point, also known as the **topic sentence**. The rest of the paragraph supplies particular details that develop and support the main point. One way to visualize the relationship between the main point and supporting information is by considering a table: the tabletop is the main point, and each of the table's legs is a supporting detail or group of details. Both professional authors and students can benefit from planning their writing by first making an outline of the topic. Outlines facilitate quick identification of the main point and supporting details without having to wade through the additional language that will exist in the fully developed essay, article, or paper. Outlining can also help readers to analyze a piece of existing writing for the same reason. The outline first summarizes the main idea in one sentence. Then, below that, it summarizes the supporting details in a numbered list. Writing the paper then consists of filling in the outline with detail, writing a paragraph for each supporting point, and adding an introduction and conclusion.

Introduction

The purpose of the introduction is to capture the reader's attention and announce the essay's main idea. Normally, the introduction contains 50-80 words, or 3-5 sentences. An introduction can begin with an interesting quote, a question, or a strong opinion—something that will **engage** the reader's interest and prompt them to keep reading. If you are writing your essay to a specific prompt, your introduction should include a **restatement or summarization** of the prompt so that the reader will have some context for your essay. Finally, your introduction should briefly state your **thesis or**

main idea: the primary thing you hope to communicate to the reader through your essay. Don't try to include all of the details and nuances of your thesis, or all of your reasons for it, in the introduction. That's what the rest of the essay is for!

Review Video: Introduction
Visit mometrix.com/academy and enter code: 961328

Thesis Statement

The thesis is the main idea of the essay. A temporary thesis, or working thesis, should be established early in the writing process because it will serve to keep the writer focused as ideas develop. This temporary thesis is subject to change as you continue to write.

The temporary thesis has two parts: a **topic** (i.e., the focus of your essay based on the prompt) and a **comment**. The comment makes an important point about the topic. A temporary thesis should be interesting and specific. Also, you need to limit the topic to a manageable scope. These three questions are useful tools to measure the effectiveness of any temporary thesis:

- Does the focus of my essay have enough interest to hold an audience?
- Is the focus of my essay specific enough to generate interest?
- Is the focus of my essay manageable for the time limit? Too broad? Too narrow?

The thesis should be a generalization rather than a fact because the thesis prepares readers for facts and details that support the thesis. The process of bringing the thesis into sharp focus may help in outlining major sections of the work. Once the thesis and introduction are complete, you can address the body of the work.

Review Video: Thesis Statements
Visit mometrix.com/academy and enter code: 691033

Supporting the Thesis

Throughout your essay, the thesis should be **explained clearly and supported** adequately by additional arguments. The thesis sentence needs to contain a clear statement of the purpose of your essay and a comment about the thesis. With the thesis statement, you have an opportunity to state what is noteworthy of this particular treatment of the prompt. Each sentence and paragraph should build on and support the thesis.

When you respond to the prompt, use parts of the passage to support your argument or defend your position. Using supporting evidence from the passage strengths your argument because readers can see your attention to the entire passage and your response to the details and facts within the passage. You can use facts, details, statistics, and direct quotations from the passage to uphold your position. Be sure to point out which information comes from the original passage and base your argument around that evidence.

Body

In an essay's introduction, the writer establishes the thesis and may indicate how the rest of the piece will be structured. In the body of the piece, the writer **elaborates** upon, **illustrates**, and **explains** the **thesis statement**. How writers arrange supporting details and their choices of paragraph types are development techniques. Writers may give examples of the concept introduced in the thesis statement. If the subject includes a cause-and-effect relationship, the author may explain its causality. A writer will explain or analyze the main idea of the piece throughout the body, often by presenting arguments for the veracity or credibility of the thesis statement. Writers may use development to define or clarify ambiguous terms. Paragraphs within the body may be organized using natural sequences, like space and time. Writers may employ **inductive reasoning**, using multiple details to establish a generalization or causal relationship, or **deductive reasoning**, proving a generalized hypothesis or proposition through a specific example or case.

Review Video: Drafting Body Paragraphs
Visit mometrix.com/academy and enter code: 724590

Paragraphs

After the introduction of a passage, a series of body paragraphs will carry a message through to the conclusion. Each paragraph should be **unified around a main point**. Normally, a good topic sentence summarizes the paragraph's main point. A topic sentence is a general sentence that gives an introduction to the paragraph.

The sentences that follow support the topic sentence. However, though it is usually the first sentence, the topic sentence can come as the final sentence to the paragraph if the earlier sentences give a clear explanation of the paragraph's topic. This allows the topic sentence to function as a concluding sentence. Overall, the paragraphs need to stay true to the main point. This means that any unnecessary sentences that do not advance the main point should be removed.

The main point of a paragraph requires adequate development (i.e., a substantial paragraph that covers the main point). A paragraph of two or three sentences does not cover a main point. This is especially true when the main point of the paragraph gives strong support to the argument of the thesis. An occasional short paragraph is fine as a transitional device. However, a well-developed argument will have paragraphs with more than a few sentences.

Methods of Developing Paragraphs

Common methods of adding substance to paragraphs include examples, illustrations, analogies, and cause and effect.

- **Examples** are supporting details to the main idea of a paragraph or a passage. When authors write about something that their audience may not understand, they can provide an example to show their point. When authors write about something that is not easily accepted, they can give examples to prove their point.
- **Illustrations** are extended examples that require several sentences. Well-selected illustrations can be a great way for authors to develop a point that may not be familiar to their audience.
- **Analogies** make comparisons between items that appear to have nothing in common. Analogies are employed by writers to provoke fresh thoughts about a subject. These comparisons may be used to explain the unfamiliar, to clarify an abstract point, or to argue a point. Although analogies are effective literary devices, they should be used carefully in arguments. Two things may be alike in some respects but completely different in others.
- **Cause and effect** is an excellent device to explain the connection between an action or situation and a particular result. One way that authors can use cause and effect is to state the effect in the topic sentence of a paragraph and add the causes in the body of the paragraph. This method can give an author's paragraphs structure, which always strengthens writing.

TYPES OF PARAGRAPHS

A **paragraph of narration** tells a story or a part of a story. Normally, the sentences are arranged in chronological order (i.e., the order that the events happened). However, flashbacks (i.e., an anecdote from an earlier time) can be included.

A **descriptive paragraph** makes a verbal portrait of a person, place, or thing. When specific details are used that appeal to one or more of the senses (i.e., sight, sound, smell, taste, and touch), authors give readers a sense of being present in the moment.

A **process paragraph** is related to time order (i.e., First, you open the bottle. Second, you pour the liquid, etc.). Usually, this describes a process or teaches readers how to perform a process.

Comparing two things draws attention to their similarities and indicates a number of differences. When authors contrast, they focus only on differences. Both comparing and contrasting may be done point-by-point, noting both the similarities and differences of each point, or in sequential paragraphs, where you discuss all the similarities and then all the differences, or vice versa.

BREAKING TEXT INTO PARAGRAPHS

For most forms of writing, you will need to use multiple paragraphs. As such, determining when to start a new paragraph is very important. Reasons for starting a new paragraph include:

- To mark off the introduction and concluding paragraphs
- To signal a shift to a new idea or topic
- To indicate an important shift in time or place
- To explain a point in additional detail
- To highlight a comparison, contrast, or cause and effect relationship

PARAGRAPH LENGTH

Most readers find that their comfort level for a paragraph is between 100 and 200 words. Shorter paragraphs cause too much starting and stopping and give a choppy effect. Paragraphs that are too long often test the attention span of readers. Two notable exceptions to this rule exist. In scientific or scholarly papers, longer paragraphs suggest seriousness and depth. In journalistic writing, constraints are placed on paragraph size by the narrow columns in a newspaper format.

The first and last paragraphs of a text will usually be the introduction and conclusion. These special-purpose paragraphs are likely to be shorter than paragraphs in the body of the work. Paragraphs in the body of the essay follow the subject's outline (e.g., one paragraph per point in short essays and a group of paragraphs per point in longer works). Some ideas require more development than others, so it is good for a writer to remain flexible. A paragraph of excessive length may be divided, and shorter ones may be combined.

COHERENT PARAGRAPHS

A smooth flow of sentences and paragraphs without gaps, shifts, or bumps will lead to paragraph **coherence**. Ties between old and new information can be smoothed using several methods:

- **Linking ideas clearly**, from the topic sentence to the body of the paragraph, is essential for a smooth transition. The topic sentence states the main point, and this should be followed by specific details, examples, and illustrations that support the topic sentence. The support may be direct or indirect. In **indirect support**, the illustrations and examples may support a sentence that in turn supports the topic directly.

- The **repetition of key words** adds coherence to a paragraph. To avoid dull language, variations of the key words may be used.
- **Parallel structures** are often used within sentences to emphasize the similarity of ideas and connect sentences giving similar information.
- Maintaining a **consistent verb tense** throughout the paragraph helps. Shifting tenses affects the smooth flow of words and can disrupt the coherence of the paragraph.

Review Video: How to Write a Good Paragraph
Visit mometrix.com/academy and enter code: 682127

SEQUENCE WORDS AND PHRASES

When a paragraph opens with the topic sentence, the second sentence may begin with a phrase like *first of all*, introducing the first supporting detail or example. The writer may introduce the second supporting item with words or phrases like *also*, *in addition*, and *besides*. The writer might introduce succeeding pieces of support with wording like, *another thing*, *moreover*, *furthermore*, or *not only that, but*. The writer may introduce the last piece of support with *lastly*, *finally*, or *last but not least*. Writers get off the point by presenting off-target items not supporting the main point. For example, a main point *my dog is not smart* is supported by the statement, *he's six years old and still doesn't answer to his name*. But *he cries when I leave for school* is not supportive, as it does not indicate lack of intelligence. Writers stay on point by presenting only supportive statements that are directly relevant to and illustrative of their main point.

Review Video: Sequence
Visit mometrix.com/academy and enter code: 489027

TRANSITIONS

Transitions between sentences and paragraphs guide readers from idea to idea and indicate relationships between sentences and paragraphs. Writers should be judicious in their use of transitions, inserting them sparingly. They should also be selected to fit the author's purpose—transitions can indicate time, comparison, and conclusion, among other purposes. Tone is also important to consider when using transitional phrases, varying the tone for different audiences. For example, in a scholarly essay, *in summary* would be preferable to the more informal *in short*.

When working with transitional words and phrases, writers usually find a natural flow that indicates when a transition is needed. In reading a draft of the text, it should become apparent where the flow is disrupted. At this point, the writer can add transitional elements during the revision process. Revising can also afford an opportunity to delete transitional devices that seem heavy handed or unnecessary.

Review Video: Transitions in Writing
Visit mometrix.com/academy and enter code: 233246

Types of Transitional Words

Time	Afterward, immediately, earlier, meanwhile, recently, lately, now, since, soon, when, then, until, before, etc.
Sequence	too, first, second, further, moreover, also, again, and, next, still, besides, finally
Comparison	similarly, in the same way, likewise, also, again, once more
Contrasting	but, although, despite, however, instead, nevertheless, on the one hand... on the other hand, regardless, yet, in contrast.
Cause and Effect	because, consequently, thus, therefore, then, to this end, since, so, as a result, if... then, accordingly
Examples	for example, for instance, such as, to illustrate, indeed, in fact, specifically
Place	near, far, here, there, to the left/right, next to, above, below, beyond, opposite, beside
Concession	granted that, naturally, of course, it may appear, although it is true that
Repetition, Summary, or Conclusion	as mentioned earlier, as noted, in other words, in short, on the whole, to summarize, therefore, as a result, to conclude, in conclusion
Addition	and, also, furthermore, moreover
Generalization	in broad terms, broadly speaking, in general

Review Video: Transitional Words and Phrases
Visit mometrix.com/academy and enter code: 197796

Review Video: What are Transition Words?
Visit mometrix.com/academy and enter code: 707563

Review Video: How to Effectively Connect Sentences
Visit mometrix.com/academy and enter code: 948325

Conclusion

Two important principles to consider when writing a conclusion are strength and closure. A strong conclusion gives the reader a sense that the author's main points are meaningful and important, and that the supporting facts and arguments are convincing, solid, and well developed. When a conclusion achieves closure, it gives the impression that the writer has stated all necessary information and points and completed the work, rather than simply stopping after a specified length. Some things to avoid when writing concluding paragraphs include:

- Introducing a completely new idea
- Beginning with obvious or unoriginal phrases like "In conclusion" or "To summarize"
- Apologizing for one's opinions or writing
- Repeating the thesis word for word rather than rephrasing it
- Believing that the conclusion must always summarize the piece

Review Video: Drafting Conclusions
Visit mometrix.com/academy and enter code: 209408

Chapter Quiz

1. Which of the following is considered the main idea of an essay?

a. Topic
b. Body
c. Theme
d. Thesis

2. Which of the following are supporting details to the main idea of a paragraph or a passage?

a. Analogies
b. Examples
c. Cause and effect
d. Transitions

3. Which of the following is NOT a transitional word or phrase in the concession category?

a. Granted that
b. Naturally
c. Broadly speaking
d. It may appear

Chapter Quiz Answer Key

1. D: The thesis is the main idea of an essay. A temporary thesis, or working thesis, should be established early in the writing process because it will serve to keep the writer focused as ideas develop. This temporary thesis is subject to change as writing continues. The thesis should be a generalization rather than a fact because the thesis prepares readers for facts and details that support the thesis. The process of bringing the thesis into sharp focus may help in outlining major sections of the work. Once the thesis and introduction are complete, the body of the work can be addressed.

2. B: Examples are supporting details to the main idea of a paragraph or a passage. When authors write about something that their audience may not understand or that is not easily accepted, they can provide an example to show their point.

3. C: Types of transitional words

Time	Afterward, immediately, earlier, meanwhile, recently, lately, now, since, soon, when, then, until, before, etc.
Sequence	Too, first, second, further, moreover, also, again, and, next, still, besides, finally
Comparison	Similarly, in the same way, likewise, also, again, once more
Contrasting	But, although, despite, however, instead, nevertheless, on the one hand... on the other hand, regardless, yet, in contrast
Cause and effect	Because, consequently, thus, therefore, then, to this end, since, so, as a result, if... then, accordingly
Examples	For example, for instance, such as, to illustrate, indeed, in fact, specifically
Place	Near, far, here, there, to the left/right, next to, above, below, beyond, opposite, beside
Concession	Granted that, naturally, of course, it may appear, although it is true that
Repetition, summary, or conclusion	As mentioned earlier, as noted, in other words, in short, on the whole, to summarize, therefore, as a result, to conclude, in conclusion
Addition	And, also, furthermore, moreover
Generalization	In broad terms, broadly speaking, in general

WRITING STYLE AND LINGUISTIC FORM

Linguistic form encodes the literal meanings of words and sentences. It comes from the phonological, morphological, syntactic, and semantic parts of a language. **Writing style** consists of different ways of encoding the meaning and indicating figurative and stylistic meanings. An author's writing style can also be referred to as his or her **voice**.

Writers' stylistic choices accomplish three basic effects on their audiences:

- They **communicate meanings** beyond linguistically dictated meanings,
- They communicate the **author's attitude**, such as persuasive or argumentative effects accomplished through style, and
- They communicate or **express feelings**.

Within style, component areas include:

- Narrative structure
- Viewpoint
- Focus
- Sound patterns
- Meter and rhythm
- Lexical and syntactic repetition and parallelism
- Writing genre
- Representational, realistic, and mimetic effects
- Representation of thought and speech
- Meta-representation (representing representation)
- Irony

- Metaphor and other indirect meanings
- Representation and use of historical and dialectal variations
- Gender-specific and other group-specific speech styles, both real and fictitious
- Analysis of the processes for inferring meaning from writing

LEVEL OF FORMALITY

The relationship between writer and reader is important in choosing a **level of formality** as most writing requires some degree of formality. **Formal writing** is for addressing a superior in a school or work environment. Business letters, textbooks, and newspapers use a moderate to high level of formality. **Informal writing** is appropriate for private letters, personal emails, and business correspondence between close associates.

For your exam, you will want to be aware of informal and formal writing. One way that this can be accomplished is to watch for shifts in point of view in the essay. For example, unless writers are using a personal example, they will rarely refer to themselves (e.g., "*I* think that *my* point is very clear.") to avoid being informal when they need to be formal.

Also, be mindful of an author who addresses his or her audience **directly** in their writing (e.g., "Readers, *like you*, will understand this argument.") as this can be a sign of informal writing. Good writers understand the need to be consistent with their level of formality. Shifts in levels of formality or point of view can confuse readers and cause them to discount the message.

CLICHÉS

Clichés are phrases that have been **overused** to the point that the phrase has no importance or has lost the original meaning. These phrases have no originality and add very little to a passage. Therefore, most writers will avoid the use of clichés. Another option is to make changes to a cliché so that it is not predictable and empty of meaning.

Examples:

> When life gives you lemons, make lemonade.
>
> Every cloud has a silver lining.

JARGON

Jargon is **specialized vocabulary** that is used among members of a certain trade or profession. Since jargon is understood by only a small audience, writers will use jargon in passages that will only be read by a specialized audience. For example, medical jargon should be used in a medical journal but not in a New York Times article. Jargon includes exaggerated language that tries to impress rather than inform. Sentences filled with jargon are not precise and are difficult to understand.

Examples:

> "He is going to *toenail* these frames for us." (Toenail is construction jargon for nailing at an angle.)
>
> "They brought in a *kip* of material today." (Kip refers to 1000 pounds in architecture and engineering.)

Slang

Slang is an **informal** and sometimes private language that is understood by some individuals. Slang terms have some usefulness, but they can have a small audience. So, most formal writing will not include this kind of language.

Examples:

> "Yes, the event was a blast!" (In this sentence, *blast* means that the event was a great experience.)
>
> "That attempt was an epic fail." (By *epic fail*, the speaker means that his or her attempt was not a success.)

Colloquialism

A colloquialism is a word or phrase that is found in informal writing. Unlike slang, **colloquial language** will be familiar to a greater range of people. However, colloquialisms are still considered inappropriate for formal writing. Colloquial language can include some slang, but these are limited to contractions for the most part.

Examples:

> "Can *y'all* come back another time?" (Y'all is a contraction of "you all.")
>
> "Will you stop him from building this *castle in the air*?" (A "castle in the air" is an improbable or unlikely event.)

Academic Language

In educational settings, students are often expected to use academic language in their schoolwork. Academic language is also commonly found in dissertations and theses, texts published by academic journals, and other forms of academic research. Academic language conventions may vary between fields, but general academic language is free of slang, regional terminology, and noticeable grammatical errors. Specific terms may also be used in academic language, and it is important to understand their proper usage. A writer's command of academic language impacts their ability to communicate in an academic or professional context. While it is acceptable to use colloquialisms, slang, improper grammar, or other forms of informal speech in social settings or at home, it is inappropriate to practice non-academic language in academic contexts.

Tone

Tone may be defined as the writer's **attitude** toward the topic, and to the audience. This attitude is reflected in the language used in the writing. The tone of a work should be **appropriate to the topic** and to the intended audience. While it may be fine to use slang or jargon in some pieces, other texts should not contain such terms. Tone can range from humorous to serious and any level in between. It may be more or less formal, depending on the purpose of the writing and its intended audience. All these nuances in tone can flavor the entire writing and should be kept in mind as the work evolves.

Word Selection

A writer's choice of words is a signature of their style. Careful thought about the use of words can improve a piece of writing. A passage can be an exciting piece to read when attention is given to the use of vivid or specific nouns rather than general ones.

Example:

General: His kindness will never be forgotten.

Specific: His thoughtful gifts and bear hugs will never be forgotten.

Attention should also be given to the kind of verbs that are used in sentences. Active verbs (e.g., run, swim) are about an action. Whenever possible, an **active verb should replace a linking verb** to provide clear examples for arguments and to strengthen a passage overall. When using an active verb, one should be sure that the verb is used in the active voice instead of the passive voice. Verbs are in the active voice when the subject is the one doing the action. A verb is in the passive voice when the subject is the recipient of an action.

Example:

Passive: The winners were called to the stage by the judges.

Active: The judges called the winners to the stage.

Conciseness

Conciseness is writing that communicates a message in the fewest words possible. Writing concisely is valuable because short, uncluttered messages allow the reader to understand the author's message more easily and efficiently. Planning is important in writing concise messages. If you have in mind what you need to write beforehand, it will be easier to make a message short and to the point. Do not state the obvious.

Revising is also important. After the message is written, make sure you have effective, pithy sentences that efficiently get your point across. When reviewing the information, imagine a conversation taking place, and concise writing will likely result.

Appropriate Kinds of Writing for Different Tasks, Purposes, and Audiences

When preparing to write a composition, consider the audience and purpose to choose the best type of writing. Three common types of writing are persuasive, expository, and narrative. **Persuasive**, or argumentative writing, is used to convince the audience to take action or agree with the author's claims. **Expository** writing is meant to inform the audience of the author's observations or research on a topic. **Narrative** writing is used to tell the audience a story and often allows more room for creativity. While task, purpose, and audience inform a writer's mode of writing, these factors also impact elements such as tone, vocabulary, and formality.

For example, students who are writing to persuade their parents to grant them some additional privilege, such as permission for a more independent activity, should use more sophisticated vocabulary and diction that sounds more mature and serious to appeal to the parental audience. However, students who are writing for younger children should use simpler vocabulary and sentence structure, as well as choose words that are more vivid and entertaining. They should treat their topics more lightly, and include humor when appropriate. Students who are writing for their classmates may use language that is more informal, as well as age-appropriate.

Review Video: Writing Purpose and Audience
Visit mometrix.com/academy and enter code: 146627

Chapter Quiz

1. Which of the following would NOT be considered formal writing?

a. Private letters
b. Business letters
c. Textbooks
d. Newspapers

2. Which of the following sentences contains a verb in the passive voice?

a. The judges called the winners to the stage for their awards.
b. Each applicant must fill out all of the forms required.
c. He raced through the copse of trees with the grace of a deer.
d. I was told that there would be food available at the party.

Chapter Quiz Answer Key

1. A: The relationship between writer and reader is important in choosing a level of formality because most writing requires some degree of formality. Formal writing is for addressing a superior in a school or work environment. Business letters, textbooks, and newspapers use a moderate to high level of formality. Informal writing is appropriate for private letters, personal emails, and business correspondence between close associates.

2. D: Attention should also be given to the kind of verbs that are used in sentences. Active verbs (e.g., run, swim) are about an action. Whenever possible, an active verb should replace a linking verb to provide clear examples for arguments and to strengthen a passage overall. When using an active verb, one should be sure that the verb is used in the active voice instead of the passive voice. Verbs are in the active voice when the subject is the one doing the action. A verb is in the passive voice when the subject is the recipient of an action.

Essays

Essays usually focus on one topic, subject, or goal. There are several types of essays, including informative, persuasive, and narrative. An essay's structure and level of formality depend on the type of essay and its goal. While narrative essays typically do not include outside sources, other types of essays often require some research and the integration of primary and secondary sources.

The basic format of an essay typically has three major parts: the introduction, the body, and the conclusion. The body is further divided into the writer's main points. Short and simple essays may have three main points, while essays covering broader ranges and going into more depth can have almost any number of main points, depending on length.

An essay's introduction should answer three questions:

1. What is the **subject** of the essay?

   If a student writes an essay about a book, the answer would include the title and author of the book and any additional information needed—such as the subject or argument of the book.

2. How does the essay **address** the subject?

   To answer this, the writer identifies the essay's organization by briefly summarizing main points and the evidence supporting them.

3. What will the essay **prove**?

This is the thesis statement, usually the opening paragraph's last sentence, clearly stating the writer's message.

The body elaborates on all the main points related to the thesis, introducing one main point at a time, and includes supporting evidence with each main point. Each body paragraph should state the point in a topic sentence, which is usually the first sentence in the paragraph. The paragraph should then explain the point's meaning, support it with quotations or other evidence, and then explain how this point and the evidence are related to the thesis. The writer should then repeat this procedure in a new paragraph for each additional main point.

The conclusion reiterates the content of the introduction, including the thesis, to remind the reader of the essay's main argument or subject. The essay writer may also summarize the highlights of the argument or description contained in the body of the essay, following the same sequence originally used in the body. For example, a conclusion might look like: Point 1 + Point 2 + Point 3 = Thesis, or Point 1 → Point 2 → Point 3 → Thesis Proof. Good organization makes essays easier for writers to compose and provides a guide for readers to follow. Well-organized essays hold attention better and are more likely to get readers to accept their theses as valid.

INFORMATIVE VS. PERSUASIVE WRITING

Informative writing, also called explanatory or expository writing, begins with the basis that something is true or factual, while **persuasive** writing strives to prove something that may or may not be true or factual. Whereas argumentative text is written to **persuade** readers to agree with the author's position, informative text merely **provides information and insight** to readers. Informative writing concentrates on **informing** readers about why or how something is as it is. This can include offering new information, explaining how a process works, and developing a concept for readers. To accomplish these objectives, the essay may name and distinguish various things within a category, provide definitions, provide details about the parts of something, explain a particular function or behavior, and give readers explanations for why a fact, object, event, or process exists or occurs.

NARRATIVE WRITING

Put simply, **narrative** writing tells a story. The most common examples of literary narratives are novels. Non-fictional biographies, autobiographies, memoirs, and histories are also narratives. Narratives should tell stories in such a way that the readers learn something or gain insight or understanding. Students can write more interesting narratives by describing events or experiences that were meaningful to them. Narratives should start with the story's actions or events, rather than long descriptions or introductions. Students should ensure that there is a point to each story by describing what they learned from the experience they narrate. To write an effective description, students should include sensory details, asking themselves what they saw, heard, felt or touched, smelled, and tasted during the experiences they describe. In narrative writing, the details should be **concrete** rather than **abstract**. Using concrete details enables readers to imagine everything that the writer describes.

Review Video: Narratives
Visit mometrix.com/academy and enter code: 280100

SENSORY DETAILS

Students need to use vivid descriptions when writing descriptive essays. Narratives should also include descriptions of characters, things, and events. Students should remember to describe not only the visual detail of what someone or something looks like, but details from other senses, as well. For example, they can contrast the feeling of a sea breeze to that of a mountain breeze, describe how they think something inedible would taste, and compare sounds they hear in the same location at different times of day and night. Readers have trouble visualizing images or imagining sensory impressions and feelings from abstract descriptions, so concrete descriptions make these more real.

Concrete vs. Abstract Descriptions in Narrative

Concrete language provides information that readers can grasp and may empathize with, while **abstract language**, which is more general, can leave readers feeling disconnected, empty, or even confused. "It was a lovely day" is abstract, but "The sun shone brightly, the sky was blue, the air felt warm, and a gentle breeze wafted across my skin" is concrete. "Ms. Couch was a good teacher" uses abstract language, giving only a general idea of the writer's opinion. But "Ms. Couch is excellent at helping us take our ideas and turn them into good essays and stories" uses concrete language, giving more specific examples of what makes Ms. Couch a good teacher. "I like writing poems but not essays" gives readers a general idea that the student prefers one genre over another, but not why. But when reading, "I like writing short poems with rhythm and rhyme, but I hate writing five-page essays that go on and on about the same ideas," readers understand that the student prefers the brevity, rhyme, and meter of short poetry over the length and redundancy of longer prose.

Autobiographical Narratives

Autobiographical narratives are narratives written by an author about an event or period in their life. Autobiographical narratives are written from one person's perspective, in first person, and often include the author's thoughts and feelings alongside their description of the event or period. Structure, style, or theme varies between different autobiographical narratives, since each narrative is personal and specific to its author and his or her experience.

Reflective Essay

A less common type of essay is the reflective essay. **Reflective essays** allow the author to reflect, or think back, on an experience and analyze what they recall. They should consider what they learned from the experience, what they could have done differently, what would have helped them during the experience, or anything else that they have realized from looking back on the experience. Reflection essays incorporate both objective reflection on one's own actions and subjective explanation of thoughts and feelings. These essays can be written for a number of experiences in a formal or informal context.

Journals and Diaries

A **journal** is a personal account of events, experiences, feelings, and thoughts. Many people write journals to express their feelings and thoughts or to help them process experiences they have had. Since journals are **private documents** not meant to be shared with others, writers may not be concerned with grammar, spelling, or other mechanics. However, authors may write journals that they expect or hope to publish someday; in this case, they not only express their thoughts and feelings and process their experiences, but they also attend to their craft in writing them. Some authors compose journals to record a particular time period or a series of related events, such as a cancer diagnosis, treatment, surviving the disease, and how these experiences have changed or affected them. Other experiences someone might include in a journal are recovering from addiction, journeys of spiritual exploration and discovery, time spent in another country, or anything else someone wants to personally document. Journaling can also be therapeutic, as some people use journals to work through feelings of grief over loss or to wrestle with big decisions.

Examples of Diaries in Literature

The Diary of a Young Girl by Dutch Jew Anne Frank (1947) contains her life-affirming, nonfictional diary entries from 1942-1944 while her family hid in an attic from World War II's genocidal Nazis. *Go Ask Alice* (1971) by Beatrice Sparks is a cautionary, fictional novel in the form of diary entries by Alice, an unhappy, rebellious teen who takes LSD, runs away from home and lives with hippies, and eventually returns home. Frank's writing reveals an intelligent, sensitive, insightful girl, raised by intellectual European parents—a girl who believes in the goodness of human nature despite surrounding atrocities. Alice, influenced by early 1970s counterculture, becomes less optimistic. However, similarities can be found between them: Frank dies in a Nazi concentration camp while the fictitious Alice dies from a drug overdose. Both young women are also unable to escape their surroundings. Additionally, adolescent searches for personal identity are evident in both books.

Review Video: Journals, Diaries, Letters, and Blogs
Visit mometrix.com/academy and enter code: 432845

Letters

Letters are messages written to other people. In addition to letters written between individuals, some writers compose letters to the editors of newspapers, magazines, and other publications, while some write "Open Letters" to be published and read by the general public. Open letters, while intended for everyone to read, may also identify a group of people or a single person whom the letter directly addresses. In everyday use, the most-used forms are business letters and personal or friendly letters. Both kinds share common elements: business or personal letterhead stationery; the writer's return address at the top; the addressee's address next; a salutation, such as "Dear [name]" or some similar opening greeting, followed by a colon in business letters or a comma in personal letters; the body of the letter, with paragraphs as indicated; and a closing, like "Sincerely/Cordially/Best regards/etc." or "Love," in intimate personal letters.

Early Letters

The Greek word for "letter" is *epistolē*, which became the English word "epistle." The earliest letters were called epistles, including the New Testament's epistles from the apostles to the Christians. In ancient Egypt, the writing curriculum in scribal schools included the epistolary genre. Epistolary novels frame a story in the form of letters. Examples of noteworthy epistolary novels include:

- *Pamela* (1740), by 18th-century English novelist Samuel Richardson
- *Shamela* (1741), Henry Fielding's satire of *Pamela* that mocked epistolary writing.
- *Lettres persanes* (1721) by French author Montesquieu
- *The Sorrows of Young Werther* (1774) by German author Johann Wolfgang von Goethe
- *The History of Emily Montague* (1769), the first Canadian novel, by Frances Brooke
- *Dracula* (1897) by Bram Stoker
- *Frankenstein* (1818) by Mary Shelley
- *The Color Purple* (1982) by Alice Walker

Blogs

The word "blog" is derived from "weblog" and refers to writing done exclusively on the internet. Readers of reputable newspapers expect quality content and layouts that enable easy reading. These expectations also apply to blogs. For example, readers can easily move visually from line to line when columns are narrow, while overly wide columns cause readers to lose their places. Blogs must also be posted with layouts enabling online readers to follow them easily. However, because the way people read on computer, tablet, and smartphone screens differs from how they read print on paper, formatting and writing blog content is more complex than writing newspaper articles. Two major principles are the bases for blog-writing rules: The first is while readers of print articles skim to estimate their length, online they must scroll down to scan; therefore, blog layouts need more subheadings, graphics, and other indications of what information follows. The second is onscreen reading can be harder on the eyes than reading printed paper, so legibility is crucial in blogs.

Rules and Rationales for Writing Blogs

1. Format all posts for smooth page layout and easy scanning.
2. Column width should not be too wide, as larger lines of text can be difficult to read
3. Headings and subheadings separate text visually, enable scanning or skimming, and encourage continued reading.
4. Bullet-pointed or numbered lists enable quick information location and scanning.
5. Punctuation is critical, so beginners should use shorter sentences until confident in their knowledge of punctuation rules.
6. Blog paragraphs should be far shorter—two to six sentences each—than paragraphs written on paper to enable "chunking" because reading onscreen is more difficult.
7. Sans-serif fonts are usually clearer than serif fonts, and larger font sizes are better.
8. Highlight important material and draw attention with **boldface**, but avoid overuse. Avoid hard-to-read *italics* and ALL CAPITALS.
9. Include enough blank spaces: overly busy blogs tire eyes and brains. Images not only break up text but also emphasize and enhance text and can attract initial reader attention.
10. Use background colors judiciously to avoid distracting the eye or making it difficult to read.
11. Be consistent throughout posts, since people read them in different orders.
12. Tell a story with a beginning, middle, and end.

Specialized Modes of Writing

Editorials

Editorials are articles in newspapers, magazines, and other serial publications. Editorials express an opinion or belief belonging to the majority of the publication's leadership. This opinion or belief generally refers to a specific issue, topic, or event. These articles are authored by a member, or a small number of members, of the publication's leadership and are often written to affect their readers, such as persuading them to adopt a stance or take a particular action.

Resumes

Resumes are brief, but formal, documents that outline an individual's experience in a certain area. Resumes are most often used for job applications. Such resumes will list the applicant's work experience, certification, and achievements or qualifications related to the position. Resumes should only include the most pertinent information. They should also use strategic formatting to highlight the applicant's most impressive experiences and achievements, to ensure the document can be read quickly and easily, and to eliminate both visual clutter and excessive negative space.

Reports

Reports summarize the results of research, new methodology, or other developments in an academic or professional context. Reports often include details about methodology and outside influences and factors. However, a report should focus primarily on the results of the research or development. Reports are objective and deliver information efficiently, sacrificing style for clear and effective communication.

Memoranda

A memorandum, also called a memo, is a formal method of communication used in professional settings. Memoranda are printed documents that include a heading listing the sender and their job title, the recipient and their job title, the date, and a specific subject line. Memoranda often include an introductory section explaining the reason and context for the memorandum. Next, a memorandum includes a section with details relevant to the topic. Finally, the memorandum will conclude with a paragraph that politely and clearly defines the sender's expectations of the recipient.

Chapter Quiz

1. The Greek word *epistolē* means:

a. Pistol.
b. Epistaxis.
c. Essay.
d. Letter.

2. What are the two major principles used to create an orderly blog?

a. The content must be interesting with various fonts and color combinations, and it should take less than 10 minutes to read in its entirety.
b. Blog layouts need more subheadings, graphics, and other indications of what information follows, and the content must be interesting with various fonts and color combinations.
c. Legibility is crucial because onscreen reading is hard on the eyes, and it should take less than 10 minutes to read in its entirety.
d. Blog layouts need more subheadings, graphics, and other indications of what information follows, and legibility is crucial because onscreen reading is hard on the eyes.

Chapter Quiz Answer Key

1. D: The Greek word for "letter" is *epistolē*, which became the English word "epistle." The earliest letters were called epistles, including the New Testament's epistles from the apostles to the Christians. In ancient Egypt, the writing curriculum in scribal schools included the epistolary genre. Epistolary novels frame a story in the form of letters.

2. D: There are two major principles that form the basis for blog-writing rules. The first is that while readers of print can skim articles to estimate their length, they must scroll down to scan something published online, meaning that blog layouts need more subheadings, graphics, and other indications of what information follows. The second principle is that onscreen reading can be harder on the eyes than reading printed paper, so legibility is crucial in blogs.

Standard English Conventions

The Eight Parts of Speech

Nouns

When you talk about a person, place, thing, or idea, you are talking about a **noun**. The two main types of nouns are **common** and **proper** nouns. Also, nouns can be abstract (i.e., general) or concrete (i.e., specific).

Common Nouns

Common nouns are generic names for people, places, and things. Common nouns are not usually capitalized.

Examples of common nouns:

People: boy, girl, worker, manager

Places: school, bank, library, home

Things: dog, cat, truck, car

Review Video: What is a Noun?
Visit mometrix.com/academy and enter code: 344028

Proper Nouns

Proper nouns name specific people, places, or things. All proper nouns are capitalized.

Examples of proper nouns:

People: Abraham Lincoln, George Washington, Martin Luther King, Jr.

Places: Los Angeles, California; New York; Asia

Things: Statue of Liberty, Earth, Lincoln Memorial

Note: When referring to the planet that we live on, capitalize *Earth*. When referring to the dirt, rocks, or land, lowercase *earth*.

General and Specific Nouns

General nouns are the names of conditions or ideas. **Specific nouns** name people, places, and things that are understood by using your senses.

General nouns:

Condition: beauty, strength

Idea: truth, peace

Specific nouns:

People: baby, friend, father

Places: town, park, city hall

Things: rainbow, cough, apple, silk, gasoline

Collective Nouns

Collective nouns are the names for a group of people, places, or things that may act as a whole. The following are examples of collective nouns: *class, company, dozen, group, herd, team,* and *public*. Collective nouns usually require an article, which denotes the noun as being a single unit. For instance, a choir is a group of singers. Even though there are many singers in a choir, the word choir is grammatically treated as a single unit. If we refer to the members of the group, and not the group itself, it is no longer a collective noun.

Incorrect: The *choir are* going to compete nationally this year.

Correct: The *choir is* going to compete nationally this year.

Incorrect: The *members* of the choir *is* competing nationally this year.

Correct: The *members* of the choir *are* competing nationally this year.

PRONOUNS

Pronouns are words that are used to stand in for nouns. A pronoun may be classified as personal, intensive, relative, interrogative, demonstrative, indefinite, and reciprocal.

Personal: *Nominative* is the case for nouns and pronouns that are the subject of a sentence. *Objective* is the case for nouns and pronouns that are an object in a sentence. *Possessive* is the case for nouns and pronouns that show possession or ownership.

Singular

	Nominative	Objective	Possessive
First Person	I	me	my, mine
Second Person	you	you	your, yours
Third Person	he, she, it	him, her, it	his, her, hers, its

Plural

	Nominative	Objective	Possessive
First Person	we	us	our, ours
Second Person	you	you	your, yours
Third Person	they	them	their, theirs

Intensive: I myself, you yourself, he himself, she herself, the (thing) itself, we ourselves, you yourselves, they themselves

Relative: which, who, whom, whose

Interrogative: what, which, who, whom, whose

Demonstrative: this, that, these, those

Indefinite: all, any, each, everyone, either/neither, one, some, several

Reciprocal: each other, one another

Review Video: Nouns and Pronouns
Visit mometrix.com/academy and enter code: 312073

VERBS

If you want to write a sentence, then you need a verb. Without a verb, you have no sentence. The verb of a sentence indicates action or being. In other words, the verb shows something's action or state of being or the action that has been done to something.

Transitive and Intransitive Verbs

A **transitive verb** is a verb whose action (e.g., drive, run, jump) indicates a receiver (e.g., car, dog, kangaroo). **Intransitive verbs** do not indicate a receiver of an action. In other words, the action of the verb does not point to a subject or object.

> **Transitive**: He plays the piano. | The piano was played by him.
>
> **Intransitive**: He plays. | John plays well.

A dictionary will tell you whether a verb is transitive or intransitive. Some verbs can be transitive and intransitive.

Action Verbs and Linking Verbs

Action verbs show what the subject is doing. In other words, an action verb shows action. Unlike most types of words, a single action verb, in the right context, can be an entire sentence. **Linking verbs** link the subject of a sentence to a noun or pronoun, or they link a subject with an adjective. You always need a verb if you want a complete sentence. However, linking verbs on their own cannot be a complete sentence.

Common linking verbs include *appear, be, become, feel, grow, look, seem, smell, sound,* and *taste.* However, any verb that shows a condition and connects to a noun, pronoun, or adjective that describes the subject of a sentence is a linking verb.

Action: He sings. | Run! | Go! | I talk with him every day. | She reads.

Linking:

> Incorrect: I am.
>
> Correct: I am John. | The roses smell lovely. | I feel tired.

Note: Some verbs are followed by words that look like prepositions, but they are a part of the verb and a part of the verb's meaning. These are known as phrasal verbs, and examples include *call off, look up,* and *drop off.*

Review Video: Action Verbs and Linking Verbs
Visit mometrix.com/academy and enter code: 743142

Voice

Transitive verbs come in active or passive **voice**. If something does an action or is acted upon, then you will know whether a verb is active or passive. When the subject of the sentence is doing the action, the verb is in **active voice**. When the subject is acted upon, the verb is in **passive voice**.

> **Active**: Jon drew the picture. (The subject *Jon* is doing the action of *drawing a picture.*)
>
> **Passive**: The picture is drawn by Jon. (The subject *picture* is receiving the action from Jon.)

Verb Tenses

A verb **tense** shows the different form of a verb to point to the time of an action. The present and past tense are indicated by the verb's form. An action in the present, *I talk,* can change form for the past: *I talked*. However, for the other tenses, an auxiliary (i.e., helping) verb is needed to show the change in form. These helping verbs include *am, are, is* | *have, has, had* | *was, were, will* (or *shall*).

Present: I talk	Present perfect: I have talked
Past: I talked	Past perfect: I had talked
Future: I will talk	Future perfect: I will have talked

Present: The action happens at the current time.

Example: He *walks* to the store every morning.

To show that something is happening right now, use the progressive present tense: I *am walking*.

Past: The action happened in the past.

Example: He *walked* to the store an hour ago.

Future: The action is going to happen later.

Example: I *will walk* to the store tomorrow.

Present perfect: The action started in the past and continues into the present or took place previously at an unspecified time.

Example: I *have walked* to the store three times today.

Past perfect: The second action happened in the past. The first action came before the second.

Example: Before I walked to the store (Action 2), I *had walked* to the library (Action 1).

Future perfect: An action that uses the past and the future. In other words, the action is complete before a future moment.

Example: When she comes for the supplies (future moment), I *will have walked* to the store (action completed before the future moment).

Review Video: Present Perfect, Past Perfect, and Future Perfect Verb Tenses
Visit mometrix.com/academy and enter code: 269472

Conjugating Verbs

When you need to change the form of a verb, you are **conjugating** a verb. The key forms of a verb are singular, present tense (dream); singular, past tense (dreamed); and the past participle (have dreamed). Note: the past participle needs a helping verb to make a verb tense. For example, I *have dreamed* of this day. The following tables demonstrate some of the different ways to conjugate a verb:

Singular

Tense	First Person	Second Person	Third Person
Present	I dream	You dream	He, she, it dreams
Past	I dreamed	You dreamed	He, she, it dreamed
Past Participle	I have dreamed	You have dreamed	He, she, it has dreamed

Plural

Tense	First Person	Second Person	Third Person
Present	We dream	You dream	They dream
Past	We dreamed	You dreamed	They dreamed
Past Participle	We have dreamed	You have dreamed	They have dreamed

Mood

There are three **moods** in English: the indicative, the imperative, and the subjunctive.

The **indicative mood** is used for facts, opinions, and questions.

Fact: You can do this.

Opinion: I think that you can do this.

Question: Do you know that you can do this?

The **imperative** is used for orders or requests.

Order: You are going to do this!

Request: Will you do this for me?

The **subjunctive mood** is for wishes and statements that go against fact.

Wish: I wish that I were famous.

Statement against fact: If I were you, I would do this. (This goes against fact because I am not you. You have the chance to do this, and I do not have the chance.)

Adjectives

An **adjective** is a word that is used to modify a noun or pronoun. An adjective answers a question: *Which one? What kind?* or *How many?* Usually, adjectives come before the words that they modify, but they may also come after a linking verb.

Which one? The *third* suit is my favorite.

What kind? This suit is *navy blue.*

How many? I am going to buy *four* pairs of socks to match the suit.

Review Video: Descriptive Text
Visit mometrix.com/academy and enter code: 174903

Articles

Articles are adjectives that are used to distinguish nouns as definite or indefinite. **Definite** nouns are preceded by the article *the* and indicate a specific person, place, thing, or idea. **Indefinite** nouns are preceded by *a* or *an* and do not indicate a specific person, place, thing, or idea. *A*, *an*, and *the* are the only articles. Note: *An* comes before words that start with a vowel sound. For example, "Are you going to get an **u**mbrella?"

> **Definite**: I lost *the* bottle that belongs to me.
>
> **Indefinite**: Does anyone have *a* bottle to share?

Review Video: Function of Articles
Visit mometrix.com/academy and enter code: 449383

Comparison with Adjectives

Some adjectives are relative and other adjectives are absolute. Adjectives that are **relative** can show the comparison between things. **Absolute** adjectives can also show comparison, but they do so in a different way. Let's say that you are reading two books. You think that one book is perfect, and the other book is not exactly perfect. It is not possible for one book to be more perfect than the other. Either you think that the book is perfect, or you think that the book is imperfect. In this case, perfect and imperfect are absolute adjectives.

Relative adjectives will show the different **degrees** of something or someone to something else or someone else. The three degrees of adjectives include positive, comparative, and superlative.

The **positive** degree is the normal form of an adjective.

> Example: This work is *difficult.* | She is *smart.*

The **comparative** degree compares one person or thing to another person or thing.

> Example: This work is *more difficult* than your work. | She is *smarter* than me.

The **superlative** degree compares more than two people or things.

> Example: This is the *most difficult* work of my life. | She is the *smartest* lady in school.

Review Video: What is an Adjective?
Visit mometrix.com/academy and enter code: 470154

Adverbs

An **adverb** is a word that is used to **modify** a verb, adjective, or another adverb. Usually, adverbs answer one of these questions: *When? Where? How?* and *Why?* The negatives *not* and *never* are considered adverbs. Adverbs that modify adjectives or other adverbs **strengthen** or **weaken** the words that they modify.

Examples:

> He walks *quickly* through the crowd.
>
> The water flows *smoothly* on the rocks.

Note: Adverbs are usually indicated by the morpheme *-ly*, which has been added to the root word. For instance, *quick* can be made into an adverb by adding *-ly* to construct *quickly*. Some words that end in *-ly* do not follow this rule and can behave as other parts of speech. Examples of adjectives ending in *-ly* include: *early, friendly, holy, lonely, silly*, and *ugly*. To know if a word that ends in *-ly* is an adjective or adverb, check your dictionary. Also, while many adverbs end in *-ly*, you need to remember that not all adverbs end in *-ly*.

Examples:

He is *never* angry.

You are *too* irresponsible to travel alone.

Review Video: What is an Adverb?
Visit mometrix.com/academy and enter code: 713951

Review Video: Adverbs that Modify Adjectives
Visit mometrix.com/academy and enter code: 122570

Comparison with Adverbs

The rules for comparing adverbs are the same as the rules for adjectives.

The **positive** degree is the standard form of an adverb.

Example: He arrives *soon*. | She speaks *softly* to her friends.

The **comparative** degree compares one person or thing to another person or thing.

Example: He arrives *sooner* than Sarah. | She speaks *more softly* than him.

The **superlative** degree compares more than two people or things.

Example: He arrives *soonest* of the group. | She speaks the *most softly* of any of her friends.

Prepositions

A **preposition** is a word placed before a noun or pronoun that shows the relationship between an object and another word in the sentence.

Common prepositions:

about	before	during	on	under
after	beneath	for	over	until
against	between	from	past	up
among	beyond	in	through	with
around	by	of	to	within
at	down	off	toward	without

Examples:

The napkin is *in* the drawer.

The Earth rotates *around* the Sun.

The needle is *beneath* the haystack.

Can you find "me" *among* the words?

Review Video: Prepositions
Visit mometrix.com/academy and enter code: 946763

Conjunctions

Conjunctions join words, phrases, or clauses and they show the connection between the joined pieces. **Coordinating conjunctions** connect equal parts of sentences. **Correlative conjunctions** show the connection between pairs. **Subordinating conjunctions** join subordinate (i.e., dependent) clauses with independent clauses.

Coordinating Conjunctions

The **coordinating conjunctions** include: *and, but, yet, or, nor, for,* and *so*

Examples:

The rock was small, *but* it was heavy.

She drove in the night, *and* he drove in the day.

Correlative Conjunctions

The **correlative conjunctions** are: *either...or* | *neither...nor* | *not only...but also*

Examples:

Either you are coming *or* you are staying.

He *not only* ran three miles *but also* swam 200 yards.

Review Video: Coordinating and Correlative Conjunctions
Visit mometrix.com/academy and enter code: 390329

Review Video: Adverb Equal Comparisons
Visit mometrix.com/academy and enter code: 231291

Subordinating Conjunctions

Common **subordinating conjunctions** include:

after	since	whenever
although	so that	where
because	unless	wherever
before	until	whether
in order that	when	while

Examples:

I am hungry *because* I did not eat breakfast.

He went home *when* everyone left.

Review Video: Subordinating Conjunctions
Visit mometrix.com/academy and enter code: 958913

Interjections

Interjections are words of exclamation (i.e., audible expression of great feeling) that are used alone or as a part of a sentence. Often, they are used at the beginning of a sentence for an introduction. Sometimes, they can be used in the middle of a sentence to show a change in thought or attitude.

Common Interjections: Hey! | Oh, | Ouch! | Please! | Wow!

Chapter Quiz

1. Which of the following is NOT considered a type of mood?

a. Indicative
b. Imperative
c. Subjunctive
d. Conjunctive

2. How many different degrees of relative adjectives are there?

a. Two
b. Three
c. Four
d. Five

3. In general, adverbs may modify all of the following, EXCEPT:

a. Another adverb.
b. Adjectives.
c. Proper nouns.
d. Verbs.

Chapter Quiz Answer Key

1. D: There are three moods in English: the indicative, the imperative, and the subjunctive.

2. B: Relative adjectives will show the different degrees of something or someone to something else or someone else. The three degrees of adjectives include positive, comparative, and superlative.

3. C: An adverb is a word that is used to modify a verb, adjective, or another adverb. Usually, adverbs answer one of the questions: *When? Where? How?* and *Why?* The negatives *not* and *never* are considered adverbs. Adverbs that modify adjectives or other adverbs strengthen or weaken the words that they modify.

Subjects and Predicates

Subjects

The **subject** of a sentence names who or what the sentence is about. The subject may be directly stated in a sentence, or the subject may be the implied *you*. The **complete subject** includes the simple subject and all of its modifiers. To find the complete subject, ask *Who* or *What* and insert the verb to complete the question. The answer, including any modifiers (adjectives, prepositional phrases, etc.), is the complete subject. To find the **simple subject**, remove all of the modifiers in the complete subject. Being able to locate the subject of a sentence helps with many problems, such as those involving sentence fragments and subject-verb agreement.

Examples:

simple subject (car)

The small, red car is the one that he wants for Christmas.

complete subject (The small, red car)

simple subject (artist)

The young artist is coming over for dinner.

complete subject (The young artist)

Review Video: Subjects in English
Visit mometrix.com/academy and enter code: 444771

In **imperative** sentences, the verb's subject is understood (e.g., [You] Run to the store), but is not actually present in the sentence. Normally, the subject comes before the verb. However, the subject comes after the verb in sentences that begin with *There are* or *There was.*

Direct:

John knows the way to the park.	Who knows the way to the park?	John
The cookies need ten more minutes.	What needs ten minutes?	The cookies
By five o'clock, Bill will need to leave.	Who needs to leave?	Bill
There are five letters on the table for him.	What is on the table?	Five letters
There were coffee and doughnuts in the house.	What was in the house?	Coffee and doughnuts

Implied:

Go to the post office for me.	Who is going to the post office?	You
Come and sit with me, please?	Who needs to come and sit?	You

PREDICATES

In a sentence, you always have a predicate and a subject. The subject tells what the sentence is about, and the **predicate** explains or describes the subject.

Think about the sentence *He sings.* In this sentence, we have a subject (He) and a predicate (sings). This is all that is needed for a sentence to be complete. Most sentences contain more information, but if this is all the information that you are given, then you have a complete sentence.

Now, let's look at another sentence: *John and Jane sing on Tuesday nights at the dance hall.*

subject — predicate

John and Jane sing on Tuesday nights at the dance hall.

Subject-Verb Agreement

Verbs **agree** with their subjects in number. In other words, singular subjects need singular verbs. Plural subjects need plural verbs. **Singular** is for **one** person, place, or thing. **Plural** is for **more than one** person, place, or thing. Subjects and verbs must also share the same point of view, as in first, second, or third person. The present tense ending *-s* is used on a verb if its subject is third person singular; otherwise, the verb's ending is not modified.

Review Video: Subject-Verb Agreement
Visit mometrix.com/academy and enter code: 479190

Number Agreement Examples:

singular subject — singular verb

Single Subject and Verb: Dan calls home.

Dan is one person. So, the singular verb *calls* is needed.

plural subject — plural verb

Plural Subject and Verb: Dan and Bob call home.

More than one person needs the plural verb *call.*

Person Agreement Examples:

First Person: I *am* walking.

Second Person: You *are* walking.

Third Person: He *is* walking.

Complications with Subject-Verb Agreement

Words Between Subject and Verb

Words that come between the simple subject and the verb have no bearing on subject-verb agreement.

Examples:

singular subject — singular verb

The joy of my life returns home tonight.

The phrase *of my life* does not influence the verb *returns.*

singular subject — singular verb

The question that still remains unanswered is "Who are you?"

Don't let the phrase "*that still remains...*" trouble you. The subject *question* goes with *is.*

Compound Subjects

A compound subject is formed when two or more nouns joined by *and*, *or*, or *nor* jointly act as the subject of the sentence.

Joined by And

When a compound subject is joined by *and*, it is treated as a plural subject and requires a plural verb.

Examples:

You and Jon (plural subject) are (plural verb) invited to come to my house.

The pencil and paper (plural subject) belong (plural verb) to me.

Joined by Or/Nor

For a compound subject joined by *or* or *nor*, the verb must agree in number with the part of the subject that is closest to the verb (italicized in the examples below).

Examples:

Today or tomorrow (subject) is (verb) the day.

Stan or Phil (subject) wants (verb) to read the book.

Neither the pen nor the book (subject) is (verb) on the desk.

Either the blanket or pillows (subject) arrive (verb) this afternoon.

Indefinite Pronouns as Subject

An indefinite pronoun is a pronoun that does not refer to a specific noun. Different indefinite pronouns may only function as a singular noun, only function as a plural noun, or change depending on how they are used.

Always Singular

Pronouns such as *each*, *either*, *everybody*, *anybody*, *somebody*, and *nobody* are always singular.

Examples:

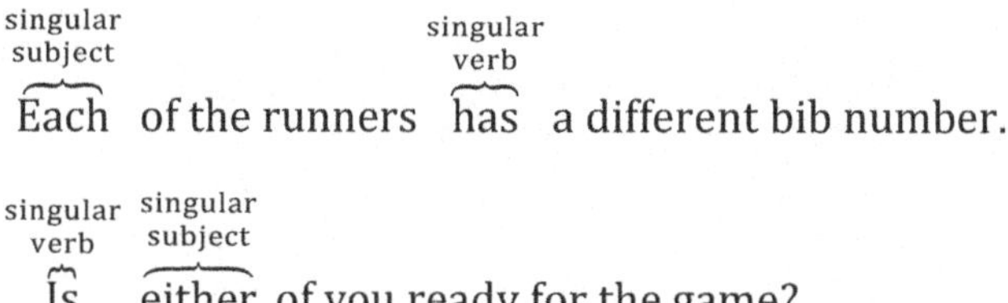

Note: The words *each* and *either* can also be used as adjectives (e.g., *each* person is unique). When one of these adjectives modifies the subject of a sentence, it is always a singular subject.

singular subject: Everybody; singular verb: grows

Everybody grows a day older every day.

singular subject: Anybody; singular verb: is

Anybody is welcome to bring a tent.

ALWAYS PLURAL

Pronouns such as *both*, *several*, and *many* are always plural.

Examples:

plural subject: Both; plural verb: were

Both of the siblings were too tired to argue.

plural subject: Many; plural verb: have tried

Many have tried, but none have succeeded.

DEPEND ON CONTEXT

Pronouns such as *some*, *any*, *all*, *none*, *more*, and *most* can be either singular or plural depending on what they are representing in the context of the sentence.

Examples:

singular subject: All; singular verb: was

All of my dog's food was still there in his bowl.

plural subject: all; plural verb: were

By the end of the night, all of my guests were already excited about coming to my next party.

OTHER CASES INVOLVING PLURAL OR IRREGULAR FORM

Some nouns are **singular in meaning but plural in form**: news, mathematics, physics, and economics.

The *news is* coming on now.

Mathematics is my favorite class.

Some nouns are plural in form and meaning, and have **no singular equivalent**: scissors and pants.

Do these *pants come* with a shirt?

The *scissors are* for my project.

Mathematical operations are **irregular** in their construction, but are normally considered to be **singular in meaning**.

> *One plus one is* two.
>
> *Three times three is* nine.

Note: Look to your **dictionary** for help when you aren't sure whether a noun with a plural form has a singular or plural meaning.

COMPLEMENTS

A complement is a noun, pronoun, or adjective that is used to give more information about the subject or verb in the sentence.

DIRECT OBJECTS

A direct object is a noun or pronoun that takes or receives the **action** of a verb. (Remember: a complete sentence does not need a direct object, so not all sentences will have them. A sentence needs only a subject and a verb.) When you are looking for a direct object, find the verb and ask *who* or *what.*

Examples:

> I took *the blanket.*
>
> Jane read *books.*

INDIRECT OBJECTS

An indirect object is a word or group of words that show how an action had an **influence** on someone or something. If there is an indirect object in a sentence, then you always have a direct object in the sentence. When you are looking for the indirect object, find the verb and ask *to/for whom or what.*

Examples:

> We taught [the old dog: indirect object] [a new trick: direct object].
>
> I gave [them: indirect object] [a math lesson: direct object].

Review Video: Direct and Indirect Objects
Visit mometrix.com/academy and enter code: 817385

PREDICATE NOMINATIVES AND PREDICATE ADJECTIVES

As we looked at previously, verbs may be classified as either action verbs or linking verbs. A linking verb is so named because it links the subject to words in the predicate that describe or define the subject. These words are called predicate nominatives (if nouns or pronouns) or predicate adjectives (if adjectives).

Examples:

My father (subject) is a lawyer (predicate nominative).

Your mother (subject) is patient (predicate adjective).

Pronoun Usage

The **antecedent** is the noun that has been replaced by a pronoun. A pronoun and its antecedent **agree** when they have the same number (singular or plural) and gender (male, female, or neutral).

Examples:

> **Singular agreement**: John (antecedent) came into town, and he (pronoun) played for us.
>
> **Plural agreement**: John and Rick (antecedent) came into town, and they (pronoun) played for us.

To determine which is the correct pronoun to use in a compound subject or object, try each pronoun **alone** in place of the compound in the sentence. Your knowledge of pronouns will tell you which one is correct.

Example:

> Bob and (I, me) will be going.
>
> Test: (1) *I will be going* or (2) *Me will be going*. The second choice cannot be correct because *me* cannot be used as the subject of a sentence. Instead, *me* is used as an object.
>
> **Answer**: Bob and I will be going.

When a pronoun is used with a noun immediately following (as in "we boys"), try the sentence **without the added noun**.

Example:

> (We/Us) boys played football last year.
>
> Test: (1) *We played football last ye*ar or (2) *Us played football last year*. Again, the second choice cannot be correct because *us* cannot be used as a subject of a sentence. Instead, *us* is used as an object.
>
> **Answer**: We boys played football last year.

Review Video: Pronoun Usage
Visit mometrix.com/academy and enter code: 666500

Review Video: What is Pronoun-Antecedent Agreement?
Visit mometrix.com/academy and enter code: 919704

A pronoun should point clearly to the **antecedent**. Here is how a pronoun reference can be unhelpful if it is puzzling or not directly stated.

antecedent pronoun

Unhelpful: Ron and Jim went to the store, and he bought soda.

Who bought soda? Ron or Jim?

antecedent pronoun

Helpful: Jim went to the store, and he bought soda.

The sentence is clear. Jim bought the soda.

Some pronouns change their form by their placement in a sentence. A pronoun that is a **subject** in a sentence comes in the **subjective case**. Pronouns that serve as **objects** appear in the **objective case**. Finally, the pronouns that are used as **possessives** appear in the **possessive case**.

Examples:

Subjective case: *He* is coming to the show.

The pronoun *He* is the subject of the sentence.

Objective case: Josh drove *him* to the airport.

The pronoun *him* is the object of the sentence.

Possessive case: The flowers are *mine*.

The pronoun *mine* shows ownership of the flowers.

The word *who* is a subjective-case pronoun that can be used as a **subject**. The word *whom* is an objective-case pronoun that can be used as an **object**. The words *who* and *whom* are common in subordinate clauses or in questions.

Examples:

subject verb

He knows who wants to come.

object verb

He knows the man whom we want at the party.

Clauses

A clause is a group of words that contains both a subject and a predicate (verb). There are two types of clauses: independent and dependent. An **independent clause** contains a complete thought, while a **dependent (or subordinate) clause** does not. A dependent clause includes a subject and a verb, and may also contain objects or complements, but it cannot stand as a complete thought without being joined to an independent clause. Dependent clauses function within sentences as adjectives, adverbs, or nouns.

Example:

independent clause: I am running | dependent clause: because I want to stay in shape.

I am running because I want to stay in shape.

The clause *I am running* is an independent clause: it has a subject and a verb, and it gives a complete thought. The clause *because I want to stay in shape* is a dependent clause: it has a subject and a verb, but it does not express a complete thought. It adds detail to the independent clause to which it is attached.

Review Video: What is a Clause?
Visit mometrix.com/academy and enter code: 940170

Review Video: Independent and Dependent Clauses
Visit mometrix.com/academy and enter code: 556903

Types of Dependent Clauses

Adjective Clauses

An **adjective clause** is a dependent clause that modifies a noun or a pronoun. Adjective clauses begin with a relative pronoun (*who, whose, whom, which,* and *that*) or a relative adverb (*where, when,* and *why*).

Also, adjective clauses come after the noun that the clause needs to explain or rename. This is done to have a clear connection to the independent clause.

Examples:

independent clause: I learned the reason | adjective clause: why I won the award.

I learned the reason why I won the award.

independent clause: This is the place | adjective clause: where I started my first job.

This is the place where I started my first job.

An adjective clause can be an essential or nonessential clause. An essential clause is very important to the sentence. **Essential clauses** explain or define a person or thing. **Nonessential clauses** give more information about a person or thing but are not necessary to define them. Nonessential clauses are set off with commas while essential clauses are not.

Examples:

essential clause: who works hard at first

A person who works hard at first can often rest later in life.

nonessential clause: who walked on the moon

Neil Armstrong, who walked on the moon, is my hero.

Review Video: Adjective Clauses and Phrases
Visit mometrix.com/academy and enter code: 520888

Adverb Clauses

An **adverb clause** is a dependent clause that modifies a verb, adjective, or adverb. In sentences with multiple dependent clauses, adverb clauses are usually placed immediately before or after the independent clause. An adverb clause is introduced with words such as *after, although, as, before, because, if, since, so, unless, when, where,* and *while.*

Examples:

(adverb clause: When you walked outside,) I called the manager.

I will go with you (adverb clause: unless you want to stay.)

Noun Clauses

A **noun clause** is a dependent clause that can be used as a subject, object, or complement. Noun clauses begin with words such as *how, that, what, whether, which, who,* and *why.* These words can also come with an adjective clause. Unless the noun clause is being used as the subject of the sentence, it should come after the verb of the independent clause.

Examples:

The real mystery is (noun clause: how you avoided serious injury.)

(noun clause: What you learn from each other) depends on your honesty with others.

Subordination

When two related ideas are not of equal importance, the ideal way to combine them is to make the more important idea an independent clause and the less important idea a dependent or subordinate clause. This is called **subordination.**

Example:

Separate ideas: The team had a perfect regular season. The team lost the championship.

Subordinated: Despite having a perfect regular season, *the team lost the championship.*

Phrases

A phrase is a group of words that functions as a single part of speech, usually a noun, adjective, or adverb. A **phrase** is not a complete thought, but it adds detail or explanation to a sentence, or renames something within the sentence.

Prepositional Phrases

One of the most common types of phrases is the prepositional phrase. A **prepositional phrase** begins with a preposition and ends with a noun or pronoun that is the object of the preposition. Normally, the prepositional phrase functions as an **adjective** or an **adverb** within the sentence.

Examples:

The picnic is on the blanket. (prepositional phrase: *on the blanket*)

I am sick with a fever today. (prepositional phrase: *with a fever*)

Among the many flowers, John found a four-leaf clover. (prepositional phrase: *Among the many flowers*)

VERBAL PHRASES

A **verbal** is a word or phrase that is formed from a verb but does not function as a verb. Depending on its particular form, it may be used as a noun, adjective, or adverb. A verbal does **not** replace a verb in a sentence.

Examples:

Correct: Walk a mile daily. (verb: *Walk*)

This is a complete sentence with the implied subject *you*.

Incorrect: To walk a mile. (verbal: *To walk*)

This is not a sentence since there is no functional verb.

There are three types of verbal: **participles**, **gerunds**, and **infinitives**. Each type of verbal has a corresponding **phrase** that consists of the verbal itself along with any complements or modifiers.

PARTICIPLES

A **participle** is a type of verbal that always functions as an adjective. The present participle always ends with *-ing*. Past participles end with *-d, -ed, -n,* or *-t*.

Examples: dance (verb) | dancing (present participle) | danced (past participle)

Participial phrases most often come right before or right after the noun or pronoun that they modify.

Examples:

participial phrase

Shipwrecked on an island, the boys started to fish for food.

participial phrase

Having been seated for five hours, we got out of the car to stretch our legs.

participial phrase

Praised for their work, the group accepted the first-place trophy.

Gerunds

A **gerund** is a type of verbal that always functions as a **noun**. Like present participles, gerunds always end with *-ing*, but they can be easily distinguished from one another by the part of speech they represent (participles always function as adjectives). Since a gerund or gerund phrase always functions as a noun, it can be used as the subject of a sentence, the predicate nominative, or the object of a verb or preposition.

Examples:

gerund

We want to be known for teaching the poor.

object of preposition

gerund

Coaching this team is the best job of my life.

subject

gerund

We like practicing our songs in the basement.

object of verb

Infinitives

An **infinitive** is a type of verbal that can function as a noun, an adjective, or an adverb. An infinitive is made of the word *to* and the basic form of the verb. As with all other types of verbal phrases, an infinitive phrase includes the verbal itself and all of its complements or modifiers.

Examples:

infinitive
To join the team is my goal in life.
noun

infinitive
The animals have enough food to eat for the night.
adjective

infinitive
People lift weights to exercise their muscles.
adverb

Review Video: Gerunds, Infinitives, and Participles
Visit mometrix.com/academy and enter code: 634263

Appositive Phrases

An **appositive** is a word or phrase that is used to explain or rename nouns or pronouns. Noun phrases, gerund phrases, and infinitive phrases can all be used as appositives.

Examples:

appositive
Terriers, hunters at heart, have been dressed up to look like lap dogs.

The noun phrase *hunters at heart* renames the noun *terriers.*

appositive
His plan, to save and invest his money, was proven as a safe approach.

The infinitive phrase explains what the plan is.

Appositive phrases can be **essential** or **nonessential**. An appositive phrase is essential if the person, place, or thing being described or renamed is too general for its meaning to be understood without the appositive.

Examples:

essential
Two of America's Founding Fathers, George Washington and Thomas Jefferson, served as presidents.

nonessential
George Washington and Thomas Jefferson, two Founding Fathers, served as presidents.

Absolute Phrases

An absolute phrase is a phrase that consists of **a noun followed by a participle**. An absolute phrase provides **context** to what is being described in the sentence, but it does not modify or explain any particular word; it is essentially independent.

Examples:

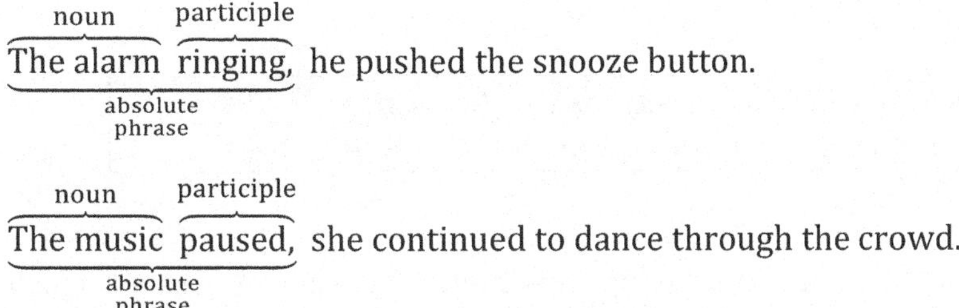

Parallelism

When multiple items or ideas are presented in a sentence in series, such as in a list, the items or ideas must be stated in grammatically equivalent ways. In other words, if one idea is stated in gerund form, the second cannot be stated in infinitive form. For example, to write, *I enjoy reading and to study* would be incorrect. An infinitive and a gerund are not equivalent. Instead, you should write *I enjoy reading and studying*. In lists of more than two, all items must be parallel.

Example:

> **Incorrect**: He stopped at the office, grocery store, and the pharmacy before heading home.
>
> The first and third items in the list of places include the article *the*, so the second item needs it as well.
>
> **Correct**: He stopped at the office, *the* grocery store, and the pharmacy before heading home.

Example:

> **Incorrect**: While vacationing in Europe, she went biking, skiing, and climbed mountains.
>
> The first and second items in the list are gerunds, so the third item must be as well.
>
> **Correct**: While vacationing in Europe, she went biking, skiing, and *mountain climbing*.

Review Video: Parallel Sentence Construction
Visit mometrix.com/academy and enter code: 831988

Sentence Purpose

There are four types of sentences: declarative, imperative, interrogative, and exclamatory.

A **declarative** sentence states a fact and ends with a period.

> *The football game starts at seven o'clock.*

An **imperative** sentence tells someone to do something and generally ends with a period. An urgent command might end with an exclamation point instead.

> *Don't forget to buy your ticket.*

An **interrogative** sentence asks a question and ends with a question mark.

> *Are you going to the game on Friday?*

An **exclamatory** sentence shows strong emotion and ends with an exclamation point.

I can't believe we won the game!

> **Review Video: Functions of a Sentence**
> Visit mometrix.com/academy and enter code: 475974

Sentence Structure

Sentences are classified by structure based on the type and number of clauses present. The four classifications of sentence structure are the following:

Simple: A simple sentence has one independent clause with no dependent clauses. A simple sentence may have **compound elements** (i.e., compound subject or verb).

Examples:

Judy [single subject] watered [single verb] the lawn.

Judy and Alan [compound subject] watered [single verb] the lawn.

Judy [single subject] watered [compound verb] the lawn and pulled [compound verb] weeds.

Judy and Alan [compound subject] watered [compound verb] the lawn and pulled [compound verb] weeds.

Compound: A compound sentence has two or more independent clauses with no dependent clauses. Usually, the independent clauses are joined with a comma and a coordinating conjunction or with a semicolon.

Examples:

The time has come, [independent clause] and we are ready. [independent clause]

I woke up at dawn; [independent clause] the sun was just coming up. [independent clause]

Complex: A complex sentence has one independent clause and at least one dependent clause.

Examples:

Although he had the flu, [dependent clause] Harry went to work. [independent clause]

Marcia got married, [independent clause] after she finished college. [dependent clause]

Compound-Complex: A compound-complex sentence has at least two independent clauses and at least one dependent clause.

Examples:

independent clause | dependent clause | independent clause
John is my friend who went to India, and he brought back souvenirs.

independent clause | independent clause | dependent clause
You may not realize this, but we heard the music that you played last night.

Review Video: Sentence Structure
Visit mometrix.com/academy and enter code: 700478

Sentence variety is important to consider when writing an essay or speech. A variety of sentence lengths and types creates rhythm, makes a passage more engaging, and gives writers an opportunity to demonstrate their writing style. Writing that uses the same length or type of sentence without variation can be boring or difficult to read. To evaluate a passage for effective sentence variety, it is helpful to note whether the passage contains diverse sentence structures and lengths. It is also important to pay attention to the way each sentence starts and avoid beginning with the same words or phrases.

Sentence Fragments

Recall that a group of words must contain at least one **independent clause** in order to be considered a sentence. If it doesn't contain even one independent clause, it is called a **sentence fragment**.

The appropriate process for **repairing** a sentence fragment depends on what type of fragment it is. If the fragment is a dependent clause, it can sometimes be as simple as removing a subordinating word (e.g., when, because, if) from the beginning of the fragment. Alternatively, a dependent clause can be incorporated into a closely related neighboring sentence. If the fragment is missing some required part, like a subject or a verb, the fix might be as simple as adding the missing part.

Examples:

Fragment: Because he wanted to sail the Mediterranean.

Removed subordinating word: He wanted to sail the Mediterranean.

Combined with another sentence: Because he wanted to sail the Mediterranean, he booked a Greek island cruise.

Run-on Sentences

Run-on sentences consist of multiple independent clauses that have not been joined together properly. Run-on sentences can be corrected in several different ways:

Join clauses properly: This can be done with a comma and coordinating conjunction, with a semicolon, or with a colon or dash if the second clause is explaining something in the first.

Example:

Incorrect: I went on the trip, we visited lots of castles.

Corrected: I went on the trip, and we visited lots of castles.

Split into separate sentences: This correction is most effective when the independent clauses are very long or when they are not closely related.

Example:

Incorrect: The drive to New York takes ten hours, my uncle lives in Boston.

Corrected: The drive to New York takes ten hours. My uncle lives in Boston.

Make one clause dependent: This is the easiest way to make the sentence correct and more interesting at the same time. It's often as simple as adding a subordinating word between the two clauses or before the first clause.

Example:

Incorrect: I finally made it to the store and I bought some eggs.

Corrected: When I finally made it to the store, I bought some eggs.

Reduce to one clause with a compound verb: If both clauses have the same subject, remove the subject from the second clause, and you now have just one clause with a compound verb.

Example:

Incorrect: The drive to New York takes ten hours, it makes me very tired.

Corrected: The drive to New York takes ten hours and makes me very tired.

Note: While these are the simplest ways to correct a run-on sentence, often the best way is to completely reorganize the thoughts in the sentence and rewrite it.

Review Video: Fragments and Run-on Sentences
Visit mometrix.com/academy and enter code: 541989

Dangling and Misplaced Modifiers

Dangling Modifiers

A dangling modifier is a dependent clause or verbal phrase that does not have a clear logical connection to a word in the sentence.

Example:

dangling modifier

Incorrect: Reading each magazine article, the stories caught my attention.

The word *stories* cannot be modified by *Reading each magazine article.* People can read, but stories cannot read. Therefore, the subject of the sentence must be a person.

dependent clause

Corrected: Reading each magazine article, I was entertained by the stories.

Example:

dangling modifier

Incorrect: Ever since childhood, my grandparents have visited me for Christmas.

The speaker in this sentence can't have been visited by her grandparents when *they* were children, since she wouldn't have been born yet. Either the modifier should be clarified or the sentence should be rearranged to specify whose childhood is being referenced.

dependent clause

Clarified: Ever since I was a child, my grandparents have visited for Christmas.

dependent clause

Rearranged: I have enjoyed my grandparents visiting for Christmas, ever since childhood.

Misplaced Modifiers

Because modifiers are grammatically versatile, they can be put in many different places within the structure of a sentence. The danger of this versatility is that a modifier can accidentally be placed where it is modifying the wrong word or where it is not clear which word it is modifying.

Example:

modifier

Incorrect: She read the book to a crowd that was filled with beautiful pictures.

The book was filled with beautiful pictures, not the crowd.

modifier

Corrected: She read the book that was filled with beautiful pictures to a crowd.

Example:

modifier

Ambiguous: Derek saw a bus nearly hit a man on his way to work.

Was Derek on his way to work or was the other man?

modifier

Derek: On his way to work, Derek saw a bus nearly hit a man.

modifier

The other man: Derek saw a bus nearly hit a man who was on his way to work.

Split Infinitives

A split infinitive occurs when a modifying word comes between the word *to* and the verb that pairs with *to*.

Example: To *clearly* explain vs. *To explain* clearly | To *softly* sing vs. *To sing* softly

Though considered improper by some, split infinitives may provide better clarity and simplicity in some cases than the alternatives. As such, avoiding them should not be considered a universal rule.

Double Negatives

Standard English allows **two negatives** only when a **positive** meaning is intended. For example, *The team was not displeased with their performance.* Double negatives to emphasize negation are not used in standard English.

Negative modifiers (e.g., never, no, and not) should not be paired with other negative modifiers or negative words (e.g., none, nobody, nothing, or neither). The modifiers *hardly, barely*, and *scarcely* are also considered negatives in standard English, so they should not be used with other negatives.

Chapter Quiz

1. Which of the following is an imperative statement?

a. John knows the way to the park.
b. There are five letters on the table for him.
c. Go to the post office for me.
d. The cookies need to cook for a few more minutes.

2. Which of the following is NOT a word used to combine nouns to make a compound subject?

a. Or
b. Nor
c. And
d. Also

3. Which of the following is always singular?

a. Each
b. Both
c. Several
d. Many

4. Identify the indirect object of the following sentence: "We taught the old dog a new trick."

a. We
b. Taught
c. The old dog
d. A new trick

5. Identify the infinitive of the following sentence: "The animals have enough food to eat for the night."

a. The animals
b. Have enough food
c. To eat
d. For the night

6. How many types of sentences are there?

a. Three
b. Four
c. Five
d. Six

7. Which of the following sentences correctly expresses the idea of parallelism?

a. He stopped at the office, grocery store, and the pharmacy before heading home.
b. While vacationing in Europe, she went biking, skiing, and climbed mountains.
c. The crowd jumped and cheered, roared and hollered, and whistled as the game concluded.
d. The flurry of blows left him staggered, discombobulated, and overwhelmed before falling.

8. Identify the phrase, "The music paused," in the following sample sentence:

"The music paused, she continued to dance through the crowd."

a. Subordinate phrase
b. Essential appositive
c. Nonessential appositive
d. Absolute phrase

Chapter Quiz Answer Key

1. C: In an imperative sentence, the verb's subject is understood without actually appearing or being named in the sentence itself. For example, in the imperative sentence, "Run to the store," the subject is the person being told to run.

2. D: A compound subject is formed when two or more nouns joined by *and*, *or*, or *nor* jointly act as the subject of the sentence.

3. A: Pronouns such as *each*, *either*, *everybody*, *anybody*, *somebody*, and *nobody* are always singular.

4. C: An indirect object is a word or group of words that show how an action had an influence on someone or something. If there is an indirect object in a sentence, then there will always be a direct object in the sentence. When looking for the indirect object, find the verb and ask *to, for whom,* or *what.*

We taught the old dog (indirect object) a new trick (direct object).

5. C: An infinitive is a type of verbal that can function as a noun, an adjective, or an adverb. An infinitive is made of the word *to* and the basic form of the verb. As with all other types of verbal phrases, an infinitive phrase includes the verbal itself and all of its complements or modifiers.

The animals have enough food to eat (infinitive) for the night. [to eat for the night: adjective]

6. B: There are four types of sentences: declarative, imperative, interrogative, and exclamatory.

7. D: When multiple items or ideas are presented in a sentence in series, such as in a list, the items or ideas must be stated in grammatically equivalent ways. In other words, if one idea is stated in gerund form, the second cannot be stated in infinitive form. For example, writing "I enjoy *reading* and *to study"* would be incorrect. An infinitive and a gerund are not equivalent. Instead, the sentence should be, "I enjoy *reading* and *studying*." In lists of more than two, all items must be parallel.

Example:

Incorrect: He stopped at the office, grocery store, and the pharmacy before heading home.

(The first and third items in the list of places include the article *the*, so the second item needs it as well.)

Correct: He stopped at the office, *the* grocery store, and the pharmacy before heading home.

8. D: An absolute phrase is a phrase that consists of a noun followed by a participle. An absolute phrase provides context to what is being described in the sentence, but it does not modify or explain any particular word; it is essentially independent.

The music (noun) paused (participle), she continued to dance through the crowd. [The music paused: absolute phrase]

End Punctuation

Periods

Use a period to end all sentences except direct questions and exclamations. Periods are also used for abbreviations.

Examples: 3 p.m. | 2 a.m. | Mr. Jones | Mrs. Stevens | Dr. Smith | Bill, Jr. | Pennsylvania Ave.

Note: An abbreviation is a shortened form of a word or phrase.

Question Marks

Question marks should be used following a **direct question**. A polite request can be followed by a period instead of a question mark.

Direct Question: What is for lunch today? | How are you? | Why is that the answer?

Polite Requests: Can you please send me the item tomorrow. | Will you please walk with me on the track.

Review Video: Question Marks
Visit mometrix.com/academy and enter code: 118471

Exclamation Marks

Exclamation marks are used after a word group or sentence that shows much feeling or has special importance. Exclamation marks should not be overused. They are saved for proper **exclamatory interjections**.

Example: We're going to the finals! | You have a beautiful car! | "That's crazy!" she yelled.

Review Video: Exclamation Points
Visit mometrix.com/academy and enter code: 199367

Commas

The comma is a punctuation mark that can help you understand connections in a sentence. Not every sentence needs a comma. However, if a sentence needs a comma, you need to put it in the right place. A comma in the wrong place (or an absent comma) will make a sentence's meaning unclear. These are some of the rules for commas:

Use Case	Example
Before a **coordinating conjunction** joining independent clauses	Bob caught three fish, and I caught two fish.
After an **introductory phrase**	After the final out, we went to a restaurant to celebrate.
After an **adverbial clause**	Studying the stars, I was awed by the beauty of the sky.
Between **items in a series**	I will bring the turkey, the pie, and the coffee.
For **interjections**	Wow, you know how to play this game.
After ***yes* and *no* responses**	No, I cannot come tomorrow.
Separate **nonessential modifiers**	John Frank, who coaches the team, was promoted today.
Separate **nonessential appositives**	Thomas Edison, an American inventor, was born in Ohio.
Separate **nouns of direct address**	You, John, are my only hope in this moment.
Separate **interrogative tags**	This is the last time, correct?
Separate **contrasts**	You are my friend, not my enemy.
Writing **dates**	July 4, 1776, is an important date to remember.
Writing **addresses**	He is meeting me at 456 Delaware Avenue, Washington, D.C., tomorrow morning.
Writing **geographical names**	Paris, France, is my favorite city.
Writing **titles**	John Smith, PhD, will be visiting your class today.
Separate **expressions like *he said***	"You can start," she said, "with an apology."

Also, you can use a comma **between coordinate adjectives** not joined with *and*. However, not all adjectives are coordinate (i.e., equal or parallel).

Incorrect: The kind, brown dog followed me home.

Correct: The kind, loyal dog followed me home.

There are two simple ways to know if your adjectives are coordinate. One, you can join the adjectives with *and*: *The kind and loyal dog*. Two, you can change the order of the adjectives: *The loyal, kind dog*.

Review Video: When to Use a Comma
Visit mometrix.com/academy and enter code: 786797

Semicolons

The semicolon is used to connect major sentence pieces of equal value. Some rules for semicolons include:

Use Case	Example
Between closely connected independent clauses **not connected with a coordinating conjunction**	You are right; we should go with your plan.
Between independent clauses **linked with a transitional word**	I think that we can agree on this; however, I am not sure about my friends.
Between items in a **series that has internal punctuation**	I have visited New York, New York; Augusta, Maine; and Baltimore, Maryland.

Review Video: How to Use Semicolons
Visit mometrix.com/academy and enter code: 370605

Colons

The colon is used to call attention to the words that follow it. A colon must come after a **complete independent clause**. The rules for colons are as follows:

Use Case	Example
After an independent clause to **make a list**	I want to learn many languages: Spanish, German, and Italian.
For **explanations**	There is one thing that stands out on your resume: responsibility.
To give a **quote**	He started with an idea: "We are able to do more than we imagine."
After the **greeting in a formal letter**	To Whom It May Concern:
Show **hours and minutes**	It is 3:14 p.m.
Separate a **title and subtitle**	The essay is titled "America: A Short Introduction to a Modern Country."

Review Video: Colons
Visit mometrix.com/academy and enter code: 868673

Parentheses

Parentheses are used for additional information. Also, they can be used to put labels for letters or numbers in a series. Parentheses should be not be used very often. If they are overused, parentheses can be a distraction instead of a help.

Examples:

Extra Information: The rattlesnake (see Image 2) is a dangerous snake of North and South America.

Series: Include in the email (1) your name, (2) your address, and (3) your question for the author.

Review Video: Parentheses
Visit mometrix.com/academy and enter code: 947743

Quotation Marks

Use quotation marks to close off **direct quotations** of a person's spoken or written words. Do not use quotation marks around indirect quotations. An indirect quotation gives someone's message without using the person's exact words. Use **single quotation marks** to close off a quotation inside a quotation.

Direct Quote: Nancy said, "I am waiting for Henry to arrive."

Indirect Quote: Henry said that he is going to be late to the meeting.

Quote inside a Quote: The teacher asked, "Has everyone read 'The Gift of the Magi'?"

Quotation marks should be used around the titles of **short works**: newspaper and magazine articles, poems, short stories, songs, television episodes, radio programs, and subdivisions of books or websites.

Examples:

"Rip Van Winkle" (short story by Washington Irving)

"O Captain! My Captain!" (poem by Walt Whitman)

Although it is not standard usage, quotation marks are sometimes used to highlight **irony** or the use of words to mean something other than their dictionary definition. This type of usage should be employed sparingly, if at all.

Examples:

The boss warned Frank that he was walking on "thin ice."	Frank is not walking on real ice. Instead, he is being warned to avoid mistakes.
The teacher thanked the young man for his "honesty."	The quotation marks around *honesty* show that the teacher does not believe the young man's explanation.

Review Video: Quotation Marks
Visit mometrix.com/academy and enter code: 884918

Periods and commas are put **inside** quotation marks. Colons and semicolons are put **outside** the quotation marks. Question marks and exclamation points are placed inside quotation marks when they are part of a quote. When the question or exclamation mark goes with the whole sentence, the mark is left outside of the quotation marks.

Examples:

Period and comma	We read "The Gift of the Magi," "The Skylight Room," and "The Cactus."
Semicolon	They watched "The Nutcracker"; then, they went home.
Exclamation mark that is a part of a quote	The crowd cheered, "Victory!"
Question mark that goes with the whole sentence	Is your favorite short story "The Tell-Tale Heart"?

APOSTROPHES

An apostrophe is used to show **possession** or the **deletion of letters in contractions**. An apostrophe is not needed with the possessive pronouns *his, hers, its, ours, theirs, whose*, and *yours*.

Singular Nouns: David's car | a book's theme | my brother's board game

Plural Nouns that end with -*s*: the scissors' handle | boys' basketball

Plural Nouns that end without -*s*: Men's department | the people's adventure

Review Video: When to Use an Apostrophe
Visit mometrix.com/academy and enter code: 213068

Review Video: Punctuation Errors in Possessive Pronouns
Visit mometrix.com/academy and enter code: 221438

HYPHENS

Hyphens are used to **separate compound words**. Use hyphens in the following cases:

Use Case	Example
Compound numbers from 21 to 99 when written out in words	This team needs twenty-five points to win the game.
Written-out fractions that are used as adjectives	The recipe says that we need a three-fourths cup of butter.
Compound adjectives that come before a noun	The well-fed dog took a nap.
Unusual compound words that would be hard to read or easily confused with other words	This is the best anti-itch cream on the market.

Note: This is not a complete set of the rules for hyphens. A dictionary is the best tool for knowing if a compound word needs a hyphen.

Review Video: Hyphens
Visit mometrix.com/academy and enter code: 981632

Dashes

Dashes are used to show a **break** or a **change in thought** in a sentence or to act as parentheses in a sentence. When typing, use two hyphens to make a dash. Do not put a space before or after the dash. The following are the functions of dashes:

Use Case	Example
Set off parenthetical statements or an **appositive with internal punctuation**	The three trees—oak, pine, and magnolia—are coming on a truck tomorrow.
Show a **break or change in tone or thought**	The first question—how silly of me—does not have a correct answer.

Ellipsis Marks

The ellipsis mark has **three** periods (…) to show when **words have been removed** from a quotation. If a **full sentence or more** is removed from a quoted passage, you need to use **four** periods to show the removed text and the end punctuation mark. The ellipsis mark should not be used at the beginning of a quotation. The ellipsis mark should also not be used at the end of a quotation unless some words have been deleted from the end of the final sentence.

Example:

> "Then he picked up the groceries…paid for them…later he went home."

Brackets

There are two main reasons to use brackets:

Use Case	Example
Placing **parentheses inside of parentheses**	The hero of this story, Paul Revere (a silversmith and industrialist [see Ch. 4]), rode through towns of Massachusetts to warn of advancing British troops.
Adding **clarification or detail to a quotation** that is not part of the quotation	The father explained, "My children are planning to attend my alma mater [State University]."

Review Video: Brackets
Visit mometrix.com/academy and enter code: 727546

Chapter Quiz

1. Which of the following correctly implements the use of parentheses?

a. The rattlesnake (see Image 2) is a dangerous snake of North and South America.
b. The rattlesnake see (Image 2) is a dangerous snake of North and South America.
c. The rattlesnake see Image (2) is a dangerous snake of North and South America.
d. The rattlesnake (see Image) (2) is a dangerous snake of North and South America.

2. Which of the following correctly describes the placement of punctuation in reference to quotations?

a. Periods and commas are put outside quotation marks; colons and semicolons go inside.
b. Periods and colons are put outside quotation marks; commas and semicolons go inside.
c. Periods and commas are put inside quotation marks; colons and semicolons go outside.
d. Periods and colons are put inside quotation marks; commas and semicolons go outside.

3. Which of the following correctly implements the use of commas?

a. He is meeting me at, 456 Delaware Avenue, Washington, D.C., tomorrow morning.
b. He is meeting me at 456 Delaware Avenue, Washington, D.C., tomorrow morning.
c. He is meeting me at 456 Delaware Avenue Washington, D.C. tomorrow morning.
d. He is meeting me at 456 Delaware Avenue, Washington, D.C. tomorrow morning.

Chapter Quiz Answer Key

1. A: Parentheses are used for additional information. Also, they can be used to put labels for letters or numbers in a series. Parentheses should be not be used very often because their overuse can become a distraction.

2. C: Periods and commas are put inside quotation marks, while colons and semicolons are put outside quotation marks. Question marks and exclamation points are placed inside quotation marks when they are part of a quote. When the question mark or exclamation point is not part of a quoted section but instead part of an entire sentence, then it is left outside of the quotation marks.

3. B: These are some of the rules for commas:

Use Case	Example
Before a **coordinating conjunction** joining independent clauses	Bob caught three fish, and I caught two fish.
After an **introductory phrase**	After the final out, we went to a restaurant to celebrate.
After an **adverbial clause**	Studying the stars, I was awed by the beauty of the sky.
Between **items in a series**	I will bring the turkey, the pie, and the coffee.
For **interjections**	Wow, you know how to play this game.
After ***yes* and *no* responses**	No, I cannot come tomorrow.
Separate **nonessential modifiers**	John Frank, who coaches the team, was promoted today.
Separate **nonessential appositives**	Thomas Edison, an American inventor, was born in Ohio.
Separate **nouns of direct address**	You, John, are my only hope in this moment.
Separate **interrogative tags**	This is the last time, correct?
Separate **contrasts**	You are my friend, not my enemy.
Writing **dates**	July 4, 1776, is an important date to remember.
Writing **addresses**	He is meeting me at 456 Delaware Avenue, Washington, D.C., tomorrow morning.
Writing **geographical names**	Paris, France, is my favorite city.
Writing **titles**	John Smith, PhD, will be visiting your class today.
Separate **expressions like "he said"**	"You can start," she said, "with an apology."

Word Confusion

Which, That, and Who

The words *which, that,* and *who* can act as **relative pronouns** to help clarify or describe a noun.

Which is used for things only.

Example: Andrew's car, *which is old and rusty,* broke down last week.

That is used for people or things. *That* is usually informal when used to describe people.

Example: Is this the only book *that Louis L'Amour wrote?*

Example: Is Louis L'Amour the author *that wrote Western novels?*

Who is used for people or for animals that have an identity or personality.

Example: Mozart was the composer *who wrote those operas.*

Example: John's dog, *who is called Max,* is large and fierce.

Homophones

Homophones are words that sound alike (or similar) but have different **spellings** and **definitions**. A homophone is a type of **homonym**, which is a pair or group of words that are pronounced or spelled the same, but do not mean the same thing.

To, Too, and Two

To can be an adverb or a preposition for showing direction, purpose, and relationship. See your dictionary for the many other ways to use *to* in a sentence.

Examples: I went to the store. | I want to go with you.

Too is an adverb that means *also, as well, very,* or *in excess.*

Examples: I can walk a mile too. | You have eaten too much.

Two is a number.

Example: You have two minutes left.

There, Their, and They're

There can be an adjective, adverb, or pronoun. Often, *there* is used to show a place or to start a sentence.

Examples: I went there yesterday. | There is something in his pocket.

Their is a pronoun that is used to show ownership.

Examples: He is their father. | This is their fourth apology this week.

They're is a contraction of *they are.*

Example: Did you know that they're in town?

Knew and New

Knew is the past tense of *know.*

Example: I knew the answer.

New is an adjective that means something is current, has not been used, or is modern.

Example: This is my new phone.

Then and Than

Then is an adverb that indicates sequence or order:

Example: I'm going to run to the library and then come home.

Than is special-purpose word used only for comparisons:

Example: Susie likes chips more than candy.

Its and It's

Its is a pronoun that shows ownership.

Example: The guitar is in its case.

It's is a contraction of *it is.*

Example: It's an honor and a privilege to meet you.

Note: The *h* in honor is silent, so *honor* starts with the vowel sound *o*, which must have the article *an*.

Your and You're

Your is a pronoun that shows ownership.

Example: This is your moment to shine.

You're is a contraction of *you are.*

Example: Yes, you're correct.

Saw and Seen

Saw is the past-tense form of *see.*

Example: I saw a turtle on my walk this morning.

Seen is the past participle of *see.*

Example: I have seen this movie before.

Affect and Effect

There are two main reasons that *affect* and *effect* are so often confused: 1) both words can be used as either a noun or a verb, and 2) unlike most homophones, their usage and meanings are closely related to each other. Here is a quick rundown of the four usage options:

Affect (n): feeling, emotion, or mood that is displayed

Example: The patient had a flat *affect*. (i.e., his face showed little or no emotion)

Affect (v): to alter, to change, to influence

Example: The sunshine *affects* the plant's growth.

Effect (n): a result, a consequence

Example: What *effect* will this weather have on our schedule?

Effect (v): to bring about, to cause to be

Example: These new rules will *effect* order in the office.

The noun form of *affect* is rarely used outside of technical medical descriptions, so if a noun form is needed on the test, you can safely select *effect*. The verb form of *effect* is not as rare as the noun form of *affect*, but it's still not all that likely to show up on your test. If you need a verb and you can't decide which to use based on the definitions, choosing *affect* is your best bet.

Homographs

Homographs are words that share the same spelling, but have different meanings and sometimes different pronunciations. To figure out which meaning is being used, you should be looking for context clues. The context clues give hints to the meaning of the word. For example, the word *spot* has many meanings. It can mean "a place" or "a stain or blot." In the sentence "After my lunch, I saw a spot on my shirt," the word *spot* means "a stain or blot." The context clues of "After my lunch" and "on my shirt" guide you to this decision. A homograph is another type of homonym.

Bank

(noun): an establishment where money is held for savings or lending

(verb): to collect or pile up

Content

(noun): the topics that will be addressed within a book

(adjective): pleased or satisfied

(verb): to make someone pleased or satisfied

Fine

(noun): an amount of money that acts a penalty for an offense

(adjective): very small or thin

(adverb): in an acceptable way

(verb): to make someone pay money as a punishment

Incense

(noun): a material that is burned in religious settings and makes a pleasant aroma

(verb): to frustrate or anger

Lead

(noun): the first or highest position

(noun): a heavy metallic element

(verb): to direct a person or group of followers

(adjective): containing lead

Object

(noun): a lifeless item that can be held and observed

(verb): to disagree

Produce

(noun): fruits and vegetables

(verb): to make or create something

Refuse

(noun): garbage or debris that has been thrown away

(verb): to not allow

Subject

(noun): an area of study

(verb): to force or subdue

Tear

(noun): a fluid secreted by the eyes

(verb): to separate or pull apart

Chapter Quiz

1. Which of the following correctly implements the word "affect"?

a. These new rules will affect order in the office.
b. What affect will this weather have on our schedule?
c. The patient had a flat affect during her examination.
d. His narcissism had a detrimental affect on everyone around him.

2. "Affect" and "effect" would be considered which of the following?

a. Homographs
b. Synonyms
c. Antonyms
d. Homophones

Chapter Quiz Answer Key

1. C: There are two main reasons that *affect* and *effect* are so often confused: 1) both words can be used as either a noun or a verb; and 2) unlike most homophones, their usage and meanings are closely related to each other. Here is a quick rundown of the four usage options:

Affect (n): feeling, emotion, or mood that is displayed

Example: The patient had a flat *affect* (i.e., his face showed little or no emotion).

Affect (v): to alter, to change, to influence

Example: The sunshine *affects* the plant's growth.

Effect (n): a result, a consequence

Example: What *effect* will this weather have on our schedule?

Effect (v): to bring about, to cause to be

Example: These new rules will *effect* order in the office.

The noun form of *affect* is rarely used outside of technical medical descriptions, so if a noun form is needed on the test, *effect* is a safe selection. The verb form of *effect* is not as rare as the noun form of *affect*, but it's still not likely to show up on a test. If a verb is needed and the definitions aren't enough of an indicator for which one to use, choosing *affect* is the safest option.

2. D: Homophones are words that sound alike (or similar) but have different spellings and definitions. A homophone is a type of homonym, which is a pair or group of words that are pronounced or spelled the same, but do not mean the same thing.

Mathematics Test

Mathematics Test Overview

The math portion of the PSAT consists of a 45-minute section in which a calculator may be used and a 25-minute section in which no calculator may be used. The calculator portion contains 31 questions and the no-calculator portion contains 17 questions.

CONCEPTS COVERED

PSAT questions fall into four categories:

- Heart of Algebra
- Problem Solving and Data Analysis
- Passport to Advanced Math
- Additional Topics in Math

The table below gives a complete breakdown of questions:

Calculator Portion	**Number of Questions**	**% of Test**
Total Questions	*31*	*100%*
Multiple Choice	27	87%
Student-Produced Response	4	13%
Content Categories		
Heart of Algebra	8	26%
Problem Solving and Data Analysis	16	52%
Passport to Advanced Math	6	19%
Additional Math Topics	1	3%
No-Calculator Portion	**Number of Questions**	**% of Test**
Total Questions	*17*	*100%*
Multiple Choice	13	76%
Student-Produced Response	4	24%
Content Categories		
Heart of Algebra	8	47%
Passport to Advanced Math	8	47%
Additional Math Topics	1	6%

USE THE PRACTICE TESTS

The best thing you can do to prepare for the PSAT is to take several practice tests and review all your wrong answers very carefully. Work back through those problems until you understand how the answer was derived and you're confident you could answer a similar problem on your own.

This guide includes a practice test with an answer key and explanations. Examples are also available on the College Board website. If you feel uncertain on a particular concept or problem type, use these tests to practice.

Foundational Math Concepts

Classifications of Numbers

Numbers are the basic building blocks of mathematics. Specific features of numbers are identified by the following terms:

Integer – any positive or negative whole number, including zero. Integers do not include fractions $\left(\frac{1}{3}\right)$, decimals (0.56), or mixed numbers $\left(7\frac{3}{4}\right)$.

Prime number – any whole number greater than 1 that has only two factors, itself and 1; that is, a number that can be divided evenly only by 1 and itself.

Composite number – any whole number greater than 1 that has more than two different factors; in other words, any whole number that is not a prime number. For example: The composite number 8 has the factors of 1, 2, 4, and 8.

Even number – any integer that can be divided by 2 without leaving a remainder. For example: 2, 4, 6, 8, and so on.

Odd number – any integer that cannot be divided evenly by 2. For example: 3, 5, 7, 9, and so on.

Decimal number – any number that uses a decimal point to show the part of the number that is less than one. Example: 1.234.

Decimal point – a symbol used to separate the ones place from the tenths place in decimals or dollars from cents in currency.

Decimal place – the position of a number to the right of the decimal point. In the decimal 0.123, the 1 is in the first place to the right of the decimal point, indicating tenths; the 2 is in the second place, indicating hundredths; and the 3 is in the third place, indicating thousandths.

The **decimal**, or base 10, system is a number system that uses ten different digits (0, 1, 2, 3, 4, 5, 6, 7, 8, 9). An example of a number system that uses something other than ten digits is the **binary**, or base 2, number system, used by computers, which uses only the numbers 0 and 1. It is thought that the decimal system originated because people had only their 10 fingers for counting.

Rational numbers include all integers, decimals, and fractions. Any terminating or repeating decimal number is a rational number.

Irrational numbers cannot be written as fractions or decimals because the number of decimal places is infinite and there is no recurring pattern of digits within the number. For example, pi (π) begins with 3.141592 and continues without terminating or repeating, so pi is an irrational number.

Real numbers are the set of all rational and irrational numbers.

Review Video: Classification of Numbers
Visit mometrix.com/academy and enter code: 461071

Review Video: Prime and Composite Numbers
Visit mometrix.com/academy and enter code: 565581

NUMBERS IN WORD FORM AND PLACE VALUE

When writing numbers out in word form or translating word form to numbers, it is essential to understand how a place value system works. In the decimal or base-10 system, each digit of a number represents how many of the corresponding place value—a specific factor of 10—are contained in the number being represented. To make reading numbers easier, every three digits to the left of the decimal place is preceded by a comma. The following table demonstrates some of the place values:

Power of 10	10^3	10^2	10^1	10^0	10^{-1}	10^{-2}	10^{-3}
Value	1,000	100	10	1	0.1	0.01	0.001
Place	thousands	hundreds	tens	ones	tenths	hundredths	thousandths

For example, consider the number 4,546.09, which can be separated into each place value like this:

4: thousands
5: hundreds
4: tens
6: ones
0: tenths
9: hundredths

This number in word form would be *four thousand five hundred forty-six and nine hundredths.*

Review Video: Place Value
Visit mometrix.com/academy and enter code: 205433

RATIONAL NUMBERS

The term **rational** means that the number can be expressed as a ratio or fraction. That is, a number, r, is rational if and only if it can be represented by a fraction $\frac{a}{b}$ where a and b are integers and b does not equal 0. The set of rational numbers includes integers and decimals. If there is no finite way to represent a value with a fraction of integers, then the number is **irrational**. Common examples of irrational numbers include: $\sqrt{5}$, $(1+\sqrt{2})$, and π.

Review Video: Rational and Irrational Numbers
Visit mometrix.com/academy and enter code: 280645

THE NUMBER LINE

A number line is a graph to see the distance between numbers. Basically, this graph shows the relationship between numbers. So a number line may have a point for zero and may show negative numbers on the left side of the line. Any positive numbers are placed on the right side of the line. For example, consider the points labeled on the following number line:

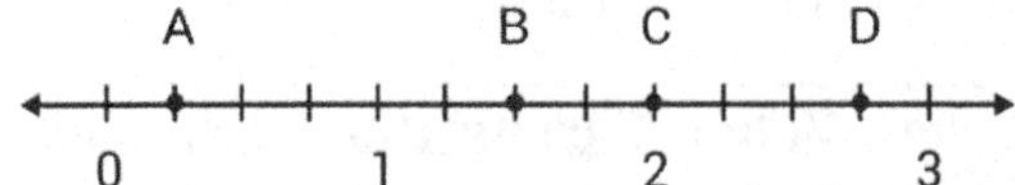

We can use the dashed lines on the number line to identify each point. Each dashed line between two whole numbers is $\frac{1}{4}$. The line halfway between two numbers is $\frac{1}{2}$.

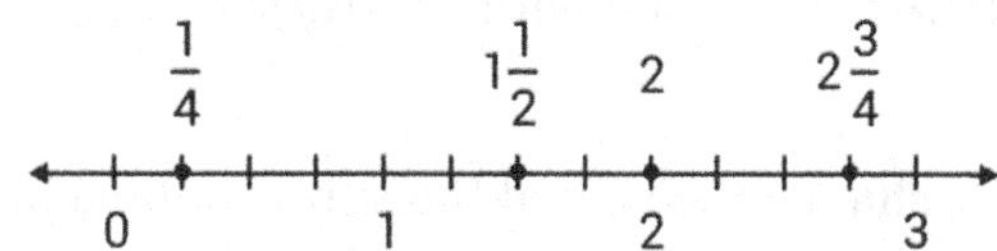

Review Video: The Number Line
Visit mometrix.com/academy and enter code: 816439

Absolute Value

A precursor to working with negative numbers is understanding what **absolute values** are. A number's absolute value is simply the distance away from zero a number is on the number line. The absolute value of a number is always positive and is written $|x|$. For example, the absolute value of 3, written as $|3|$, is 3 because the distance between 0 and 3 on a number line is three units. Likewise, the absolute value of –3, written as $|-3|$, is 3 because the distance between 0 and –3 on a number line is three units. So $|3| = |-3|$.

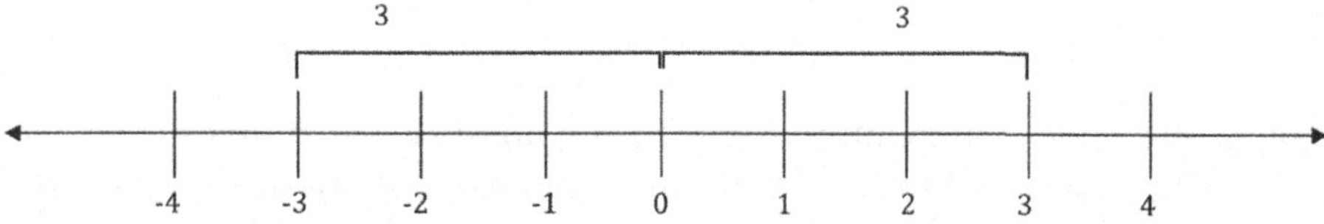

Review Video: Absolute Value
Visit mometrix.com/academy and enter code: 314669

Operations

An **operation** is simply a mathematical process that takes some value(s) as input(s) and produces an output. Elementary operations are often written in the following form: *value operation value*. For instance, in the expression $1 + 2$ the values are 1 and 2 and the operation is addition. Performing the operation gives the output of 3. In this way we can say that $1 + 2$ and 3 are equal, or $1 + 2 = 3$.

Addition

Addition increases the value of one quantity by the value of another quantity (both called **addends**). Example: $2 + 4 = 6$ or $8 + 9 = 17$. The result is called the **sum**. With addition, the order does not matter, $4 + 2 = 2 + 4$.

When adding signed numbers, if the signs are the same simply add the absolute values of the addends and apply the original sign to the sum. For example, $(+4) + (+8) = +12$ and $(-4) + (-8) = -12$. When the original signs are different, take the absolute values of the addends and subtract the smaller value from the larger value, then apply the original sign of the larger value to the difference. Example: $(+4) + (-8) = -4$ and $(-4) + (+8) = +4$.

Subtraction

Subtraction is the opposite operation to addition; it decreases the value of one quantity (the **minuend**) by the value of another quantity (the **subtrahend**). For example, $6 - 4 = 2$ or $17 - 8 = 9$. The result is called the **difference**. Note that with subtraction, the order does matter, $6 - 4 \neq 4 - 6$.

For subtracting signed numbers, change the sign of the subtrahend and then follow the same rules used for addition. Example: $(+4) - (+8) = (+4) + (-8) = -4$

Multiplication

Multiplication can be thought of as repeated addition. One number (the **multiplier**) indicates how many times to add the other number (the **multiplicand**) to itself. Example: $3 \times 2 = 2 + 2 + 2 = 6$. With multiplication, the order does not matter, $2 \times 3 = 3 \times 2$ or $3 + 3 = 2 + 2 + 2$, either way the result (the **product**) is the same.

If the signs are the same, the product is positive when multiplying signed numbers. Example: $(+4) \times (+8) = +32$ and $(-4) \times (-8) = +32$. If the signs are opposite, the product is negative. Example: $(+4) \times (-8) = -32$ and $(-4) \times (+8) = -32$. When more than two factors are multiplied together, the sign of the product is determined by how many negative factors are present. If there are an odd number of negative factors then the product is negative, whereas an even number of negative factors indicates a positive product. Example: $(+4) \times (-8) \times (-2) = +64$ and $(-4) \times (-8) \times (-2) = -64$.

Division

Division is the opposite operation to multiplication; one number (the **divisor**) tells us how many parts to divide the other number (the **dividend**) into. The result of division is called the **quotient**. Example: $20 \div 4 = 5$. If 20 is split into 4 equal parts, each part is 5. With division, the order of the numbers does matter, $20 \div 4 \neq 4 \div 20$.

The rules for dividing signed numbers are similar to multiplying signed numbers. If the dividend and divisor have the same sign, the quotient is positive. If the dividend and divisor have opposite signs, the quotient is negative. Example: $(-4) \div (+8) = -0.5$.

Review Video: Mathematical Operations
Visit mometrix.com/academy and enter code: 208095

Parentheses

Parentheses are used to designate which operations should be done first when there are multiple operations. Example: $4 - (2 + 1) = 1$; the parentheses tell us that we must add 2 and 1, and then subtract the sum from 4, rather than subtracting 2 from 4 and then adding 1 (this would give us an answer of 3).

Review Video: Mathematical Parentheses
Visit mometrix.com/academy and enter code: 978600

Exponents

An **exponent** is a superscript number placed next to another number at the top right. It indicates how many times the base number is to be multiplied by itself. Exponents provide a shorthand way to write what would be a longer mathematical expression, Example: $2^4 = 2 \times 2 \times 2 \times 2$. A number with an exponent of 2 is said to be "squared," while a number with an exponent of 3 is said to be "cubed." The value of a number raised to an exponent is called its power. So 8^4 is read as "8 to the 4th power," or "8 raised to the power of 4."

Review Video: Introduction to Exponents
Visit mometrix.com/academy and enter code: 600998

Roots

A **root**, such as a square root, is another way of writing a fractional exponent. Instead of using a superscript, roots use the radical symbol ($\sqrt{\ }$) to indicate the operation. A radical will have a number underneath the bar, and may sometimes have a number in the upper left: $\sqrt[n]{a}$, read as "the nth root of a." The relationship between radical notation and exponent notation can be described by this equation:

$$\sqrt[n]{a} = a^{\frac{1}{n}}$$

The two special cases of $n = 2$ and $n = 3$ are called square roots and cube roots. If there is no number to the upper left, the radical is understood to be a square root ($n = 2$). Nearly all of the roots you encounter will be square roots. A square root is the same as a number raised to the one-half power. When we say that a is the square root of b ($a = \sqrt{b}$), we mean that a multiplied by itself equals b: ($a \times a = b$).

A **perfect square** is a number that has an integer for its square root. There are 10 perfect squares from 1 to 100: 1, 4, 9, 16, 25, 36, 49, 64, 81, 100 (the squares of integers 1 through 10).

Review Video: Roots
Visit mometrix.com/academy and enter code: 795655

Review Video: Square Root and Perfect Squares
Visit mometrix.com/academy and enter code: 648063

Word Problems and Mathematical Symbols

When working on word problems, you must be able to translate verbal expressions or "math words" into math symbols. This chart contains several "math words" and their appropriate symbols:

Phrase	Symbol
equal, is, was, will be, has, costs, gets to, is the same as, becomes	$=$
times, of, multiplied by, product of, twice, doubles, halves, triples	$\times$
divided by, per, ratio of/to, out of	$\div$
plus, added to, sum, combined, and, more than, totals of	$+$
subtracted from, less than, decreased by, minus, difference between	$-$
what, how much, original value, how many, a number, a variable	x, n, etc.

Examples of Translated Mathematical Phrases

- The phrase four more than twice a number can be written algebraically as $2x + 4$.
- The phrase half a number decreased by six can be written algebraically as $\frac{1}{2}x - 6$.
- The phrase the sum of a number and the product of five and that number can be written algebraically as $x + 5x$.

- You may see a test question that says, "Olivia is constructing a bookcase from seven boards. Two of them are for vertical supports and five are for shelves. The height of the bookcase is twice the width of the bookcase. If the seven boards total 36 feet in length, what will be the height of Olivia's bookcase?" You would need to make a sketch and then create the equation to determine the width of the shelves. The height can be represented as double the width. (If x represents the width of the shelves in feet, then the height of the bookcase is $2x$. Since the seven boards total 36 feet, $2x + 2x + x + x + x + x + x = 36$ or $9x = 36$; $x = 4$. The height is twice the width, or 8 feet.)

SUBTRACTION WITH REGROUPING

A great way to make use of some of the features built into the decimal system would be regrouping when attempting longform subtraction operations. When subtracting within a place value, sometimes the minuend is smaller than the subtrahend, **regrouping** enables you to 'borrow' a unit from a place value to the left in order to get a positive difference. For example, consider subtracting 189 from 525 with regrouping.

First, set up the subtraction problem in vertical form:

$$\begin{array}{r} 525 \\ -\ 189 \\ \hline \end{array}$$

Notice that the numbers in the ones and tens columns of 525 are smaller than the numbers in the ones and tens columns of 189. This means you will need to use regrouping to perform subtraction:

$$\begin{array}{rrrr} & 5 & 2 & 5 \\ - & 1 & 8 & 9 \\ \hline \end{array}$$

To subtract 9 from 5 in the ones column you will need to borrow from the 2 in the tens columns:

$$\begin{array}{rrrr} & 5 & 1 & 15 \\ - & 1 & 8 & 9 \\ \hline & & & 6 \end{array}$$

Next, to subtract 8 from 1 in the tens column you will need to borrow from the 5 in the hundreds column:

$$\begin{array}{rrrr} & 4 & 11 & 15 \\ - & 1 & 8 & 9 \\ \hline & & 3 & 6 \end{array}$$

Last, subtract the 1 from the 4 in the hundreds column:

$$\begin{array}{rrrr} & 4 & 11 & 15 \\ - & 1 & 8 & 9 \\ \hline & 3 & 3 & 6 \end{array}$$

Review Video: Subtracting Large Numbers
Visit mometrix.com/academy and enter code: 603350

ORDER OF OPERATIONS

The **order of operations** is a set of rules that dictates the order in which we must perform each operation in an expression so that we will evaluate it accurately. If we have an expression that includes multiple different operations, the order of operations tells us which operations to do first. The most common mnemonic for the order of operations is **PEMDAS**, or "Please Excuse My Dear Aunt Sally." PEMDAS stands for parentheses, exponents, multiplication, division, addition, and subtraction. It is important to understand that multiplication and division have equal precedence, as do addition and subtraction, so those pairs of operations are simply worked from left to right in order.

For example, evaluating the expression $5 + 20 \div 4 \times (2 + 3)^2 - 6$ using the correct order of operations would be done like this:

- **P:** Perform the operations inside the parentheses: $(2 + 3) = 5$
- **E:** Simplify the exponents: $(5)^2 = 5 \times 5 = 25$
  - The expression now looks like this: $5 + 20 \div 4 \times 25 - 6$
- **MD:** Perform multiplication and division from left to right: $20 \div 4 = 5$; then $5 \times 25 = 125$
  - The expression now looks like this: $5 + 125 - 6$
- **AS:** Perform addition and subtraction from left to right: $5 + 125 = 130$; then $130 - 6 = 124$

Review Video: Order of Operations
Visit mometrix.com/academy and enter code: 259675

The properties of exponents are as follows:

Property	Description
$a^1 = a$	Any number to the power of 1 is equal to itself
$1^n = 1$	The number 1 raised to any power is equal to 1
$a^0 = 1$	Any number raised to the power of 0 is equal to 1
$a^n \times a^m = a^{n+m}$	Add exponents to multiply powers of the same base number
$a^n \div a^m = a^{n-m}$	Subtract exponents to divide powers of the same base number
$(a^n)^m = a^{n \times m}$	When a power is raised to a power, the exponents are multiplied
$(a \times b)^n = a^n \times b^n$ $(a \div b)^n = a^n \div b^n$	Multiplication and division operations inside parentheses can be raised to a power. This is the same as each term being raised to that power.
$a^{-n} = \frac{1}{a^n}$	A negative exponent is the same as the reciprocal of a positive exponent

Note that exponents do not have to be integers. Fractional or decimal exponents follow all the rules above as well. Example: $5^{\frac{1}{4}} \times 5^{\frac{3}{4}} = 5^{\frac{1}{4}+\frac{3}{4}} = 5^1 = 5$.

Review Video: Properties of Exponents
Visit mometrix.com/academy and enter code: 532558

Factors and Greatest Common Factor

Factors are numbers that are multiplied together to obtain a **product**. For example, in the equation $2 \times 3 = 6$, the numbers 2 and 3 are factors. A **prime number** has only two factors (1 and itself), but other numbers can have many factors.

A **common factor** is a number that divides exactly into two or more other numbers. For example, the factors of 12 are 1, 2, 3, 4, 6, and 12, while the factors of 15 are 1, 3, 5, and 15. The common factors of 12 and 15 are 1 and 3.

A **prime factor** is also a prime number. Therefore, the prime factors of 12 are 2 and 3. For 15, the prime factors are 3 and 5.

The **greatest common factor** (**GCF**) is the largest number that is a factor of two or more numbers. For example, the factors of 15 are 1, 3, 5, and 15; the factors of 35 are 1, 5, 7, and 35. Therefore, the greatest common factor of 15 and 35 is 5.

Review Video: Factors
Visit mometrix.com/academy and enter code: 920086

Review Video: Prime Numbers and Factorization
Visit mometrix.com/academy and enter code: 760669

Review Video: Greatest Common Factor and Least Common Multiple
Visit mometrix.com/academy and enter code: 838699

Multiples and Least Common Multiple

Often listed out in multiplication tables, **multiples** are integer increments of a given factor. In other words, dividing a multiple by the factor will result in an integer. For example, the multiples of 7 include: $1 \times 7 = 7, 2 \times 7 = 14, 3 \times 7 = 21, 4 \times 7 = 28, 5 \times 7 = 35$. Dividing 7, 14, 21, 28, or 35 by 7 will result in the integers 1, 2, 3, 4, and 5, respectively.

The least common multiple (**LCM**) is the smallest number that is a multiple of two or more numbers. For example, the multiples of 3 include 3, 6, 9, 12, 15, etc.; the multiples of 5 include 5, 10, 15, 20, etc. Therefore, the least common multiple of 3 and 5 is 15.

Review Video: Multiples
Visit mometrix.com/academy and enter code: 626738

Fractions

A **fraction** is a number that is expressed as one integer written above another integer, with a dividing line between them $\left(\frac{x}{y}\right)$. It represents the **quotient** of the two numbers "x divided by y." It can also be thought of as x out of y equal parts.

The top number of a fraction is called the **numerator**, and it represents the number of parts under consideration. The 1 in $\frac{1}{4}$ means that 1 part out of the whole is being considered in the calculation. The bottom number of a fraction is called the **denominator**, and it represents the total number of equal parts. The 4 in $\frac{1}{4}$ means that the whole consists of 4 equal parts. A fraction cannot have a denominator of zero; this is referred to as "*undefined*."

Fractions can be manipulated, without changing the value of the fraction, by multiplying or dividing (but not adding or subtracting) both the numerator and denominator by the same number. If you divide both numbers by a common factor, you are **reducing** or simplifying the fraction. Two fractions that have the same value but are expressed differently are known as **equivalent fractions**. For example, $\frac{2}{10}, \frac{3}{15}, \frac{4}{20}$, and $\frac{5}{25}$ are all equivalent fractions. They can also all be reduced or simplified to $\frac{1}{5}$.

When two fractions are manipulated so that they have the same denominator, this is known as finding a **common denominator**. The number chosen to be that common denominator should be the least common multiple of the two original denominators. Example: $\frac{3}{4}$ and $\frac{5}{6}$; the least common multiple of 4 and 6 is 12. Manipulating to achieve the common denominator: $\frac{3}{4} = \frac{9}{12}; \frac{5}{6} = \frac{10}{12}$.

Review Video: Overview of Fractions
Visit mometrix.com/academy and enter code: 262335

Proper Fractions and Mixed Numbers

A fraction whose denominator is greater than its numerator is known as a **proper fraction**, while a fraction whose numerator is greater than its denominator is known as an **improper fraction**. Proper fractions have values *less than one* and improper fractions have values *greater than one*.

A **mixed number** is a number that contains both an integer and a fraction. Any improper fraction can be rewritten as a mixed number. Example: $\frac{8}{3} = \frac{6}{3} + \frac{2}{3} = 2 + \frac{2}{3} = 2\frac{2}{3}$. Similarly, any mixed number can be rewritten as an improper fraction. Example: $1\frac{3}{5} = 1 + \frac{3}{5} = \frac{5}{5} + \frac{3}{5} = \frac{8}{5}$.

Review Video: Improper Fractions and Mixed Numbers
Visit mometrix.com/academy and enter code: 211077

Adding and Subtracting Fractions

If two fractions have a common denominator, they can be added or subtracted simply by adding or subtracting the two numerators and retaining the same denominator. If the two fractions do not already have the same denominator, one or both of them must be manipulated to achieve a common denominator before they can be added or subtracted. Example: $\frac{1}{2} + \frac{1}{4} = \frac{2}{4} + \frac{1}{4} = \frac{3}{4}$.

Review Video: Adding and Subtracting Fractions
Visit mometrix.com/academy and enter code: 378080

MULTIPLYING FRACTIONS

Two fractions can be multiplied by multiplying the two numerators to find the new numerator and the two denominators to find the new denominator. Example: $\frac{1}{3} \times \frac{2}{3} = \frac{1\times 2}{3\times 3} = \frac{2}{9}$.

DIVIDING FRACTIONS

Two fractions can be divided by flipping the numerator and denominator of the second fraction and then proceeding as though it were a multiplication problem. Example: $\frac{2}{3} \div \frac{3}{4} = \frac{2}{3} \times \frac{4}{3} = \frac{8}{9}$.

Review Video: Multiplying and Dividing Fractions
Visit mometrix.com/academy and enter code: 473632

MULTIPLYING A MIXED NUMBER BY A WHOLE NUMBER OR A DECIMAL

When multiplying a mixed number by something, it is usually best to convert it to an improper fraction first. Additionally, if the multiplicand is a decimal, it is most often simplest to convert it to a fraction. For instance, to multiply $4\frac{3}{8}$ by 3.5, begin by rewriting each quantity as a whole number plus a proper fraction. Remember, a mixed number is a fraction added to a whole number and a decimal is a representation of the sum of fractions, specifically tenths, hundredths, thousandths, and so on:

$$4\frac{3}{8} \times 3.5 = \left(4 + \frac{3}{8}\right) \times \left(3 + \frac{1}{2}\right)$$

Next, the quantities being added need to be expressed with the same denominator. This is achieved by multiplying and dividing the whole number by the denominator of the fraction. Recall that a whole number is equivalent to that number divided by 1:

$$= \left(\frac{4}{1} \times \frac{8}{8} + \frac{3}{8}\right) \times \left(\frac{3}{1} \times \frac{2}{2} + \frac{1}{2}\right)$$

When multiplying fractions, remember to multiply the numerators and denominators separately:

$$= \left(\frac{4 \times 8}{1 \times 8} + \frac{3}{8}\right) \times \left(\frac{3 \times 2}{1 \times 2} + \frac{1}{2}\right)$$
$$= \left(\frac{32}{8} + \frac{3}{8}\right) \times \left(\frac{6}{2} + \frac{1}{2}\right)$$

Now that the fractions have the same denominators, they can be added:

$$= \frac{35}{8} \times \frac{7}{2}$$

Finally, perform the last multiplication and then simplify:

$$= \frac{35 \times 7}{8 \times 2} = \frac{245}{16} = \frac{240}{16} + \frac{5}{16} = 15\frac{5}{16}$$

DECIMALS

Decimals are one way to represent parts of a whole. Using the place value system, each digit to the right of a decimal point denotes the number of units of a corresponding *negative* power of ten. For example, consider the decimal 0.24. We can use a model to represent the decimal. Since a dime is worth one-tenth of a dollar and a penny is worth one-hundredth of a dollar, one possible model to represent this fraction is to have 2 dimes representing the 2 in the tenths place and 4 pennies representing the 4 in the hundredths place:

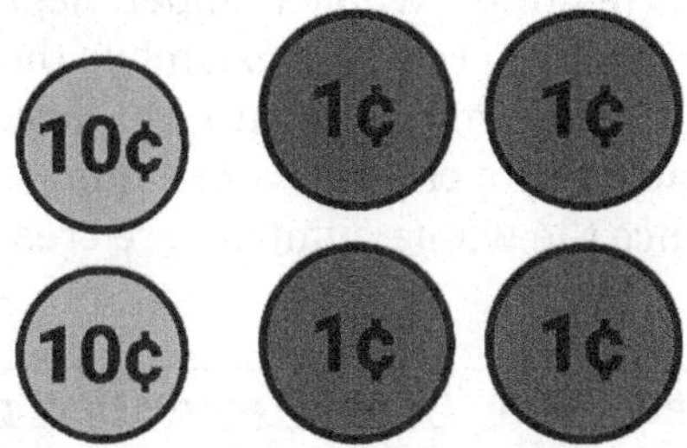

To write the decimal as a fraction, put the decimal in the numerator with 1 in the denominator. Multiply the numerator and denominator by tens until there are no more decimal places. Then simplify the fraction to lowest terms. For example, converting 0.24 to a fraction:

$$0.24 = \frac{0.24}{1} = \frac{0.24 \times 100}{1 \times 100} = \frac{24}{100} = \frac{6}{25}$$

Review Video: Decimals
Visit mometrix.com/academy and enter code: 837268

Operations with Decimals

Adding and Subtracting Decimals

When adding and subtracting decimals, the decimal points must always be aligned. Adding decimals is just like adding regular whole numbers. Example: $4.5 + 2.0 = 6.5$.

If the problem-solver does not properly align the decimal points, an incorrect answer of 4.7 may result. An easy way to add decimals is to align all of the decimal points in a vertical column visually. This will allow you to see exactly where the decimal should be placed in the final answer. Begin adding from right to left. Add each column in turn, making sure to carry the number to the left if a column adds up to more than 9. The same rules apply to the subtraction of decimals.

Review Video: Adding and Subtracting Decimals
Visit mometrix.com/academy and enter code: 381101

Multiplying Decimals

A simple multiplication problem has two components: a **multiplicand** and a **multiplier**. When multiplying decimals, work as though the numbers were whole rather than decimals. Once the final product is calculated, count the number of places to the right of the decimal in both the multiplicand and the multiplier. Then, count that number of places from the right of the product and place the decimal in that position.

For example, 12.3×2.56 has a total of three places to the right of the respective decimals. Multiply 123×256 to get 31,488. Now, beginning on the right, count three places to the left and insert the decimal. The final product will be 31.488.

Review Video: How to Multiply Decimals
Visit mometrix.com/academy and enter code: 731574

Dividing Decimals

Every division problem has a **divisor** and a **dividend**. The dividend is the number that is being divided. In the problem $14 \div 7$, 14 is the dividend and 7 is the divisor. In a division problem with decimals, the divisor must be converted into a whole number. Begin by moving the decimal in the divisor to the right until a whole number is created. Next, move the decimal in the dividend the same number of spaces to the right. For example, 4.9 into 24.5 would become 49 into 245. The decimal was moved one space to the right to create a whole number in the divisor, and then the same was done for the dividend. Once the whole numbers are created, the problem is carried out normally: $245 \div 49 = 5$.

Review Video: How to Divide Decimals
Visit mometrix.com/academy and enter code: 560690

Review Video: Dividing Decimals by Whole Numbers
Visit mometrix.com/academy and enter code: 535669

Percentages

Percentages can be thought of as fractions that are based on a whole of 100; that is, one whole is equal to 100%. The word **percent** means "per hundred." Percentage problems are often presented in three main ways:

- Find what percentage of some number another number is.
  - Example: What percentage of 40 is 8?
- Find what number is some percentage of a given number.
  - Example: What number is 20% of 40?
- Find what number another number is a given percentage of.
  - Example: What number is 8 20% of?

There are three components in each of these cases: a **whole** (W), a **part** (P), and a **percentage** (%). These are related by the equation: $P = W \times \%$. This can easily be rearranged into other forms that may suit different questions better: $\% = \frac{P}{W}$ and $W = \frac{P}{\%}$. Percentage problems are often also word problems. As such, a large part of solving them is figuring out which quantities are what. For example, consider the following word problem:

In a school cafeteria, 7 students choose pizza, 9 choose hamburgers, and 4 choose tacos. What percentage of student choose tacos?

To find the whole, you must first add all of the parts: $7 + 9 + 4 = 20$. The percentage can then be found by dividing the part by the whole $\left(\% = \frac{P}{W}\right)$: $\frac{4}{20} = \frac{20}{100} = 20\%$.

Review Video: Computation with Percentages
Visit mometrix.com/academy and enter code: 693099

Converting Between Percentages, Fractions, and Decimals

Converting decimals to percentages and percentages to decimals is as simple as moving the decimal point. To *convert from a decimal to a percentage*, move the decimal point **two places to the right**. To *convert from a percentage to a decimal*, move it **two places to the left**. It may be helpful to remember that the percentage number will always be larger than the equivalent decimal number. Example:

$$0.23 = 23\% \quad 5.34 = 534\% \quad 0.007 = 0.7\%$$
$$700\% = 7.00 \quad 86\% = 0.86 \quad 0.15\% = 0.0015$$

To convert a fraction to a decimal, simply divide the numerator by the denominator in the fraction. To convert a decimal to a fraction, put the decimal in the numerator with 1 in the denominator. Multiply the numerator and denominator by tens until there are no more decimal places. Then simplify the fraction to lowest terms. For example, converting 0.24 to a fraction:

$$0.24 = \frac{0.24}{1} = \frac{0.24 \times 100}{1 \times 100} = \frac{24}{100} = \frac{6}{25}$$

Fractions can be converted to a percentage by finding equivalent fractions with a denominator of 100. Example:

$$\frac{7}{10} = \frac{70}{100} = 70\% \quad \frac{1}{4} = \frac{25}{100} = 25\%$$

To convert a percentage to a fraction, divide the percentage number by 100 and reduce the fraction to its simplest possible terms. Example:

$$60\% = \frac{60}{100} = \frac{3}{5} \quad 96\% = \frac{96}{100} = \frac{24}{25}$$

Review Video: Converting Fractions to Percentages and Decimals
Visit mometrix.com/academy and enter code: 306233

Review Video: Converting Percentages to Decimals and Fractions
Visit mometrix.com/academy and enter code: 287297

Review Video: Converting Decimals to Fractions and Percentages
Visit mometrix.com/academy and enter code: 986765

Review Video: Converting Decimals, Improper Fractions, and Mixed Numbers
Visit mometrix.com/academy and enter code: 696924

Heart of Algebra

Heart of Algebra Overview

The questions in this section will cover a range of topics in algebra. Students will be tested on their ability to analyze and solve linear equations and systems of equations. They will also need to be able to create these equations to represent a relationship between two or more quantities and solve problems. Along with linear equations, students will need to be able to create and solve linear inequalities. Some questions will also require the student to interpret formulas and rearrange them to solve the problem.

Question Types in Heart of Algebra

The **heart of algebra** section will test your knowledge of the following:

- Create, solve, or interpret a **linear expression or equation in one variable** that represents a context.
  - The expression or equation will have rational coefficients, and multiple steps may be required to simplify the expression, simplify the equation, or solve for the variable in the equation.
- Create, solve, or interpret **linear inequalities in one variable** that represent a context.
  - The inequality will have rational coefficients, and multiple steps may be required to simplify or solve for the variable.
- Build a linear function that models a linear relationship between two quantities.
  - The student will describe a linear relationship that models a context using either an equation in two variables or function notation.
  - The equation or function will have rational coefficients, and multiple steps may be required to build and simplify the equation or function.
- Create, solve, and interpret **systems of linear inequalities** in two variables.
  - The student will analyze one or more constraints that exist between two variables by creating, solving, or interpreting an inequality in two variables or a system of inequalities in two variables to represent a context.
  - Multiple steps may be required to create the inequality or system of inequalities or to determine whether a given point is in the solution set.
- Create, solve, and interpret **systems of two linear equations** in two variables.
  - The student will analyze one or more constraints that exist between two variables by creating, solving, or analyzing a system of linear equations to represent a context.
  - The equations will have rational coefficients, and multiple steps may be required to simplify or solve the system.
- Algebraically solve linear equations (or inequalities) in one variable.
  - The equation (or inequality) will have rational coefficients and may require multiple steps to solve for the variable; the equation may yield no solution, one solution, or infinitely many solutions.
  - The student may also be asked to determine the value of a constant or coefficient for an equation with no solution or infinitely many solutions.
- Algebraically solve systems of two linear equations in two variables.
  - The equations will have rational coefficients, and the system may yield no solution, one solution, or infinitely many solutions.
  - The student may also be asked to determine the value of a constant or coefficient of an equation in which the system has no solution, one solution, or infinitely many solutions.
- Interpret the variables and constants in expressions for linear functions within the context presented.
  - The student will make connections between a context and the linear equation that models the context and will identify or describe the real-life meaning of a constant term, a variable, or a feature of the given equation.

- Understand connections between algebraic and graphical representations.
  - The student will select a graph described by a given linear equation, select a linear equation that describes a given graph, determine the equation of a line given a verbal description of its graph, determine key features of the graph of a linear function from its equation, or determine how a graph may be affected by a change in its equation.

Other Necessary Skills

Translating Verbal Expressions into Mathematical Language

You must be able to translate **verbal expressions** into mathematical language. These may be simple or complex algebraic expressions (linear, quadratic, or exponential); you must be able to simplify these expressions using order of operations. You may be asked to determine an algebraic model involving costs or interest and then use that model to perform a calculation. You may be given a geometric situation involving area or perimeter, in which you have to write and simplify an expression. These problems may be complex and require sketches in order to choose or produce a correct answer.

Modeling Scenarios with Linear Equations

You should expect to be given a real-world scenario and the linear function associated with that scenario. You may be asked to identify variable terms or constant terms from the given function as well as interpret their meanings in the given real-world situation. You may see a test question like "The school van begins a field trip with 14 gallons of gasoline. After traveling 120 miles, the van has 8 gallons of gasoline. If this relationship is modeled by the linear function $f(x) = -20x + 280$, what does the x represent?" Or you might be asked what -20 and 280 represent in the given function.

Systems of Three Equations

This test typically has one problem with a system of three equations. Usually, the graphs as well as the equations are given. The key point is that the only solutions to this graph are the points at which all three graphs coincide or intersect. For example, the graph might include a circle, a parabola, and a line. There are no solutions to the given system if all three graphs do not intersect at one or more points. If the three graphs intersect at one point, then there is one solution to the given system, and that solution is the point of intersection. If the line intersects the circle at two points, and the line also intersects the parabola at the same exact two points, there are two solutions to the given system, and those solutions are the points of intersection. This system has at most two solutions.

Terms and Coefficients

Mathematical expressions consist of a combination of one or more values arranged in terms that are added together. As such, an expression could be just a single number, including zero. A **variable term** is the product of a real number, also called a **coefficient**, and one or more variables, each of which may be raised to an exponent. Expressions may also include numbers without a variable, called **constants** or **constant terms**. The expression $6s^2$, for example, is a single term where the coefficient is the real number 6 and the variable term is s^2. Note that if a term is written as simply a variable to some exponent, like t^2, then the coefficient is 1, because $t^2 = 1t^2$.

Linear Expressions

A **single variable linear expression** is the sum of a single variable term, where the variable has no exponent, and a constant, which may be zero. For instance, the expression $2w + 7$ has $2w$ as the variable term and 7 as the constant term. It is important to realize that terms are separated by addition or subtraction. Since an expression is a sum of terms, expressions such as $5x - 3$ can be written as $5x + (-3)$ to emphasize that the constant term is negative. A real-world example of a single variable linear expression is the perimeter of a square, four times the side length, often expressed: $4s$.

In general, a **linear expression** is the sum of any number of variable terms so long as none of the variables have an exponent. For example, $3m + 8n - \frac{1}{4}p + 5.5q - 1$ is a linear expression, but $3y^3$ is not. In the same way, the expression for the perimeter of a general triangle, the sum of the side lengths $(a + b + c)$ is considered to be linear, but the expression for the area of a square, the side length squared $(s^2)$is not.

LINEAR EQUATIONS

Equations that can be written as $ax + b = 0$, where $a \neq 0$, are referred to as **one variable linear equations**. A solution to such an equation is called a **root**. In the case where we have the equation $5x + 10 = 0$, if we solve for x we get a solution of $x = -2$. In other words, the root of the equation is -2. This is found by first subtracting 10 from both sides, which gives $5x = -10$. Next, simply divide both sides by the coefficient of the variable, in this case 5, to get $x = -2$. This can be checked by plugging -2 back into the original equation $(5)(-2) + 10 = -10 + 10 = 0$.

The **solution set** is the set of all solutions of an equation. In our example, the solution set would simply be -2. If there were more solutions (there usually are in multivariable equations) then they would also be included in the solution set. When an equation has no true solutions, it is referred to as an **empty set**. Equations with identical solution sets are **equivalent equations**. An **identity** is a term whose value or determinant is equal to 1.

Linear equations can be written many ways. Below is a list of some forms linear equations can take:

- **Standard Form**: $Ax + By = C$; the slope is $\frac{-A}{B}$ and the y-intercept is $\frac{C}{B}$
- **Slope Intercept Form**: $y = mx + b$, where m is the slope and b is the y-intercept
- **Point-Slope Form**: $y - y_1 = m(x - x_1)$, where m is the slope and (x_1, y_1) is a point on the line
- **Two-Point Form**: $\frac{y-y_1}{x-x_1} = \frac{y_2-y_1}{x_2-x_1}$, where (x_1, y_1) and (x_2, y_2) are two points on the given line
- **Intercept Form**: $\frac{x}{x_1} + \frac{y}{y_1} = 1$, where $(x_1, 0)$ is the point at which a line intersects the x-axis, and $(0, y_1)$ is the point at which the same line intersects the y-axis

Review Video: Slope-Intercept and Point-Slope Forms
Visit mometrix.com/academy and enter code: 113216

Review Video: Linear Equations Basics
Visit mometrix.com/academy and enter code: 793005

SOLVING ONE-VARIABLE LINEAR EQUATIONS

Multiply all terms by the lowest common denominator to eliminate any fractions. Look for addition or subtraction to undo so you can isolate the variable on one side of the equal sign. Divide both sides by the coefficient of the variable. When you have a value for the variable, substitute this value into the original equation to make sure you have a true equation. Consider the following example:

Kim's savings are represented by the table below. Represent her savings, using an equation.

X (Months)	Y (Total Savings)
2	$1,300
5	$2,050
9	$3,050
11	$3,550
16	$4,800

The table shows a function with a constant rate of change, or slope, of 250. Given the points on the table, the slopes can be calculated as $\frac{(2{,}050-1300)}{(5-2)}$, $\frac{(3{,}050-2{,}050)}{(9-5)}$, $\frac{(3{,}550-3{,}050)}{(11-9)}$, and $\frac{(4{,}800-3{,}550)}{(16-11)}$, each of which equals 250. Thus, the table shows a constant rate of change, indicating a linear function. The slope-intercept form of a linear equation is written as $y = mx + b$, where m represents the slope and b represents the y-intercept. Substituting the slope into this form gives $y = 250x + b$. Substituting corresponding x- and y-values from any point into this equation will give the y-intercept, or b. Using the point, $(2, 1{,}300)$, gives $1{,}300 = 250(2) + b$, which simplifies as $b = 800$. Thus, her savings may be represented by the equation, $y = 250x + 800$.

Rules for Manipulating Equations

Like Terms

Like terms are terms in an equation that have the same variable, regardless of whether or not they also have the same coefficient. This includes terms that *lack* a variable; all constants (i.e., numbers without variables) are considered like terms. If the equation involves terms with a variable raised to different powers, the like terms are those that have the variable raised to the same power.

For example, consider the equation $x^2 + 3x + 2 = 2x^2 + x - 7 + 2x$. In this equation, 2 and -7 are like terms; they are both constants. $3x$, x, and $2x$ are like terms, they all include the variable x raised to the first power. x^2 and $2x^2$ are like terms, they both include the variable x, raised to the second power. $2x$ and $2x^2$ are not like terms; although they both involve the variable x, the variable is not raised to the same power in both terms. The fact that they have the same coefficient, 2, is not relevant.

Review Video: Rules for Manipulating Equations
Visit mometrix.com/academy and enter code: 838871

Carrying Out the Same Operation on Both Sides of an Equation

When solving an equation, the general procedure is to carry out a series of operations on both sides of an equation, choosing operations that will tend to simplify the equation when doing so. The reason why the same operation must be carried out on both sides of the equation is because that leaves the meaning of the equation unchanged, and yields a result that is equivalent to the original equation. This would not be the case if we carried out an operation on one side of an equation and not the other. Consider what an equation means: it is a statement that two values or expressions are equal. If we carry out the same operation on both sides of the equation—add 3 to both sides, for example—then the two sides of the equation are changed in the same way, and so remain equal. If we do that to only one side of the equation—add 3 to one side but not the other—then that wouldn't be true; if we change one side of the equation but not the other then the two sides are no longer equal.

Advantage of Combining Like Terms

Combining like terms refers to adding or subtracting like terms—terms with the same variable—and therefore reducing sets of like terms to a single term. The main advantage of doing this is that it simplifies the equation. Often, combining like terms can be done as the first step in solving an equation, though it can also be done later, such as after distributing terms in a product.

For example, consider the equation $2(x + 3) + 3(2 + x + 3) = -4$. The 2 and the 3 in the second set of parentheses are like terms, and we can combine them, yielding $2(x + 3) + 3(x + 5) = -4$. Now we can carry out the multiplications implied by the parentheses, distributing the outer 2 and 3 accordingly: $2x + 6 + 3x + 15 = -4$. The $2x$ and the $3x$ are like terms, and we can add them together: $5x + 6 + 15 = -4$. Now, the constants 6, 15, and -4 are also like terms, and we can combine them as well: subtracting 6 and 15 from both sides of the equation, we get $5x = -4 - 6 - 15$, or $5x = -25$, which simplifies further to $x = -5$.

Review Video: Solving Equations by Combining Like Terms
Visit mometrix.com/academy and enter code: 668506

Canceling Terms on Opposite Sides of an Equation

Two terms on opposite sides of an equation can be canceled if and only if they *exactly* match each other. They must have the same variable raised to the same power and the same coefficient. For example, in the equation $3x + 2x^2 + 6 = 2x^2 - 6$, $2x^2$ appears on both sides of the equation and can be canceled, leaving $3x + 6 = -6$. The 6 on each side of the equation *cannot* be canceled, because it is added on one side of the equation and subtracted on the other. While they cannot be canceled, however, the 6 and -6 are like terms and can be combined, yielding $3x = -12$, which simplifies further to $x = -4$.

It's also important to note that the terms to be canceled must be independent terms and cannot be part of a larger term. For example, consider the equation $2(x + 6) = 3(x + 4) + 1$. We cannot cancel the x's, because even though they match each other they are part of the larger terms $2(x + 6)$ and $3(x + 4)$. We must first distribute the 2 and 3, yielding $2x + 12 = 3x + 12 + 1$. Now we see that the terms with the x's do not match, but the 12s do, and can be canceled, leaving $2x = 3x + 1$, which simplifies to $x = -1$.

Process for Manipulating Equations

Isolating Variables

To **isolate a variable** means to manipulate the equation so that the variable appears by itself on one side of the equation, and does not appear at all on the other side. Generally, an equation or inequality is considered to be solved once the variable is isolated and the other side of the equation or inequality is simplified as much as possible. In the case of a two-variable equation or inequality, only one variable needs to be isolated; it will not usually be possible to simultaneously isolate both variables.

For a linear equation—an equation in which the variable only appears raised to the first power—isolating a variable can be done by first moving all the terms with the variable to one side of the equation and all other terms to the other side. (*Moving* a term really means adding the inverse of the term to both sides; when a term is *moved* to the other side of the equation its sign is flipped.)

Then combine like terms on each side. Finally, divide both sides by the coefficient of the variable, if applicable. The steps need not necessarily be done in this order, but this order will always work.

Review Video: Solving One-Step Equations
Visit mometrix.com/academy and enter code: 777004

Equations with More Than One Solution

Some types of non-linear equations, such as equations involving squares of variables, may have more than one solution. For example, the equation $x^2 = 4$ has two solutions: 2 and –2. Equations with absolute values can also have multiple solutions: $|x| = 1$ has the solutions $x = 1$ and $x = -1$.

It is also possible for a linear equation to have more than one solution, but only if the equation is true regardless of the value of the variable. In this case, the equation is considered to have infinitely many solutions, because any possible value of the variable is a solution. We know a linear equation has infinitely many solutions if when we combine like terms the variables cancel, leaving a true statement. For example, consider the equation $2(3x + 5) = x + 5(x + 2)$. Distributing, we get $6x + 10 = x + 5x + 10$; combining like terms gives $6x + 10 = 6x + 10$, and the $6x$-terms cancel to leave $10 = 10$. This is clearly true, so the original equation is true for any value of x. We could also have canceled the 10s leaving $0 = 0$, but again this is clearly true—in general if both sides of the equation match exactly, it has infinitely many solutions.

Equations with No Solution

Some types of non-linear equations, such as equations involving squares of variables, may have no solution. For example, the equation $x^2 = -2$ has no solutions in the real numbers, because the square of any real number must be positive. Similarly, $|x| = -1$ has no solution, because the absolute value of a number is always positive.

It is also possible for an equation to have no solution even if does not involve any powers greater than one, absolute values, or other special functions. For example, the equation $2(x + 3) + x = 3x$ has no solution. We can see that if we try to solve it: first we distribute, leaving $2x + 6 + x = 3x$. But now if we try to combine all the terms with the variable, we find that they cancel: we have $3x$ on the left and $3x$ on the right, canceling to leave us with $6 = 0$. This is clearly false. In general, whenever the variable terms in an equation cancel leaving different constants on both sides, it means that the equation has no solution. (If we are left with the *same* constant on both sides, the equation has infinitely many solutions instead.)

Features of Equations That Require Special Treatment

Linear Equations

A linear equation is an equation in which variables only appear by themselves: not multiplied together, not with exponents other than one, and not inside absolute value signs or any other functions. For example, the equation $x + 1 - 3x = 5 - x$ is a linear equation; while x appears multiple times, it never appears with an exponent other than one, or inside any function. The two-variable equation $2x - 3y = 5 + 2x$ is also a linear equation. In contrast, the equation $x^2 - 5 = 3x$ is *not* a linear equation, because it involves the term x^2. $\sqrt{x} = 5$ is not a linear equation, because it involves a square root. $(x - 1)^2 = 4$ is not a linear equation because even though there's no exponent on the x directly, it appears as part of an expression that is squared. The two-variable equation $x + xy - y = 5$ is not a linear equation because it includes the term xy, where two variables are multiplied together.

Linear equations can always be solved (or shown to have no solution) by combining like terms and performing simple operations on both sides of the equation. Some non-linear equations can be solved by similar methods, but others may require more advanced methods of solution, if they can be solved analytically at all.

Solving Equations Involving Roots

In an equation involving roots, the first step is to isolate the term with the root, if possible, and then raise both sides of the equation to the appropriate power to eliminate it. Consider an example equation, $2\sqrt{x+1}-1=3$. In this case, begin by adding 1 to both sides, yielding $2\sqrt{x+1}=4$, and then dividing both sides by 2, yielding $\sqrt{x+1}=2$. Now square both sides, yielding $x+1=4$. Finally, subtracting 1 from both sides yields $x=3$.

Squaring both sides of an equation may, however, yield a spurious solution—a solution to the squared equation that is *not* a solution of the original equation. It's therefore necessary to plug the solution back into the original equation to make sure it works. In this case, it does: $2\sqrt{3+1}-1=2\sqrt{4}-1=2(2)-1=4-1=3$.

The same procedure applies for other roots as well. For example, given the equation $3+\sqrt[3]{2x}=5$, we can first subtract 3 from both sides, yielding $\sqrt[3]{2x}=2$ and isolating the root. Raising both sides to the third power yields $2x=2^3$; i.e., $2x=8$. We can now divide both sides by 2 to get $x=4$.

Review Video: Solving Equations Involving Roots
Visit mometrix.com/academy and enter code: 297670

Solving Equations with Exponents

To solve an equation involving an exponent, the first step is to isolate the variable with the exponent. We can then take the appropriate root of both sides to eliminate the exponent. For instance, for the equation $2x^3+17=5x^3-7$, we can subtract $5x^3$ from both sides to get $-3x^3+17=-7$, and then subtract 17 from both sides to get $-3x^3=-24$. Finally, we can divide both sides by –3 to get $x^3=8$. Finally, we can take the cube root of both sides to get $x=\sqrt[3]{8}=2$.

One important but often overlooked point is that equations with an exponent greater than 1 may have more than one answer. The solution to $x^2=9$ isn't simply $x=3$; it's $x=\pm 3$ (that is, $x=3$ or $x=-3$). For a slightly more complicated example, consider the equation $(x-1)^2-1=3$. Adding 1 to both sides yields $(x-1)^2=4$; taking the square root of both sides yields $x-1=2$. We can then add 1 to both sides to get $x=3$. However, there's a second solution. We also have the possibility that $x-1=-2$, in which case $x=-1$. Both $x=3$ and $x=-1$ are valid solutions, as can be verified by substituting them both into the original equation.

Review Video: Solving Equations with Exponents
Visit mometrix.com/academy and enter code: 514557

Solving Equations with Absolute Values

When solving an equation with an absolute value, the first step is to isolate the absolute value term. We then consider two possibilities: when the expression inside the absolute value is positive or when it is negative. In the former case, the expression in the absolute value equals the expression on the other side of the equation; in the latter, it equals the additive inverse of that expression—the expression times negative one. We consider each case separately and finally check for spurious solutions.

For instance, consider solving $|2x - 1| + x = 5$ for x. We can first isolate the absolute value by moving the x to the other side: $|2x - 1| = -x + 5$. Now, we have two possibilities. First, that $2x - 1$ is positive, and hence $2x - 1 = -x + 5$. Rearranging and combining like terms yields $3x = 6$, and hence $x = 2$. The other possibility is that $2x - 1$ is negative, and hence $2x - 1 = -(-x + 5) = x - 5$. In this case, rearranging and combining like terms yields $x = -4$. Substituting $x = 2$ and $x = -4$ back into the original equation, we see that they are both valid solutions.

Note that the absolute value of a sum or difference applies to the sum or difference as a whole, not to the individual terms; in general, $|2x - 1|$ is not equal to $|2x + 1|$ or to $|2x| - 1$.

Spurious Solutions

A **spurious solution** may arise when we square both sides of an equation as a step in solving it or under certain other operations on the equation. It is a solution to the squared or otherwise modified equation that is *not* a solution of the original equation. To identify a spurious solution, it's useful when you solve an equation involving roots or absolute values to plug the solution back into the original equation to make sure it's valid.

Choosing Which Variable to Isolate in Two-Variable Equations

Similar to methods for a one-variable equation, solving a two-variable equation involves isolating a variable: manipulating the equation so that a variable appears by itself on one side of the equation, and not at all on the other side. However, in a two-variable equation, you will usually only be able to isolate one of the variables; the other variable may appear on the other side along with constant terms, or with exponents or other functions.

Often one variable will be much more easily isolated than the other, and therefore that's the variable you should choose. If one variable appears with various exponents, and the other is only raised to the first power, the latter variable is the one to isolate: given the equation $a^2 + 2b = a^3 + b + 3$, the b only appears to the first power, whereas a appears squared and cubed, so b is the variable that can be solved for: combining like terms and isolating the b on the left side of the equation, we get $b = a^3 - a^2 + 3$. If both variables are equally easy to isolate, then it's best to isolate the independent variable, if one is defined; if the two variables are x and y, the convention is that y is the independent variable.

Graphical Solutions to Equations and Inequalities

When equations are shown graphically, they are usually shown on a **Cartesian coordinate plane**. The Cartesian coordinate plane consists of two number lines placed perpendicular to each other and intersecting at the zero point, also known as the origin. The horizontal number line is known as the x-axis, with positive values to the right of the origin, and negative values to the left of the origin. The vertical number line is known as the y-axis, with positive values above the origin, and negative values below the origin. Any point on the plane can be identified by an ordered pair in the form (x, y), called coordinates. The x-value of the coordinate is called the abscissa, and the y-value of the coordinate is called the ordinate. The two number lines divide the plane into **four quadrants**: I, II, III, and IV.

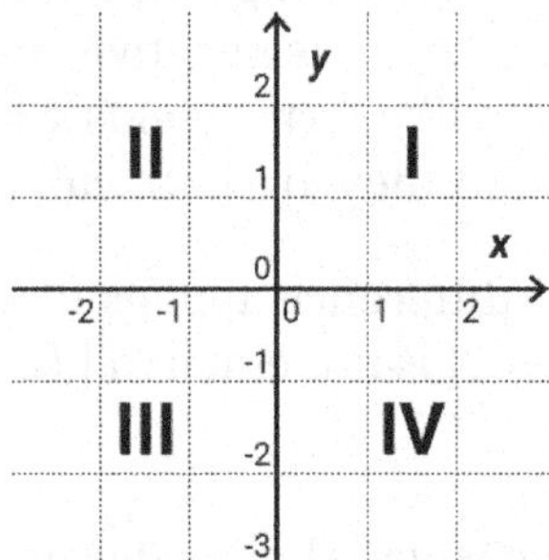

Note that in quadrant I $x > 0$ and $y > 0$, in quadrant II $x < 0$ and $y > 0$, in quadrant III $x < 0$ and $y < 0$, and in quadrant IV $x > 0$ and $y < 0$.

Recall that if the value of the slope of a line is positive, the line slopes upward from left to right. If the value of the slope is negative, the line slopes downward from left to right. If the y-coordinates are the same for two points on a line, the slope is 0 and the line is a **horizontal line**. If the x-coordinates are the same for two points on a line, there is no slope and the line is a **vertical line**. Two or more lines that have equivalent slopes are **parallel lines**. **Perpendicular lines** have slopes that are negative reciprocals of each other, such as $\frac{a}{b}$ and $\frac{-b}{a}$.

Review Video: Cartesian Coordinate Plane and Graphing
Visit mometrix.com/academy and enter code: 115173

Graphing Equations in Two Variables

One way of graphing an equation in two variables is to plot enough points to get an idea for its shape and then draw the appropriate curve through those points. A point can be plotted by substituting in a value for one variable and solving for the other. If the equation is linear, we only need two points and can then draw a straight line between them.

For example, consider the equation $y = 2x - 1$. This is a linear equation—both variables only appear raised to the first power—so we only need two points. When $x = 0$, $y = 2(0) - 1 = -1$. When $x = 2$, $y = 2(2) - 1 = 3$. We can therefore choose the points $(0, -1)$ and $(2, 3)$, and draw a line between them:

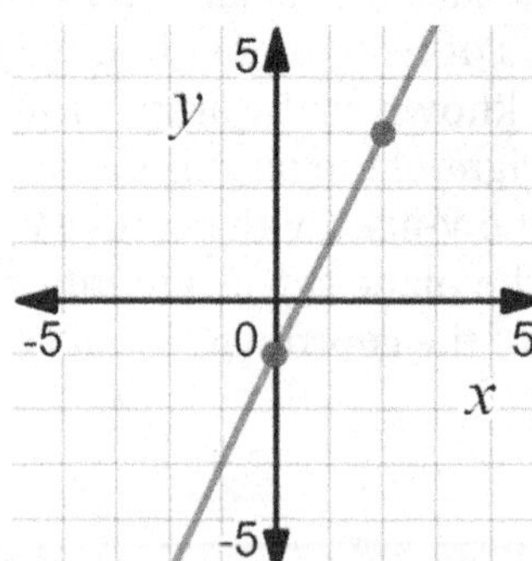

Working with Inequalities

Commonly in algebra and other upper-level fields of math you find yourself working with mathematical expressions that do not equal each other. The statement comparing such expressions with symbols such as $<$ (less than) or $>$ (greater than) is called an *inequality*. An example of an inequality is $7x > 5$. To solve for x, simply divide both sides by 7 and the solution is shown to be $x > \frac{5}{7}$. Graphs of the solution set of inequalities are represented on a number line. Open circles are used to show that an expression approaches a number but is never quite equal to that number.

> **Review Video: Solving Multi-Step Inequalities**
> Visit mometrix.com/academy and enter code: 347842
>
> **Review Video: Solving Inequalities Using All 4 Basic Operations**
> Visit mometrix.com/academy and enter code: 401111

Conditional inequalities are those with certain values for the variable that will make the condition true and other values for the variable where the condition will be false. **Absolute inequalities** can have any real number as the value for the variable to make the condition true, while there is no real number value for the variable that will make the condition false. Solving inequalities is done by following the same rules for solving equations with the exception that when multiplying or dividing by a negative number the direction of the inequality sign must be flipped or reversed. **Double inequalities** are situations where two inequality statements apply to the same variable expression. Example: $-c < ax + b < c$.

> **Review Video: Conditional and Absolute Inequalities**
> Visit mometrix.com/academy and enter code: 980164

Determining Solutions to Inequalities

To determine whether a coordinate is a solution of an inequality, you can substitute the values of the coordinate into the inequality, simplify, and check whether the resulting statement holds true. For instance, to determine whether $(-2,4)$ is a solution of the inequality $y \geq -2x + 3$, substitute the values into the inequality, $4 \geq -2(-2) + 3$. Simplify the right side of the inequality and the result is $4 \geq 7$, which is a false statement. Therefore, the coordinate is not a solution of the inequality. You can also use this method to determine which part of the graph of an inequality is shaded. The graph of $y \geq -2x + 3$ includes the solid line $y = -2x + 3$ and, since it excludes the point $(-2,4)$ to the left of the line, it is shaded to the right of the line.

> **Review Video: Graphing Linear Inequalities**
> Visit mometrix.com/academy and enter code: 439421

Flipping Inequality Signs

When given an inequality, we can always turn the entire inequality around, swapping the two sides of the inequality and changing the inequality sign. For instance, $x + 2 > 2x - 3$ is equivalent to $2x - 3 < x + 2$. Aside from that, normally the inequality does not change if we carry out the same operation on both sides of the inequality. There is, however, one principal exception: if we *multiply* or *divide* both sides of the inequality by a *negative number*, the inequality is flipped. For example, if we take the inequality $-2x < 6$ and divide both sides by -2, the inequality flips and we are left with $x > -3$. This *only* applies to multiplication and division, and only with negative numbers. Multiplying or dividing both sides by a positive number, or adding or subtracting any number regardless of sign, does not flip the inequality. Another special case that flips the inequality sign is when reciprocals are used. For instance, $3 > 2$ but the relation of the reciprocals is $\frac{1}{2} < \frac{1}{3}$.

Compound Inequalities

A **compound inequality** is an equality that consists of two inequalities combined with *and* or *or*. The two components of a proper compound inequality must be of opposite type: that is, one must be greater than (or greater than or equal to), the other less than (or less than or equal to). For instance, "$x + 1 < 2$ or $x + 1 > 3$" is a compound inequality, as is "$2x \geq 4$ and $2x \leq 6$." An *and* inequality can be written more compactly by having one inequality on each side of the common part: "$2x \geq 1$ and $2x \leq 6$," can also be written as $1 \leq 2x \leq 6$.

In order for the compound inequality to be meaningful, the two parts of an *and* inequality must overlap; otherwise, no numbers satisfy the inequality. On the other hand, if the two parts of an *or* inequality overlap, then *all* numbers satisfy the inequality and as such the inequality is usually not meaningful.

Solving a compound inequality requires solving each part separately. For example, given the compound inequality "$x + 1 < 2$ or $x + 1 > 3$," the first inequality, $x + 1 < 2$, reduces to $x < 1$, and the second part, $x + 1 > 3$, reduces to $x > 2$, so the whole compound inequality can be written as "$x < 1$ or $x > 2$." Similarly, $1 \leq 2x \leq 6$ can be solved by dividing each term by 2, yielding $\frac{1}{2} \leq x \leq 3$.

Review Video: Compound Inequalities
Visit mometrix.com/academy and enter code: 786318

Solving Inequalities Involving Absolute Values

To solve an inequality involving an absolute value, first isolate the term with the absolute value. Then proceed to treat the two cases separately as with an absolute value equation, but flipping the inequality in the case where the expression in the absolute value is negative (since that essentially involves multiplying both sides by –1.) The two cases are then combined into a compound inequality; if the absolute value is on the greater side of the inequality, then it is an *or* compound inequality, if on the lesser side, then it's an *and*.

Consider the inequality $2 + |x - 1| \geq 3$. We can isolate the absolute value term by subtracting 2 from both sides: $|x - 1| \geq 1$. Now, we're left with the two cases $x - 1 \geq 1$ or $x - 1 \leq -1$: note that in the latter, negative case, the inequality is flipped. $x - 1 \geq 1$ reduces to $x \geq 2$, and $x - 1 \leq -1$ reduces to $x \leq 0$. Since in the inequality $|x - 1| \geq 1$ the absolute value is on the greater side, the two cases combine into an *or* compound inequality, so the final, solved inequality is "$x \leq 0$ or $x \geq 2$."

Review Video: Solving Absolute Value Inequalities
Visit mometrix.com/academy and enter code: 997008

Solving Inequalities Involving Square Roots

Solving an inequality with a square root involves two parts. First, we solve the inequality as if it were an equation, isolating the square root and then squaring both sides of the equation. Second, we restrict the solution to the set of values of x for which the value inside the square root sign is non-negative.

For example, in the inequality, $\sqrt{x-2}+1<5$, we can isolate the square root by subtracting 1 from both sides, yielding $\sqrt{x-2}<4$. Squaring both sides of the inequality yields $x-2<16$, so $x<18$. Since we can't take the square root of a negative number, we also require the part inside the square root to be non-negative. In this case, that means $x-2\geq 0$. Adding 2 to both sides of the inequality yields $x\geq 2$. Our final answer is a compound inequality combining the two simple inequalities: $x\geq 2$ and $x<18$, or $2\leq x<18$.

Note that we only get a compound inequality if the two simple inequalities are in opposite directions; otherwise, we take the one that is more restrictive.

The same technique can be used for other even roots, such as fourth roots. It is *not*, however, used for cube roots or other odd roots—negative numbers *do* have cube roots, so the condition that the quantity inside the root sign cannot be negative does not apply.

Review Video: Solving Inequalities Involving Square Roots
Visit mometrix.com/academy and enter code: 800288

Special Circumstances

Sometimes an inequality involving an absolute value or an even exponent is true for all values of x, and we don't need to do any further work to solve it. This is true if the inequality, once the absolute value or exponent term is isolated, says that term is greater than a negative number (or greater than or equal to zero). Since an absolute value or a number raised to an even exponent is *always* non-negative, this inequality is always true.

Graphical Solutions to Inequalities

Graphing Simple Inequalities

To graph a simple inequality, we first mark on the number line the value that signifies the end point of the inequality. If the inequality is strict (involves a less than or greater than), we use a hollow circle; if it is not strict (less than or equal to or greater than or equal to), we use a solid circle. We then fill in the part of the number line that satisfies the inequality: to the left of the marked point for less than (or less than or equal to), to the right for greater than (or greater than or equal to).

For example, we would graph the inequality $x<5$ by putting a hollow circle at 5 and filling in the part of the line to the left:

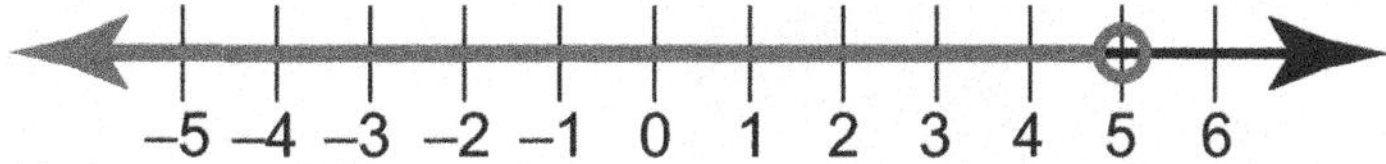

Graphing Compound Inequalities

To graph a compound inequality, we fill in both parts of the inequality for an *or* inequality, or the overlap between them for an *and* inequality. More specifically, we start by plotting the endpoints of each inequality on the number line. For an *or* inequality, we then fill in the appropriate side of the line for each inequality. Typically, the two component inequalities do not overlap, which means the shaded part is *outside* the two points. For an *and* inequality, we instead fill in the part of the line that meets both inequalities.

For the inequality "$x \leq -3$ or $x > 4$," we first put a solid circle at –3 and a hollow circle at 4. We then fill the parts of the line *outside* these circles:

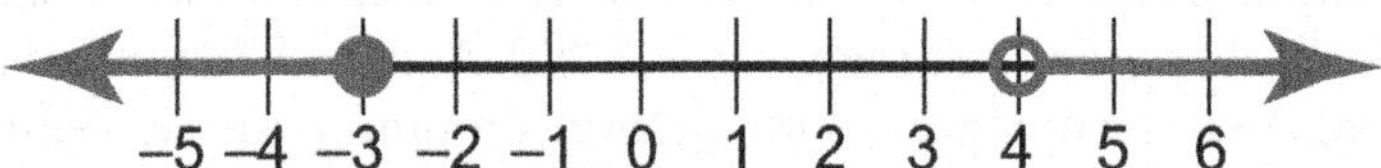

Graphing Inequalities Including Absolute Values

An inequality with an absolute value can be converted to a compound inequality. To graph the inequality, first convert it to a compound inequality, and then graph that normally. If the absolute value is on the greater side of the inequality, we end up with an *or* inequality; we plot the endpoints of the inequality on the number line and fill in the part of the line *outside* those points. If the absolute value is on the smaller side of the inequality, we end up with an *and* inequality; we plot the endpoints of the inequality on the number line and fill in the part of the line *between* those points.

For example, the inequality $|x + 1| \geq 4$ can be rewritten as $x \geq 3$ or $x \leq -5$. We place solid circles at the points 3 and –5 and fill in the part of the line *outside* them:

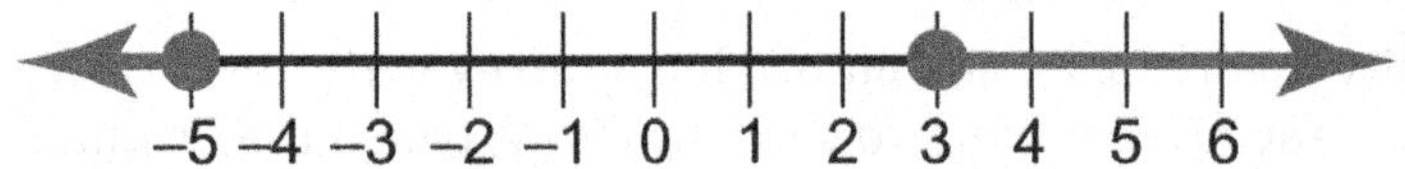

Graphing Inequalities in Two Variables

To graph an inequality in two variables, we first graph the border of the inequality. This means graphing the equation that we get if we replace the inequality sign with an equals sign. If the inequality is strict ($>$ or $<$), we graph the border with a dashed or dotted line; if it is not strict ($\geq$ or $\leq$), we use a solid line. We can then test any point not on the border to see if it satisfies the inequality. If it does, we shade in that side of the border; if not, we shade in the other side. As an example, consider $y > 2x + 2$. To graph this inequality, we first graph the border, $y = 2x + 2$. Since it is a strict inequality, we use a dashed line. Then, we choose a test point. This can be any point not on the border; in this case, we will choose the origin, (0,0). (This makes the calculation easy and is generally a good choice unless the border passes through the origin.) Putting this into the original inequality, we get $0 > 2(0) + 2$, i.e., $0 > 2$. This is *not* true, so we shade in the side of the border that does *not* include the point (0,0):

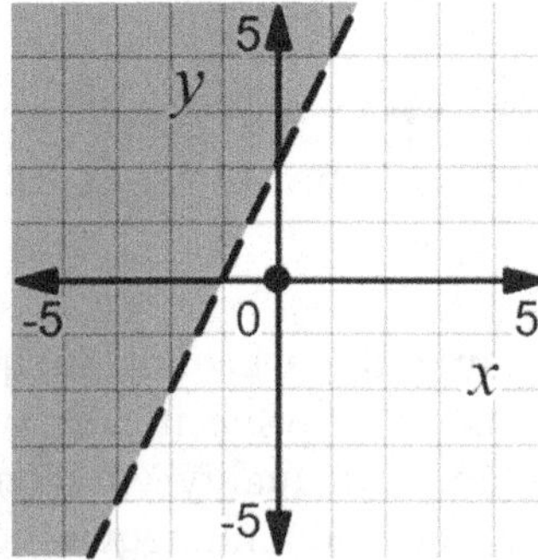

Graphing Compound Inequalities in Two Variables

One way to graph a compound inequality in two variables is to first graph each of the component inequalities. For an *and* inequality, we then shade in only the parts where the two graphs overlap; for an *or* inequality, we shade in any region that pertains to either of the individual inequalities.

Consider the graph of "$y \geq x - 1$ and $y \leq -x$":

We first shade in the individual inequalities:

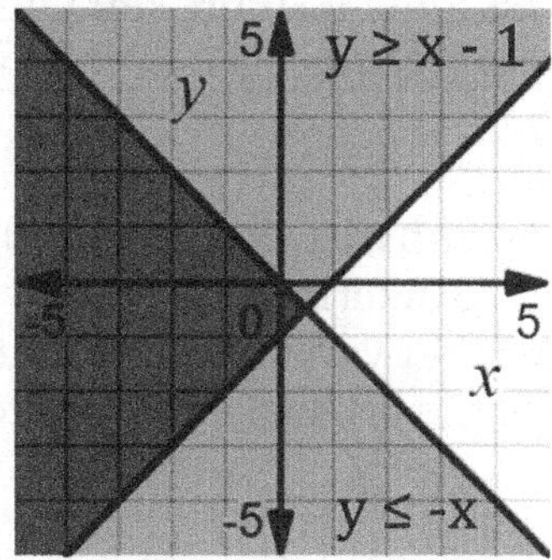

Now, since the compound inequality has an *and*, we only leave shaded the overlap—the part that pertains to *both* inequalities:

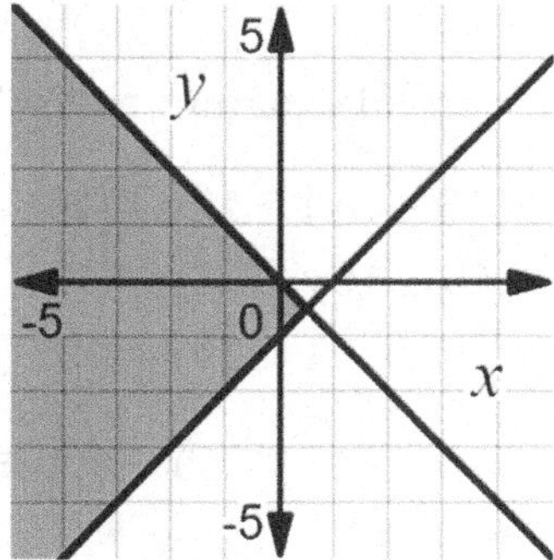

If instead the inequality had been "$y \geq x - 1$ or $y \leq -x$," our final graph would involve the *total* shaded area:

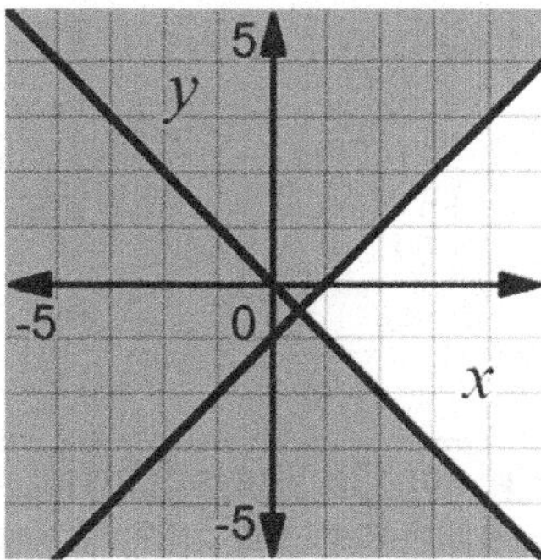

Review Video: Graphing Solutions to Inequalities
Visit mometrix.com/academy and enter code: 391281

Solving Systems of Equations

A **system of equations** is a set of simultaneous equations that all use the same variables. A solution to a system of equations must be true for each equation in the system. **Consistent systems** are those with at least one solution. **Inconsistent systems** are systems of equations that have no solution.

Review Video: Solving Systems and Linear Equations
Visit mometrix.com/academy and enter code: 746745

Substitution

To solve a system of linear equations by **substitution**, start with the easier equation and solve for one of the variables. Express this variable in terms of the other variable. Substitute this expression in the other equation and solve for the other variable. The solution should be expressed in the form (x, y). Substitute the values into both of the original equations to check your answer. Consider the following system of equations:

$$x + 6y = 15$$
$$3x - 12y = 18$$

Solving the first equation for x: $x = 15 - 6y$

Substitute this value in place of x in the second equation, and solve for y:

$$\begin{aligned} 3(15 - 6y) - 12y &= 18 \\ 45 - 18y - 12y &= 18 \\ 30y &= 27 \\ y &= \frac{27}{30} = \frac{9}{10} = 0.9 \end{aligned}$$

Plug this value for y back into the first equation to solve for x:

$$x = 15 - 6(0.9) = 15 - 5.4 = 9.6$$

Check both equations if you have time:

$$\begin{aligned} 9.6 + 6(0.9) &= 15 \\ 9.6 + 5.4 &= 15 \\ 15 &= 15 \end{aligned} \qquad \begin{aligned} 3(9.6) - 12(0.9) &= 18 \\ 28.8 - 10.8 &= 18 \\ 18 &= 18 \end{aligned}$$

Therefore, the solution is $(9.6,0.9)$.

Review Video: The Substitution Method
Visit mometrix.com/academy and enter code: 565151

Elimination

To solve a system of equations using **elimination**, begin by rewriting both equations in standard form $Ax + By = C$. Check to see if the coefficients of one pair of like variables add to zero. If not, multiply one or both of the equations by a non-zero number to make one set of like variables add to zero. Add the two equations to solve for one of the variables. Substitute this value into one of the original equations to solve for the other variable. Check your work by substituting into the other equation. Now, let's look at solving the following system using the elimination method:

$$5x + 6y = 4$$
$$x + 2y = 4$$

If we multiply the second equation by -3, we can eliminate the y-terms:

$$5x + 6y = 4$$
$$-3x - 6y = -12$$

Add the equations together and solve for x:

$$2x = -8$$
$$x = \frac{-8}{2} = -4$$

Plug the value for x back in to either of the original equations and solve for y:

$$-4 + 2y = 4$$
$$y = \frac{4+4}{2} = 4$$

Check both equations if you have time:

$$5(-4) + 6(4) = 4 \qquad -4 + 2(4) = 4$$
$$-20 + 24 = 4 \qquad -4 + 8 = 4$$
$$4 = 4 \qquad 4 = 4$$

Therefore, the solution is $(-4,4)$.

Review Video: The Elimination Method
Visit mometrix.com/academy and enter code: 449121

GRAPHICALLY

To solve a system of linear equations **graphically**, plot both equations on the same graph. The solution of the equations is the point where both lines cross. If the lines do not cross (are parallel), then there is **no solution**.

For example, consider the following system of equations:

$$y = 2x + 7$$
$$y = -x + 1$$

Since these equations are given in slope-intercept form, they are easy to graph; the y-intercepts of the lines are (0,7) and (0,1). The respective slopes are 2 and –1, thus the graphs look like this:

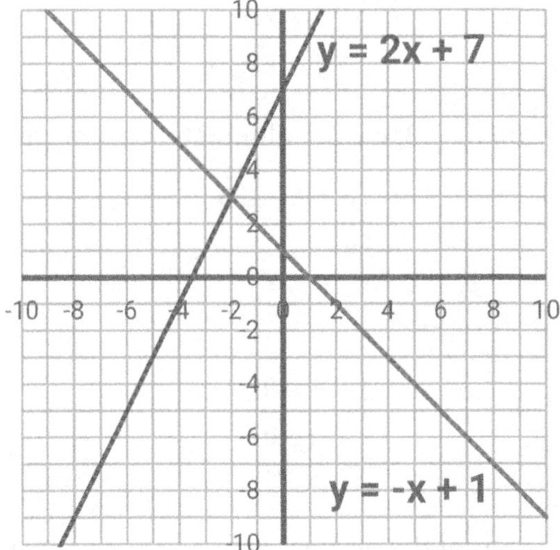

The two lines intersect at the point $(-2,3)$, thus this is the solution to the system of equations.

Solving a system graphically is generally only practical if both coordinates of the solution are integers; otherwise the intersection will lie between gridlines on the graph and the coordinates will be difficult or impossible to determine exactly. It also helps if, as in this example, the equations are in slope-intercept form or some other form that makes them easy to graph. Otherwise, another method of solution (by substitution or elimination) is likely to be more useful.

Review Video: Solving Systems by Graphing
Visit mometrix.com/academy and enter code: 634812

Solving Systems of Equations Using the Trace Feature

Using the trace feature on a calculator requires that you rewrite each equation, isolating the y-variable on one side of the equal sign. Enter both equations in the graphing calculator and plot the graphs simultaneously. Use the trace cursor to find where the two lines cross. Use the zoom feature if necessary to obtain more accurate results. Always check your answer by substituting into the original equations. The trace method is likely to be less accurate than other methods due to the resolution of graphing calculators but is a useful tool to provide an approximate answer.

Calculations Using Points

Sometimes you need to perform calculations using only points on a graph as input data. Using points, you can determine what the **midpoint** and **distance** are. If you know the equation for a line, you can calculate the distance between the line and the point.

To find the **midpoint** of two points (x_1, y_1) and (x_2, y_2), average the x-coordinates to get the x-coordinate of the midpoint, and average the y-coordinates to get the y-coordinate of the midpoint. The formula is: $\left(\frac{x_1+x_2}{2}, \frac{y_1+y_2}{2}\right)$.

The **distance** between two points is the same as the length of the hypotenuse of a right triangle with the two given points as endpoints, and the two sides of the right triangle parallel to the x-axis and y-axis, respectively. The length of the segment parallel to the x-axis is the difference between the x-coordinates of the two points. The length of the segment parallel to the y-axis is the difference between the y-coordinates of the two points. Use the Pythagorean theorem $a^2 + b^2 = c^2$ or $c = \sqrt{a^2 + b^2}$ to find the distance. The formula is $d = \sqrt{(x_2 - x_1)^2 + (y_2 - y_1)^2}$.

When a line is in the format $Ax + By + C = 0$, where A, B, and C are coefficients, you can use a point (x_1, y_1) not on the line and apply the formula $d = \frac{|Ax_1 + By_1 + C|}{\sqrt{A^2 + B^2}}$ to find the distance between the line and the point (x_1, y_1).

Review Video: Calculations Using Points on a Graph
Visit mometrix.com/academy and enter code: 883228

Problem Solving and Data Analysis

Problem Solving and Data Analysis Overview

The questions in this section will require students to create and analyze relationships. They will solve single-step and multistep problems using ratios, rates, proportions, and percentages. Some questions will also require students to describe relationships that are presented graphically. In addition, students should be able to analyze and summarize both qualitative and quantitative data.

Question Types in Problem Solving and Data Analysis

The problem solving and data analysis section will test your knowledge of the following:

- Use ratios, rates, proportional relationships, and scale drawings to solve single- and multistep problems.
  - The student will use a proportional relationship between two variables to solve a multistep problem to determine a ratio or rate; calculate a ratio or rate and then solve a multistep problem; or take a given ratio or rate and solve a multistep problem.
- Solve single- and multistep problems involving **percentages**.
  - The student will solve a multistep problem to determine a percentage; calculate a percentage and then solve a multistep problem; or take a given percentage and solve a multistep problem.
- Solve single- and multistep problems involving **measurement quantities, units,** and **unit conversion.**
  - The student will solve a multistep problem to determine a unit rate;
  - calculate a unit rate and then solve a multistep problem;
  - solve a multistep problem to complete a unit conversion;
  - solve a multistep problem to calculate density;
  - or use the concept of density to solve a multistep problem.
- Given a scatterplot, use **linear**, **quadratic**, or **exponential models** to describe how the variables are related.
  - The student will, given a scatterplot, select the equation of a line or curve of best fit;
  - interpret the line in the context of the situation;

- or use the line or curve of best fit to make a prediction.
- Use the relationship between two variables to investigate **key features of the graph**.
    - The student will make connections between the graphical representation of a relationship and properties of the graph by selecting the graph that represents the properties described, or using the graph to identify a value or set of values.
- Compare linear growth with exponential growth.
    - The student will infer the connection between two variables given a context in order to determine what type of model fits best.
- Use two-way tables to summarize categorical data and relative frequencies, and calculate conditional probability.
    - The student will summarize categorical data or use categorical data to calculate conditional frequencies, conditional probabilities, association of variables, or independence of events.
- Make inferences about **population parameters** based on **sample data**.
    - The student will estimate a population parameter given the results from a random sample of the population.
    - The sample statistics may mention confidence intervals and measurement error that the student should understand and make use of, but need not calculate.
- Use statistics to investigate **measures of center of data** and analyze **shape**, **center**, and **spread**.
    - The student will calculate measures of center and/or spread for a given set of data or use given statistics to compare two separate sets of data.
    - The measures of center that may be calculated include mean, median, and mode, and the measures of spread that may be calculated include range.
    - When comparing two data sets, the student may investigate mean, median, mode, range, and/or standard deviation.
- Evaluate reports to **make inferences**, justify **conclusions**, and determine appropriateness of **data collection methods**.
    - The reports may consist of tables, graphs, or text summaries.

PROPORTIONS

A proportion is a relationship between two quantities that dictates how one changes when the other changes. A **direct proportion** describes a relationship in which a quantity increases by a set amount for every increase in the other quantity, or decreases by that same amount for every decrease in the other quantity. Example: Assuming a constant driving speed, the time required for a car trip increases as the distance of the trip increases. The distance to be traveled and the time required to travel are directly proportional.

An **inverse proportion** is a relationship in which an increase in one quantity is accompanied by a decrease in the other, or vice versa. Example: the time required for a car trip decreases as the speed increases and increases as the speed decreases, so the time required is inversely proportional to the speed of the car.

Review Video: Proportions
Visit mometrix.com/academy and enter code: 505355

Ratios

A **ratio** is a comparison of two quantities in a particular order. Example: If there are 14 computers in a lab, and the class has 20 students, there is a student to computer ratio of 20 to 14, commonly written as $20:14$. Ratios are normally reduced to their smallest whole number representation, so $20:14$ would be reduced to $10:7$ by dividing both sides by 2.

Review Video: Ratios
Visit mometrix.com/academy and enter code: 996914

Constant of Proportionality

When two quantities have a proportional relationship, there exists a **constant of proportionality** between the quantities. The product of this constant and one of the quantities is equal to the other quantity. For example, if one lemon costs \$0.25, two lemons cost \$0.50, and three lemons cost \$0.75, there is a proportional relationship between the total cost of lemons and the number of lemons purchased. The constant of proportionality is the **unit price**, namely \$0.25/lemon. Notice that the total price of lemons, t, can be found by multiplying the unit price of lemons, p, and the number of lemons, n: $t = pn$.

Work/Unit Rate

Unit rate expresses a quantity of one thing in terms of one unit of another. For example, if you travel 30 miles every two hours, a unit rate expresses this comparison in terms of one hour: in one hour you travel 15 miles, so your unit rate is 15 miles per hour. Other examples are how much one ounce of food costs (price per ounce) or figuring out how much one egg costs out of the dozen (price per 1 egg, instead of price per 12 eggs). The denominator of a unit rate is always 1. Unit rates are used to compare different situations to solve problems. For example, to make sure you get the best deal when deciding which kind of soda to buy, you can find the unit rate of each. If soda #1 costs \$1.50 for a 1-liter bottle, and soda #2 costs \$2.75 for a 2-liter bottle, it would be a better deal to buy soda #2, because its unit rate is only \$1.375 per 1-liter, which is cheaper than soda #1. Unit rates can also help determine the length of time a given event will take. For example, if you can paint 2 rooms in 4.5 hours, you can determine how long it will take you to paint 5 rooms by solving for the unit rate per room and then multiplying that by 5.

Review Video: Rates and Unit Rates
Visit mometrix.com/academy and enter code: 185363

Slope

On a graph with two points, (x_1, y_1) and (x_2, y_2), the **slope** is found with the formula $m = \frac{y_2 - y_1}{x_2 - x_1}$; where $x_1 \neq x_2$ and m stands for slope. If the value of the slope is **positive**, the line has an *upward direction* from left to right. If the value of the slope is **negative**, the line has a *downward direction* from left to right. Consider the following example:

A new book goes on sale in bookstores and online stores. In the first month, 5,000 copies of the book are sold. Over time, the book continues to grow in popularity. The data for the number of copies sold is in the table below.

# of Months on Sale	1	2	3	4	5
# of Copies Sold (In Thousands)	5	10	15	20	25

So, the number of copies that are sold and the time that the book is on sale is a proportional relationship. In this example, an equation can be used to show the data: $y = 5x$, where x is the number of months that the book is on sale. Also, y is the number of copies sold. So, the slope of the corresponding line is $\frac{\text{rise}}{\text{run}} = \frac{5}{1} = 5$.

Review Video: Finding the Slope of a Line
Visit mometrix.com/academy and enter code: 766664

Finding an Unknown in Equivalent Expressions

It is often necessary to apply information given about a rate or proportion to a new scenario. For example, if you know that Jedha can run a marathon (26.2 miles) in 3 hours, how long would it take her to run 10 miles at the same pace? Start by setting up equivalent expressions:

$$\frac{26.2 \text{ mi}}{3 \text{ hr}} = \frac{10 \text{ mi}}{x \text{ hr}}$$

Now, cross multiply and solve for x:

$$26.2x = 30$$
$$x = \frac{30}{26.2} = \frac{15}{13.1}$$
$$x \approx 1.15 \text{ hrs } or \text{ 1 hr 9 min}$$

So, at this pace, Jedha could run 10 miles in about 1.15 hours or about 1 hour and 9 minutes.

Review Video: Cross Multiply Fractions
Visit mometrix.com/academy and enter code: 893904

Metric Measurement Prefixes

Giga-	One billion	1 *giga*watt is one billion watts
Mega-	One million	1 *mega*hertz is one million hertz
Kilo-	One thousand	1 *kilo*gram is one thousand grams
Deci-	One-tenth	1 *deci*meter is one-tenth of a meter
Centi-	One-hundredth	1 *centi*meter is one-hundredth of a meter
Milli-	One-thousandth	1 *milli*liter is one-thousandth of a liter
Micro-	One-millionth	1 *micro*gram is one-millionth of a gram

Review Video: Metric System Conversion - How the Metric System Works
Visit mometrix.com/academy and enter code: 163709

Measurement Conversion

When converting between units, the goal is to maintain the same meaning but change the way it is displayed. In order to go from a larger unit to a smaller unit, multiply the number of the known amount by the equivalent amount. When going from a smaller unit to a larger unit, divide the number of the known amount by the equivalent amount.

For complicated conversions, it may be helpful to set up conversion fractions. In these fractions, one fraction is the **conversion factor**. The other fraction has the unknown amount in the numerator. So, the known value is placed in the denominator. Sometimes, the second fraction has the known value from the problem in the numerator and the unknown in the denominator. Multiply the two fractions to get the converted measurement. Note that since the numerator and the denominator of the factor are equivalent, the value of the fraction is 1. That is why we can say that the result in the new units is equal to the result in the old units even though they have different numbers.

It can often be necessary to chain known conversion factors together. As an example, consider converting 512 square inches to square meters. We know that there are 2.54 centimeters in an inch and 100 centimeters in a meter, and we know we will need to square each of these factors to achieve the conversion we are looking for.

$$\frac{512\text{ in}^2}{1} \times \left(\frac{2.54\text{ cm}}{1\text{ in}}\right)^2 \times \left(\frac{1\text{ m}}{100\text{ cm}}\right)^2 = \frac{512\,\cancel{\text{in}^2}}{1} \times \left(\frac{6.4516\,\cancel{\text{cm}^2}}{1\,\cancel{\text{in}^2}}\right) \times \left(\frac{1\text{ m}^2}{10{,}000\,\cancel{\text{cm}^2}}\right) = 0.330\text{ m}^2$$

Review Video: Measurement Conversions
Visit mometrix.com/academy and enter code: 316703

Common Units and Equivalents

Metric Equivalents

1000 μg (microgram)	1 mg
1000 mg (milligram)	1 g
1000 g (gram)	1 kg
1000 kg (kilogram)	1 metric ton
1000 mL (milliliter)	1 L
1000 μm (micrometer)	1 mm
1000 mm (millimeter)	1 m
100 cm (centimeter)	1 m
1000 m (meter)	1 km

Distance and Area Measurement

Unit	Abbreviation	US equivalent	Metric equivalent
Inch	in	1 inch	2.54 centimeters
Foot	ft	12 inches	0.305 meters
Yard	yd	3 feet	0.914 meters
Mile	mi	5280 feet	1.609 kilometers
Acre	ac	4840 square yards	0.405 hectares
Square Mile	sq. mi. or mi.^{2}	640 acres	2.590 square kilometers

CAPACITY MEASUREMENTS

Unit	Abbreviation	US equivalent	Metric equivalent
Fluid Ounce	fl oz	8 fluid drams	29.573 milliliters
Cup	c	8 fluid ounces	0.237 liter
Pint	pt.	16 fluid ounces	0.473 liter
Quart	qt.	2 pints	0.946 liter
Gallon	gal.	4 quarts	3.785 liters
Teaspoon	t or tsp.	1 fluid dram	5 milliliters
Tablespoon	T or tbsp.	4 fluid drams	15 or 16 milliliters
Cubic Centimeter	cc or cm^3	0.271 drams	1 milliliter

WEIGHT MEASUREMENTS

Unit	Abbreviation	US equivalent	Metric equivalent
Ounce	oz	16 drams	28.35 grams
Pound	lb	16 ounces	453.6 grams
Ton	tn.	2,000 pounds	907.2 kilograms

VOLUME AND WEIGHT MEASUREMENT CLARIFICATIONS

Always be careful when using ounces and fluid ounces. They are not equivalent.

1 pint = 16 fluid ounces	1 fluid ounce ≠ 1 ounce
1 pound = 16 ounces	1 pint ≠ 1 pound

Having one pint of something does not mean you have one pound of it. In the same way, just because something weighs one pound does not mean that its volume is one pint.

In the United States, the word "ton" by itself refers to a short ton or a net ton. Do not confuse this with a long ton (also called a gross ton) or a metric ton (also spelled *tonne*), which have different measurement equivalents.

$$1 \text{ US ton} = 2000 \text{ pounds} \quad \neq \quad 1 \text{ metric ton} = 1000 \text{ kilograms}$$

PROBABILITY

Probability is the likelihood of a certain outcome occurring for a given event. An **event** is any situation that produces a result. It could be something as simple as flipping a coin or as complex as launching a rocket. Determining the probability of an outcome for an event can be equally simple or complex. As such, there are specific terms used in the study of probability that need to be understood:

- **Compound event**—an event that involves two or more independent events (rolling a pair of dice and taking the sum)
- **Desired outcome** (or success)—an outcome that meets a particular set of criteria (a roll of 1 or 2 if we are looking for numbers less than 3)
- **Independent events**—two or more events whose outcomes do not affect one another (two coins tossed at the same time)
- **Dependent events**—two or more events whose outcomes affect one another (two cards drawn consecutively from the same deck)
- **Certain outcome**—probability of outcome is 100% or 1

- **Impossible outcome**—probability of outcome is 0% or 0
- **Mutually exclusive outcomes**—two or more outcomes whose criteria cannot all be satisfied in a single event (a coin coming up heads and tails on the same toss)
- **Random variable**—refers to all possible outcomes of a single event which may be discrete or continuous.

Review Video: Intro to Probability
Visit mometrix.com/academy and enter code: 212374

SAMPLE SPACE

The total set of all possible results of a test or experiment is called a **sample space**, or sometimes a universal sample space. The sample space, represented by one of the variables S, Ω, or U (for universal sample space) has individual elements called outcomes. Other terms for outcome that may be used interchangeably include elementary outcome, simple event, or sample point. The number of outcomes in a given sample space could be infinite or finite, and some tests may yield multiple unique sample sets. For example, tests conducted by drawing playing cards from a standard deck would have one sample space of the card values, another sample space of the card suits, and a third sample space of suit-denomination combinations. For most tests, the sample spaces considered will be finite.

An **event**, represented by the variable E, is a portion of a sample space. It may be one outcome or a group of outcomes from the same sample space. If an event occurs, then the test or experiment will generate an outcome that satisfies the requirement of that event. For example, given a standard deck of 52 playing cards as the sample space, and defining the event as the collection of face cards, then the event will occur if the card drawn is a J, Q, or K. If any other card is drawn, the event is said to have not occurred.

For every sample space, each possible outcome has a specific likelihood, or probability, that it will occur. The probability measure, also called the **distribution**, is a function that assigns a real number probability, from zero to one, to each outcome. For a probability measure to be accurate, every outcome must have a real number probability measure that is greater than or equal to zero and less than or equal to one. Also, the probability measure of the sample space must equal one, and the probability measure of the union of multiple outcomes must equal the sum of the individual probability measures.

Probabilities of events are expressed as real numbers from zero to one. They give a numerical value to the chance that a particular event will occur. The probability of an event occurring is the sum of the probabilities of the individual elements of that event. For example, in a standard deck of 52 playing cards as the sample space and the collection of face cards as the event, the probability of drawing a specific face card is $\frac{1}{52} = 0.019$, but the probability of drawing any one of the twelve face cards is $12(0.019) = 0.228$. Note that rounding of numbers can generate different results. If you multiplied 12 by the fraction $\frac{1}{52}$ before converting to a decimal, you would get the answer $\frac{12}{52} = 0.231$.

Theoretical and Experimental Probability

Theoretical probability can usually be determined without actually performing the event. The likelihood of an outcome occurring, or the probability of an outcome occurring, is given by the formula:

$$P(A) = \frac{\text{Number of acceptable outcomes}}{\text{Number of possible outcomes}}$$

Note that $P(A)$ is the probability of an outcome A occurring, and each outcome is just as likely to occur as any other outcome. If each outcome has the same probability of occurring as every other possible outcome, the outcomes are said to be equally likely to occur. The total number of acceptable outcomes must be less than or equal to the total number of possible outcomes. If the two are equal, then the outcome is certain to occur and the probability is 1. If the number of acceptable outcomes is zero, then the outcome is impossible and the probability is 0. For example, if there are 20 marbles in a bag and 5 are red, then the theoretical probability of randomly selecting a red marble is 5 out of 20, $\left(\frac{5}{20} = \frac{1}{4}, 0.25, \text{or } 25\%\right)$.

If the theoretical probability is unknown or too complicated to calculate, it can be estimated by an experimental probability. **Experimental probability**, also called empirical probability, is an estimate of the likelihood of a certain outcome based on repeated experiments or collected data. In other words, while theoretical probability is based on what *should* happen, experimental probability is based on what *has* happened. Experimental probability is calculated in the same way as theoretical probability, except that actual outcomes are used instead of possible outcomes. The more experiments performed or datapoints gathered, the better the estimate should be.

Theoretical and experimental probability do not always line up with one another. Theoretical probability says that out of 20 coin-tosses, 10 should be heads. However, if we were actually to toss 20 coins, we might record just 5 heads. This doesn't mean that our theoretical probability is incorrect; it just means that this particular experiment had results that were different from what was predicted. A practical application of empirical probability is the insurance industry. There are no set functions that define lifespan, health, or safety. Insurance companies look at factors from hundreds of thousands of individuals to find patterns that they then use to set the formulas for insurance premiums.

Review Video: Empirical Probability
Visit mometrix.com/academy and enter code: 513468

Objective and Subjective Probability

Objective probability is based on mathematical formulas and documented evidence. Examples of objective probability include raffles or lottery drawings where there is a pre-determined number of possible outcomes and a predetermined number of outcomes that correspond to an event. Other cases of objective probability include probabilities of rolling dice, flipping coins, or drawing cards. Most gambling games are based on objective probability.

In contrast, **subjective probability** is based on personal or professional feelings and judgments. Often, there is a lot of guesswork following extensive research. Areas where subjective probability is applicable include sales trends and business expenses. Attractions set admission prices based on subjective probabilities of attendance based on varying admission rates in an effort to maximize their profit.

Complement of an Event

Sometimes it may be easier to calculate the possibility of something not happening, or the **complement of an event**. Represented by the symbol $\bar{A}$, the complement of A is the probability that event A does not happen. When you know the probability of event A occurring, you can use the formula $P(\bar{A}) = 1 - P(A)$, where $P(\bar{A})$ is the probability of event A not occurring, and $P(A)$ is the probability of event A occurring.

Addition Rule

The **addition rule** for probability is used for finding the probability of a compound event. Use the formula $P(A \cup B) = P(A) + P(B) - P(A \cap B)$, where $P(A \cap B)$ is the probability of both events occurring to find the probability of a compound event. The probability of both events occurring at the same time must be subtracted to eliminate any overlap in the first two probabilities.

Conditional Probability

Given two events A and B, the **conditional probability** $P(A|B)$ is the probability that event A will occur, given that event B has occurred. The conditional probability cannot be calculated simply from $P(A)$ and $P(B)$; these probabilities alone do not give sufficient information to determine the conditional probability. It can, however, be determined if you are also given the probability of the intersection of events A and B, $P(A \cap B)$, the probability that events A and B both occur. Specifically, $P(A|B) = \frac{P(A \cap B)}{P(B)}$. For instance, suppose you have a jar containing two red marbles and two blue marbles, and you draw two marbles at random. Consider event A being the event that the first marble drawn is red, and event B being the event that the second marble drawn is blue. If we want to find the probability that B occurs given that A occurred, $P(B|A)$, then we can compute it using the fact that $P(A)$ is $\frac{1}{2}$, and $P(A \cap B)$ is $\frac{1}{3}$. (The latter may not be obvious, but may be determined by finding the product of $\frac{1}{2}$ and $\frac{2}{3}$). Therefore $P(B|A) = \frac{P(A \cap B)}{P(A)} = \frac{1/3}{1/2} = \frac{2}{3}$.

Conditional Probability in Everyday Situations

Conditional probability often arises in everyday situations in, for example, estimating the risk or benefit of certain activities. The conditional probability of having a heart attack given that you exercise daily may be smaller than the overall probability of having a heart attack. The conditional probability of having lung cancer given that you are a smoker is larger than the overall probability of having lung cancer. Note that changing the order of the conditional probability changes the meaning: the conditional probability of having lung cancer given that you are a smoker is a very different thing from the probability of being a smoker given that you have lung cancer. In an extreme case, suppose that a certain rare disease is caused only by eating a certain food, but even then, it is unlikely. Then the conditional probability of having that disease given that you eat the dangerous food is nonzero but low, but the conditional probability of having eaten that food given that you have the disease is 100%!

Review Video: Conditional Probability
Visit mometrix.com/academy and enter code: 397924

INDEPENDENCE

The conditional probability $P(A|B)$ is the probability that event A will occur given that event B occurs. If the two events are independent, we do not expect that whether or not event B occurs should have any effect on whether or not event A occurs. In other words, we expect $P(A|B) = P(A)$.

This can be proven using the usual equations for conditional probability and the joint probability of independent events. The conditional probability $P(A|B) = \frac{P(A\cap B)}{P(B)}$. If A and B are independent, then $P(A \cap B) = P(A)P(B)$. So $P(A|B) = \frac{P(A)P(B)}{P(B)} = P(A)$. By similar reasoning, if A and B are independent then $P(B|A) = P(B)$.

MULTIPLICATION RULE

The **multiplication rule** can be used to find the probability of two independent events occurring using the formula $P(A \cap B) = P(A) \times P(B)$, where $P(A \cap B)$ is the probability of two independent events occurring, $P(A)$ is the probability of the first event occurring, and $P(B)$ is the probability of the second event occurring.

The multiplication rule can also be used to find the probability of two dependent events occurring using the formula $P(A \cap B) = P(A) \times P(B|A)$, where $P(A \cap B)$ is the probability of two dependent events occurring and $P(B|A)$ is the probability of the second event occurring after the first event has already occurred.

Use a **combination of the multiplication** rule and the rule of complements to find the probability that at least one outcome of the element will occur. This is given by the general formula $P(\text{at least one event occurring}) = 1 - P(\text{no outcomes occurring})$. For example, to find the probability that at least one even number will show when a pair of dice is rolled, find the probability that two odd numbers will be rolled (no even numbers) and subtract from one. You can always use a tree diagram or make a chart to list the possible outcomes when the sample space is small, such as in the dice-rolling example, but in most cases it will be much faster to use the multiplication and complement formulas.

Review Video: Multiplication Rule
Visit mometrix.com/academy and enter code: 782598

UNION AND INTERSECTION OF TWO SETS OF OUTCOMES

If A and B are each a set of elements or outcomes from an experiment, then the **union** (symbol ∪) of the two sets is the set of elements found in set A or set B. For example, if $A = \{2, 3, 4\}$ and $B = \{3, 4, 5\}$, $A \cup B = \{2, 3, 4, 5\}$. Note that the outcomes 3 and 4 appear only once in the union. For statistical events, the union is equivalent to "or"; $P(A \cup B)$ is the same thing as $P(A \text{ or } B)$. The **intersection** (symbol ∩) of two sets is the set of outcomes common to both sets. For the above sets A and B, $A \cap B = \{3, 4\}$. For statistical events, the intersection is equivalent to "and"; $P(A \cap B)$ is the same thing as $P(A \text{ and } B)$. It is important to note that union and intersection operations commute. That is:

$$A \cup B = B \cup A \text{ and } A \cap B = B \cap A$$

Permutations and Combinations

When trying to calculate the probability of an event using the $\frac{\text{desired outcomes}}{\text{total outcomes}}$ formula, you may frequently find that there are too many outcomes to individually count them. **Permutation** and **combination formulas** offer a shortcut to counting outcomes. A permutation is an arrangement of a specific number of a set of objects in a specific order. The number of **permutations** of r items given a set of n items can be calculated as ${}_nP_r = \frac{n!}{(n-r)!}$. Combinations are similar to permutations, except there are no restrictions regarding the order of the elements. While ABC is considered a different permutation than BCA, ABC and BCA are considered the same combination. The number of **combinations** of r items given a set of n items can be calculated as ${}_nC_r = \frac{n!}{r!(n-r)!}$ or ${}_nC_r = \frac{{}_nP_r}{r!}$.

Suppose you want to calculate how many different 5-card hands can be drawn from a deck of 52 cards. This is a combination since the order of the cards in a hand does not matter. There are 52 cards available, and 5 to be selected. Thus, the number of different hands is ${}_{52}C_5 = \frac{52!}{5! \times 47!} =$ 2,598,960.

Review Video: Probability - Permutation and Combination
Visit mometrix.com/academy and enter code: 907664

Tree Diagram

For a simple sample space, possible outcomes may be determined by using a **tree diagram** or an organized chart. In either case, you can easily draw or list out the possible outcomes. For example, to determine all the possible ways three objects can be ordered, you can draw a tree diagram:

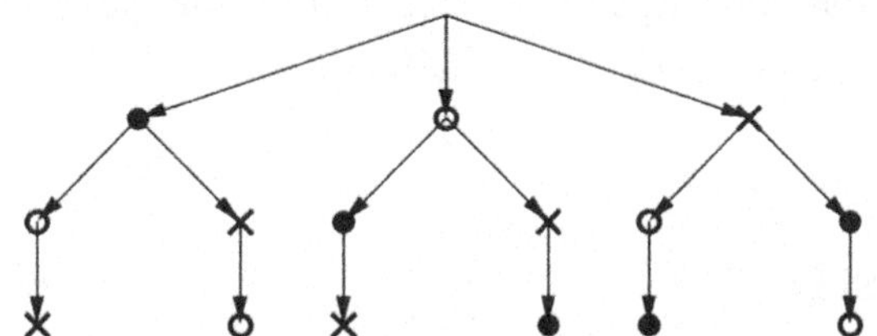

Review Video: Tree Diagrams
Visit mometrix.com/academy and enter code: 829158

You can also make a chart to list all the possibilities:

First object	Second object	Third object
●	x	o
●	o	x
o	●	x
o	x	●
x	●	o
x	o	●

Either way, you can easily see there are six possible ways the three objects can be ordered.

If two events have no outcomes in common, they are said to be **mutually exclusive**. For example, in a standard deck of 52 playing cards, the event of all card suits is mutually exclusive to the event of all card values. If two events have no bearing on each other so that one event occurring has no influence on the probability of another event occurring, the two events are said to be independent. For example, rolling a standard six-sided die multiple times does not change that probability that a particular number will be rolled from one roll to the next. If the outcome of one event does affect the probability of the second event, the two events are said to be dependent. For example, if cards are drawn from a deck, the probability of drawing an ace after an ace has been drawn is different than the probability of drawing an ace if no ace (or no other card, for that matter) has been drawn.

In probability, the **odds in favor of an event** are the number of times the event will occur compared to the number of times the event will not occur. To calculate the odds in favor of an event, use the formula $\frac{P(A)}{1-P(A)}$, where $P(A)$ is the probability that the event will occur. Many times, odds in favor is given as a ratio in the form $\frac{a}{b}$ or $a:b$, where a is the probability of the event occurring and b is the complement of the event, the probability of the event not occurring. If the odds in favor are given as 2:5, that means that you can expect the event to occur two times for every 5 times that it does not occur. In other words, the probability that the event will occur is $\frac{2}{2+5}=\frac{2}{7}$.

In probability, the **odds against an event** are the number of times the event will not occur compared to the number of times the event will occur. To calculate the odds against an event, use the formula $\frac{1-P(A)}{P(A)}$, where $P(A)$ is the probability that the event will occur. Many times, odds against is given as a ratio in the form $\frac{b}{a}$ or $b:a$, where b is the probability the event will not occur (the complement of the event) and a is the probability the event will occur. If the odds against an event are given as 3:1, that means that you can expect the event to not occur 3 times for every one time it does occur. In other words, 3 out of every 4 trials will fail.

Two-Way Frequency Tables

If we have a two-way frequency table, it is generally a straightforward matter to read off the probabilities of any two events A and B, as well as the joint probability of both events occurring, $P(A \cap B)$. We can then find the conditional probability $P(A|B)$ by calculating $P(A|B) = \frac{P(A\cap B)}{P(B)}$. We could also check whether or not events are independent by verifying whether $P(A)P(B) = P(A\cap B)$.

For example, a certain store's recent T-shirt sales:

	Small	Medium	Large	Total
Blue	25	40	35	100
White	27	25	22	74
Black	8	23	15	46
Total	60	88	72	220

Suppose we want to find the conditional probability that a customer buys a black shirt (event A), given that the shirt he buys is size small (event B). From the table, the probability $P(B)$ that a customer buys a small shirt is $\frac{60}{220} = \frac{3}{11}$. The probability $P(A \cap B)$ that he buys a small, black shirt is $\frac{8}{220} = \frac{2}{55}$. The conditional probability $P(A|B)$ that he buys a black shirt, given that he buys a small shirt, is therefore $P(A|B) = \frac{2/55}{3/11} = \frac{2}{15}$.

Similarly, if we want to check whether the event a customer buys a blue shirt, A, is independent of the event that a customer buys a medium shirt, B. From the table, $P(A) = \frac{100}{220} = \frac{5}{11}$ and $P(B) = \frac{88}{220} = \frac{4}{10}$. Also, $P(A \cap B) = \frac{40}{220} = \frac{2}{11}$. Since $\left(\frac{5}{11}\right)\left(\frac{4}{10}\right) = \frac{20}{110} = \frac{2}{11}$, $P(A)P(B) = P(A \cap B)$ and these two events are indeed independent.

Expected Value

Expected value is a method of determining the expected outcome in a random situation. It is a sum of the weighted probabilities of the possible outcomes. Multiply the probability of an event occurring by the weight assigned to that probability (such as the amount of money won or lost). A practical application of the expected value is to determine whether a game of chance is really fair. If the sum of the weighted probabilities is equal to zero, the game is generally considered fair because the player has a fair chance to at least break even. If the expected value is less than zero, then players are expected to lose more than they win. For example, a lottery drawing might allow the player to choose any three-digit number, 000–999. The probability of choosing the winning number is 1:1000. If it costs \$1 to play, and a winning number receives \$500, the expected value is $\left(-\$1 \times \frac{999}{1,000}\right) + \left(\$499 \times \frac{1}{1,000}\right) = -\$0.50$. You can expect to lose on average 50 cents for every dollar you spend.

Review Video: Expected Value
Visit mometrix.com/academy and enter code: 643554

Expected Value and Simulators

A die roll simulator will show the results of n rolls of a die. The result of each die roll may be recorded. For example, suppose a die is rolled 100 times. All results may be recorded. The numbers of 1s, 2s, 3s, 4s, 5s, and 6s, may be counted. The experimental probability of rolling each number will equal the ratio of the frequency of the rolled number to the total number of rolls. As the number of rolls increases, or approaches infinity, the experimental probability will approach the theoretical probability of $\frac{1}{6}$. Thus, the expected value for the roll of a die is shown to be $\left(1 \times \frac{1}{6}\right) + \left(2 \times \frac{1}{6}\right) + \left(3 \times \frac{1}{6}\right) + \left(4 \times \frac{1}{6}\right) + \left(5 \times \frac{1}{6}\right) + \left(6 \times \frac{1}{6}\right)$, or 3.5.

Statistics

Statistics is the branch of mathematics that deals with collecting, recording, interpreting, illustrating, and analyzing large amounts of **data**. The following terms are often used in the discussion of data and **statistics**:

- **Data** – the collective name for pieces of information (singular is datum)
- **Quantitative data** – measurements (such as length, mass, and speed) that provide information about quantities in numbers
- **Qualitative data** – information (such as colors, scents, tastes, and shapes) that cannot be measured using numbers
- **Discrete data** – information that can be expressed only by a specific value, such as whole or half numbers. (e.g., since people can be counted only in whole numbers, a population count would be discrete data.)
- **Continuous data** – information (such as time and temperature) that can be expressed by any value within a given range
- **Primary data** – information that has been collected directly from a survey, investigation, or experiment, such as a questionnaire or the recording of daily temperatures. (Primary data that has not yet been organized or analyzed is called **raw data**.)
- **Secondary data** – information that has been collected, sorted, and processed by the researcher
- **Ordinal data** – information that can be placed in numerical order, such as age or weight
- **Nominal data** – information that *cannot* be placed in numerical order, such as names or places

Data Collection

Population

In statistics, the **population** is the entire collection of people, plants, etc., that data can be collected from. For example, a study to determine how well students in local schools perform on a standardized test would have a population of all the students enrolled in those schools, although a study may include just a small sample of students from each school. A **parameter** is a numerical value that gives information about the population, such as the mean, median, mode, or standard deviation. Remember that the symbol for the mean of a population is μ and the symbol for the standard deviation of a population is σ.

Sample

A **sample** is a portion of the entire population. Whereas a parameter helped describe the population, a **statistic** is a numerical value that gives information about the sample, such as mean, median, mode, or standard deviation. Keep in mind that the symbols for mean and standard deviation are different when they are referring to a sample rather than the entire population. For a sample, the symbol for mean is $\bar{x}$ and the symbol for standard deviation is s. The mean and standard deviation of a sample may or may not be identical to that of the entire population due to a sample only being a subset of the population. However, if the sample is random and large enough, statistically significant values can be attained. Samples are generally used when the population is too large to justify including every element or when acquiring data for the entire population is impossible.

Inferential Statistics

Inferential statistics is the branch of statistics that uses samples to make predictions about an entire population. This type of statistic is often seen in political polls, where a sample of the population is questioned about a particular topic or politician to gain an understanding of the attitudes of the entire population of the country. Often, exit polls are conducted on election days using this method. Inferential statistics can have a large margin of error if you do not have a valid sample.

Sampling Distribution

Statistical values calculated from various samples of the same size make up the **sampling distribution**. For example, if several samples of identical size are randomly selected from a large population and then the mean of each sample is calculated, the distribution of values of the means would be a sampling distribution.

The **sampling distribution of the mean** is the distribution of the sample mean, $\bar{x}$, derived from random samples of a given size. It has three important characteristics. First, the mean of the sampling distribution of the mean is equal to the mean of the population that was sampled. Second, assuming the standard deviation is non-zero, the standard deviation of the sampling distribution of the mean equals the standard deviation of the sampled population divided by the square root of the sample size. This is sometimes called the standard error. Finally, as the sample size gets larger, the sampling distribution of the mean gets closer to a normal distribution via the central limit theorem.

Survey Study

A **survey study** is a method of gathering information from a small group in an attempt to gain enough information to make accurate general assumptions about the population. Once a survey study is completed, the results are then put into a summary report.

Survey studies are generally in the format of surveys, interviews, or questionnaires as part of an effort to find opinions of a particular group or to find facts about a group.

It is important to note that the findings from a survey study are only as accurate as the sample chosen from the population.

Correlational Studies

Correlational studies seek to determine how much one variable is affected by changes in a second variable. For example, correlational studies may look for a relationship between the amount of time a student spends studying for a test and the grade that student earned on the test or between student scores on college admissions tests and student grades in college.

It is important to note that correlational studies cannot show a cause and effect, but rather can show only that two variables are or are not potentially correlated.

Experimental Studies

Experimental studies take correlational studies one step farther, in that they attempt to prove or disprove a cause-and-effect relationship. These studies are performed by conducting a series of experiments to test the hypothesis. For a study to be scientifically accurate, it must have both an experimental group that receives the specified treatment and a control group that does not get the treatment. This is the type of study pharmaceutical companies do as part of drug trials for new medications. Experimental studies are only valid when the proper scientific method has been followed. In other words, the experiment must be well-planned and executed without bias in the testing process, all subjects must be selected at random, and the process of determining which subject is in which of the two groups must also be completely random.

Observational Studies

Observational studies are the opposite of experimental studies. In observational studies, the tester cannot change or in any way control all of the variables in the test. For example, a study to determine which gender does better in math classes in school is strictly observational. You cannot change a person's gender, and you cannot change the subject being studied. The big downfall of observational studies is that you have no way of proving a cause-and-effect relationship because you cannot control outside influences. Events outside of school can influence a student's performance in school, and observational studies cannot take that into consideration.

Random Samples

For most studies, a **random sample** is necessary to produce valid results. Random samples should not have any particular influence to cause sampled subjects to behave one way or another. The goal is for the random sample to be a **representative sample**, or a sample whose characteristics give an accurate picture of the characteristics of the entire population. To accomplish this, you must make sure you have a proper **sample size**, or an appropriate number of elements in the sample.

Biases

In statistical studies, biases must be avoided. **Bias** is an error that causes the study to favor one set of results over another. For example, if a survey to determine how the country views the president's job performance only speaks to registered voters in the president's party, the results will be skewed because a disproportionately large number of responders would tend to show approval, while a disproportionately large number of people in the opposite party would tend to express disapproval. **Extraneous variables** are, as the name implies, outside influences that can affect the outcome of a study. They are not always avoidable but could trigger bias in the result.

Dispersion

A **measure of dispersion** is a single value that helps to "interpret" the measure of central tendency by providing more information about how the data values in the set are distributed about the measure of central tendency. The measure of dispersion helps to eliminate or reduce the disadvantages of using the mean, median, or mode as a single measure of central tendency, and give a more accurate picture of the dataset as a whole. To have a measure of dispersion, you must know or calculate the range, standard deviation, or variance of the data set.

Range

The **range** of a set of data is the difference between the greatest and lowest values of the data in the set. To calculate the range, you must first make sure the units for all data values are the same, and then identify the greatest and lowest values. If there are multiple data values that are equal for the highest or lowest, just use one of the values in the formula. Write the answer with the same units as the data values you used to do the calculations.

Review Video: Statistical Range
Visit mometrix.com/academy and enter code: 778541

Sample Standard Deviation

Standard deviation is a measure of dispersion that compares all the data values in the set to the mean of the set to give a more accurate picture. To find the **standard deviation of a sample**, use the formula

$$s = \sqrt{\frac{\sum_{i=1}^{n}(x_i - \bar{x})^2}{n-1}}$$

Note that s is the standard deviation of a sample, x_i represents the individual values in the data set, $\bar{x}$ is the mean of the data values in the set, and n is the number of data values in the set. The higher the value of the standard deviation is, the greater the variance of the data values from the mean. The units associated with the standard deviation are the same as the units of the data values.

Review Video: Standard Deviation
Visit mometrix.com/academy and enter code: 419469

Sample Variance

The **variance of a sample** is the square of the sample standard deviation (denoted s^2). While the mean of a set of data gives the average of the set and gives information about where a specific data value lies in relation to the average, the variance of the sample gives information about the degree to which the data values are spread out and tells you how close an individual value is to the average compared to the other values. The units associated with variance are the same as the units of the data values squared.

Percentile

Percentiles and quartiles are other methods of describing data within a set. **Percentiles** tell what percentage of the data in the set fall below a specific point. For example, achievement test scores are often given in percentiles. A score at the 80th percentile is one which is equal to or higher than 80 percent of the scores in the set. In other words, 80 percent of the scores were lower than that score.

Quartiles are percentile groups that make up quarter sections of the data set. The first quartile is the 25th percentile. The second quartile is the 50th percentile; this is also the median of the dataset. The third quartile is the 75th percentile.

Skewness

Skewness is a way to describe the symmetry or asymmetry of the distribution of values in a dataset. If the distribution of values is symmetrical, there is no skew. In general the closer the mean of a data set is to the median of the data set, the less skew there is. Generally, if the mean is to the right of the median, the data set is *positively skewed*, or right-skewed, and if the mean is to the left of the median, the data set is *negatively skewed*, or left-skewed. However, this rule of thumb is not infallible. When the data values are graphed on a curve, a set with no skew will be a perfect bell curve.

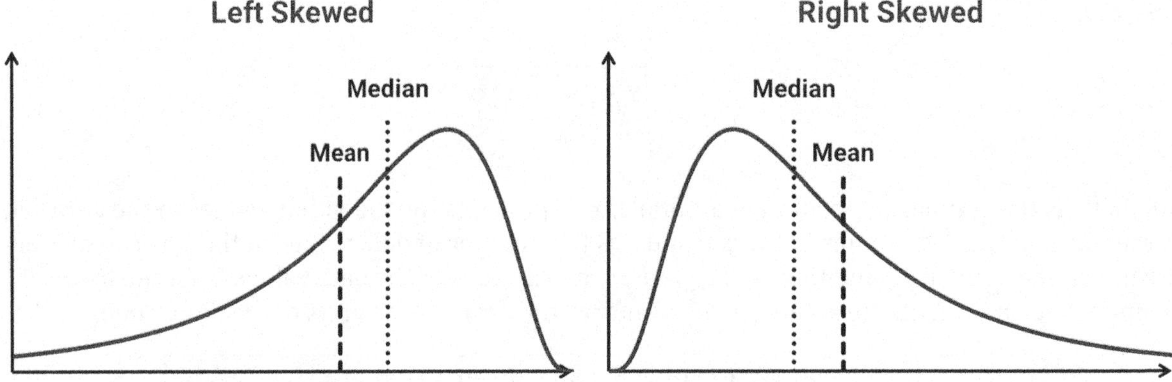

To estimate skew, use the formula:

$$\text{skew} = \frac{\sqrt{n(n-1)}}{n-2}\left(\frac{\frac{1}{n}\sum_{i=1}^{n}(x_i-\bar{x})^3}{\left(\frac{1}{n}\sum_{i=1}^{n}(x_i-\bar{x})^2\right)^{\frac{3}{2}}}\right)$$

Note that n is the datapoints in the set, x_i is the ith value in the set, and $\bar{x}$ is the mean of the set.

Review Video: Skew
Visit mometrix.com/academy and enter code: 661486

Unimodal vs. Bimodal

If a distribution has a single peak, it would be considered **unimodal**. If it has two discernible peaks it would be considered **bimodal**. Bimodal distributions may be an indication that the set of data being considered is actually the combination of two sets of data with significant differences. A **uniform distribution** is a distribution in which there is *no distinct peak or variation* in the data. No values or ranges are particularly more common than any other values or ranges.

Outlier

An outlier is an extremely high or extremely low value in the data set. It may be the result of measurement error, in which case, the outlier is not a valid member of the data set. However, it may also be a valid member of the distribution. Unless a measurement error is identified, the experimenter cannot know for certain if an outlier is or is not a member of the distribution. There are arbitrary methods that can be employed to designate an extreme value as an outlier. One method designates an outlier (or possible outlier) to be any value less than $Q_1 - 1.5(IQR)$ or any value greater than $Q_3 + 1.5(IQR)$.

Data Analysis

Simple Regression

In statistics, **simple regression** is using an equation to represent a relation between independent and dependent variables. The independent variable is also referred to as the explanatory variable or the predictor and is generally represented by the variable x in the equation. The dependent variable, usually represented by the variable y, is also referred to as the response variable. The equation may be any type of function – linear, quadratic, exponential, etc. The best way to handle this task is to use the regression feature of your graphing calculator. This will easily give you the curve of best fit and provide you with the coefficients and other information you need to derive an equation.

LINE OF BEST FIT

In a scatter plot, the **line of best fit** is the line that best shows the trends of the data. The line of best fit is given by the equation $\hat{y} = ax + b$, where a and b are the regression coefficients. The regression coefficient a is also the slope of the line of best fit, and b is also the y-coordinate of the point at which the line of best fit crosses the y-axis. Not every point on the scatter plot will be on the line of best fit. The differences between the y-values of the points in the scatter plot and the corresponding y-values according to the equation of the line of best fit are the residuals. The line of best fit is also called the least-squares regression line because it is also the line that has the lowest sum of the squares of the residuals.

CORRELATION COEFFICIENT

The **correlation coefficient** is the numerical value that indicates how strong the relationship is between the two variables of a linear regression equation. A correlation coefficient of –1 is a perfect negative correlation. A correlation coefficient of +1 is a perfect positive correlation. Correlation coefficients close to –1 or +1 are very strong correlations. A correlation coefficient equal to zero indicates there is no correlation between the two variables. This test is a good indicator of whether or not the equation for the line of best fit is accurate. The formula for the correlation coefficient is

$$r = \frac{\sum_{i=1}^{n}(x_i - \bar{x})(y_i - \bar{y})}{\sqrt{\sum_{i=1}^{n}(x_i - \bar{x})^2}\sqrt{\sum_{i=1}^{n}(y_i - \bar{y})^2}}$$

where r is the correlation coefficient, n is the number of data values in the set, (x_i, y_i) is a point in the set, and $\bar{x}$ and $\bar{y}$ are the means.

Z-SCORE

A **z-score** is an indication of how many standard deviations a given value falls from the sample mean. To calculate a z-score, use the formula:

$$\frac{x - \bar{x}}{\sigma}$$

In this formula x is the data value, $\bar{x}$ is the mean of the sample data, and σ is the standard deviation of the population. If the z-score is positive, the data value lies above the mean. If the z-score is negative, the data value falls below the mean. These scores are useful in interpreting data such as standardized test scores, where every piece of data in the set has been counted, rather than just a small random sample. In cases where standard deviations are calculated from a random sample of the set, the z-scores will not be as accurate.

CENTRAL LIMIT THEOREM

According to the **central limit theorem**, regardless of what the original distribution of a sample is, the distribution of the means tends to get closer and closer to a normal distribution as the sample size gets larger and larger (this is necessary because the sample is becoming more all-encompassing of the elements of the population). As the sample size gets larger, the distribution of the sample mean will approach a normal distribution with a mean of the population mean and a variance of the population variance divided by the sample size.

MEASURES OF CENTRAL TENDENCY

A **measure of central tendency** is a statistical value that gives a reasonable estimate for the center of a group of data. There are several different ways of describing the measure of central tendency. Each one has a unique way it is calculated, and each one gives a slightly different perspective on the data set. Whenever you give a measure of central tendency, always make sure the units are the same. If the data has different units, such as hours, minutes, and seconds, convert all the data to the same unit, and use the same unit in the measure of central tendency. If no units are given in the data, do not give units for the measure of central tendency.

MEAN

The **statistical mean** of a group of data is the same as the arithmetic average of that group. To find the mean of a set of data, first convert each value to the same units, if necessary. Then find the sum of all the values, and count the total number of data values, making sure you take into consideration each individual value. If a value appears more than once, count it more than once. Divide the sum of the values by the total number of values and apply the units, if any. Note that the mean does not have to be one of the data values in the set, and may not divide evenly.

$$\text{mean} = \frac{\text{sum of the data values}}{\text{quantity of data values}}$$

For instance, the mean of the data set {88, 72, 61, 90, 97, 68, 88, 79, 86, 93, 97, 71, 80, 84, 89} would be the sum of the fifteen numbers divided by 15:

$$\frac{88 + 72 + 61 + 90 + 97 + 68 + 88 + 79 + 86 + 93 + 97 + 71 + 80 + 84 + 89}{15} = \frac{1242}{15}$$
$$= 82.8$$

While the mean is relatively easy to calculate and averages are understood by most people, the mean can be very misleading if it is used as the sole measure of central tendency. If the data set has outliers (data values that are unusually high or unusually low compared to the rest of the data values), the mean can be very distorted, especially if the data set has a small number of values. If unusually high values are countered with unusually low values, the mean is not affected as much. For example, if five of twenty students in a class get a 100 on a test, but the other 15 students have an average of 60 on the same test, the class average would appear as 70. Whenever the mean is skewed by outliers, it is always a good idea to include the median as an alternate measure of central tendency.

A **weighted mean**, or weighted average, is a mean that uses "weighted" values. The formula is weighted mean $= \frac{w_1x_1+w_2x_2+w_3x_3...+w_nx_n}{w_1+w_2+w_3+\cdots+w_n}$. Weighted values, such as $w_1, w_2, w_3, ... w_n$ are assigned to each member of the set $x_1, x_2, x_3, ... x_n$. When calculating the weighted mean, make sure a weight value for each member of the set is used.

Review Video: All About Averages
Visit mometrix.com/academy and enter code: 176521

MEDIAN

The **statistical median** is the value in the middle of the set of data. To find the median, list all data values in order from smallest to largest or from largest to smallest. Any value that is repeated in the set must be listed the number of times it appears. If there are an odd number of data values, the median is the value in the middle of the list. If there is an even number of data values, the median is the arithmetic mean of the two middle values.

For example, the median of the data set {88, 72, 61, 90, 97, 68, 88, 79, 86, 93, 97, 71, 80, 84, 88} is 86 since the ordered set is {61, 68, 71, 72, 79, 80, 84, **86**, 88, 88, 88, 90, 93, 97, 97}.

The big disadvantage of using the median as a measure of central tendency is that is relies solely on a value's relative size as compared to the other values in the set. When the individual values in a set of data are evenly dispersed, the median can be an accurate tool. However, if there is a group of rather large values or a group of rather small values that are not offset by a different group of values, the information that can be inferred from the median may not be accurate because the distribution of values is skewed.

Mode

The **statistical mode** is the data value that occurs the greatest number of times in the data set. It is possible to have exactly one mode, more than one mode, or no mode. To find the mode of a set of data, arrange the data like you do to find the median (all values in order, listing all multiples of data values). Count the number of times each value appears in the data set. If all values appear an equal number of times, there is no mode. If one value appears more than any other value, that value is the mode. If two or more values appear the same number of times, but there are other values that appear fewer times and no values that appear more times, all of those values are the modes.

For example, the mode of the data set {**88**, 72, 61, 90, 97, 68, **88**, 79, 86, 93, 97, 71, 80, 84, **88**} is 88.

The main disadvantage of the mode is that the values of the other data in the set have no bearing on the mode. The mode may be the largest value, the smallest value, or a value anywhere in between in the set. The mode only tells which value or values, if any, occurred the greatest number of times. It does not give any suggestions about the remaining values in the set.

Review Video: Mean, Median, and Mode
Visit mometrix.com/academy and enter code: 286207

Frequency Tables

Frequency tables show how frequently each unique value appears in a set. A **relative frequency table** is one that shows the proportions of each unique value compared to the entire set. Relative frequencies are given as percentages; however, the total percent for a relative frequency table will not necessarily equal 100 percent due to rounding. An example of a frequency table with relative frequencies is below.

Favorite Color	Frequency	Relative Frequency
Blue	4	13%
Red	7	22%
Green	3	9%
Purple	6	19%
Cyan	12	38%

Review Video: Data Interpretation of Graphs
Visit mometrix.com/academy and enter code: 200439

CIRCLE GRAPHS

Circle graphs, also known as *pie charts*, provide a visual depiction of the relationship of each type of data compared to the whole set of data. The circle graph is divided into sections by drawing radii to create central angles whose percentage of the circle is equal to the individual data's percentage of the whole set. Each 1% of data is equal to 3.6° in the circle graph. Therefore, data represented by a 90° section of the circle graph makes up 25% of the whole. When complete, a circle graph often looks like a pie cut into uneven wedges. The pie chart below shows the data from the frequency table referenced earlier where people were asked their favorite color.

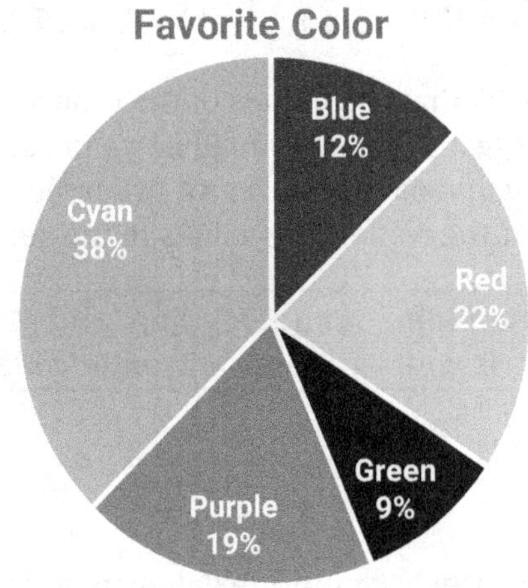

PICTOGRAPHS

A **pictograph** is a graph, generally in the horizontal orientation, that uses pictures or symbols to represent the data. Each pictograph must have a key that defines the picture or symbol and gives the quantity each picture or symbol represents. Pictures or symbols on a pictograph are not always shown as whole elements. In this case, the fraction of the picture or symbol shown represents the same fraction of the quantity a whole picture or symbol stands for. For example, a row with $3\frac{1}{2}$ ears of corn, where each ear of corn represents 100 stalks of corn in a field, would equal $3\frac{1}{2} \times 100 = 350$ stalks of corn in the field.

Review Video: Pictographs
Visit mometrix.com/academy and enter code: 147860

Line Graphs

Line graphs have one or more lines of varying styles (solid or broken) to show the different values for a set of data. The individual data are represented as ordered pairs, much like on a Cartesian plane. In this case, the x- and y-axes are defined in terms of their units, such as dollars or time. The individual plotted points are joined by line segments to show whether the value of the data is increasing (line sloping upward), decreasing (line sloping downward), or staying the same (horizontal line). Multiple sets of data can be graphed on the same line graph to give an easy visual comparison. An example of this would be graphing achievement test scores for different groups of students over the same time period to see which group had the greatest increase or decrease in performance from year to year (as shown below).

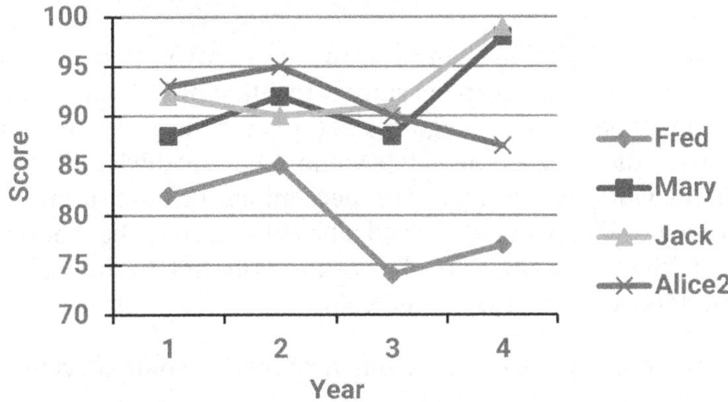

Review Video: How to Create a Line Graph
Visit mometrix.com/academy and enter code: 480147

Line Plots

A **line plot**, also known as a *dot plot*, has plotted points that are not connected by line segments. In this graph, the horizontal axis lists the different possible values for the data, and the vertical axis lists the number of times the individual value occurs. A single dot is graphed for each value to show the number of times it occurs. This graph is more closely related to a bar graph than a line graph. Do not connect the dots in a line plot or it will misrepresent the data.

Review Video: Line Plot
Visit mometrix.com/academy and enter code: 754610

Stem and Leaf Plots

A **stem and leaf plot** is useful for depicting groups of data that fall into a range of values. Each piece of data is separated into two parts: the first, or left, part is called the stem; the second, or right, part is called the leaf. Each stem is listed in a column from smallest to largest. Each leaf that has the common stem is listed in that stem's row from smallest to largest. For example, in a set of two-digit numbers, the digit in the tens place is the stem, and the digit in the ones place is the leaf. With a stem and leaf plot, you can easily see which subset of numbers (10s, 20s, 30s, etc.) is the largest. This information is also readily available by looking at a histogram, but a stem and leaf plot also allows you to look closer and see exactly which values fall in that range. Using a sample set of test scores (82, 88, 92, 93, 85, 90, 92, 95, 74, 88, 90, 91, 78, 87, 98, 99), we can assemble a stem and leaf plot like the one below.

Test Scores

Stem	Leaf
7	4 8
8	2 5 7 8 8
9	0 0 1 2 2 3 5 8 9

Review Video: Stem and Leaf Plots
Visit mometrix.com/academy and enter code: 302339

Bar Graphs

A **bar graph** is one of the few graphs that can be drawn correctly in two different configurations – both horizontally and vertically. A bar graph is similar to a line plot in the way the data is organized on the graph. Both axes must have their categories defined for the graph to be useful. Rather than placing a single dot to mark the point of the data's value, a bar, or thick line, is drawn from zero to the exact value of the data, whether it is a number, percentage, or other numerical value. Longer bar lengths correspond to greater data values. To read a bar graph, read the labels for the axes to find the units being reported. Then, look where the bars end in relation to the scale given on the corresponding axis and determine the associated value.

The bar chart below represents the responses from our favorite-color survey.

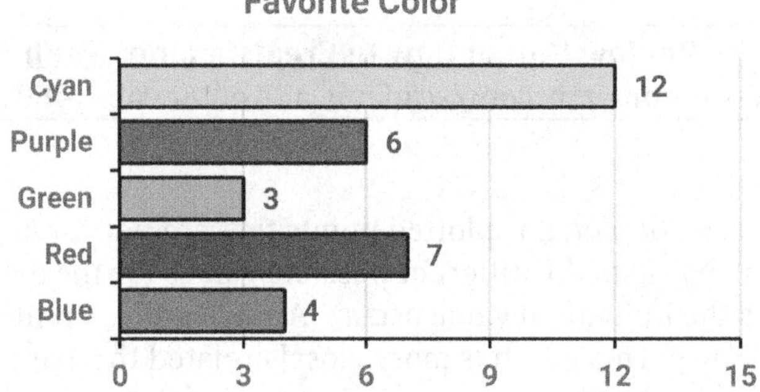

Histograms

At first glance, a **histogram** looks like a vertical bar graph. The difference is that a bar graph has a separate bar for each piece of data and a histogram has one continuous bar for each *range* of data. For example, a histogram may have one bar for the range 0–9, one bar for 10–19, etc. While a bar graph has numerical values on one axis, a histogram has numerical values on both axes. Each range is of equal size, and they are ordered left to right from lowest to highest. The height of each column on a histogram represents the number of data values within that range. Like a stem and leaf plot, a histogram makes it easy to glance at the graph and quickly determine which range has the greatest quantity of values. A simple example of a histogram is below.

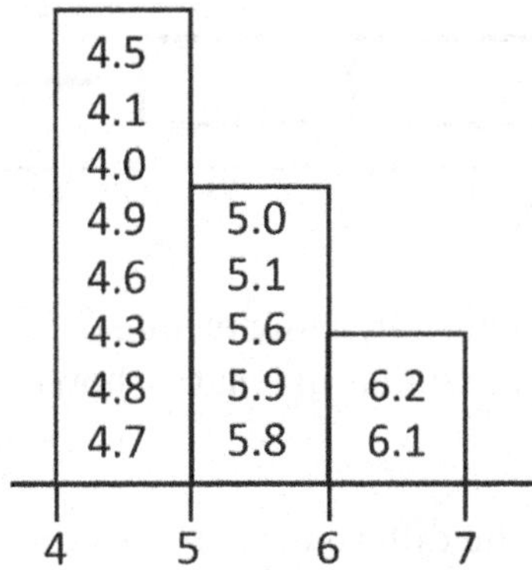

5-Number Summary

The **5-number summary** of a set of data gives a very informative picture of the set. The five numbers in the summary include the minimum value, maximum value, and the three quartiles. This information gives the reader the range and median of the set, as well as an indication of how the data is spread about the median.

Box and Whisker Plots

A **box-and-whiskers plot** is a graphical representation of the 5-number summary. To draw a box-and-whiskers plot, plot the points of the 5-number summary on a number line. Draw a box whose ends are through the points for the first and third quartiles. Draw a vertical line in the box through the median to divide the box in half. Draw a line segment from the first quartile point to the minimum value, and from the third quartile point to the maximum value.

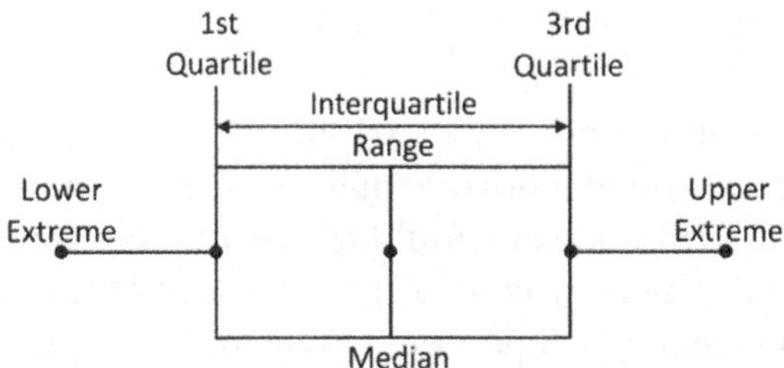

Review Video: Box and Whisker Plots
Visit mometrix.com/academy and enter code: 810817

Example

Given the following data (32, 28, 29, 26, 35, 27, 30, 31, 27, 32), we first sort it into numerical order: 26, 27, 27, 28, 29, 30, 31, 32, 32, 35. We can then find the median. Since there are ten values, we take the average of the 5th and 6th values to get 29.5. We find the lower quartile by taking the median of the data smaller than the median. Since there are five values, we take the 3rd value, which is 27. We find the upper quartile by taking the median of the data larger than the overall median, which is 32. Finally, we note our minimum and maximum, which are simply the smallest and largest values in the set: 26 and 35, respectively. Now we can create our box plot:

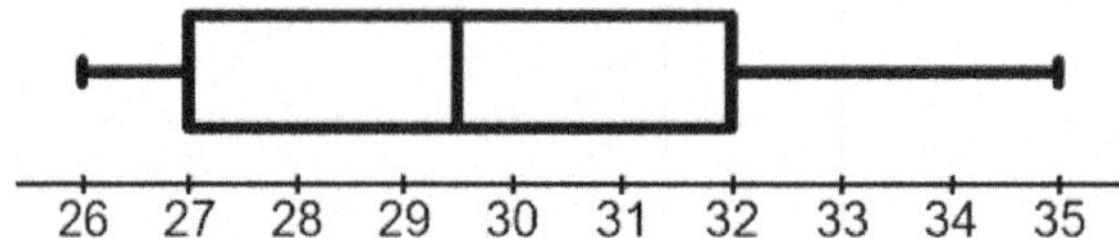

This plot is fairly "long" on the right whisker, showing one or more unusually high values (but not quite outliers). The other quartiles are similar in length, showing a fairly even distribution of data.

INTERQUARTILE RANGE

The **interquartile range, or IQR**, is the difference between the upper and lower quartiles. It measures how the data is dispersed: a high IQR means that the data is more spread out, while a low IQR means that the data is clustered more tightly around the median. To find the IQR, subtract the lower quartile value (Q_1) from the upper quartile value (Q_3).

EXAMPLE

To find the upper and lower quartiles, we first find the median and then take the median of all values above it and all values below it. In the following data set (16, 18, 13, 24, 16, 51, 32, 21, 27, 39), we first rearrange the values in numerical order: 13, 16, 16, 18, 21, 24, 27, 32, 39, 51. There are 10 values, so the median is the average of the 5th and 6th: $\frac{21+24}{2} = \frac{45}{2} = 22.5$. We do not actually need this value to find the upper and lower quartiles. We look at the set of numbers below the median: 13, 16, 16, 18, 21. There are five values, so the 3rd is the median (16), or the value of the lower quartile (Q_1). Then we look at the numbers above the median: 24, 27, 32, 39, 51. Again there are five values, so the 3rd is the median (32), or the value of the upper quartile (Q_3). We find the IQR by subtracting Q_1 from Q_3: $32 - 16 = 16$.

68-95-99.7 RULE

The **68–95–99.7 rule** describes how a normal distribution of data should appear when compared to the mean. This is also a description of a normal bell curve. According to this rule, 68 percent of the data values in a normally distributed set should fall within one standard deviation of the mean (34 percent above and 34 percent below the mean), 95 percent of the data values should fall within two standard deviations of the mean (47.5 percent above and 47.5 percent below the mean), and 99.7 percent of the data values should fall within three standard deviations of the mean, again, equally distributed on either side of the mean. This means that only 0.3 percent of all data values should fall more than three standard deviations from the mean. On the graph below, the normal curve is centered on the y-axis. The x-axis labels are how many standard deviations away from the center you are. Therefore, it is easy to see how the 68-95-99.7 rule can apply.

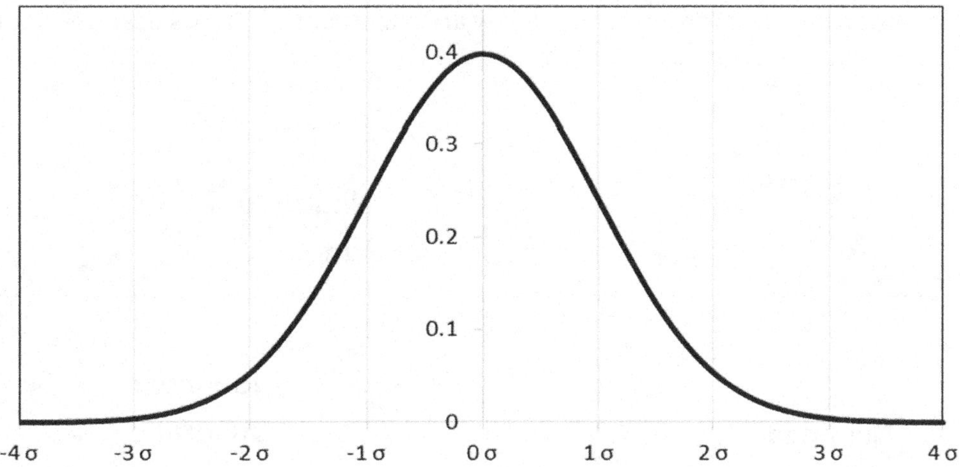

Bivariate Data

Bivariate data is simply data from two different variables. (The prefix *bi-* means *two*.) In a *scatter plot*, each value in the set of data is plotted on a grid similar to a Cartesian plane, where each axis represents one of the two variables. By looking at the pattern formed by the points on the grid, you can often determine whether or not there is a relationship between the two variables, and what that relationship is, if it exists. The variables may be directly proportionate, inversely proportionate, or show no proportion at all. It may also be possible to determine if the data is linear, and if so, to find an equation to relate the two variables. The following scatter plot shows the relationship between preference for brand "A" and the age of the consumers surveyed.

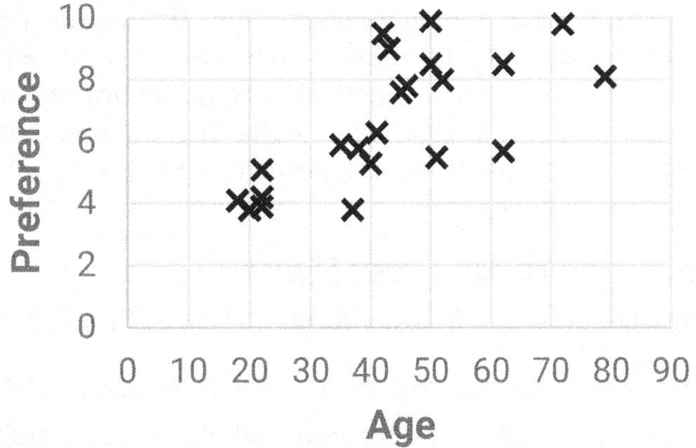

Scatter Plots

Scatter plots are also useful in determining the type of function represented by the data and finding the simple regression. Linear scatter plots may be positive or negative. Nonlinear scatter plots are generally exponential or quadratic. Below are some common types of scatter plots:

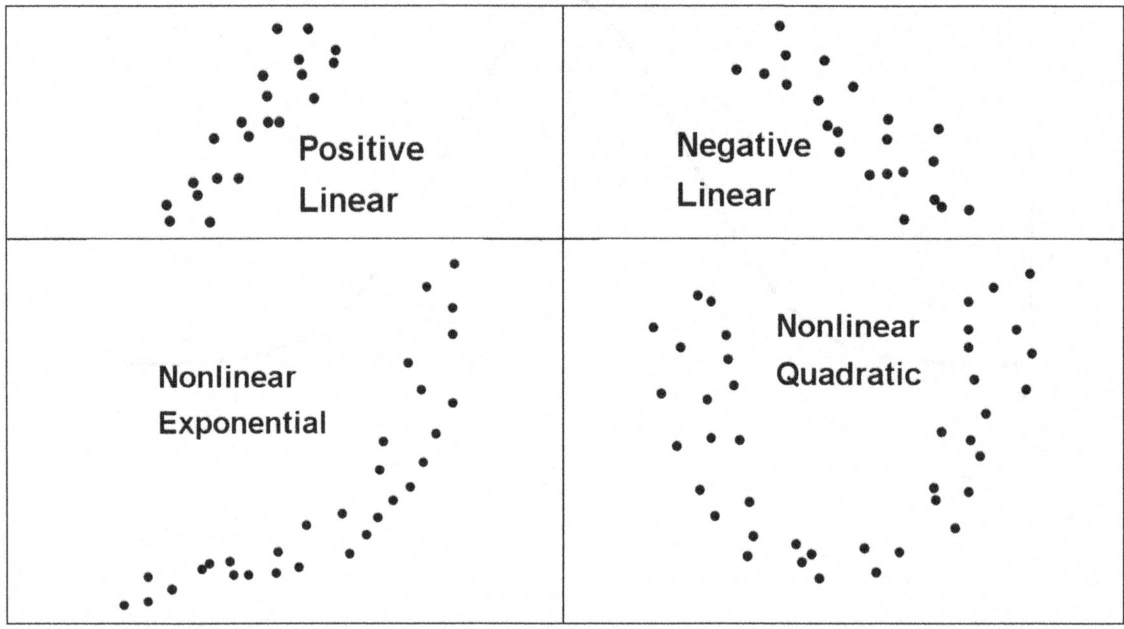

Review Video: What is a Scatter Plot?
Visit mometrix.com/academy and enter code: 596526

Passport to Advanced Math

Passport to Advanced Math Overview

In this section, the questions will deal with more advanced equations and expressions. Students need to be able to create quadratic and exponential equations that model a context. They also need to be able to solve these equations. Students should also be able to create equivalent expressions that involve radicals and rational exponents. Like the Heart of Algebra section, this section will test systems of equations. These systems, however, will involve one linear and one quadratic equation in two variables. Finally, students should be able to perform operations such as addition, subtraction, and multiplication on polynomials.

Question Types in Passport to Advanced Math

The passport to advanced math section will test your knowledge of the following:

- Create a **quadratic** or **exponential function** or equation that models a context.
    - The equation will have rational coefficients and may require multiple steps to simplify or solve the equation.
- Determine the most suitable form of an expression or equation to **reveal a particular trait**, given a context.

- Create **equivalent expressions** involving **rational exponents** and **radicals**, including simplifying or rewriting in other forms.
- Create an **equivalent form** of an algebraic expression by using structure and fluency with operations.
- Solve a quadratic equation having **rational coefficients**.
    - The equation can be presented in a wide range of forms to reward attending to algebraic structure and can require manipulation in order to solve.
- Add, subtract, and multiply **polynomial expressions** and simplify the result.
    - The expressions will have rational coefficients.
- Solve an equation in one variable that contains **radicals** or contains the **variable in the denominator** of a fraction.
    - The equation will have rational coefficients, and the student may be required to identify when a resulting solution is extraneous.
- Solve a system of one linear equation and one quadratic equation.
    - The equations will have rational coefficients.
- Rewrite simple rational expressions.
    - Students will add, subtract, multiply, or divide two rational expressions or divide two polynomial expressions and simplify the result.
    - The expressions will have rational coefficients.
- Interpret parts of **nonlinear expressions** in terms of their context.
    - Students will make connections between a context and the nonlinear equation that models the context to identify or describe the real-life meaning of a constant term, a variable, or a feature of the given equation.
- Understand the **relationship between zeros** and **factors of polynomials**, and use that knowledge to sketch graphs.
    - Students will use properties of factorable polynomials to solve conceptual problems relating to zeros, such as determining whether an expression is a factor of a polynomial based on other information provided.
- Understand a **nonlinear relationship** between two variables by making connections between their **algebraic** and **graphical representations**.
    - The student will select a graph corresponding to a given nonlinear equation; interpret graphs in the context of solving systems of equations; select a nonlinear equation corresponding to a given graph; determine the equation of a curve given a verbal description of a graph; determine key features of the graph of a linear function from its equation; or determine the impact on a graph of a change in the defining equation.
- Use **function notation**, and interpret statements using function notation.
    - The student will use function notation to solve conceptual problems related to transformations and compositions of functions.
- Use structure to **isolate or identify a quantity of interest** in an expression or isolate a quantity of interest in an equation.
    - The student will rearrange an equation or formula to isolate a single variable or a quantity of interest.

Solving a System of Equations Consisting of a Linear Equation and a Quadratic Equation

Algebraically

Generally, the simplest way to solve a system of equations consisting of a linear equation and a quadratic equation algebraically is through the method of substitution. One possible strategy is to solve the linear equation for y and then substitute that expression into the quadratic equation. After expansion and combining like terms, this will result in a new quadratic equation for x, which, like all quadratic equations, may have zero, one, or two solutions. Plugging each solution for x back into one of the original equations will then produce the corresponding value of y.

For example, consider the following system of equations:

$$x + y = 1$$
$$y = (x + 3)^2 - 2$$

We can solve the linear equation for y to yield $y = -x + 1$. Substituting this expression into the quadratic equation produces $-x + 1 = (x + 3)^2 - 2$. We can simplify this equation:

$$\begin{aligned} -x + 1 &= (x + 3)^2 - 2 \\ -x + 1 &= x^2 + 6x + 9 - 2 \\ -x + 1 &= x^2 + 6x + 7 \\ 0 &= x^2 + 7x + 6 \end{aligned}$$

This quadratic equation can be factored as $(x + 1)(x + 6) = 0$. It therefore has two solutions: $x_1 = -1$ and $x_2 = -6$. Plugging each of these back into the original linear equation yields $y_1 = -x_1 + 1 = -(-1) + 1 = 2$ and $y_2 = -x_2 + 1 = -(-6) + 1 = 7$. Thus, this system of equations has two solutions, $(-1,2)$ and $(-6,7)$.

It may help to check your work by putting each x- and y-value back into the original equations and verifying that they do provide a solution.

Graphically

To solve a system of equations consisting of a linear equation and a quadratic equation graphically, plot both equations on the same graph. The linear equation will, of course, produce a straight line, while the quadratic equation will produce a parabola. These two graphs will intersect at zero, one, or two points; each point of intersection is a solution of the system.

For example, consider the following system of equations:

$$y = -2x + 2$$
$$y = -2x^2 + 4x + 2$$

The linear equation describes a line with a y-intercept of $(0,2)$ and a slope of -2.

To graph the quadratic equation, we can first find the vertex of the parabola: the x-coordinate of the vertex is $h = -\frac{b}{2a} = -\frac{4}{2(-2)} = 1$, and the y-coordinate is $k = -2(1)^2 + 4(1) + 2 = 4$. Thus, the vertex lies at $(1,4)$. To get a feel for the rest of the parabola, we can plug in a few more values of x to find more points; by putting in $x = 2$ and $x = 3$ in the quadratic equation, we find that the points

(2,2) and $(3, -4)$ lie on the parabola; by symmetry, so must $(0, 2)$ and $(-1, -4)$. We can now plot both equations:

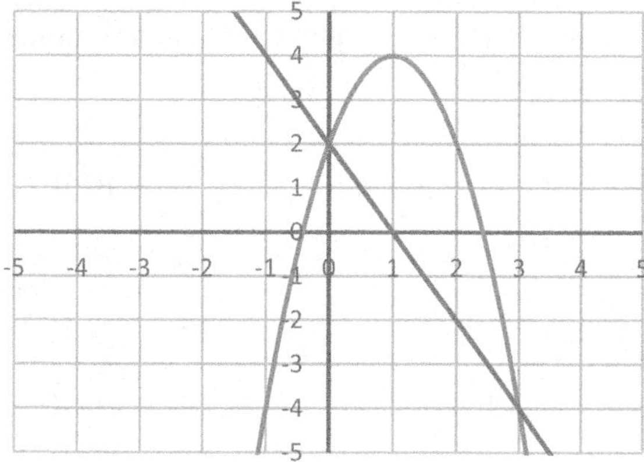

These two curves intersect at the points (0,2) and $(3, -4)$, thus these are the solutions of the equation.

> **Review Video: Solving a System of Equations Consisting of a Linear Equation and Quadratic Equations**
> Visit mometrix.com/academy and enter code: 194870

MONOMIALS AND POLYNOMIALS

A **monomial** is a single constant, variable, or product of constants and variables, such as 7, x, $2x$, or x^3y. There will never be addition or subtraction symbols in a monomial. Like monomials have like variables, but they may have different coefficients. **Polynomials** are algebraic expressions that use addition and subtraction to combine two or more monomials. Two terms make a **binomial**, three terms make a **trinomial**, etc. The **degree of a monomial** is the sum of the exponents of the variables. The **degree of a polynomial** is the highest degree of any individual term.

> **Review Video: Polynomials**
> Visit mometrix.com/academy and enter code: 305005

SIMPLIFYING POLYNOMIALS

Simplifying polynomials requires combining like terms. The like terms in a polynomial expression are those that have the same variable raised to the same power. It is often helpful to connect the like terms with arrows or lines in order to separate them from the other monomials. Once you have determined the like terms, you can rearrange the polynomial by placing them together. Remember to include the sign that is in front of each term. Once the like terms are placed together, you can apply each operation and simplify. When adding and subtracting polynomials, only add and subtract the **coefficient**, or the number part; the variable and exponent stay the same.

> **Review Video: Adding and Subtracting Polynomials**
> Visit mometrix.com/academy and enter code: 124088

The FOIL Method

In general, multiplying polynomials is done by multiplying each term in one polynomial by each term in the other and adding the results. In the specific case for multiplying binomials, there is a useful acronym, FOIL, that can help you make sure to cover each combination of terms. The **FOIL method** for $(Ax + By)(Cx + Dy)$ would be:

F	Multiply the *first* terms of each binomial	$(\overbrace{Ax}^{first} + By)(\overbrace{Cx}^{first} + Dy)$	ACx^2
O	Multiply the *outer* terms	$(\overbrace{Ax}^{outer} + By)(Cx + \overbrace{Dy}^{outer})$	$ADxy$
I	Multiply the *inner* terms	$(Ax + \overbrace{By}^{inner})(\overbrace{Cx}^{inner} + Dy)$	$BCxy$
L	Multiply the *last* terms of each binomial	$(Ax + \overbrace{By}^{last})(Cx + \overbrace{Dy}^{last})$	BDy^2

Then, add up the result of each and combine like terms: $ACx^2 + (AD + BC)xy + BDy^2$.

For example, using the FOIL method on binomials $(x + 2)$ and $(x - 3)$:

$$\begin{aligned} &\text{First:} & (\boxed{x} + 2)(\boxed{x} + (-3)) &\rightarrow & (x)(x) &= x^2 \\ &\text{Outer:} & (\boxed{x} + 2)(x + \boxed{(-3)}) &\rightarrow & (x)(-3) &= -3x \\ &\text{Inner:} & (x + \boxed{2})(\boxed{x} + (-3)) &\rightarrow & (2)(x) &= 2x \\ &\text{Last:} & (x + \boxed{2})(x + \boxed{(-3)}) &\rightarrow & (2)(-3) &= -6 \end{aligned}$$

This results in: $(x^2) + (-3x) + (2x) + (-6)$

Combine like terms: $x^2 + (-3 + 2)x + (-6) = x^2 - x - 6$

Review Video: Multiplying Terms Using the FOIL Method
Visit mometrix.com/academy and enter code: 854792

Dividing Polynomials

Use long division to divide a polynomial by either a monomial or another polynomial of equal or lesser degree.

When **dividing by a monomial**, divide each term of the polynomial by the monomial.

When **dividing by a polynomial**, begin by arranging the terms of each polynomial in order of one variable. You may arrange in ascending or descending order, but be consistent with both polynomials. To get the first term of the quotient, divide the first term of the dividend by the first term of the divisor. Multiply the first term of the quotient by the entire divisor and subtract that product from the dividend. Repeat for the second and successive terms until you either get a remainder of zero or a remainder whose degree is less than the degree of the divisor. If the quotient has a remainder, write the answer as a mixed expression in the form:

$$\text{quotient} + \frac{\text{remainder}}{\text{divisor}}$$

For example, we can evaluate the following expression in the same way as long division:

$$\frac{x^3 - 3x^2 - 2x + 5}{x - 5}$$

$$\begin{array}{r}
x^2 + 2x + 8 \\
x - 5 \,\overline{)\, x^3 - 3x^2 - 2x + 5} \\
-\underline{(x^3 - 5x^2)} \\
2x^2 - 2x \\
-\underline{(2x^2 - 10x)} \\
8x + 5 \\
-\underline{(8x - 40)} \\
45
\end{array}$$

$$\frac{x^3 - 3x^2 - 2x + 5}{x - 5} = x^2 + 2x + 8 + \frac{45}{x - 5}$$

When **factoring** a polynomial, first check for a common monomial factor, that is, look to see if each coefficient has a common factor or if each term has an x in it. If the factor is a trinomial but not a perfect trinomial square, look for a factorable form, such as one of these:

$$x^2 + (a + b)x + ab = (x + a)(x + b)$$
$$(ac)x^2 + (ad + bc)x + bd = (ax + b)(cx + d)$$

For factors with four terms, look for groups to factor. Once you have found the factors, write the original polynomial as the product of all the factors. Make sure all of the polynomial factors are prime. Monomial factors may be *prime* or *composite*. Check your work by multiplying the factors to make sure you get the original polynomial.

Below are patterns of some special products to remember to help make factoring easier:

- Perfect trinomial squares: $x^2 + 2xy + y^2 = (x + y)^2$ or $x^2 - 2xy + y^2 = (x - y)^2$
- Difference between two squares: $x^2 - y^2 = (x + y)(x - y)$
- Sum of two cubes: $x^3 + y^3 = (x + y)(x^2 - xy + y^2)$
    - Note: the second factor is *not* the same as a perfect trinomial square, so do not try to factor it further.
- Difference between two cubes: $x^3 - y^3 = (x - y)(x^2 + xy + y^2)$
    - Again, the second factor is *not* the same as a perfect trinomial square.
- Perfect cubes: $x^3 + 3x^2y + 3xy^2 + y^3 = (x + y)^3$ and $x^3 - 3x^2y + 3xy^2 - y^3 = (x - y)^3$

RATIONAL EXPRESSIONS

Rational expressions are fractions with polynomials in both the numerator and the denominator; the value of the polynomial in the denominator cannot be equal to zero. Be sure to keep track of values that make the denominator of the original expression zero as the final result inherits the same restrictions. For example, a denominator of $x - 3$ indicates that the expression is not defined when $x = 3$ and, as such, regardless of any operations done to the expression, it remains undefined there.

To **add or subtract** rational expressions, first find the common denominator, then rewrite each fraction as an equivalent fraction with the common denominator. Finally, add or subtract the numerators to get the numerator of the answer, and keep the common denominator as the denominator of the answer.

When **multiplying** rational expressions, factor each polynomial and cancel like factors (a factor which appears in both the numerator and the denominator). Then, multiply all remaining factors in the numerator to get the numerator of the product, and multiply the remaining factors in the denominator to get the denominator of the product. Remember: cancel entire factors, not individual terms.

To **divide** rational expressions, take the reciprocal of the divisor (the rational expression you are dividing by) and multiply by the dividend.

Review Video: Rational Expressions
Visit mometrix.com/academy and enter code: 415183

Simplifying Rational Expressions

To simplify a rational expression, factor the numerator and denominator completely. Factors that are the same and appear in the numerator and denominator have a ratio of 1. For example, look at the following expression:

$$\frac{x-1}{1-x^2}$$

The denominator, $(1-x^2)$, is a difference of squares. It can be factored as $(1-x)(1+x)$. The factor $1-x$ and the numerator $x-1$ are opposites and have a ratio of -1. Rewrite the numerator as $-1(1-x)$. So, the rational expression can be simplified as follows:

$$\frac{x-1}{1-x^2}=\frac{-1(1-x)}{(1-x)(1+x)}=\frac{-1}{1+x}$$

Note that since the original expression is only defined for $x \neq \{-1, 1\}$, the simplified expression has the same restrictions.

Review Video: Reducing Rational Expressions
Visit mometrix.com/academy and enter code: 788868

Algebraic Theorems

According to the **fundamental theorem of algebra**, every non-constant, single-variable polynomial has exactly as many roots as the polynomial's highest exponent. For example, if x^4 is the largest exponent of a term, the polynomial will have exactly 4 roots. However, some of these roots may have multiplicity or be complex numbers. For instance, in the polynomial function $f(x) = x^4 - 4x + 3$, the only real root is 1, though it has multiplicity of 2 – that is, it occurs twice. The other two roots, $(-1 - i\sqrt{2})$ and $(-1 + i\sqrt{2})$, are complex, consisting of both real and non-real components.

The **remainder theorem** is useful for determining the remainder when a polynomial is divided by a binomial. The remainder theorem states that if a polynomial function $f(x)$ is divided by a binomial $x - a$, where a is a real number, the remainder of the division will be the value of $f(a)$. If $f(a) = 0$, then a is a root of the polynomial.

The **factor theorem** is related to the remainder theorem and states that if $f(a) = 0$ then $(x - a)$ is a factor of the function.

According to the **rational root theorem,** any rational root of a polynomial function $f(x) = a_n x^n + a_{n-1}x^{n-1} + \cdots + a_1 x + a_0$ with integer coefficients will, when reduced to its lowest terms, be a positive or negative fraction such that the numerator is a factor of a_0 and the denominator is a factor of a_n. For instance, if the polynomial function $f(x) = x^3 + 3x^2 - 4$ has any rational roots, the numerators of those roots can only be factors of 4 (1, 2, 4), and the denominators can only be factors of 1 (1). The function in this example has roots of 1 (or $\frac{1}{1}$) and -2 (or $\frac{-2}{1}$).

Solving Quadratic Equations

Quadratic equations are a special set of trinomials of the form $y = ax^2 + bx + c$ that occur commonly in math and real-world applications. The **roots** of a quadratic equation are the solutions that satisfy the equation when $y = 0$; in other words, where the graph touches the x-axis. There are several ways to determine these solutions including using the quadratic formula, factoring, completing the square, and graphing the function.

Review Video: Quadratic Equations Overview
Visit mometrix.com/academy and enter code: 476276

Review Video: Solutions of a Quadratic Equation on a Graph
Visit mometrix.com/academy and enter code: 328231

Quadratic Formula

The **quadratic formula** is used to solve quadratic equations when other methods are more difficult. To use the quadratic formula to solve a quadratic equation, begin by rewriting the equation in standard form $ax^2 + bx + c = 0$, where a, b, and c are coefficients. Once you have identified the values of the coefficients, substitute those values into the quadratic formula

$$x = \frac{-b \pm \sqrt{b^2 - 4ac}}{2a}$$

Evaluate the equation and simplify the expression. Again, check each root by substituting into the original equation. In the quadratic formula, the portion of the formula under the radical ($b^2 - 4ac$) is called the **discriminant**. If the discriminant is zero, there is only one root: $-\frac{b}{2a}$. If the discriminant is positive, there are two different real roots. If the discriminant is negative, there are no real roots; you will instead find complex roots. Often these solutions don't make sense in context and are ignored.

Review Video: Using the Quadratic Formula
Visit mometrix.com/academy and enter code: 163102

Factoring

To solve a quadratic equation by factoring, begin by rewriting the equation in standard form, $x^2 + bx + c = 0$. Remember that the goal of factoring is to find numbers f and g such that

$(x+f)(x+g) = x^2 + (f+g)x + fg$, in other words $(f+g) = b$ and $fg = c$. This can be a really useful method when b and c are integers. Determine the factors of c and look for pairs that could sum to b.

For example, consider finding the roots of $x^2 + 6x - 16 = 0$. The factors of -16 include, -4 and 4, -8 and 2, -2 and 8, -1 and 16, and 1 and -16. The factors that sum to 6 are -2 and 8. Write these factors as the product of two binomials, $0 = (x-2)(x+8)$. Finally, since these binomials multiply together to equal zero, set them each equal to zero and solve each for x. This results in $x - 2 = 0$, which simplifies to $x = 2$ and $x + 8 = 0$, which simplifies to $x = -8$. Therefore, the roots of the equation are 2 and -8.

Review Video: Factoring Quadratic Equations
Visit mometrix.com/academy and enter code: 336566

Completing the Square

One way to find the roots of a quadratic equation is to find a way to manipulate it such that it follows the form of a perfect square $(x^2 + 2px + p^2)$ by adding and subtracting a constant. This process is called **completing the square**. In other words, if you are given a quadratic that is not a perfect square, $x^2 + bx + c = 0$, you can find a constant d that could be added in to make it a perfect square:

$$x^2 + bx + c + (d - d) = 0; \{\text{Let } b = 2p \text{ and } c + d = p^2\}$$

then:

$$x^2 + 2px + p^2 - d = 0 \text{ and } d = \frac{b^2}{4} - c$$

Once you have completed the square you can find the roots of the resulting equation:

$$\begin{aligned} x^2 + 2px + p^2 - d &= 0 \\ (x+p)^2 &= d \\ x + p &= \pm\sqrt{d} \\ x &= -p \pm \sqrt{d} \end{aligned}$$

It is worth noting that substituting the original expressions into this solution gives the same result as the quadratic formula where $a = 1$:

$$x = -p \pm \sqrt{d} = -\frac{b}{2} \pm \sqrt{\frac{b^2}{4} - c} = -\frac{b}{2} \pm \frac{\sqrt{b^2 - 4c}}{2} = \frac{-b \pm \sqrt{b^2 - 4c}}{2}$$

Completing the square can be seen as arranging block representations of each of the terms to be as close to a square as possible and then filling in the gaps. For example, consider the quadratic expression $x^2 + 6x + 2$:

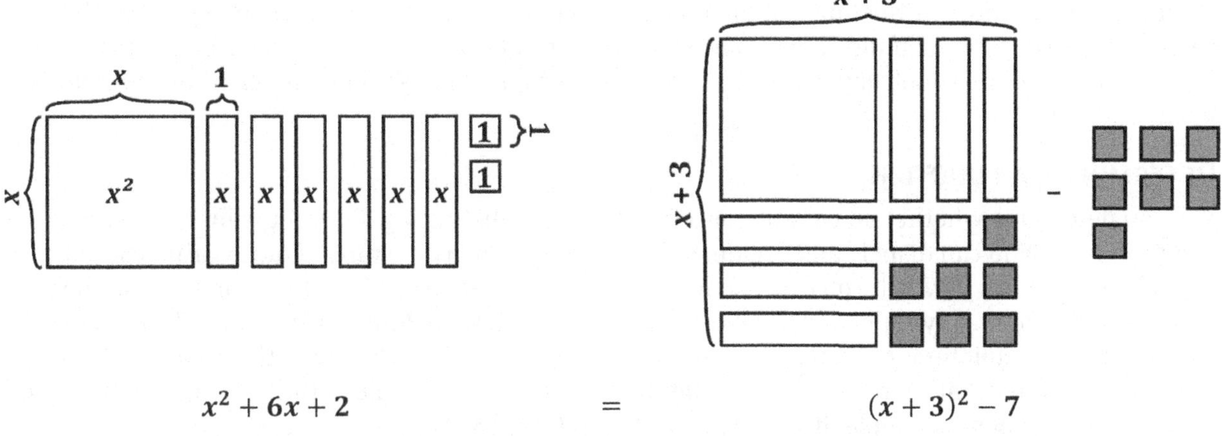

$$x^2 + 6x + 2 \quad = \quad (x + 3)^2 - 7$$

Review Video: Completing the Square
Visit mometrix.com/academy and enter code: 982479

Using Given Roots to Find Quadratic Equation

One way to find the roots of a quadratic equation is to factor the equation and use the **zero product property**, setting each factor of the equation equal to zero to find the corresponding root. We can use this technique in reverse to find an equation given its roots. Each root corresponds to a linear equation which in turn corresponds to a factor of the quadratic equation.

For example, we can find a quadratic equation whose roots are $x = 2$ and $x = -1$. The root $x = 2$ corresponds to the equation $x - 2 = 0$, and the root $x = -1$ corresponds to the equation $x + 1 = 0$.

These two equations correspond to the factors $(x - 2)$ and $(x + 1)$, from which we can derive the equation $(x - 2)(x + 1) = 0$, or $x^2 - x - 2 = 0$.

Any integer multiple of this entire equation will also yield the same roots, as the integer will simply cancel out when the equation is factored. For example, $2x^2 - 2x - 4 = 0$ factors as $2(x - 2)(x + 1) = 0$.

Function and Relation

When expressing functional relationships, the **variables** x and y are typically used. These values are often written as the **coordinates** (x, y). The x-value is the independent variable and the y-value is the dependent variable. A **relation** is a set of data in which there is not a unique y-value for each x-value in the dataset. This means that there can be two of the same x-values assigned to different y-values. A relation is simply a relationship between the x- and y-values in each coordinate but does not apply to the relationship between the values of x and y in the data set. A **function** is a relation where one quantity depends on the other. For example, the amount of money that you make depends on the number of hours that you work. In a function, each x-value in the data set has one unique y-value because the y-value depends on the x-value.

FUNCTIONS

A function has exactly one value of **output variable** (dependent variable) for each value of the **input variable** (independent variable). The set of all values for the input variable (here assumed to be x) is the domain of the function, and the set of all corresponding values of the output variable (here assumed to be y) is the range of the function. When looking at a graph of an equation, the easiest way to determine if the equation is a function or not is to conduct the vertical line test. If a vertical line drawn through any value of x crosses the graph in more than one place, the equation is not a function.

DETERMINING A FUNCTION

You can determine whether an equation is a **function** by substituting different values into the equation for x. You can display and organize these numbers in a data table. A **data table** contains the values for x and y, which you can also list as coordinates. In order for a function to exist, the table cannot contain any repeating x-values that correspond with different y-values. If each x-coordinate has a unique y-coordinate, the table contains a function. However, there can be repeating y-values that correspond with different x-values. An example of this is when the function contains an exponent. Example: if $x^2 = y$, $2^2 = 4$, and $(-2)^2 = 4$.

Review Video: Definition of a Function
Visit mometrix.com/academy and enter code: 784611

FINDING THE DOMAIN AND RANGE OF A FUNCTION

The **domain** of a function $f(x)$ is the set of all input values for which the function is defined. The **range** of a function $f(x)$ is the set of all possible output values of the function—that is, of every possible value of $f(x)$, for any value of x in the function's domain. For a function expressed in a table, every input-output pair is given explicitly. To find the domain, we just list all the x-values and to find the range, we just list all the values of $f(x)$. Consider the following example:

x	-1	4	2	1	0	3	8	6
$f(x)$	3	0	3	-1	-1	2	4	6

In this case, the domain would be $\{-1, 4, 2, 1, 0, 3, 8, 6\}$ or, putting them in ascending order, $\{-1, 0, 1, 2, 3, 4, 6, 8\}$. (Putting the values in ascending order isn't strictly necessary, but generally makes the set easier to read.) The range would be $\{3, 0, 3, -1, -1, 2, 4, 6\}$. Note that some of these values appear more than once. This is entirely permissible for a function; while each value of x must be matched to a unique value of $f(x)$, the converse is not true. We don't need to list each value more than once, so eliminating duplicates, the range is $\{3, 0, -1, 2, 4, 6\}$, or, putting them in ascending order, $\{-1, 0, 2, 3, 4, 6\}$.

Note that by definition of a function, no input value can be matched to more than one output value. It is good to double-check to make sure that the data given follows this and is therefore actually a function.

Review Video: Domain and Range
Visit mometrix.com/academy and enter code: 778133

Review Video: Domain and Range of Quadratic Functions
Visit mometrix.com/academy and enter code: 331768

Writing a Function Rule Using a Table

If given a set of data, place the corresponding x- and y-values into a table and analyze the relationship between them. Consider what you can do to each x-value to obtain the corresponding y-value. Try adding or subtracting different numbers to and from x and then try multiplying or dividing different numbers to and from x. If none of these **operations** give you the y-value, try combining the operations. Once you find a rule that works for one pair, make sure to try it with each additional set of ordered pairs in the table. If the same operation or combination of operations satisfies each set of coordinates, then the table contains a function. The rule is then used to write the equation of the function in "$y = f(x)$" form.

Direct and Inverse Variations of Variables

Variables that vary directly are those that either both increase at the same rate or both decrease at the same rate. For example, in the functions $y = kx$ or $y = kx^n$, where k and n are positive, the value of y increases as the value of x increases and decreases as the value of x decreases.

Variables that vary inversely are those where one increases while the other decreases. For example, in the functions $y = \frac{k}{x}$ or $y = \frac{k}{x^n}$ where k and n are positive, the value of y increases as the value of x decreases and decreases as the value of x increases.

In both cases, k is the constant of variation.

Properties of Functions

There are many different ways to classify functions based on their structure or behavior. Important features of functions include:

- **End behavior**: the behavior of the function at extreme values ($f(x)$ as $x \to \pm\infty$)
- **y-intercept**: the value of the function at $f(0)$
- **Roots**: the values of x where the function equals zero ($f(x) = 0$)
- **Extrema**: minimum or maximum values of the function or where the function changes direction ($f(x) \geq k$ or $f(x) \leq k$)

Classification of Functions

An **invertible function** is defined as a function, $f(x)$, for which there is another function, $f^{-1}(x)$, such that $f^{-1}(f(x)) = x$. For example, if $f(x) = 3x - 2$ the inverse function, $f^{-1}(x)$, can be found:

$$x = 3(f^{-1}(x)) - 2$$
$$\frac{x+2}{3} = f^{-1}(x)$$

$$f^{-1}(f(x)) = \frac{3x - 2 + 2}{3}$$
$$= \frac{3x}{3}$$
$$= x$$

Note that $f^{-1}(x)$ is a valid function over all values of x.

In a **one-to-one function**, each value of x has exactly one value for y on the coordinate plane (this is the definition of a function) and each value of y has exactly one value for x. While the vertical line test will determine if a graph is that of a function, the horizontal line test will determine if a function is a one-to-one function. If a horizontal line drawn at any value of y intersects the graph in more than one place, the graph is not that of a one-to-one function. Do not make the mistake of using the horizontal line test exclusively in determining if a graph is that of a one-to-one function. A one-to-one function must pass both the vertical line test and the horizontal line test. As such, one-to-one functions are invertible functions.

A **many-to-one function** is a function whereby the relation is a function, but the inverse of the function is not a function. In other words, each element in the domain is mapped to one and only one element in the range. However, one or more elements in the range may be mapped to the same element in the domain. A graph of a many-to-one function would pass the vertical line test, but not the horizontal line test. This is why many-to-one functions are not invertible.

A **monotone function** is a function whose graph either constantly increases or constantly decreases. Examples include the functions $f(x) = x$, $f(x) = -x$, or $f(x) = x^3$.

An **even function** has a graph that is symmetric with respect to the y-axis and satisfies the equation $f(x) = f(-x)$. Examples include the functions $f(x) = x^2$ and $f(x) = ax^n$, where a is any real number and n is a positive even integer.

An **odd function** has a graph that is symmetric with respect to the origin and satisfies the equation $f(x) = -f(-x)$. Examples include the functions $f(x) = x^3$ and $f(x) = ax^n$, where a is any real number and n is a positive odd integer.

Review Video: Even and Odd Functions
Visit mometrix.com/academy and enter code: 278985

Constant functions are given by the equation $f(x) = b$, where b is a real number. There is no independent variable present in the equation, so the function has a constant value for all x. The graph of a constant function is a horizontal line of slope 0 that is positioned b units from the x-axis. If b is positive, the line is above the x-axis; if b is negative, the line is below the x-axis.

Identity functions are identified by the equation $f(x) = x$, where every value of the function is equal to its corresponding value of x. The only zero is the point (0,0). The graph is a line with a slope of 1.

In **linear functions**, the value of the function changes in direct proportion to x. The rate of change, represented by the slope on its graph, is constant throughout. The standard form of a linear equation is $ax + cy = d$, where a, c, and d are real numbers. As a function, this equation is commonly in the form $y = mx + b$ or $f(x) = mx + b$ where $m = -\frac{a}{c}$ and $b = \frac{d}{c}$. This is known as the slope-intercept form, because the coefficients give the slope of the graphed function (m) and its y-intercept (b). Solve the equation $mx + b = 0$ for x to get $x = -\frac{b}{m}$, which is the only zero of the function. The domain and range are both the set of all real numbers.

Review Video: Linear Functions
Visit mometrix.com/academy and enter code: 699478

Algebraic functions are those that exclusively use polynomials and roots. These would include polynomial functions, rational functions, square root functions, and all combinations of these functions, such as polynomials as the radicand. These combinations may be joined by addition, subtraction, multiplication, or division, but may not include variables as exponents.

Review Video: Common Functions
Visit mometrix.com/academy and enter code: 629798

Absolute Value Functions

An **absolute value function** is in the format $f(x) = |ax + b|$. Like other functions, the domain is the set of all real numbers. However, because absolute value indicates positive numbers, the range is limited to positive real numbers. To find the zero of an absolute value function, set the portion inside the absolute value sign equal to zero and solve for x. An absolute value function is also known as a piecewise function because it must be solved in pieces—one for if the value inside the absolute value sign is positive, and one for if the value is negative. The function can be expressed as:

$$f(x) = \begin{cases} ax + b \text{ if } ax + b \geq 0 \\ -(ax + b) \text{ if } ax + b < 0 \end{cases}$$

This will allow for an accurate statement of the range. The graph of an example absolute value function, $f(x) = |2x - 1|$, is below:

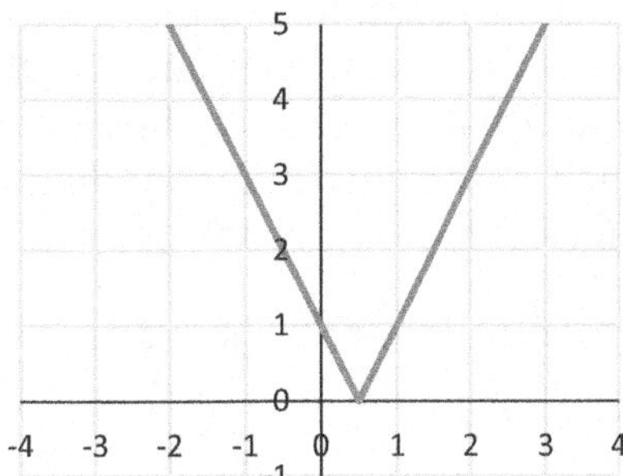

Piecewise Functions

A **piecewise function** is a function that has different definitions on two or more different intervals. The following, for instance, is one example of a piecewise-defined function:

$$f(x) = \begin{cases} x^2, & x < 0 \\ x, & 0 \leq x \leq 2 \\ (x-2)^2, & x > 2 \end{cases}$$

To graph this function, you would simply graph each part separately in the appropriate domain. The final graph would look like this:

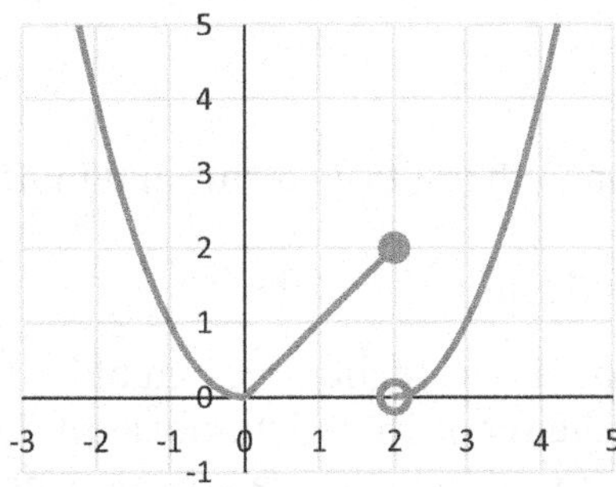

Note the filled and hollow dots at the discontinuity at $x = 2$. This is important to show which side of the graph that point corresponds to. Because $f(x) = x$ on the closed interval $0 \leq x \leq 2$, $f(2) = 2$. The point $(2, 2)$ is therefore marked with a filled circle, and the point (2,0), which is the endpoint of the rightmost $(x-2)^2$ part of the graph but *not actually part of the function*, is marked with a hollow dot to indicate this.

Review Video: Piecewise Functions
Visit mometrix.com/academy and enter code: 707921

Quadratic Functions

A **quadratic function** is a function in the form $y = ax^2 + bx + c$, where a does not equal 0. While a linear function forms a line, a quadratic function forms a **parabola**, which is a u-shaped figure that either opens upward or downward. A parabola that opens upward is said to be a **positive quadratic function,** and a parabola that opens downward is said to be a **negative quadratic function**. The shape of a parabola can differ, depending on the values of a, b, and c. All parabolas contain a **vertex**, which is the highest possible point, the **maximum**, or the lowest possible point, the **minimum**. This is the point where the graph begins moving in the opposite direction. A quadratic function can have zero, one, or two solutions, and therefore zero, one, or two x-intercepts. Recall that the x-intercepts are referred to as the zeros, or roots, of a function. A quadratic function will have only one y-intercept. Understanding the basic components of a quadratic function can give you an idea of the shape of its graph.

Example graph of a positive quadratic function, $x^2 + 2x - 3$:

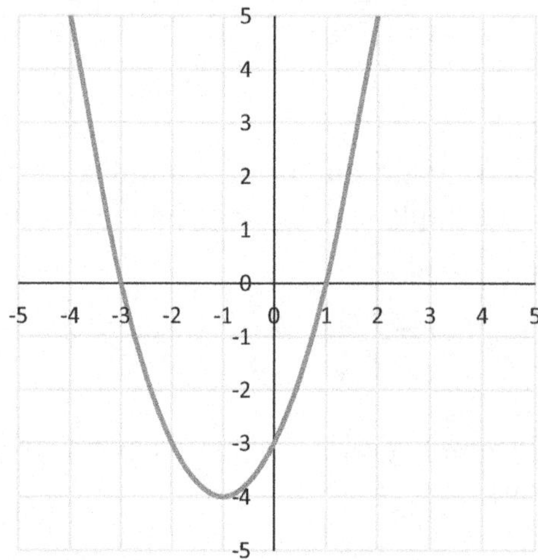

Polynomial Functions

A **polynomial function** is a function with multiple terms and multiple powers of x, such as:

$$f(x) = a_n x^n + a_{n-1} x^{n-1} + a_{n-2} x^{n-2} + \cdots + a_1 x + a_0$$

where n is a non-negative integer that is the highest exponent in the polynomial and $a_n \neq 0$. The domain of a polynomial function is the set of all real numbers. If the greatest exponent in the polynomial is even, the polynomial is said to be of even degree and the range is the set of real numbers that satisfy the function. If the greatest exponent in the polynomial is odd, the polynomial is said to be odd and the range, like the domain, is the set of all real numbers.

Rational Functions

A **rational function** is a function that can be constructed as a ratio of two polynomial expressions: $f(x) = \frac{p(x)}{q(x)}$, where $p(x)$ and $q(x)$ are both polynomial expressions and $q(x) \neq 0$. The domain is the set of all real numbers, except any values for which $q(x) = 0$. The range is the set of real numbers that satisfies the function when the domain is applied. When you graph a rational function, you will have vertical asymptotes wherever $q(x) = 0$. If the polynomial in the numerator is of lesser degree than the polynomial in the denominator, the x-axis will also be a horizontal asymptote. If the numerator and denominator have equal degrees, there will be a horizontal asymptote not on the x-axis. If the degree of the numerator is exactly one greater than the degree of the denominator, the graph will have an oblique, or diagonal, asymptote. The asymptote will be along the line $y = \frac{p_n}{q_{n-1}}x + \frac{p_{n-1}}{q_{n-1}}$, where p_n and q_{n-1} are the coefficients of the highest degree terms in their respective polynomials.

Square Root Functions

A **square root function** is a function that contains a radical and is in the format $f(x) = \sqrt{ax + b}$. The domain is the set of all real numbers that yields a positive radicand or a radicand equal to zero. Because square root values are assumed to be positive unless otherwise identified, the range is all real numbers from zero to infinity. To find the zero of a square root function, set the radicand equal to zero and solve for x. The graph of a square root function is always to the right of the zero and always above the x-axis.

Example graph of a square root function, $f(x) = \sqrt{2x + 1}$:

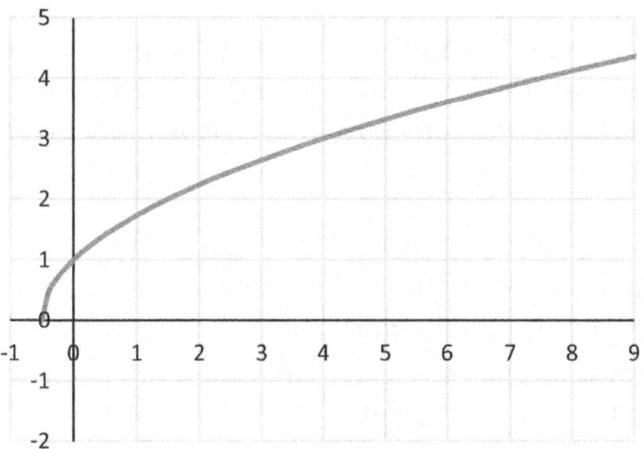

Manipulation of Functions

Translation occurs when values are added to or subtracted from the x- or y-values. If a constant is added to the y-portion of each point, the graph shifts up. If a constant is subtracted from the y-portion of each point, the graph shifts down. This is represented by the expression $f(x) \pm k$, where k is a constant. If a constant is added to the x-portion of each point, the graph shifts left. If a constant is subtracted from the x-portion of each point, the graph shifts right. This is represented by the expression $f(x \pm k)$, where k is a constant.

Stretching, compression, and reflection occur when different parts of a function are multiplied by different groups of constants. If the function as a whole is multiplied by a real number constant greater than 1, $(k \times f(x))$, the graph is stretched vertically. If k in the previous equation is greater than zero but less than 1, the graph is compressed vertically. If k is less than zero, the graph is reflected about the x-axis, in addition to being either stretched or compressed vertically if k is less than or greater than -1, respectively. If instead, just the x-term is multiplied by a constant greater than 1 $(f(k \times x))$, the graph is compressed horizontally. If k in the previous equation is greater than zero but less than 1, the graph is stretched horizontally. If k is less than zero, the graph is reflected about the y-axis, in addition to being either stretched or compressed horizontally if k is greater than or less than –1, respectively.

Review Video: Manipulation of Functions
Visit mometrix.com/academy and enter code: 669117

Applying the Basic Operations to Functions

For each of the basic operations, we will use these functions as examples: $f(x) = x^2$ and $g(x) = x$.

To find the sum of two functions f and g, assuming the domains are compatible, simply add the two functions together: $(f + g)(x) = f(x) + g(x) = x^2 + x$.

To find the difference of two functions f and g, assuming the domains are compatible, simply subtract the second function from the first: $(f - g)(x) = f(x) - g(x) = x^2 - x$.

To find the product of two functions f and g, assuming the domains are compatible, multiply the two functions together: $(f \times g)(x) = f(x) \times g(x) = x^2 \times x = x^3$.

To find the quotient of two functions f and g, assuming the domains are compatible, divide the first function by the second: $\frac{f}{g}(x) = \frac{f(x)}{g(x)} = \frac{x^2}{x} = x\,; x \neq 0$.

The example given in each case is fairly simple, but on a given problem, if you are looking only for the value of the sum, difference, product, or quotient of two functions at a particular x-value, it may be simpler to solve the functions individually and then perform the given operation using those values.

The composite of two functions f and g, written as $(f \circ g)(x)$ simply means that the output of the second function is used as the input of the first. This can also be written as $f(g(x))$. In general, this can be solved by substituting $g(x)$ for all instances of x in $f(x)$ and simplifying. Using the example functions $f(x) = x^2 - x + 2$ and $g(x) = x + 1$, we can find that $(f \circ g)(x)$ or $f(g(x))$ is equal to $f(x + 1) = (x + 1)^2 - (x + 1) + 2$, which simplifies to $x^2 + x + 2$.

It is important to note that $(f \circ g)(x)$ is not necessarily the same as $(g \circ f)(x)$. The process is not always commutative like addition or multiplication expressions. It *can* be commutative, but most often this is not the case.

Step Functions

The double brackets indicate a step function. For a step function, the value inside the double brackets is rounded down to the nearest integer. The graph of the function $f_0(x) = [\![x]\!]$ appears on the left graph. In comparison $f(x) = 2\left[\!\left[\frac{1}{3}(x - 1)\right]\!\right]$ is on the right graph. The coefficient of 2 shows that it's stretched vertically by a factor of 2 (so there's a vertical distance of 2 units between successive "steps"). The coefficient of $\frac{1}{3}$ in front of the x shows that it's stretched horizontally by a factor of 3 (so each "step" is three units long), and the $x - 1$ shows that it's displaced one unit to the right.

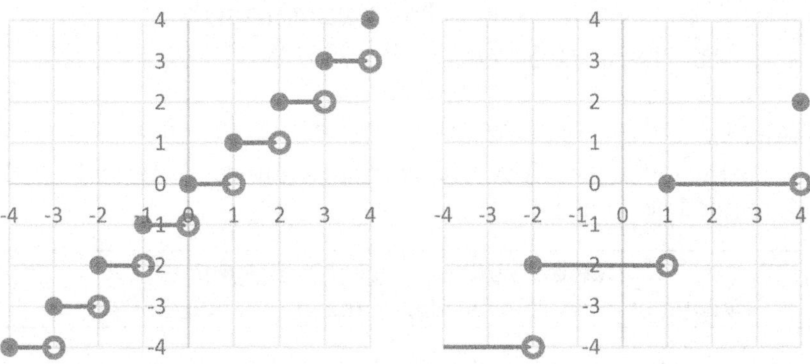

TRANSCENDENTAL FUNCTIONS

Transcendental functions are all functions that are non-algebraic. Any function that includes logarithms, trigonometric functions, variables as exponents, or any combination that includes any of these is not algebraic in nature, even if the function includes polynomials or roots.

EXPONENTIAL FUNCTIONS

Exponential functions are equations that have the format $y = b^x$, where base $b > 0$ and $b \neq 1$. The exponential function can also be written $f(x) = b^x$. Recall the properties of exponents, like the product of terms with the same base is equal to the base raised to the sum of the exponents ($a^x \times a^y = a^{x+y}$) and a term with an exponent that is raised to an exponent is equal to the base of the original term raised to the product of the exponents: $((a^x)^y = a^{xy})$. The graph of an example exponential function, $f(x) = 2^x$, is below:

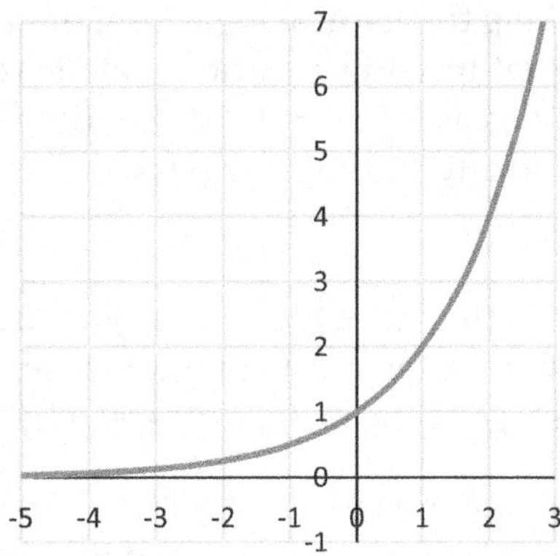

Note in the graph that the y-value approaches zero to the left and infinity to the right. One of the key features of an exponential function is that there will be one end that goes off to infinity and another that asymptotically approaches a lower bound. Common forms of exponential functions include:

Geometric sequences: $a_n = a_1 \times r^{n-1}$, where a_n is the value of the nth term, a_1 is the initial value, r is the common ratio, and n is the number of terms. Note that $a_1 \times r^{1-1} = a_1 \times r^0 = a_1 \times 1 = a_1$.

Population growth: $f(t) = ae^{rt}$, where $f(t)$ is the population at time $t \geq 0$, a is the initial population, e is the mathematical constant known as Euler's number, and r is the growth rate.

Review Video: Population Growth
Visit mometrix.com/academy and enter code: 109278

Compound interest: $f(t) = P\left(1 + \frac{r}{n}\right)^{nt}$, where $f(t)$ is the account value at a certain number of time periods $t \geq 0$, P is the initial principal balance, r is the interest rate, and n is the number of times the interest is applied per time period.

Review Video: Interest Functions
Visit mometrix.com/academy and enter code: 559176

General exponential growth or decay: $f(t) = a(1 + r)^t$, where $f(t)$ is the future count, a is the current or initial count, r is the growth or decay rate, and t is the time.

For example, suppose the initial population of a town was 1,200 people. The annual population growth is 5%. The current population is 2,400. To find out how much time has passed since the town was founded, we can use the following function:

$$2{,}400 = 1{,}200e^{0.05t}.$$

The general form for population growth may be represented as $f(t) = ae^{rt}$, where $f(t)$ represents the current population, a represents the initial population, r represents the growth rate, and t represents the time. Thus, substituting the initial population, current population, and rate into this form gives the equation above.

The number of years that have passed were found by first dividing both sides of the equation by 1,200. Doing so gives $2 = e^{0.05t}$. Taking the natural logarithm of both sides gives $\ln(2) = ln(e^{0.05t})$. Applying the power property of logarithms, the equation may be rewritten as $\ln(2) = 0.05t \times \ln(e)$, which simplifies as $\ln(2) = 0.05t$. Dividing both sides of this equation by 0.05 gives $t \approx 13.86$. Thus, approximately 13.86 years passed.

Logarithmic Functions

Logarithmic functions are equations that have the format $y = \log_b x$ or $f(x) = \log_b x$. The base b may be any number except one; however, the most common bases for logarithms are base 10 and base e. The log base e is the natural logarithm, or ln, expressed by the function $f(x) = \ln x$.

Any logarithm that does not have an assigned value of b is assumed to be base 10: $\log x = \log_{10} x$. Exponential functions and logarithmic functions are related in that one is the inverse of the other. If $f(x) = b^x$, then $f^{-1}(x) = \log_b x$. This can perhaps be expressed more clearly by the two equations: $y = b^x$ and $x = \log_b y$.

The following properties apply to logarithmic expressions:

Property	Description
$\log_b 1 = 0$	The log of 1 is equal to 0 for any base
$\log_b b = 1$	The log of the base is equal to 1
$\log_b b^p = p$	The log of the base raised to a power is equal to that power
$\log_b MN = \log_b M + \log_b N$	The log of a product is the sum of the log of each factor
$\log_b \frac{M}{N} = \log_b M - \log_b N$	The log of a quotient is equal to the log of the dividend minus the log of the divisor
$\log_b M^p = p \log_b M$	The log of a value raised to a power is equal to the power times the log of the value

The graph of an example logarithmic function, $f(x) = \log_2(x + 2)$, is below:

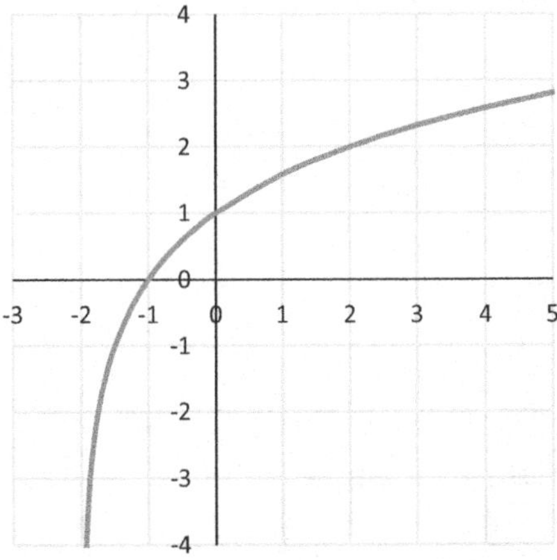

Review Video: Logarithmic Function
Visit mometrix.com/academy and enter code: 658985

Trigonometric Functions

Trigonometric functions are periodic, meaning that they repeat the same form over and over. The basic trigonometric functions are sine (abbreviated 'sin'), cosine (abbreviated 'cos'), and tangent (abbreviated 'tan'). The simplest way to think of them is as describing the ratio of the side lengths of a right triangle in relation to the angles of the triangle.

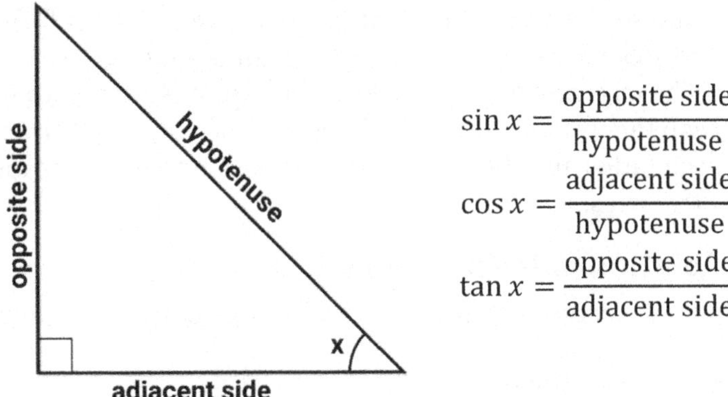

$$\sin x = \frac{\text{opposite side}}{\text{hypotenuse}}$$

$$\cos x = \frac{\text{adjacent side}}{\text{hypotenuse}}$$

$$\tan x = \frac{\text{opposite side}}{\text{adjacent side}}$$

Using sine as an example, trigonometric functions take the form $f(x) = A\sin(Bx + C) + D$, where the **amplitude** is simply equal to A. The **period** is the distance between successive peaks or troughs, essentially the length of the repeated pattern. In this form, the period is equal to $\frac{2\pi}{B}$. As for C, this is the **phase shift** or the horizontal shift of the function. The last term, D, is the vertical shift and determines the **midline** as $y = D$.

For instance, consider the function $f(x) = 2 + \frac{3}{2}\sin\left(\pi x + \frac{\pi}{2}\right)$. Here, $A = \frac{3}{2}$, $B = \pi$, $C = \frac{\pi}{2}$, and $D = 2$, so the midline is at $y = 2$, the amplitude is $\frac{3}{2}$, and the period is $\frac{2\pi}{\pi} = 2$. To graph this function, we center the sine wave on the midline and extend it to a height above and below the midline equal to the amplitude—so this graph would have a minimum value of $2 - \frac{3}{2} = \frac{1}{2}$ and a maximum of $2 + \frac{3}{2} = \frac{7}{2}$. So, the function would be graphed as follows:

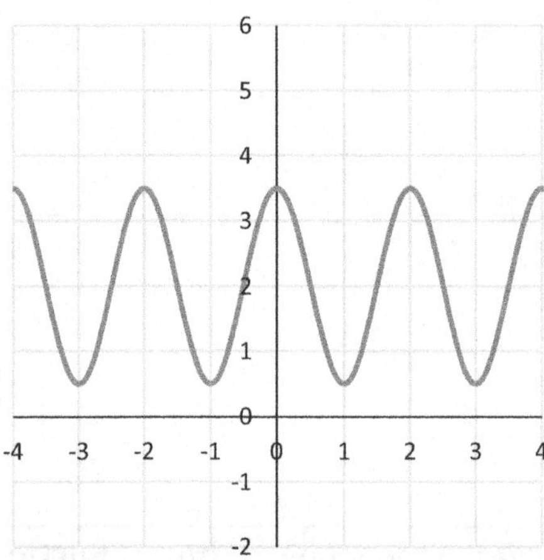

Additional Topics in Math

Additional Topics in Math Overview

Questions in this section will test geometric and trigonometric concepts and the Pythagorean theorem. The student should be familiar with geometric concepts such as volume, radius, diameter, chord length, angle, arc, and sector area. The questions will give certain information about a figure and require the student to solve for some missing information. Any required volume formulas will be provided on the test. The trigonometry questions will require students to use trigonometric ratios and the Pythagorean theorem to solve problems dealing with right triangles. The student should be able to use these ratios and the Pythagorean theorem to solve for missing lengths and angle measures in right triangles.

Question Types in Additional Topics in Math

The additional topics in math section will test your knowledge of the following:

- Solve problems using **volume formulas**.
  - The student will use given information about figures, such as length of a side, area of a face, or volume of a solid, to calculate missing information.

- Any required volume formulas will be provided to students either on the formula sheet or within the question.
- Use **trigonometric ratios** and the **Pythagorean theorem** to solve applied problems involving right triangles.
  - The student will use information about triangle side lengths or angles presented in a context to calculate missing information using the Pythagorean theorem and/or trigonometric ratios.
- Add, subtract, multiply, divide, and simplify **complex numbers**.
- Convert between **degrees** and **radians** and use radians to determine **arc lengths**; use trigonometric functions of radian measure.
  - The student will convert between angle measures in degrees and radians in order to calculate arc lengths by recognizing the relationship between an angle measured in radians and an arc length, evaluating trigonometric functions of angles in radians.
- Apply **theorems about circles** to find arc lengths, angle measures, chord lengths, and areas of sectors.
  - The student will use given information about circles and lines to calculate missing values for radius, diameter, chord length, angle, arc, and sector area.
- Use concepts and theorems about **congruence and similarity** to solve problems about lines, angles, and triangles.
  - The student will use theorems about triangles and intersecting lines to determine missing lengths and angle measures of triangles.
  - The student may also be asked to provide a missing length or angle to satisfy a given theorem.
- Use the relationship between **similarity**, **right triangles**, and **trigonometric ratios**; use the relationship between sine and cosine of **complementary angles**.
  - The student will use trigonometry and theorems about triangles and intersecting lines to determine missing lengths and angle measures of right triangles.
  - The student may also be asked to provide a missing length or angle that would satisfy a given theorem.
- Create or use an equation in two variables to solve a problem about a **circle in the coordinate plane**.
  - The student will create an equation or use properties of an equation of a circle to demonstrate or determine a property of the circle's graph.

Basic Trigonometric Functions

Sine

The **sine** (sin) function has a period of 360° or 2π radians. This means that its graph makes one complete cycle every 360° or 2π. Because $\sin 0 = 0$, the graph of $y = \sin x$ begins at the origin, with the x-axis representing the angle measure, and the y-axis representing the sine of the angle. The graph of the sine function is a smooth curve that begins at the origin, peaks at the point $\left(\frac{\pi}{2}, 1\right)$, crosses the x-axis at $(\pi, 0)$, has its lowest point at $\left(\frac{3\pi}{2}, -1\right)$, and returns to the x-axis to complete one cycle at $(2\pi, 0)$.

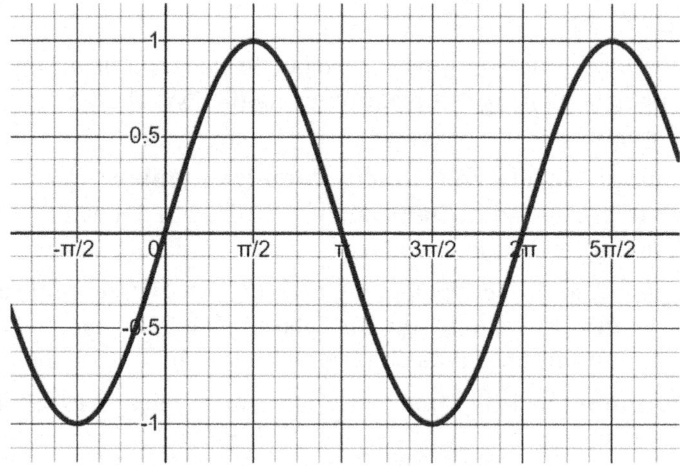

Review Video: Sine
Visit mometrix.com/academy and enter code: 193339

COSINE

The **cosine** (cos) function also has a period of 360° or 2π radians, which means that its graph also makes one complete cycle every 360° or 2π. Because $\cos 0° = 1$, the graph of $y = \cos x$ begins at the point $(0, 1)$, with the x-axis representing the angle measure, and the y-axis representing the cosine of the angle. The graph of the cosine function is a smooth curve that begins at the point $(0,1)$, crosses the x-axis at the point $\left(\frac{\pi}{2}, 0\right)$, has its lowest point at $(\pi, -1)$, crosses the x-axis again at the point $\left(\frac{3\pi}{2}, 0\right)$, and returns to a peak at the point $(2\pi, 1)$ to complete one cycle.

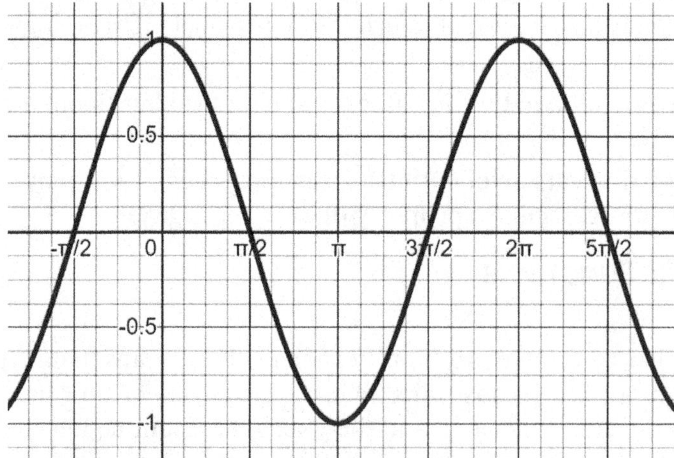

Review Video: Cosine
Visit mometrix.com/academy and enter code: 361120

TANGENT

The **tangent** (tan) function has a period of 180° or π radians, which means that its graph makes one complete cycle every 180° or π radians. The x-axis represents the angle measure, and the y-axis represents the tangent of the angle. The graph of the tangent function is a series of smooth curves that cross the x-axis at every 180° or π radians and have an asymptote every $k \times 90°$ or $\frac{k\pi}{2}$ radians, where k is an odd integer. This can be explained by the fact that the tangent is calculated by dividing the sine by the cosine, since the cosine equals zero at those asymptote points.

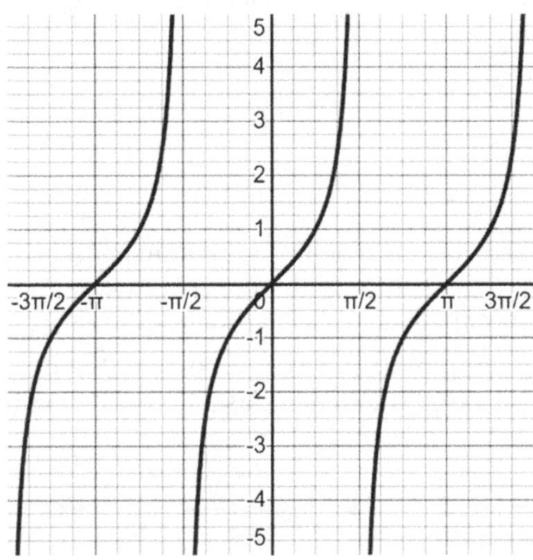

Review Video: Tangent
Visit mometrix.com/academy and enter code: 947639

Complex Numbers

Complex numbers consist of a real component and an imaginary component. Complex numbers are expressed in the form $a + bi$ with real component a and imaginary component bi. The imaginary unit i is equal to $\sqrt{-1}$. That means $i^2 = -1$. The imaginary unit provides a way to find the square root of a negative number. For example, $\sqrt{-25}$ is $5i$. You should expect questions asking you to add, subtract, multiply, divide, and simplify complex numbers. You may see a question that says, "Add $3 + 2i$ and $5 - 7i$" or "Subtract $4 + i\sqrt{5}$ from $2 + i\sqrt{5}$." Or you may see a question that says, "Multiply $6 + 2i$ by $8 - 4i$" or "Divide $1 - 3i$ by $9 - 7i$."

Operations on Complex Numbers

Operations with complex numbers resemble operations with variables in algebra. When adding or subtracting complex numbers, you can only combine like terms—real terms with real terms and imaginary terms with imaginary terms. For example, if you are asked to simplify the expression $-2 + 4i - (-3 + 7i) - 5i$, you should first remove the parentheses to yield $-2 + 4i + 3 - 7i - 5i$. Combining like terms yields $1 - 8i$. One interesting aspect of imaginary numbers is that if i has an exponent greater than 1, it can be simplified. Example: $i^2 = -1$, $i^3 = -i$, and $i^4 = 1$. When multiplying complex numbers, remember to simplify each i with an exponent greater than 1. For example, you might see a question that says, "Simplify $(2 - i)(3 + 2i)$." You need to distribute and multiply to get $6 + 4i - 3i - 2i^2$. This is further simplified to $6 + i - 2(-1)$, or $8 + i$.

Simplifying Expressions with Complex Denominators

If an expression contains an i in the denominator, it must be simplified. Remember, roots cannot be left in the denominator of a fraction. Since i is equivalent to $\sqrt{-1}$, i cannot be left in the denominator of a fraction. You must rationalize the denominator of a fraction that contains a complex denominator by multiplying the numerator and denominator by the conjugate of the denominator. The conjugate of the complex number $a + bi$ is $a - bi$. You can simplify $\frac{2}{5i}$ by simply multiplying $\frac{2}{5i} \times \frac{i}{i}$, which yields $-\frac{2}{5}i$. And you can simplify $\frac{5+3i}{2-4i}$ by multiplying $\frac{5+3i}{2-4i} \times \frac{2+4i}{2+4i}$. This yields $\frac{10+20i+6i-12}{4-8i+8i+16}$ which simplifies to $\frac{-2+26i}{20}$ or $\frac{-1+13i}{10}$, which can also be written as $-\frac{1}{10} + \frac{13}{10}i$.

Points and Lines

A **point** is a fixed location in space, has no size or dimensions, and is commonly represented by a dot. A **line** is a set of points that extends infinitely in two opposite directions. It has length, but no width or depth. A line can be defined by any two distinct points that it contains. A **line segment** is a portion of a line that has definite endpoints. A **ray** is a portion of a line that extends from a single point on that line in one direction along the line. It has a definite beginning, but no ending.

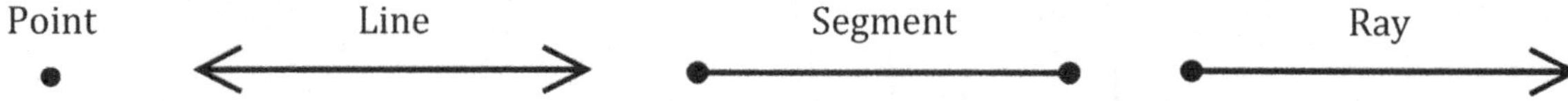

Interactions between Lines

Intersecting lines are lines that have exactly one point in common. **Concurrent lines** are multiple lines that intersect at a single point. **Perpendicular lines** are lines that intersect at right angles. They are represented by the symbol ⊥. The shortest distance from a line to a point not on the line is a perpendicular segment from the point to the line. **Parallel lines** are lines in the same plane that have no points in common and never meet. It is possible for lines to be in different planes, have no points in common, and never meet, but they are not parallel because they are in different planes.

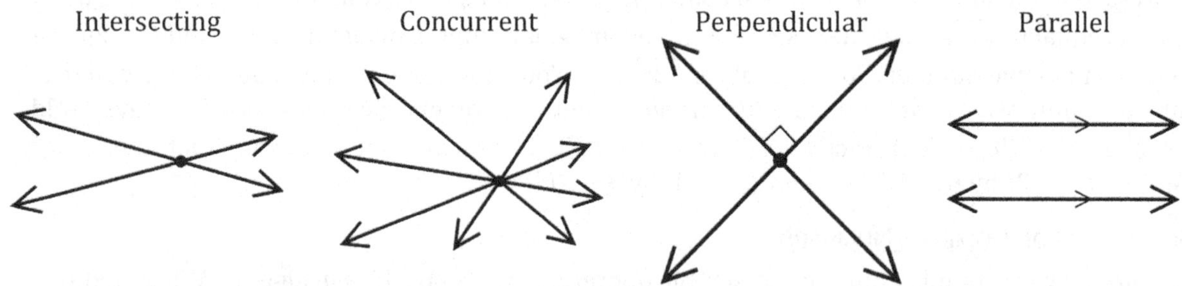

Review Video: Parallel and Perpendicular Lines
Visit mometrix.com/academy and enter code: 815923

A **transversal** is a line that intersects at least two other lines, which may or may not be parallel to one another. A transversal that intersects parallel lines is a common occurrence in geometry. A **bisector** is a line or line segment that divides another line segment into two equal lengths. A

perpendicular bisector of a line segment is composed of points that are equidistant from the endpoints of the segment it is dividing.

Transversal Bisector Perpendicular bisector

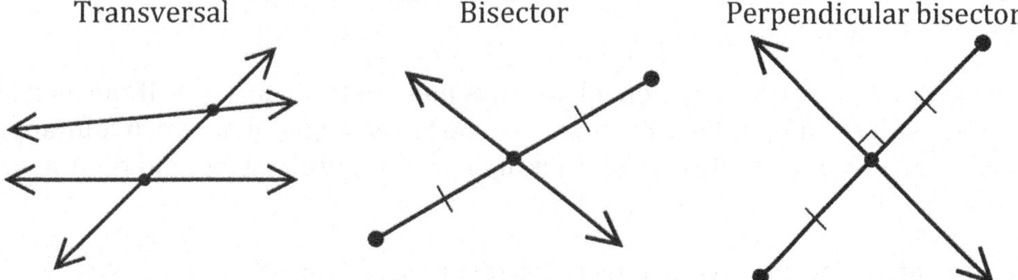

The **projection of a point on a line** is the point at which a perpendicular line drawn from the given point to the given line intersects the line. This is also the shortest distance from the given point to the line. The **projection of a segment on a line** is a segment whose endpoints are the points formed when perpendicular lines are drawn from the endpoints of the given segment to the given line. This is similar to the length a diagonal line appears to be when viewed from above.

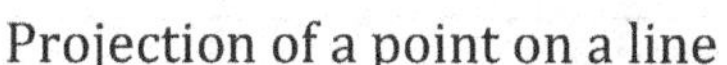

Projection of a segment on a line

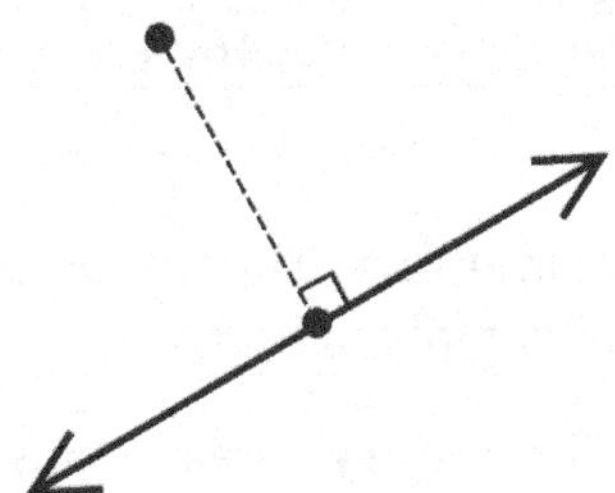

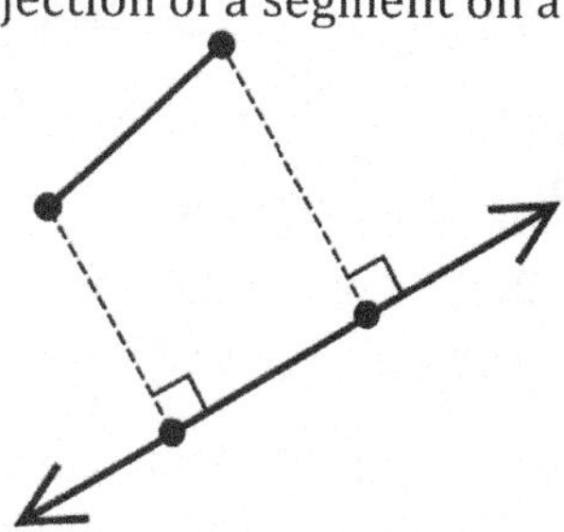

PLANES

A **plane** is a two-dimensional flat surface defined by three non-collinear points. A plane extends an infinite distance in all directions in those two dimensions. It contains an infinite number of points, parallel lines and segments, intersecting lines and segments, as well as parallel or intersecting rays. A plane will never contain a three-dimensional figure or skew lines, which are lines that don't intersect and are not parallel. Two given planes are either parallel or they intersect at a line. A plane may intersect a circular conic surface to form **conic sections**, such as a parabola, hyperbola, circle or ellipse.

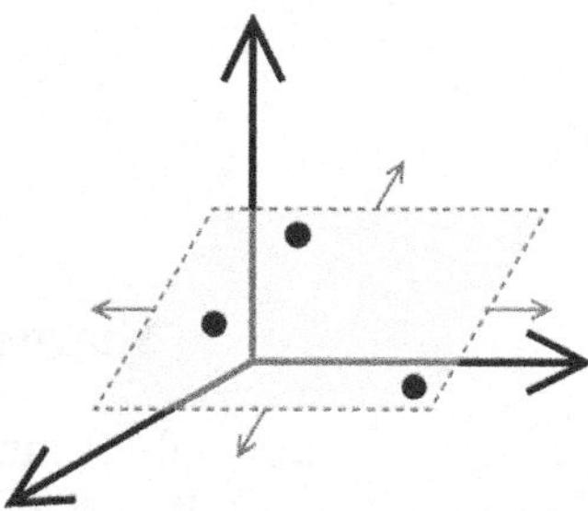

Review Video: Lines and Planes
Visit mometrix.com/academy and enter code: 554267

Angles and Vertices

An **angle** is formed when two lines or line segments meet at a common point. It may be a common starting point for a pair of segments or rays, or it may be the intersection of lines. Angles are represented by the symbol ∠.

The **vertex** is the point at which two segments or rays meet to form an angle. If the angle is formed by intersecting rays, lines, and/or line segments, the vertex is the point at which four angles are formed. The pairs of angles opposite one another are called vertical angles, and their measures are equal.

- An **acute** angle is an angle with a degree measure less than 90°.
- A **right** angle is an angle with a degree measure of exactly 90°.
- An **obtuse** angle is an angle with a degree measure greater than 90° but less than 180°.
- A **straight angle** is an angle with a degree measure of exactly 180°. This is also a semicircle.
- A **reflex angle** is an angle with a degree measure greater than 180° but less than 360°.

A **full angle** is an angle with a degree measure of exactly 360°. This is also a circle.

Review Video: Angles
Visit mometrix.com/academy and enter code: 264624

Relationships Between Angles

Two angles whose sum is exactly 90° are said to be **complementary**. The two angles may or may not be adjacent. In a right triangle, the two acute angles are complementary.

Two angles whose sum is exactly 180° are said to be **supplementary**. The two angles may or may not be adjacent. Two intersecting lines always form two pairs of supplementary angles. Adjacent supplementary angles will always form a straight line.

Two angles that have the same vertex and share a side are said to be **adjacent**. Vertical angles are not adjacent because they share a vertex but no common side.

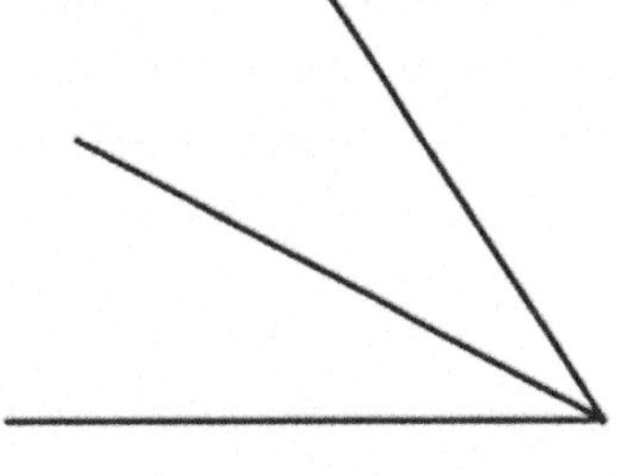

Adjacent
Share vertex and side

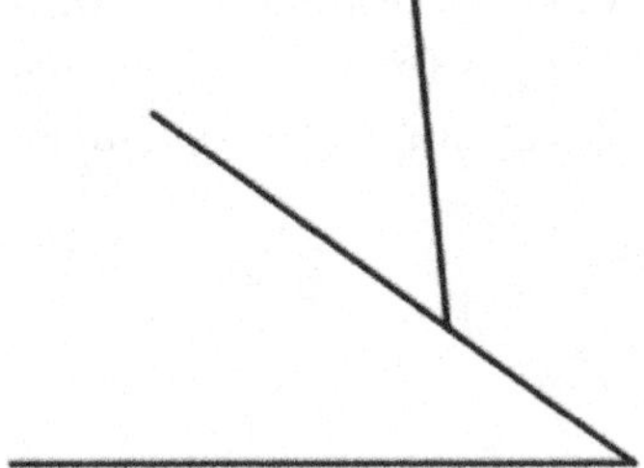

Not adjacent
Share part of a side, but not vertex

When two parallel lines are cut by a transversal, the angles that are between the two parallel lines are **interior angles**. In the diagram below, angles 3, 4, 5, and 6 are interior angles.

When two parallel lines are cut by a transversal, the angles that are outside the parallel lines are **exterior angles**. In the diagram below, angles 1, 2, 7, and 8 are exterior angles.

When two parallel lines are cut by a transversal, the angles that are in the same position relative to the transversal and a parallel line are **corresponding angles**. The diagram below has four pairs of corresponding angles: angles 1 and 5, angles 2 and 6, angles 3 and 7, and angles 4 and 8. Corresponding angles formed by parallel lines are congruent.

When two parallel lines are cut by a transversal, the two interior angles that are on opposite sides of the transversal are called **alternate interior angles**. In the diagram below, there are two pairs of alternate interior angles: angles 3 and 6, and angles 4 and 5. Alternate interior angles formed by parallel lines are congruent.

When two parallel lines are cut by a transversal, the two exterior angles that are on opposite sides of the transversal are called **alternate exterior angles**.

In the diagram below, there are two pairs of alternate exterior angles: angles 1 and 8, and angles 2 and 7. Alternate exterior angles formed by parallel lines are congruent.

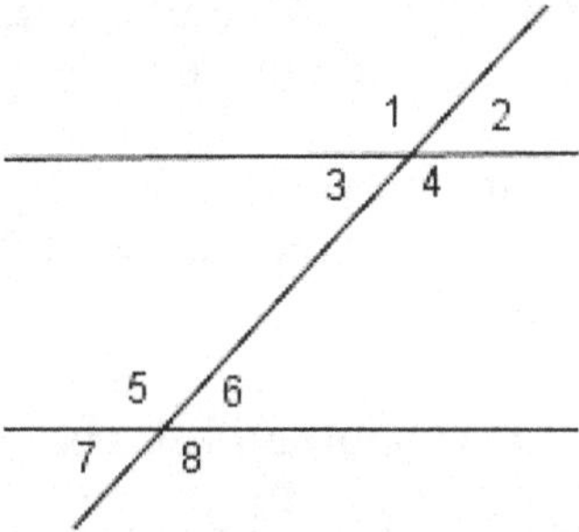

When two lines intersect, four angles are formed. The non-adjacent angles at this vertex are called vertical angles. Vertical angles are congruent. In the diagram, $\angle ABD \cong \angle CBE$ and $\angle ABC \cong \angle DBE$. The other pairs of angles, $(\angle ABC, \angle CBE)$ and $(\angle ABD, \angle DBE)$, are supplementary, meaning the pairs sum to 180°.

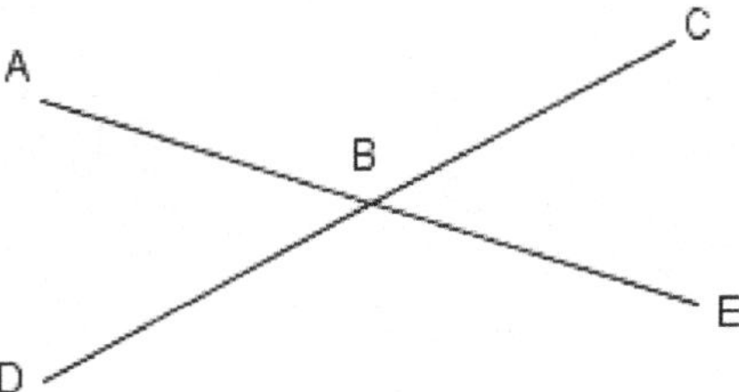

Polygons

A **polygon** is a closed, two-dimensional figure with three or more straight line segments called **sides**. The point at which two sides of a polygon intersect is called the **vertex**. In a polygon, the number of sides is always equal to the number of vertices. A polygon with all sides congruent and all angles equal is called a **regular polygon**. Common polygons are:

$$\begin{aligned} \text{Triangle} &= 3 \text{ sides} \\ \text{Quadrilateral} &= 4 \text{ sides} \\ \text{Pentagon} &= 5 \text{ sides} \\ \text{Hexagon} &= 6 \text{ sides} \\ \text{Heptagon} &= 7 \text{ sides} \\ \text{Octagon} &= 8 \text{ sides} \\ \text{Nonagon} &= 9 \text{ sides} \\ \text{Decagon} &= 10 \text{ sides} \\ \text{Dodecagon} &= 12 \text{ sides} \end{aligned}$$

More generally, an n-gon is a polygon that has n angles and n sides.

Review Video: Intro to Polygons
Visit mometrix.com/academy and enter code: 271869

The sum of the interior angles of an n-sided polygon is $(n - 2) \times 180°$. For example, in a triangle $n = 3$. So the sum of the interior angles is $(3 - 2) \times 180° = 180°$. In a quadrilateral, $n = 4$, and the sum of the angles is $(4 - 2) \times 180° = 360°$.

Review Video: Sum of Interior Angles
Visit mometrix.com/academy and enter code: 984991

Convex and Concave Polygons

A **convex polygon** is a polygon whose diagonals all lie within the interior of the polygon. A **concave polygon** is a polygon with a least one diagonal that is outside the polygon. In the diagram below, quadrilateral $ABCD$ is concave because diagonal $\overline{AC}$ lies outside the polygon and quadrilateral $EFGH$ is convex because both diagonals lie inside the polygon.

Concave

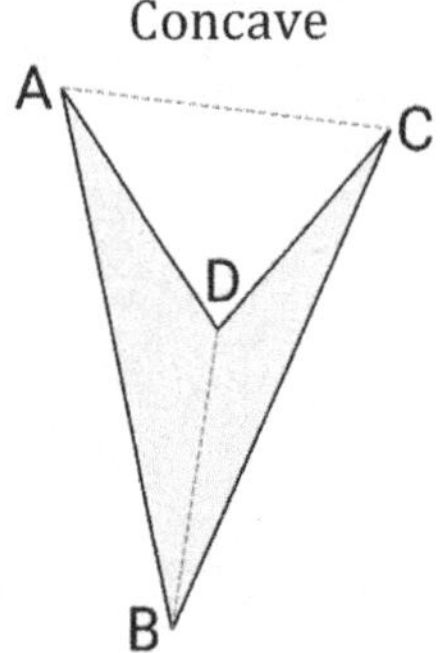

Convex

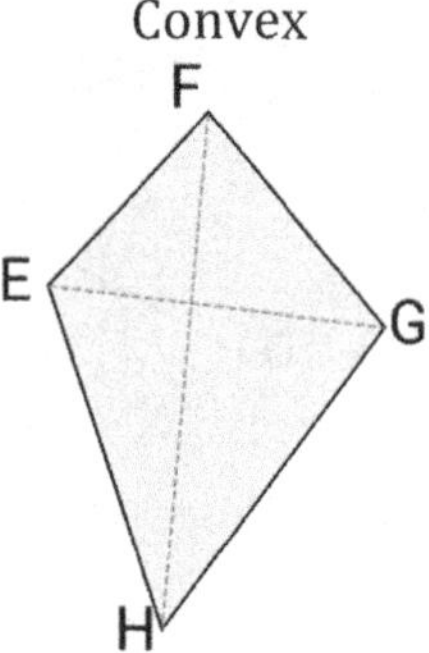

Apothem and Radius

A line segment from the center of a polygon that is perpendicular to a side of the polygon is called the **apothem**. A line segment from the center of a polygon to a vertex of the polygon is called a

radius. In a regular polygon, the apothem can be used to find the area of the polygon using the formula $A = \frac{1}{2}ap$, where a is the apothem, and p is the perimeter.

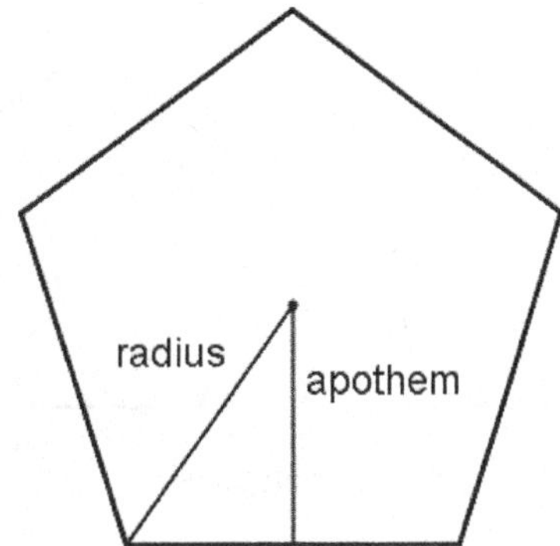

A **diagonal** is a line segment that joins two non-adjacent vertices of a polygon. The number of diagonals a polygon has can be found by using the formula:

$$\text{number of diagonals} = \frac{n(n-3)}{2}$$

Note that n is the number of sides in the polygon. This formula works for all polygons, not just regular polygons.

CONGRUENCE AND SIMILARITY

Congruent figures are geometric figures that have the same size and shape. All corresponding angles are equal, and all corresponding sides are equal. Congruence is indicated by the symbol ≅.

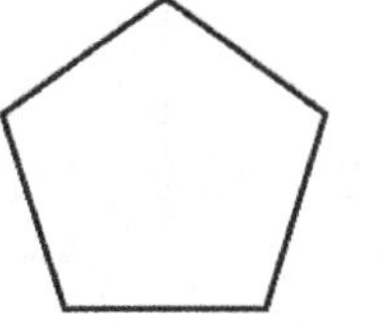 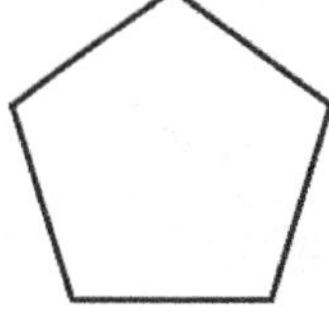

Congruent polygons

Similar figures are geometric figures that have the same shape, but do not necessarily have the same size. All corresponding angles are equal, and all corresponding sides are proportional, but they do not have to be equal. It is indicated by the symbol ~.

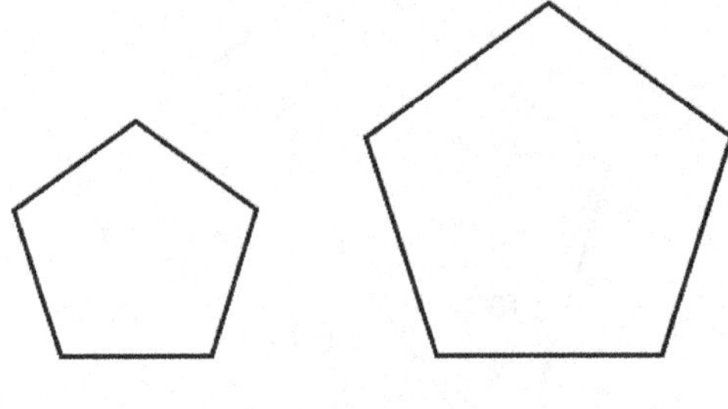

Similar polygons

Note that all congruent figures are also similar, but not all similar figures are congruent.

Review Video: What is a Congruent Shape?
Visit mometrix.com/academy and enter code: 492281

LINE OF SYMMETRY

A line that divides a figure or object into congruent parts is called a **line of symmetry**. An object may have no lines of symmetry, one line of symmetry, or multiple (i.e., more than one) lines of symmetry.

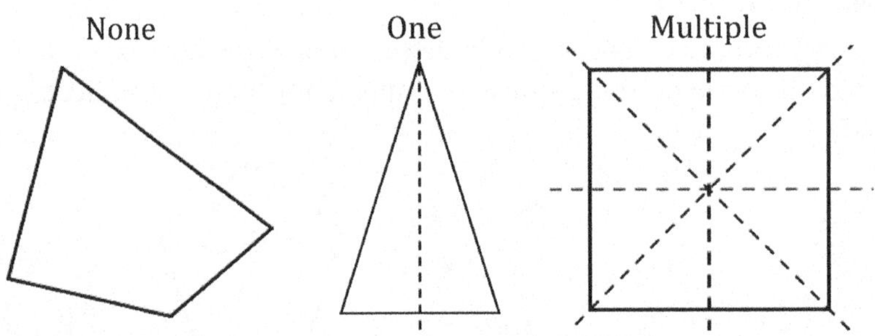

Review Video: Symmetry
Visit mometrix.com/academy and enter code: 528106

TRIANGLES

A triangle is a three-sided figure with the sum of its interior angles being 180°. The **perimeter of any triangle** is found by summing the three side lengths; $P = a + b + c$. For an equilateral triangle, this is the same as $P = 3a$, where a is any side length, since all three sides are the same length.

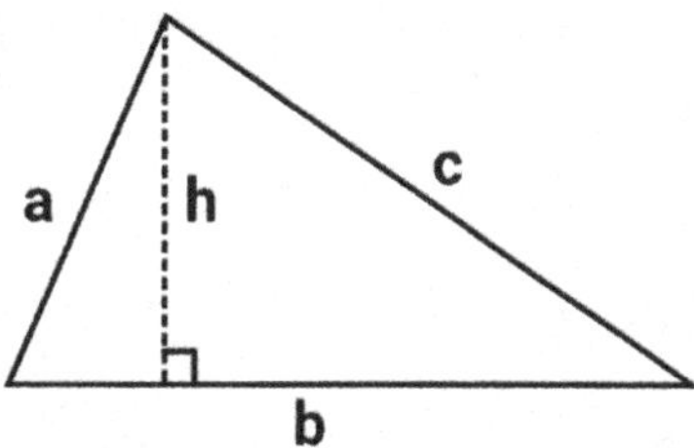

Review Video: Proof that a Triangle is 180 Degrees
Visit mometrix.com/academy and enter code: 687591

Review Video: Area and Perimeter of a Triangle
Visit mometrix.com/academy and enter code: 853779

The **area of any triangle** can be found by taking half the product of one side length referred to as the base, often given the variable b and the perpendicular distance from that side to the opposite vertex called the altitude or height and given the variable h. In equation form that is $A = \frac{1}{2}bh$. Another formula that works for any triangle is $A = \sqrt{s(s-a)(s-b)(s-c)}$, where s is the semiperimeter: $\frac{a+b+c}{2}$, and a, b, and c are the lengths of the three sides. Special cases include isosceles triangles, $A = \frac{1}{2}b\sqrt{a^2 - \frac{b^2}{4}}$, where b is the unique side and a is the length of one of the two congruent sides, and equilateral triangles, $A = \frac{\sqrt{3}}{4}a^2$, where a is the length of a side.

Review Video: Area of Any Triangle
Visit mometrix.com/academy and enter code: 138510

PARTS OF A TRIANGLE

An **altitude** of a triangle is a line segment drawn from one vertex perpendicular to the opposite side. In the diagram that follows, $\overline{BE}$, $\overline{AD}$, and $\overline{CF}$ are altitudes. The length of an altitude is also called the height of the triangle. The three altitudes in a triangle are always concurrent. The point of concurrency of the altitudes of a triangle, O, is called the **orthocenter**. Note that in an obtuse triangle, the orthocenter will be outside the triangle, and in a right triangle, the orthocenter is the vertex of the right angle.

A **median** of a triangle is a line segment drawn from one vertex to the midpoint of the opposite side. In the diagram that follows, $\overline{BH}$, $\overline{AG}$, and $\overline{CI}$ are medians. This is not the same as the altitude, except the altitude to the base of an isosceles triangle and all three altitudes of an equilateral triangle. The point of concurrency of the medians of a triangle, T, is called the **centroid**. This is the same point as the orthocenter only in an equilateral triangle. Unlike the orthocenter, the centroid is always inside the triangle. The centroid can also be considered the exact center of the triangle. Any shape triangle can be perfectly balanced on a tip placed at the centroid. The centroid is also the point that is two-thirds the distance from the vertex to the opposite side.

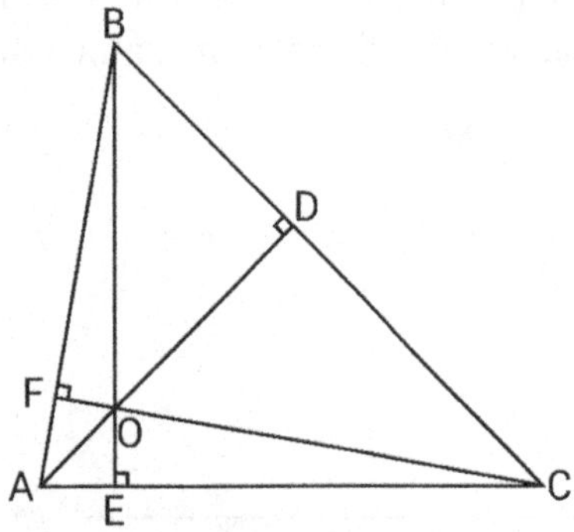

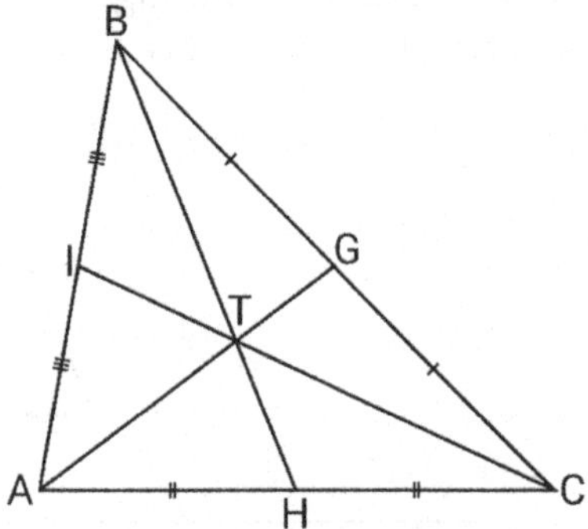

Review Video: Centroid, Incenter, Circumcenter, and Orthocenter
Visit mometrix.com/academy and enter code: 598260

CLASSIFICATIONS OF TRIANGLES

A **scalene triangle** is a triangle with no congruent sides. A scalene triangle will also have three angles of different measures. The angle with the largest measure is opposite the longest side, and the angle with the smallest measure is opposite the shortest side. An **acute triangle** is a triangle whose three angles are all less than 90°. If two of the angles are equal, the acute triangle is also an **isosceles triangle**. An isosceles triangle will also have two congruent angles opposite the two congruent sides. If the three angles are all equal, the acute triangle is also an **equilateral triangle**. An equilateral triangle will also have three congruent angles, each 60°. All equilateral triangles are also acute triangles. An **obtuse triangle** is a triangle with exactly one angle greater than 90°. The other two angles may or may not be equal. If the two remaining angles are equal, the obtuse triangle is also an isosceles triangle. A **right triangle** is a triangle with exactly one angle equal to 90°. All right triangles follow the Pythagorean theorem. A right triangle can never be acute or obtuse.

The table below illustrates how each descriptor places a different restriction on the triangle:

Sides \ Angles	**Acute:** **All angles < 90°**	**Obtuse:** **One angle > 90°**	**Right:** **One angle = 90°**
Scalene: **No equal side lengths**	$90° > \angle a > \angle b > \angle c$ $x > y > z$	$\angle a > 90° > \angle b > \angle c$ $x > y > z$	$90° = \angle a > \angle b > \angle c$ $x > y > z$
Isosceles: **Two equal side lengths**	$90° > \angle a, \angle b, or\ \angle c$ $\angle b = \angle c, \quad y = z$	$\angle a > 90° > \angle b = \angle c$ $x > y = z$	$\angle a = 90°$ $\angle b = \angle c = 45°$ $x > y = z$
Equilateral: **Three equal side lengths**	$60° = \angle a = \angle b = \angle c$ $x = y = z$		

Review Video: Introduction to Types of Triangles
Visit mometrix.com/academy and enter code: 511711

General Rules for Triangles

The **triangle inequality theorem** states that the sum of the measures of any two sides of a triangle is always greater than the measure of the third side. If the sum of the measures of two sides were equal to the third side, a triangle would be impossible because the two sides would lie flat across the third side and there would be no vertex. If the sum of the measures of two of the sides was less than the third side, a closed figure would be impossible because the two shortest sides would never meet. In other words, for a triangle with sides lengths A, B, and C: $A + B > C$, $B + C > A$, and $A + C > B$.

The sum of the measures of the interior angles of a triangle is always 180°. Therefore, a triangle can never have more than one angle greater than or equal to 90°.

In any triangle, the angles opposite congruent sides are congruent, and the sides opposite congruent angles are congruent. The largest angle is always opposite the longest side, and the smallest angle is always opposite the shortest side.

The line segment that joins the midpoints of any two sides of a triangle is always parallel to the third side and exactly half the length of the third side.

Review Video: General Rules (Triangle Inequality Theorem)
Visit mometrix.com/academy and enter code: 166488

Similarity and Congruence Rules

Similar triangles are triangles whose corresponding angles are equal and whose corresponding sides are proportional. Represented by AAA. Similar triangles whose corresponding sides are congruent are also congruent triangles.

Triangles can be shown to be **congruent** in 5 ways:

- **SSS**: Three sides of one triangle are congruent to the three corresponding sides of the second triangle.
- **SAS**: Two sides and the included angle (the angle formed by those two sides) of one triangle are congruent to the corresponding two sides and included angle of the second triangle.
- **ASA**: Two angles and the included side (the side that joins the two angles) of one triangle are congruent to the corresponding two angles and included side of the second triangle.
- **AAS**: Two angles and a non-included side of one triangle are congruent to the corresponding two angles and non-included side of the second triangle.
- **HL**: The hypotenuse and leg of one right triangle are congruent to the corresponding hypotenuse and leg of the second right triangle.

Review Video: Similar Triangles
Visit mometrix.com/academy and enter code: 398538

Pythagorean Theorem

The side of a triangle opposite the right angle is called the **hypotenuse**. The other two sides are called the legs. The Pythagorean theorem states a relationship among the legs and hypotenuse of a right triangle: $(a^2 + b^2 = c^2)$, where a and b are the lengths of the legs of a right triangle, and c is the length of the hypotenuse. Note that this formula will only work with right triangles.

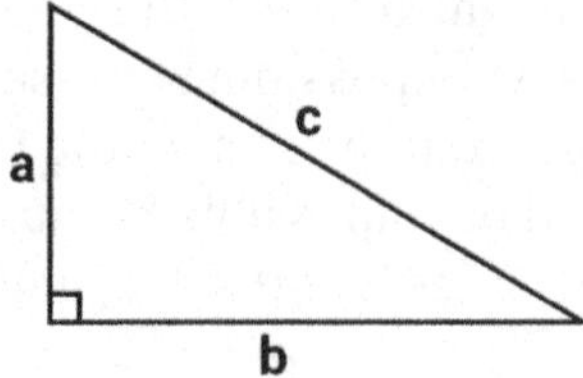

Review Video: Pythagorean Theorem
Visit mometrix.com/academy and enter code: 906576

TRIGONOMETRIC FORMULAS

In the diagram below, angle C is the right angle, and side c is the hypotenuse. Side a is the side opposite to angle A and side b is the side opposite to angle B. Using ratios of side lengths as a means to calculate the sine, cosine, and tangent of an acute angle only works for right triangles.

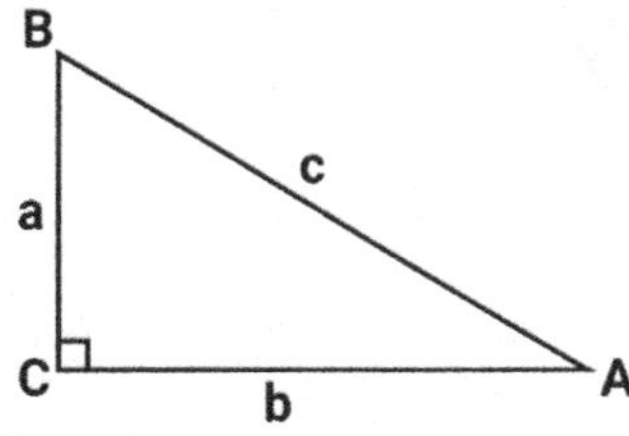

$$\sin A = \frac{\text{opposite side}}{\text{hypotenuse}} = \frac{a}{c} \qquad \csc A = \frac{1}{\sin A} = \frac{\text{hypotenuse}}{\text{opposite side}} = \frac{c}{a}$$

$$\cos A = \frac{\text{adjacent side}}{\text{hypotenuse}} = \frac{b}{c} \qquad \sec A = \frac{1}{\cos A} = \frac{\text{hypotenuse}}{\text{adjacent side}} = \frac{c}{b}$$

$$\tan A = \frac{\text{opposite side}}{\text{adjacent side}} = \frac{a}{b} \qquad \cot A = \frac{1}{\tan A} = \frac{\text{adjacent side}}{\text{opposite side}} = \frac{b}{a}$$

LAWS OF SINES AND COSINES

The **law of sines** states that $\frac{\sin A}{a} = \frac{\sin B}{b} = \frac{\sin C}{c}$, where A, B, and C are the angles of a triangle, and a, b, and c are the sides opposite their respective angles. This formula will work with all triangles, not just right triangles.

The **law of cosines** is given by the formula $c^2 = a^2 + b^2 - 2ab(\cos C)$, where a, b, and c are the sides of a triangle, and C is the angle opposite side c. This is a generalized form of the Pythagorean theorem that can be used on any triangle.

Review Video: Law of Sines
Visit mometrix.com/academy and enter code: 206844

Review Video: Law of Cosines
Visit mometrix.com/academy and enter code: 158911

QUADRILATERALS

A **quadrilateral** is a closed two-dimensional geometric figure that has four straight sides. The sum of the interior angles of any quadrilateral is 360°.

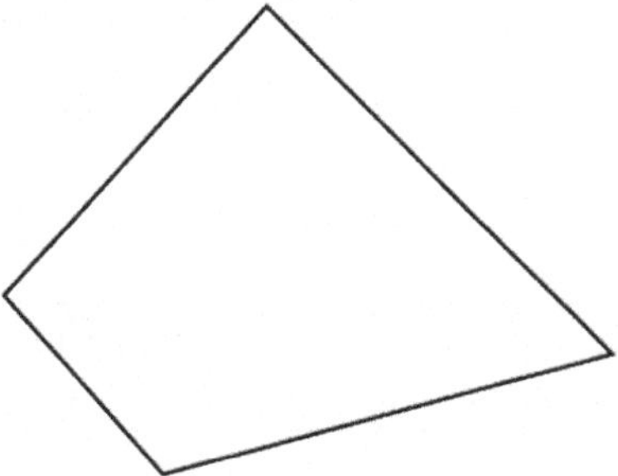

Review Video: Diagonals of Parallelograms, Rectangles, and Rhombi
Visit mometrix.com/academy and enter code: 320040

KITE

A **kite** is a quadrilateral with two pairs of adjacent sides that are congruent. A result of this is perpendicular diagonals. A kite can be concave or convex and has one line of symmetry.

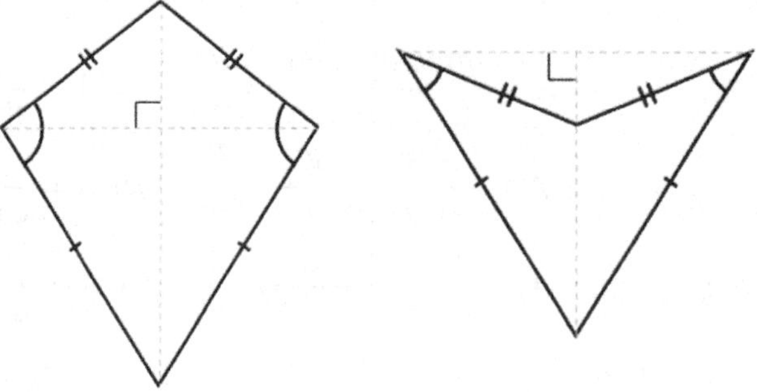

TRAPEZOID

Trapezoid: A trapezoid is defined as a quadrilateral that has at least one pair of parallel sides. There are no rules for the second pair of sides. So, there are no rules for the diagonals and no lines of symmetry for a trapezoid.

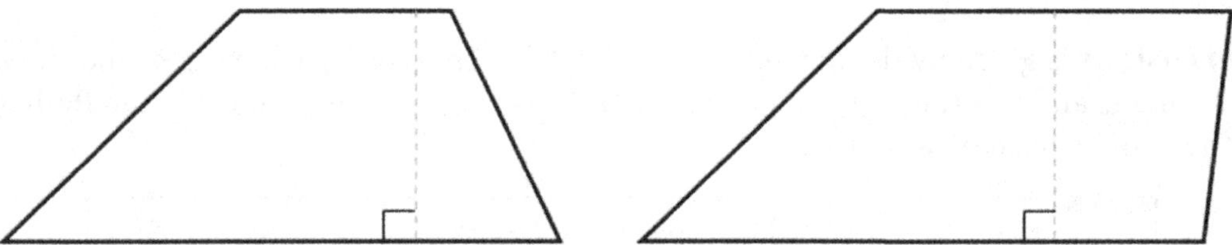

The **area of a trapezoid** is found by the formula $A = \frac{1}{2}h(b_1 + b_2)$, where h is the height (segment joining and perpendicular to the parallel bases), and b_1 and b_2 are the two parallel sides (bases). Do not use one of the other two sides as the height unless that side is also perpendicular to the parallel bases.

The **perimeter of a trapezoid** is found by the formula $P = a + b_1 + c + b_2$, where a, b_1, c, and b_2 are the four sides of the trapezoid.

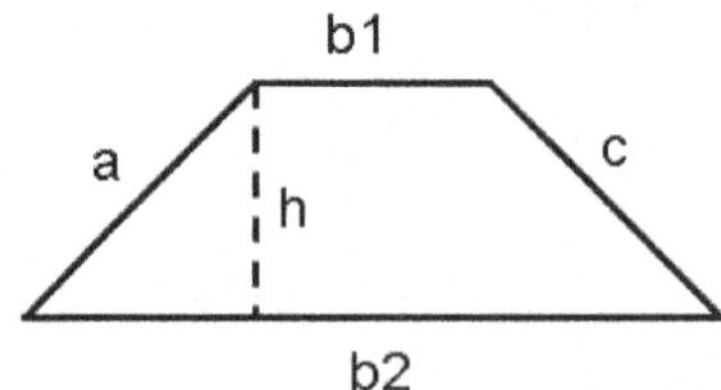

Review Video: Area and Perimeter of a Trapezoid
Visit mometrix.com/academy and enter code: 587523

Isosceles trapezoid: A trapezoid with equal base angles. This gives rise to other properties including: the two nonparallel sides have the same length, the two non-base angles are also equal, and there is one line of symmetry through the midpoints of the parallel sides.

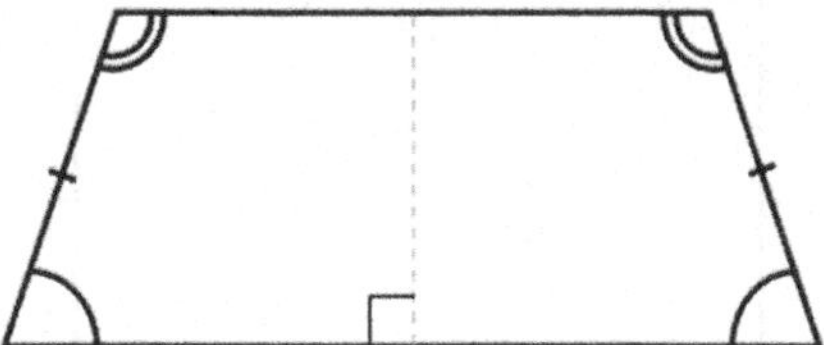

Parallelogram

A **parallelogram** is a quadrilateral that has two pairs of opposite parallel sides. As such it is a special type of trapezoid. The sides that are parallel are also congruent. The opposite interior angles are always congruent, and the consecutive interior angles are supplementary. The diagonals of a parallelogram divide each other. Each diagonal divides the parallelogram into two congruent triangles. A parallelogram has no line of symmetry, but does have 180-degree rotational symmetry about the midpoint.

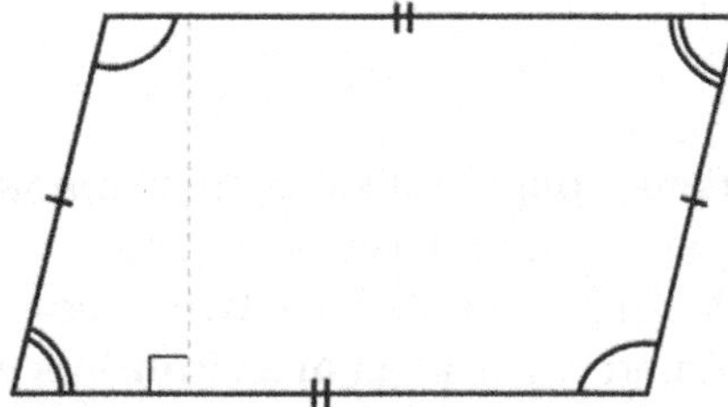

The **area of a parallelogram** is found by the formula $A = bh$, where b is the length of the base, and h is the height. Note that the base and height correspond to the length and width in a rectangle, so this formula would apply to rectangles as well. Do not confuse the height of a parallelogram with the length of the second side. The two are only the same measure in the case of a rectangle.

The **perimeter of a parallelogram** is found by the formula $P = 2a + 2b$ or $P = 2(a + b)$, where a and b are the lengths of the two sides.

Review Video: How to Find the Area and Perimeter of a Parallelogram
Visit mometrix.com/academy and enter code: 718313

Rectangle

A **rectangle** is a quadrilateral with four right angles. All rectangles are parallelograms and trapezoids, but not all parallelograms or trapezoids are rectangles. The diagonals of a rectangle are congruent. Rectangles have two lines of symmetry (through each pair of opposing midpoints) and 180-degree rotational symmetry about the midpoint.

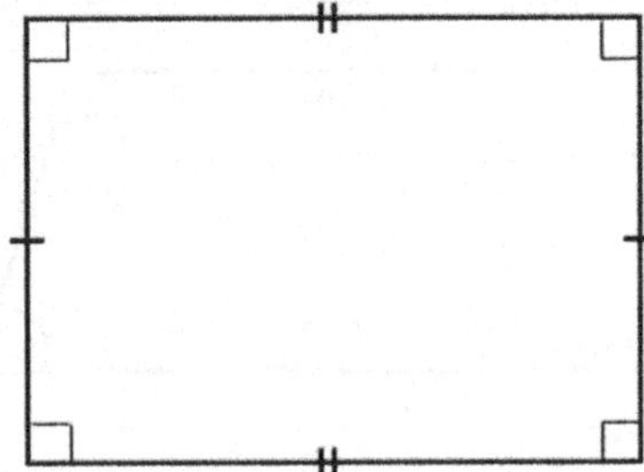

The **area of a rectangle** is found by the formula $A = lw$, where A is the area of the rectangle, l is the length (usually considered to be the longer side) and w is the width (usually considered to be the shorter side). The numbers for l and w are interchangeable.

The **perimeter of a rectangle** is found by the formula $P = 2l + 2w$ or $P = 2(l + w)$, where l is the length, and w is the width. It may be easier to add the length and width first and then double the result, as in the second formula.

Rhombus

A **rhombus** is a quadrilateral with four congruent sides. All rhombuses are parallelograms and kites; thus, they inherit all the properties of both types of quadrilaterals. The diagonals of a rhombus are perpendicular to each other. Rhombi have two lines of symmetry (along each of the diagonals) and 180° rotational symmetry. The **area of a rhombus** is half the product of the diagonals: $A = \frac{d_1 d_2}{2}$ and the perimeter of a rhombus is: $P = 2\sqrt{(d_1)^2 + (d_2)^2}$.

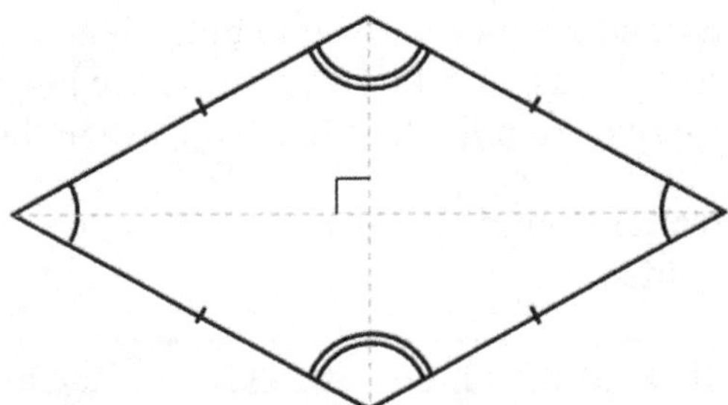

Square

A **square** is a quadrilateral with four right angles and four congruent sides. Squares satisfy the criteria of all other types of quadrilaterals. The diagonals of a square are congruent and perpendicular to each other. Squares have four lines of symmetry (through each pair of opposing midpoints and along each of the diagonals) as well as 90° rotational symmetry about the midpoint.

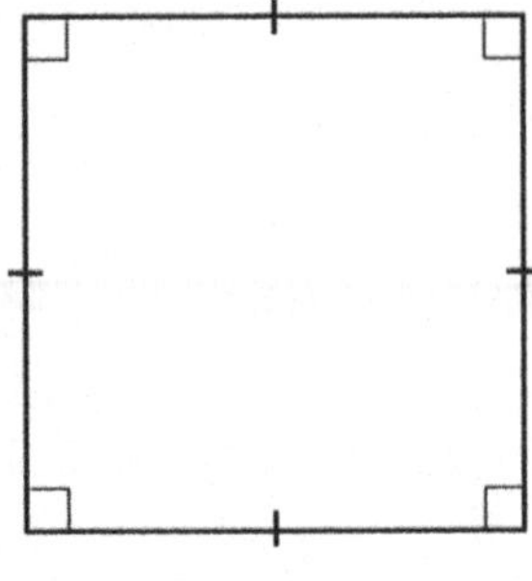

The **area of a square** is found by using the formula $A = s^2$, where s is the length of one side. The **perimeter of a square** is found by using the formula $P = 4s$, where s is the length of one side. Because all four sides are equal in a square, it is faster to multiply the length of one side by 4 than to add the same number four times. You could use the formulas for rectangles and get the same answer.

Review Video: Area and Perimeter of Rectangles and Squares
Visit mometrix.com/academy and enter code: 428109

Hierarchy of Quadrilaterals

The hierarchy of quadrilaterals is as follows:

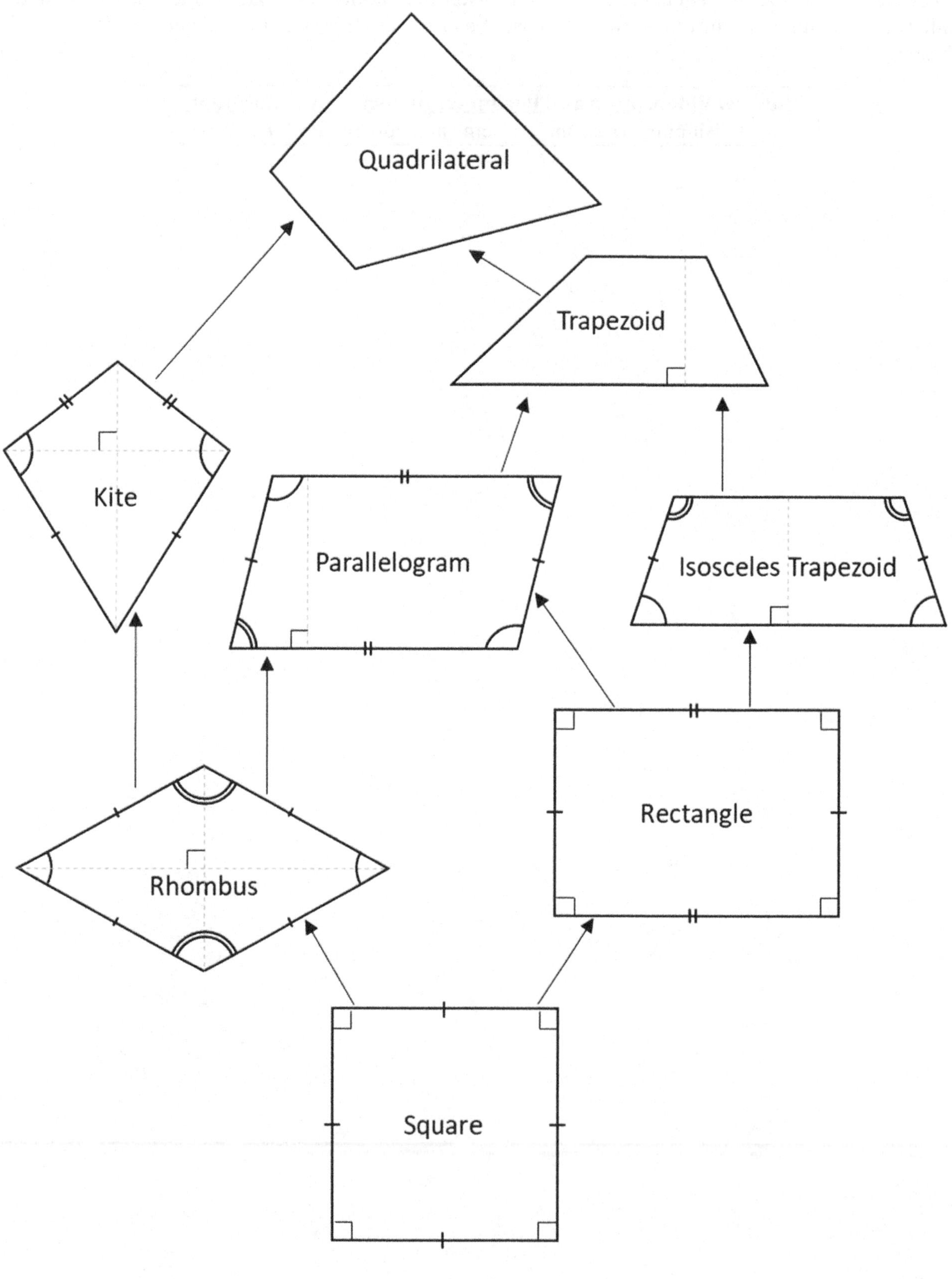

Circles

The **center** of a circle is the single point from which every point on the circle is **equidistant**. The **radius** is a line segment that joins the center of the circle and any one point on the circle. All radii of a circle are equal. Circles that have the same center but not the same length of radii are **concentric**. The **diameter** is a line segment that passes through the center of the circle and has both endpoints on the circle. The length of the diameter is exactly twice the length of the radius. Point O in the diagram below is the center of the circle, segments $\overline{OX}$, $\overline{OY}$, and $\overline{OZ}$ are radii; and segment $\overline{XZ}$ is a diameter.

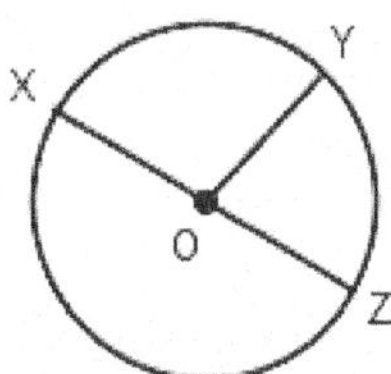

Review Video: Points of a Circle
Visit mometrix.com/academy and enter code: 420746

Review Video: The Diameter, Radius, and Circumference of Circles
Visit mometrix.com/academy and enter code: 448988

The **area of a circle** is found by the formula $A = \pi r^2$, where r is the length of the radius. If the diameter of the circle is given, remember to divide it in half to get the length of the radius before proceeding.

The **circumference** of a circle is found by the formula $C = 2\pi r$, where r is the radius. Again, remember to convert the diameter if you are given that measure rather than the radius.

Review Video: Area and Circumference of a Circle
Visit mometrix.com/academy and enter code: 243015

Inscribed and Circumscribed Figures

These terms can both be used to describe a given arrangement of figures, depending on perspective. If each of the vertices of figure A lie on figure B, then it can be said that figure A is **inscribed** in figure B, but it can also be said that figure B is **circumscribed** about figure A. The following table and examples help to illustrate the concept. Note that the figures cannot both be circles, as they would be completely overlapping and neither would be inscribed or circumscribed.

Given	Description	Equivalent Description	Figures
Each of the sides of a pentagon is tangent to a circle	The circle is inscribed in the pentagon	The pentagon is circumscribed about the circle	
Each of the vertices of a pentagon lie on a circle	The pentagon is inscribed in the circle	The circle is circumscribed about the pentagon	

Arcs

An **arc** is a portion of a circle. Specifically, an arc is the set of points between and including two points on a circle. An arc does not contain any points inside the circle. When a segment is drawn from the endpoints of an arc to the center of the circle, a sector is formed. A **minor arc** is an arc that has a measure less than 180°. A **major arc** is an arc that has a measure of at least 180°. Every minor arc has a corresponding major arc that can be found by subtracting the measure of the minor arc from 360°. A **semicircle** is an arc whose endpoints are the endpoints of the diameter of a circle. A semicircle is exactly half of a circle.

Arc length is the length of that portion of the circumference between two points on the circle. The formula for arc length is $s = \frac{\pi r\theta}{180°}$, where s is the arc length, r is the length of the radius, and θ is the angular measure of the arc in degrees, or $s = r\theta$, where θ is the angular measure of the arc in radians (2π radians $= 360$ degrees).

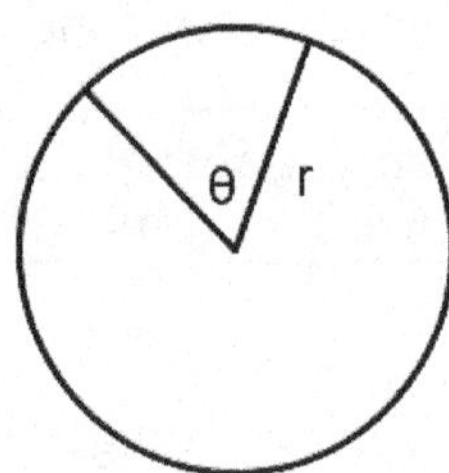

Angles of Circles

A **central angle** is an angle whose vertex is the center of a circle and whose legs intercept an arc of the circle. The measure of a central angle is equal to the measure of the minor arc it intercepts.

An **inscribed angle** is an angle whose vertex lies on a circle and whose legs contain chords of that circle. The portion of the circle intercepted by the legs of the angle is called the intercepted arc. The measure of the intercepted arc is exactly twice the measure of the inscribed angle. In the following diagram, angle ABC is an inscribed angle. $\widehat{AC} = 2(\text{m}\angle ABC)$.

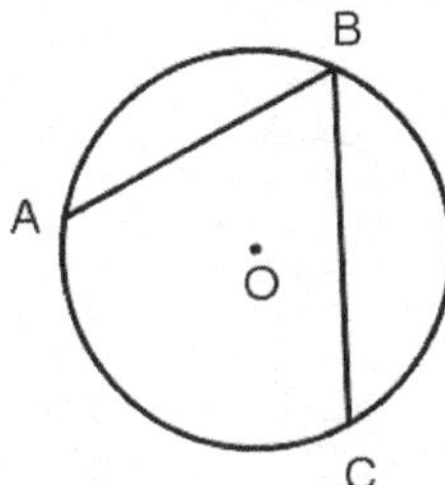

Any angle inscribed in a semicircle is a right angle. The intercepted arc is 180°, making the inscribed angle half that, or 90°. In the diagram below, angle ABC is inscribed in semicircle ABC, making angle ABC equal to 90°.

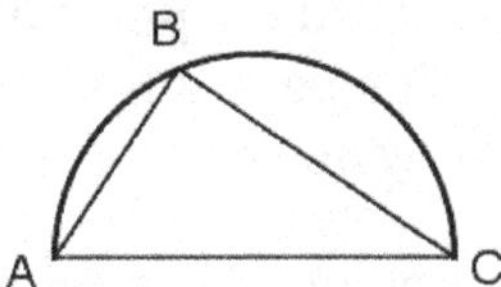

Review Video: Arcs and Angles of Circles
Visit mometrix.com/academy and enter code: 652838

SECANTS, CHORDS, AND TANGENTS

A **secant** is a line that intersects a circle in two points. The segment of a secant line that is contained within the circle is called a **chord**. Two secants may intersect inside the circle, on the circle, or outside the circle. When the two secants intersect on the circle, an inscribed angle is formed. When two secants intersect inside a circle, the measure of each of two vertical angles is equal to half the sum of the two intercepted arcs. Consider the following diagram where $\text{m}\angle AEB = \frac{1}{2}(\widehat{AB} + \widehat{CD})$ and $\text{m}\angle BEC = \frac{1}{2}(\widehat{BC} + \widehat{AD})$.

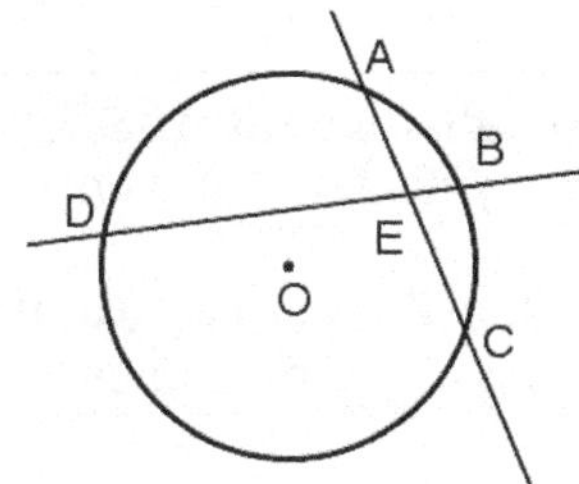

When two secants intersect outside a circle, the measure of the angle formed is equal to half the difference of the two arcs that lie between the two secants. In the diagram below, $m\angle AEB = \frac{1}{2}(\widehat{AB} - \widehat{CD})$.

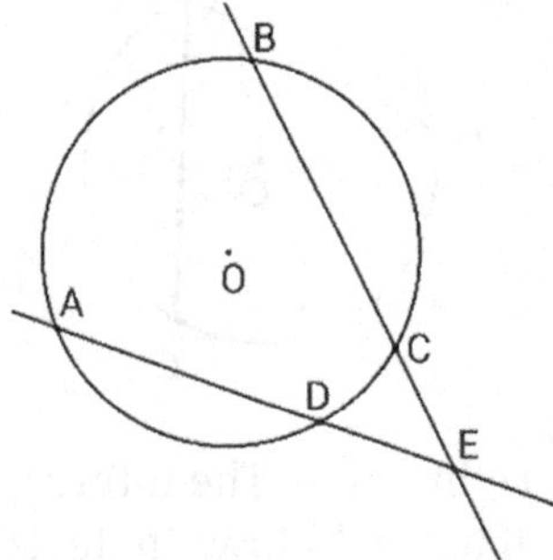

A **tangent** is a line in the same plane as a circle that touches the circle in exactly one point. The point at which a tangent touches a circle is called the **point of tangency**. While a line segment can be tangent to a circle as part of a line that is tangent, it is improper to say a tangent can be simply a line segment that touches the circle in exactly one point.

In the diagram below, $\overleftrightarrow{EB}$ is a secant and contains chord $\overline{EB}$, and $\overleftrightarrow{CD}$ is tangent to circle A. Notice that $\overline{FB}$ is not tangent to the circle. $\overline{FB}$ is a line segment that touches the circle in exactly one point, but if the segment were extended, it would touch the circle in a second point. In the diagram below, point B is the point of tangency.

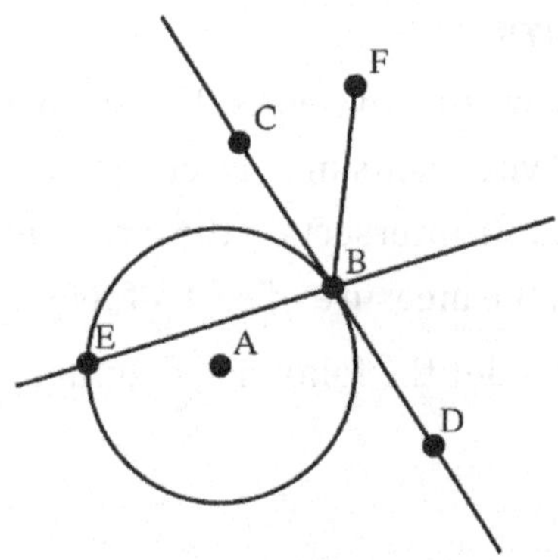

Review Video: Secants, Chords, and Tangents
Visit mometrix.com/academy and enter code: 258360

Review Video: Tangent Lines of a Circle
Visit mometrix.com/academy and enter code: 780167

SECTORS

A **sector** is the portion of a circle formed by two radii and their intercepted arc. While the arc length is exclusively the points that are also on the circumference of the circle, the sector is the entire area bounded by the arc and the two radii.

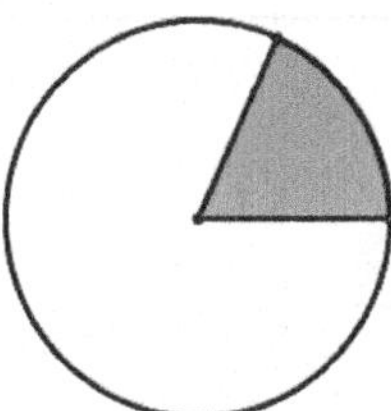

The **area of a sector** of a circle is found by the formula, $A = \frac{\theta r^2}{2}$, where A is the area, θ is the measure of the central angle in radians, and r is the radius. To find the area with the central angle in degrees, use the formula, $A = \frac{\theta \pi r^2}{360}$, where θ is the measure of the central angle and r is the radius.

SOLIDS

The **surface area of a solid object** is the area of all sides or exterior surfaces. For objects such as prisms and pyramids, a further distinction is made between base surface area (B) and lateral surface area (LA). For a prism, the total surface area (SA) is $SA = LA + 2B$. For a pyramid or cone, the total surface area is $SA = LA + B$.

The **surface area of a sphere** can be found by the formula $A = 4\pi r^2$, where r is the radius. The volume is given by the formula $V = \frac{4}{3}\pi r^3$, where r is the radius. Both quantities are generally given in terms of π.

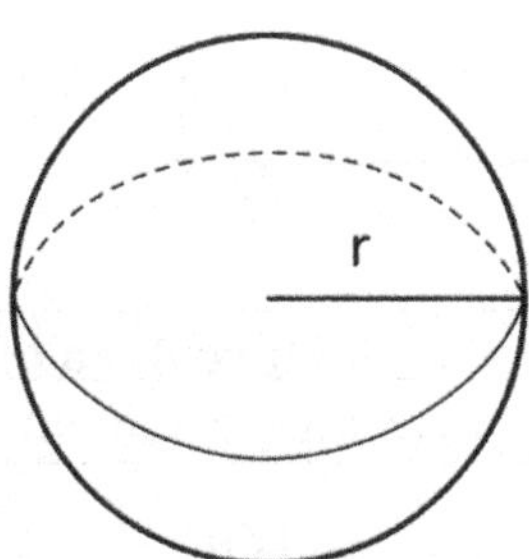

Review Video: Volume and Surface Area of a Sphere
Visit mometrix.com/academy and enter code: 786928

The **volume of any prism** is found by the formula $V = Bh$, where B is the area of the base, and h is the height (perpendicular distance between the bases). The surface area of any prism is the sum of the areas of both bases and all sides. It can be calculated as $SA = 2B + Ph$, where P is the perimeter of the base.

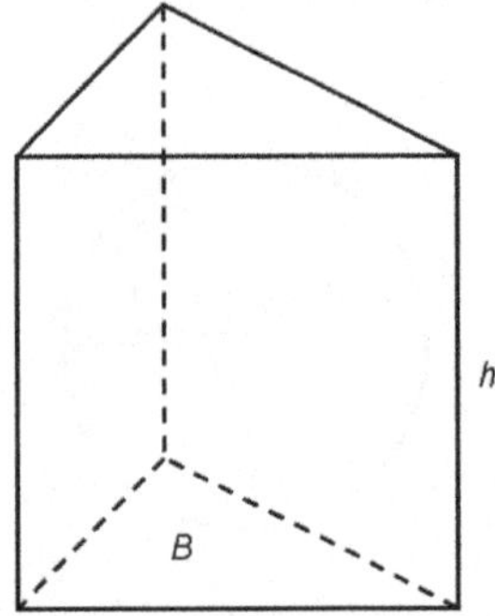

Review Video: Volume and Surface Area of a Prism
Visit mometrix.com/academy and enter code: 420158

For a **rectangular prism**, the volume can be found by the formula $V = lwh$, where V is the volume, l is the length, w is the width, and h is the height. The surface area can be calculated as $SA = 2lw + 2hl + 2wh$ or $SA = 2(lw + hl + wh)$.

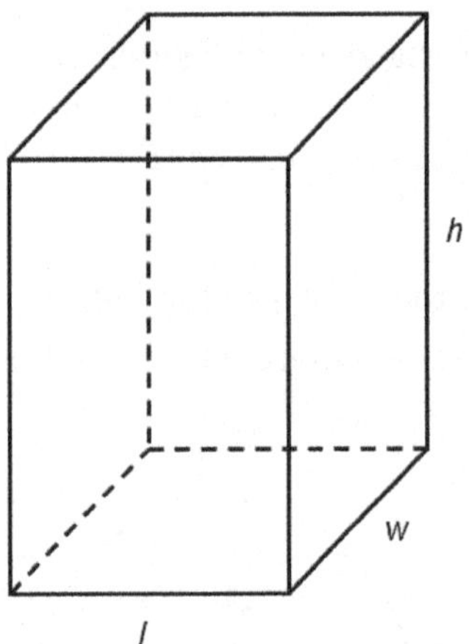

Review Video: Volume and Surface Area of a Rectangular Prism
Visit mometrix.com/academy and enter code: 282814

The **volume of a cube** can be found by the formula $V = s^3$, where s is the length of a side. The surface area of a cube is calculated as $SA = 6s^2$, where SA is the total surface area and s is the length of a side. These formulas are the same as the ones used for the volume and surface area of a rectangular prism, but simplified since all three quantities (length, width, and height) are the same.

Review Video: Volume and Surface Area of a Cube
Visit mometrix.com/academy and enter code: 664455

The **volume of a cylinder** can be calculated by the formula $V = \pi r^2 h$, where r is the radius, and h is the height. The surface area of a cylinder can be found by the formula $SA = 2\pi r^2 + 2\pi rh$. The first term is the base area multiplied by two, and the second term is the perimeter of the base multiplied by the height.

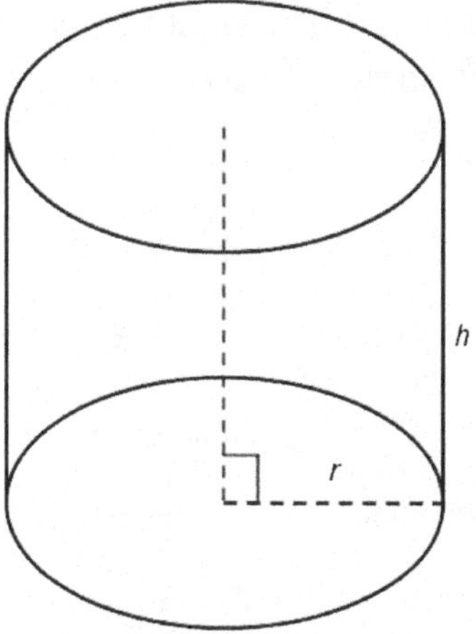

Review Video: Finding the Volume and Surface Area of a Right Circular Cylinder
Visit mometrix.com/academy and enter code: 226463

The **volume of a pyramid** is found by the formula $V = \frac{1}{3}Bh$, where B is the area of the base, and h is the height (perpendicular distance from the vertex to the base). Notice this formula is the same as $\frac{1}{3}$ times the volume of a prism. Like a prism, the base of a pyramid can be any shape.

Finding the **surface area of a pyramid** is not as simple as the other shapes we've looked at thus far. If the pyramid is a right pyramid, meaning the base is a regular polygon and the vertex is directly over the center of that polygon, the surface area can be calculated as $SA = B + \frac{1}{2}Ph_s$, where P is the perimeter of the base, and h_s is the slant height (distance from the vertex to the midpoint of one side of the base). If the pyramid is irregular, the area of each triangle side must be calculated individually and then summed, along with the base.

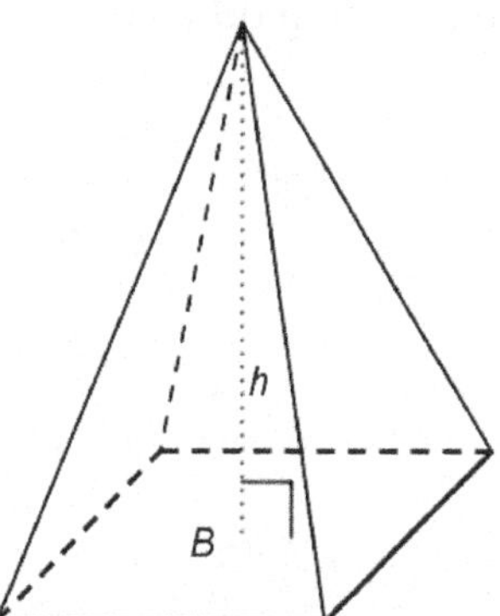

Review Video: Finding the Volume and Surface Area of a Pyramid
Visit mometrix.com/academy and enter code: 621932

The **volume of a cone** is found by the formula $V = \frac{1}{3}\pi r^2 h$, where r is the radius, and h is the height. Notice this is the same as $\frac{1}{3}$ times the volume of a cylinder. The surface area can be calculated as $SA = \pi r^2 + \pi rs$, where s is the slant height. The slant height can be calculated using the Pythagorean theorem to be $\sqrt{r^2 + h^2}$, so the surface area formula can also be written as $SA = \pi r^2 + \pi r\sqrt{r^2 + h^2}$.

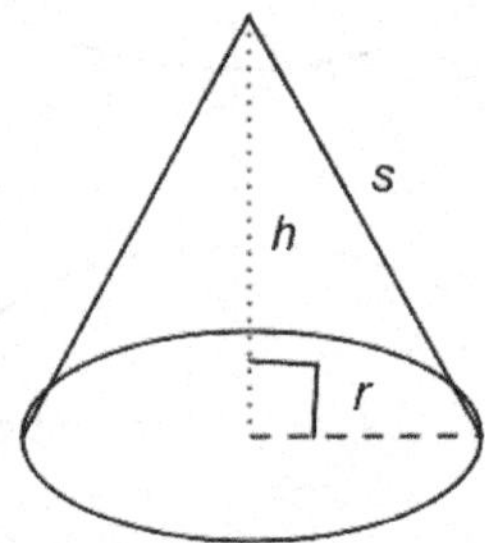

Review Video: Volume and Surface Area of a Right Circular Cone
Visit mometrix.com/academy and enter code: 573574

Degrees, Radians, and the Unit Circle

It is important to understand the deep connection between trigonometry and circles. Specifically, the two main units, **degrees** (°) and **radians** (rad), that are used to measure angles are related this way: 360° in one full circle and 2π radians in one full circle: ($360° = 2\pi$ rad). The conversion factor relating the two is often stated as $\frac{180°}{\pi}$. For example, to convert $\frac{3\pi}{2}$ radians to degrees, multiply by the conversion factor: $\frac{3\pi}{2} \times \frac{180°}{\pi} = 270°$. As another example, to convert 60° to radians, divide by the conversion factor or multiply by the reciprocal: $60° \times \frac{\pi}{180°} = \frac{\pi}{3}$ radians.

Recall that the standard equation for a circle is $(x - h)^2 + (y - k)^2 = r^2$. A **unit circle** is a circle with a radius of 1 ($r = 1$) that has its center at the origin ($h = 0, k = 0$). Thus, the equation for the unit circle simplifies from the standard equation down to $x^2 + y^2 = 1$.

Standard position is the position of an angle of measure θ whose vertex is at the origin, the initial side crosses the unit circle at the point $(1, 0)$, and the terminal side crosses the unit circle at some other point (a, b). In the standard position, $\sin\theta = b$, $\cos\theta = a$, and $\tan\theta = \frac{b}{a}$.

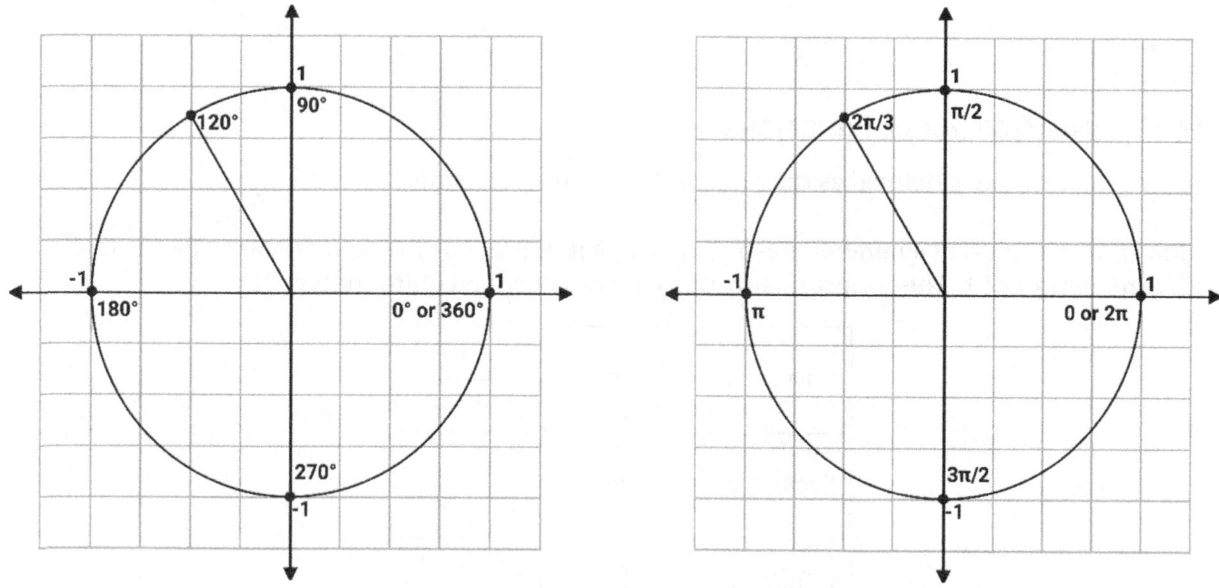

Review Video: Unit Circles and Standard Position
Visit mometrix.com/academy and enter code: 333922

TABLE OF COMMONLY ENCOUNTERED ANGLES

$0° = 0$ radians, $30° = \frac{\pi}{6}$ radians, $45° = \frac{\pi}{4}$ radians, $60° = \frac{\pi}{3}$ radians, and $90° = \frac{\pi}{2}$ radians

$\sin 0° = 0$	$\cos 0° = 1$	$\tan 0° = 0$
$\sin 30° = \frac{1}{2}$	$\cos 30° = \frac{\sqrt{3}}{2}$	$\tan 30° = \frac{\sqrt{3}}{3}$
$\sin 45° = \frac{\sqrt{2}}{2}$	$\cos 45° = \frac{\sqrt{2}}{2}$	$\tan 45° = 1$
$\sin 60° = \frac{\sqrt{3}}{2}$	$\cos 60° = \frac{1}{2}$	$\tan 60° = \sqrt{3}$
$\sin 90° = 1$	$\cos 90° = 0$	$\tan 90° =$ undefined
$\csc 0° =$ undefined	$\sec 0° = 1$	$\cot 0° =$ undefined
$\csc 30° = 2$	$\sec 30° = \frac{2\sqrt{3}}{3}$	$\cot 30° = \sqrt{3}$
$\csc 45° = \sqrt{2}$	$\sec 45° = \sqrt{2}$	$\cot 45° = 1$
$\csc 60° = \frac{2\sqrt{3}}{3}$	$\sec 60° = 2$	$\cot 60° = \frac{\sqrt{3}}{3}$
$\csc 90° = 1$	$\sec 90° =$ undefined	$\cot 90° = 0$

The values in the upper half of this table are values you should have memorized or be able to find quickly and those in the lower half can easily be determined as the reciprocal of the corresponding function.

DEFINED AND RECIPROCAL FUNCTIONS

The tangent function is defined as the ratio of the sine to the cosine: $\tan x = \frac{\sin x}{\cos x}$.

To take the reciprocal of a number means to place that number as the denominator of a fraction with a numerator of 1. The reciprocal functions are thus defined quite simply.

Cosecant	$\csc x$	$\frac{1}{\sin x}$
Secant	$\sec x$	$\frac{1}{\cos x}$
Cotangent	$\cot x$	$\frac{1}{\tan x}$

It is important to know these reciprocal functions, but they are not as commonly used as the three basic functions.

Review Video: Defined and Reciprocal Functions
Visit mometrix.com/academy and enter code: 996431

INVERSE FUNCTIONS

Each of the trigonometric functions accepts an angular measure, either degrees or radians, and gives a numerical value as the output. The inverse functions do the opposite; they accept a numerical value and give an angular measure as the output.

The inverse of sine, or arcsine, commonly written as either $\sin^{-1} x$ or $\arcsin x$, gives the angle whose sine is x. Similarly:

The inverse of $\cos x$ is written as $\cos^{-1} x$ or $\arccos x$ and means the angle whose cosine is x.
The inverse of $\tan x$ is written as $\tan^{-1} x$ or $\arctan x$ and means the angle whose tangent is x.
The inverse of $\csc x$ is written as $\csc^{-1} x$ or $\text{arccsc}\, x$ and means the angle whose cosecant is x.
The inverse of $\sec x$ is written as $\sec^{-1} x$ or $\text{arcsec}\, x$ and means the angle whose secant is x.

The inverse of $\cot x$ is written as $\cot^{-1} x$ or $\operatorname{arccot} x$ and means the angle whose cotangent is x.

Review Video: Inverse Trig Functions
Visit mometrix.com/academy and enter code: 156054

IMPORTANT NOTE ABOUT SOLVING TRIGONOMETRIC EQUATIONS

When solving for an angle with a known trigonometric value, you must consider the sign and include all angles with that value. Your calculator will probably only give one value as an answer, typically in the following ranges:

- For $\sin^{-1} x$, $\left[-\frac{\pi}{2}, \frac{\pi}{2}\right]$ or $[-90°, 90°]$
- For $\cos^{-1} x$, $[0, \pi]$ or $[0°, 180°]$
- For $\tan^{-1} x$, $\left[-\frac{\pi}{2}, \frac{\pi}{2}\right]$ or $[-90°, 90°]$

It is important to determine if there is another angle in a different quadrant that also satisfies the problem. To do this, find the other quadrant(s) with the same sign for that trigonometric function and find the angle that has the same reference angle. Then check whether this angle is also a solution.

- In the first quadrant, all six trigonometric functions are positive.
- In the second quadrant, sin and csc are positive.
- In the third quadrant, tan and cot are positive.
- In the fourth quadrant, cos and sec are positive.

If you remember the phrase, "ALL Students Take Classes," you will be able to remember the sign of each trigonometric function in each quadrant. ALL represents all the signs in the first quadrant. The "S" in "Students" represents the sine function and its reciprocal in the second quadrant. The "T" in "Take" represents the tangent function and its reciprocal in the third quadrant. The "C" in "Classes" represents the cosine function and its reciprocal.

TRIGONOMETRIC IDENTITIES

SUM AND DIFFERENCE

To find the sine, cosine, or tangent of the sum or difference of two angles, use one of the following formulas where α and β are two angles with known sine, cosine, or tangent values as needed:

$$\sin(\alpha \pm \beta) = \sin \alpha \cos \beta \pm \cos \alpha \sin \beta$$
$$\cos(\alpha \pm \beta) = \cos \alpha \cos \beta \mp \sin \alpha \sin \beta$$
$$\tan(\alpha \pm \beta) = \frac{\tan \alpha \pm \tan \beta}{1 \mp \tan \alpha \tan \beta}$$

HALF ANGLE

To find the sine or cosine of half of a known angle, use the following formulas where θ is an angle with a known exact cosine value:

$$\sin\left(\frac{\theta}{2}\right) = \pm\sqrt{\frac{(1-cos\theta)}{2}}$$

$$\cos\left(\frac{\theta}{2}\right) = \pm\sqrt{\frac{(1+\cos\theta)}{2}}$$

To determine the sign of the answer, you must recognize which quadrant the given angle is in and apply the correct sign for the trigonometric function you are using. If you need to find an expression for the exact sine or cosine of an angle that you do not know, such as sine 22.5°, you can rewrite the given angle as a half angle, such as $\sin\left(\frac{45°}{2}\right)$, and use the formula above:

$$\sin\left(\frac{45°}{2}\right) = \pm\sqrt{\frac{(1-\cos(45°))}{2}} = \pm\sqrt{\frac{\left(1-\frac{\sqrt{2}}{2}\right)}{2}} = \pm\sqrt{\frac{(2-\sqrt{2})}{4}} = \pm\frac{1}{2}\sqrt{(2-\sqrt{2})}$$

To find the tangent or cotangent of half of a known angle, use the following formulas where θ is an angle with known exact sine and cosine values:

$$\tan\frac{\theta}{2} = \frac{sin\theta}{1+\cos\theta}$$

$$\cot\frac{\theta}{2} = \frac{\sin\theta}{1-\cos\theta}$$

These formulas will work for finding the tangent or cotangent of half of any angle unless the cosine of θ happens to make the denominator of the identity equal to 0.

The Pythagorean theorem states that $a^2 + b^2 = c^2$ for all right triangles. The trigonometric identity that derives from this principle is stated in this way: $\sin^2\theta + \cos^2\theta = 1$.

Dividing each term by either $\sin^2\theta$ or $\cos^2\theta$ yields two other identities, respectively:

$$1 + \cot^2\theta = \csc^2\theta$$

$$\tan^2\theta + 1 = \sec^2\theta$$

Review Video: Sum and Difference Trigonometric Identities
Visit mometrix.com/academy and enter code: 468838

Double Angles

In each case, use one of the double angle formulas. To find the sine or cosine of twice a known angle, use one of the following formulas:

$$\sin(2\theta) = 2\sin\theta\cos\theta$$

$$\begin{aligned}\cos(2\theta) &= \cos^2\theta - \sin^2\theta \\ &= 2\cos^2\theta - 1 \\ &= 1 - 2\sin^2\theta\end{aligned}$$

To find the tangent or cotangent of twice a known angle, use the formulas where θ is an angle with known exact sine, cosine, tangent, and cotangent values:

$$\tan(2\theta) = \frac{2\tan\theta}{1-\tan^2\theta}$$

$$\cot(2\theta) = \frac{\cot\theta - \tan\theta}{2}$$

Products

To find the product of the sines and cosines of two different angles, use one of the following formulas where α and β are two unique angles:

$$\sin\alpha\sin\beta = \frac{1}{2}[\cos(\alpha-\beta) - \cos(\alpha+\beta)]$$

$$\cos\alpha\cos\beta = \frac{1}{2}[\cos(\alpha+\beta) + \cos(\alpha-\beta)]$$

$$\sin\alpha\cos\beta = \frac{1}{2}[\sin(\alpha+\beta) + \sin(\alpha-\beta)]$$

$$\cos\alpha\sin\beta = \frac{1}{2}[\sin(\alpha+\beta) - \sin(\alpha-\beta)]$$

Review Video: Half-Angle, Double Angle, and Product Trig Identities
Visit mometrix.com/academy and enter code: 274252

Complementary

The trigonometric cofunction identities use the trigonometric relationships of complementary angles (angles whose sum is 90°). These are:

$$\cos x = \sin(90° - x)$$

$$\csc x = \sec(90° - x)$$

$$\cot x = \tan(90° - x)$$

Domain, Range, and Asymptotes in Trigonometry

The domain is the set of all possible real number values of x on the graph of a trigonometric function. Some graphs will impose limits on the values of x.

The range is the set of all possible real number values of y on the graph of a trigonometric function. Some graphs will impose limits on the values of y.

Asymptotes are lines that the graph of a trigonometric function approaches but never reaches. Asymptotes exist for values of x in the graphs of the tangent, cotangent, secant, and cosecant. The sine and cosine graphs do not have any asymptotes.

DOMAIN, RANGE, AND ASYMPTOTES OF THE SIX TRIGONOMETRIC FUNCTIONS

The domain, range, and asymptotes for each of the trigonometric functions are as follows:

- In the **sine** function, the domain is all real numbers, the range is $-1 \leq y \leq 1$, and there are no asymptotes.
- In the **cosine** function, the domain is all real numbers, the range is $-1 \leq y \leq 1$, and there are no asymptotes.
- In the **tangent** function, the domain is $x \in \mathbb{R}; x \neq \frac{\pi}{2} + k\pi$, the range is all real numbers, and the asymptotes are the lines $x = \frac{\pi}{2} + k\pi$.
- In the **cosecant** function, the domain is $x \in \mathbb{R}; x \neq k\pi$, the range is $(-\infty, -1]$ and $[1, \infty)$, and the asymptotes are the lines $x = k\pi$.
- In the **secant** function, the domain is $x \in \mathbb{R}; x \neq \frac{\pi}{2} + k\pi$, the range is $(-\infty, 1]$ and $[1, \infty)$, and the asymptotes are the lines $x = \frac{\pi}{2} + k\pi$.
- In the **cotangent** function, the domain is $x \in \mathbb{R}; x \neq k\pi$, the range is all real numbers, and the asymptotes are the lines $x = k\pi$.

In each of the above cases, k represents any integer.

RECTANGULAR AND POLAR COORDINATES

Rectangular coordinates are those that lie on the square grids of the Cartesian plane. They should be quite familiar to you. The polar coordinate system is based on a circular graph, rather than the square grid of the Cartesian system. Points in the polar coordinate system are in the format (r, θ), where r is the distance from the origin (think radius of the circle) and θ is the smallest positive angle (moving counterclockwise around the circle) made with the positive horizontal axis.

To convert a point from rectangular (x, y) format to polar (r, θ) format, use the formula (x, y) to $(r, \theta) \Rightarrow r = \sqrt{x^2 + y^2}; \theta = \arctan\frac{y}{x}$ when $x \neq 0$.

If x is positive, use the positive square root value for r. If x is negative, use the negative square root value for r. If $x = 0$, use the following rules:

- If $y = 0$, then $\theta = 0$.
- If $y > 0$, then $\theta = \frac{\pi}{2}$.
- If $y < 0$, then $\theta = \frac{3\pi}{2}$.

To convert a point from polar (r, θ) format to rectangular (x, y) format, use the formula (r, θ) to $(x, y) \Rightarrow x = r\cos\theta\ ; y = r\sin\theta$.

De Moivre's Theorem

De Moivre's theorem is used to find the powers of complex numbers (numbers that contain the imaginary number i) written in polar form. Given a trigonometric expression that contains i, such as $z = r\cos x + ir\sin x$, where r is a real number and x is an angle measurement in polar form, use the formula $z^n = r^n(\cos nx + i\sin nx)$, where r and n are real numbers, x is the angle measure in polar form, and i is the imaginary number $i = \sqrt{-1}$. The expression $\cos x + i\sin x$ can be written $\text{cis}\, x$, making the formula appear in the format $z^n = r^n \text{ cis } nx$.

Note that De Moivre's theorem is only for angles in polar form. If you are given an angle in degrees, you must convert to polar form before using the formula.

Student-Produced Response

This test includes some questions that are not multiple choice. Instead, they require you to solve the problem, then fill the exact number into a grid very similar to the one you used to enter your name and address on the form. The grid has a row of four boxes on top, with a column of numbers 0–9, a slash, and a decimal beneath each box.

To fill in the grid, write your answer in the boxes on top, then fill in the corresponding circle underneath. Use the slash to indicate fractions. It's a machine-scored test, so you don't get any credit for the number you write on top — that's strictly to help you fill in the circles correctly. If your answer doesn't fill up all four columns, that's okay. And it doesn't matter whether you left-justify or right-justify your answers. What does matter is that the circles be filled in correctly.

If You Can't Write It Using the Characters Provided, It's Not Right

No student-produced response will be a negative number or a percentage. If you get a negative number, you've made a mistake. Percentages should be expressed as a ratio or decimal; for example, 50% can be written as .50.

Start on the Left

There are a few reasons to start with the first box every time. For one thing, it's faster. It will also help you be as precise as possible. If your answer is <1, though, don't use a leading 0 before the decimal. This test omits the 0 from column one to help you be as precise as possible. For decimals, use as many columns as you can. Don't round or truncate answers. If you calculate an answer to be .125, enter the full number, not .13.

Repeat a Repeating Decimal

Repeating decimals such as .666666 are only counted correct if you fill all the available columns. Either .666 or .667 will get credit. However, .66 will be counted as wrong.

Don't Use Mixed Numbers

If you try to write 2 ½, the computer will think you've written 21/2 and count it wrong. Instead, use the improper fraction form of such numbers; for example, 2 ½ = 5/2.

Use Your Calculator

You brought a calculator; use it. Work the problem twice to make sure you entered all the numbers correctly.

Check Your Work

More than any other questions in the math section, student-produced responses need to be double-checked. Try working the problem backward, plugging answers back into the original equation.

It's Okay to Get Multiple Answers

Some questions may have more than one answer. In that case, any correct answer will do.

In General

Approach the problem systematically. Take time to understand what is being asked for. In many cases, there is a drawing or graph that you can write on. Draw lines, jot notes, do whatever is necessary to create a visual picture and to allow you to understand what is being asked.

PSAT Practice Test #1

Reading

Questions 1-9 are based on the following passage.

This passage is adapted from Louisa May Alcott, Little Women, *originally published in 1868.*

"Christmas won't be Christmas without any presents," grumbled Jo, lying on the rug.

"It's so dreadful to be poor!" sighed Meg, looking down at her old dress.

"I don't think it's fair for some girls to have plenty of pretty things, and other girls nothing at all," added little Amy, with an injured sniff.

"We've got Father and Mother, and each other," said Beth contentedly from her corner.

The four young faces on which the firelight shone brightened at the cheerful words, but darkened again as Jo said sadly, "We haven't got Father, and shall not have him for a long time." She didn't say "perhaps never," but each silently added it, thinking of Father far away, where the fighting was.

Nobody spoke for a minute; then Meg said in an altered tone, "You know the reason Mother proposed not having any presents this Christmas was because it is going to be a hard winter for everyone. She thinks we ought not to spend money for pleasure, when our men in the army are suffering so. We can't do much, but we can make our little sacrifices, and ought to do it gladly. But I am afraid I don't," and Meg shook her head, as she thought regretfully of all the pretty things she wanted.

"But I don't think the little we should spend would do any good. We've each got a dollar, and the army wouldn't be much helped by our giving that. I agree not to expect anything from Mother or you, but I do want to buy Undine and Sintram for myself. I've wanted it so long," said Jo, who was a bookworm.

"I planned to spend mine in new music," said Beth, with a little sigh, which no one heard but the hearth brush and kettle-holder.

"I shall get a nice box of Faber's drawing pencils; I really need them," said Amy decidedly.

"Mother didn't say anything about our money, and she won't wish us to give up everything. Let's each buy what we want, and have a little fun; I'm sure we work hard enough to earn it," cried Jo, examining the heels of her shoes in a gentlemanly manner.

"I know I do—teaching those tiresome children nearly all day, when I'm longing to enjoy myself at home," began Meg, in the complaining tone again.

"You don't have half such a hard time as I do," said Jo. "How would you like to be shut up for hours with a nervous, fussy old lady, who keeps you trotting, is never satisfied, and worries you till you're ready to fly out the window or cry?"

"It's naughty to fret, but I do think washing dishes and keeping things tidy is the worst work in the world. It makes me cross, and my hands get so stiff, I can't practice well at all." And Beth looked at her rough hands with a sigh that anyone could hear that time.

"I don't believe any of you suffer as I do," cried Amy, "for you don't have to go to school with impertinent girls, who plague you if you don't know your lessons, and laugh at your dresses, and label your father if he isn't rich, and insult you when your nose isn't nice."

"If you mean libel, I'd say so, and not talk about labels, as if Papa was a pickle bottle," advised Jo, laughing.

1. Which choice gives the best summary of the problems presented in this passage?

A) The sisters do not have as much money to spend as they would like, and Amy is made fun of at school.
B) Mother forbade any presents this Christmas, and the sisters are unhappy with their responsibilities.
C) Father is away at war, money is scarce, and the sisters are unhappy with their responsibilities.
D) Beth is tired of cleaning and washing dishes, and Father is away at war.

2. Which of the following selections provides the best evidence that this passage takes place during a time of war?

A) Lines 1-2 ("Christmas won't ... any presents")
B) Lines 14-15 ("We haven't ... long time.")
C) Lines 22-24 ("She thinks ... suffering so")
D) Lines 30-31 ("But I ... any good")

3. Based on what is stated in the passage, what do you know to be true about Father?

A) He wants his daughters to spend their money on themselves.
B) He wants his daughters to buy things for each other.
C) He is likely to die in the war.
D) He is not likely to return home in time for Christmas.

4. Which sister does NOT specify what she wants to buy with her money?

A) Amy
B) Beth
C) Jo
D) Meg

5. As used in line 8, the word "injured" most nearly means

A) In Pain
B) Offended
C) Sympathetic
D) Sickly

6. Based on the context of the passage, a reader who is unfamiliar with "Undine and Sintram" mentioned in line 35 could conclude it is the name of which of these?

A) A perfume
B) A work of art
C) A work of literature
D) A work of music

7. What do lines 39-40 ("no one ... kettle-holder") tell the reader about where Beth is located in the room?

A) She is next to the stove.
B) She is next to the window.
C) She is next to the kitchen table.
D) She is next to the fireplace.

8. In line 63, Beth complains of not being able to practice well. To what sort of practicing is Beth referring?

A) Practicing music
B) Practicing drawing
C) Practicing housekeeping
D) Practicing schoolwork

9. Which of the following sentences best describes the theme of this passage?

A) Children should not be required to work outside the home.
B) In time of war, everyone should make sacrifices for the good of the country.
C) Not everyone has the same problems, but everyone has problems.
D) Money should only be spent on oneself, because no one else deserves it.

Questions 10-20 are based on the following two passages.

Both passages are adapted from addresses given by Abraham Lincoln. The first is his Second Inaugural Address *and the second is his* Gettysburg Address.

Passage 1

At this second appearing to take the oath of the Presidential office there is less occasion for an extended address than there was at the first. Then a statement somewhat in detail of a course to be pursued seemed fitting and proper. Now, at the expiration of four years, during which public declarations have been constantly called forth on every point and phase of the great contest which still absorbs the attention and engrosses the energies of the nation, little that is new could be presented. The progress of our arms, upon which all else chiefly depends, is as well known to the public as to myself, and it is, I trust, reasonably satisfactory and encouraging to all. With high hope for the future, no prediction in regard to it is ventured.

On the occasion corresponding to this four years ago all thoughts were anxiously directed to an impending civil war. All dreaded it, all sought to avert it. While the inaugural address was being delivered from this place, devoted altogether to saving the Union without war, insurgent agents were in the city seeking to destroy it without war—seeking to dissolve the Union and divide effects by negotiation. Both parties deprecated war, but one of them would make war rather than let the nation survive, and the other would accept war rather than let it perish, and the war came.

One-eighth of the whole population were colored slaves, not distributed generally over the Union, but localized in the southern part of it. These slaves constituted a peculiar and powerful interest. All knew that this interest was somehow the cause of the war. To strengthen, perpetuate, and extend this interest was the object for which the insurgents would rend the Union even by war, while the Government claimed no right to do more than to restrict the territorial enlargement of it. Neither party expected for the war the magnitude or the duration which it has already attained. Neither anticipated that the cause of the conflict might cease with or even before the conflict itself should cease. Each looked for an easier triumph, and a result less fundamental and astounding. Both read the same Bible and pray to the same God, and each invokes His aid against the other. It may seem strange that any men should dare to ask a just God's assistance in wringing their bread from the sweat of other men's faces, but let us judge not, that we be not judged. The prayers of both could not be answered. That of neither has been answered fully. The Almighty has His own purposes. "Woe unto the world because of offenses; for it must needs be that offenses come, but woe to that man by whom the offense cometh." If we shall suppose that American slavery is one of those offenses which, in the providence of God, must needs come, but which, having continued through His appointed time, He now wills to remove, and that He gives to both North and South this terrible war as the woe due to those by whom the offense came, shall we discern therein any departure from those divine attributes which the believers in a living God always ascribe to Him? Fondly do we hope, fervently do we pray, that this mighty scourge of war may speedily pass away. Yet, if God wills that it continue until all the wealth piled by the bondsman's two hundred and fifty years of unrequited toil shall be sunk, and until every drop of blood drawn with the lash shall be paid by another drawn with the sword, as was said three thousand years ago, so still it must be said "the judgments of the Lord are true and righteous altogether."

With malice toward none, with charity for all, with firmness in the right as God gives us to see the right, let us strive on to finish the work we are in, to bind up the nation's wounds, to care for him who shall have borne the battle and for his widow and his orphan, to do all which may achieve and cherish a just and lasting peace among ourselves and with all nations.

Passage 2

Four score and seven years ago our fathers brought forth on this continent, a new nation, conceived in Liberty, and dedicated to the proposition that all men are created equal.

Now we are engaged in a great civil war, testing whether that nation, or any nation so conceived and so dedicated, can long endure. We are met on a great battle-field of that war. We have come to dedicate a portion of that field, as a final resting place for those who here gave their lives that that nation might live. It is altogether fitting and proper that we should do this.

But, in a larger sense, we cannot dedicate -- we cannot consecrate -- we cannot hallow -- this ground. The brave men, living and dead, who struggled here, have consecrated it, far above our poor power to add or detract. The world will little note, nor long remember what we say here, but it can never forget what they did here. It is for us the living, rather, to be dedicated here to the unfinished work which they who fought here have thus far so nobly advanced. It is rather for us to be here dedicated to the great task remaining before us: that from these honored dead we take increased devotion to that cause for which they gave the last full measure of devotion; that we here highly resolve that these dead shall not have died in vain; that this nation, under God, shall have a new birth of freedom; and that government of the people, by the people, for the people shall not perish from the earth.

10. Why does the author discuss his first inaugural address in Passage 1?

A) To prove that the country could have gone in a different direction.
B) To illustrate how the country had changed since his first inauguration.
C) To show how much he improved the country during his first term.
D) To explain that the country was once a place of peace.

11. In line 36 of Passage 1, the word "peculiar" most nearly means

A) Odd
B) Bizarre
C) Specific
D) Appropriate

12. In lines 62-69 of Passage 1, the author states, "If we shall suppose that... [God] gives to both North and South this terrible war as the woe due to those by whom the offense came..." Which of the following does he provide as evidence of this supposition?

A) Lines 44-46 ("Neither party ... already attained")
B) Lines 50-53 ("Both read ... the other")
C) Lines 60-62 ("Woe unto ... offense cometh")
D) Lines 75-83 ("Yet, if God ... righteous altogether")

13. What is the purpose of lines 84-92 of Passage 1 ("With malice ... all nations.")?

A) It is a sober remembrance for all who died during the American Civil War.
B) It is a warning that America could face new conflicts with other nations.
C) It is an attempt to forge a new feeling of union and caring between the North and the South.
D) It is a plea to other nations to seek peaceful solutions to conflicts with the United States.

14. Which sentence from Passage 1 supports the idea that the author believed the North and the South did not have equally justifiable reasons for taking part in the war?

A) Lines 28-32 ("Both parties ... war came")
B) Lines 37-38 ("All knew ... the war")
C) Line 46-48 ("Neither anticipated ... should cease")
D) Lines 49-50 ("Each looked ... and astounding")

15. How does the author unite the themes of war and religion in Passage 1?

A) He suggests that the war and its end are parts of God's plan.
B) He says that no man would ask God to help him win a war.
C) He insists that it is God's responsibility, not his own, to resolve the war.
D) He quotes from the Bible liberally to extend an address he knew was too short.

16. In lines 19-22 of Passage 2, the author writes that "the world will little note, nor long remember what we say here, but it can never forget what they did here." Which rhetorical device does the author use?

A) Epiphora
B) Anaphora
C) Repetition
D) Parallelism

17. In line 33 of Passage 2, what is the author most likely emphasizing when he speaks of "freedom"?

A) Freedom from war
B) Freedom for all citizens
C) Freedom to own slaves
D) Freedom to worship God

18. Which of the following comes closest to summarizing the main idea of Passage 2?

A) In dedicating this ground, we must moreover save our democracy so soldiers did not die in vain.
B) In dedicating this ground, we must consecrate and hallow it to honor the soldiers living and dead.
C) In dedicating this ground, we must ensure the world remembers what we said and they did here.
D) In dedicating this ground, we must complete soldiers' unfinished work by declaring a cease-fire.

19. Which idea is overtly included in both passages?

A) Achieving an enduring peace
B) The Civil War being God's will
C) Completing some ongoing tasks
D) Wishing the war would end soon

20. How would the experience of reading Passage 1, a transcript of a speech, most likely differ from seeing and hearing the address delivered in person?

A) The author likely was angry while delivering his address, and this anger is lost in its transcription.
B) The author's original address was much longer than the version that was later transcribed.
C) The author was an impressively tall man and appeared more intimidating when he leaned toward his audience.
D) The author would have been able to use his voice to heighten the emotion in his address.

Questions 21-29 are based on the following passage.

This passage is adapted from Franklin Roosevelt's 1941 State of the Union Address.

Many subjects connected with our social economy call for immediate improvement. We should bring more citizens under the coverage of old-age pensions and unemployment insurance. We should widen the opportunities for adequate medical care. We should plan a better system by which persons deserving or needing gainful employment may obtain it.

I have called for personal sacrifice. And I am assured of the willingness of almost all Americans to respond to that call. A part of the sacrifice means the payment of more money in taxes. In my Budget Message, I will recommend that a greater portion of this great defense program be paid for from taxation than we are paying for today. No person should try, or be allowed, to get rich out of the program; and the principle of tax payments in accordance with ability to pay should be constantly before our eyes to guide our legislation. If the Congress maintains these principles, the voters, putting patriotism ahead of pocketbooks, will give you their applause.

In the future days, which we seek to make secure, we look forward to a world founded upon four essential human freedoms. The first is freedom of speech and expression—everywhere in the world. The second is freedom of every person to worship God in his own way—everywhere in the world. The third is freedom from want—which, translated into world terms, means economic understandings which will secure to every nation a healthy peacetime life for its inhabitants—everywhere in the world. The fourth is freedom from fear—which, translated into world terms, means a world-wide reduction of armaments to such a point and in such a thorough fashion that no nation will be in a position to commit an act of physical aggression against any neighbor—anywhere in the world.

That is no vision of a distant millennium. It is a definite basis for a kind of world attainable in our own time and generation. That kind of world is the very antithesis of the so-called new order of tyranny which the dictators seek to create with the crash of a bomb. To that new order we oppose the greater conception—the moral order. A good society is able to face schemes of world domination and foreign revolutions alike without fear.

Since the beginning of our American history, we have been engaged in change—in a perpetual peaceful revolution—a revolution which goes on steadily, quietly adjusting itself to changing conditions—without the concentration camp or the quick-lime in the ditch. The world order which we seek is the cooperation of free countries, working together in a friendly, civilized society.

This nation has placed its destiny in the hands and heads and hearts of its millions of free men and women; and its faith in freedom under the guidance of God. Freedom means the supremacy of human rights everywhere. Our support goes to those who struggle to gain those rights and keep them. Our strength is our unity of purpose. To that high concept there can be no end save victory.

21. Which of the following does the author give as an example of the "personal sacrifice" mentioned in line 10?

A) Higher taxation
B) Military service
C) Arms reduction
D) Four freedoms

22. Which of the following describes a major theme of the passage?

A) It is important for all people to have access to the benefits of an old-age system that supports citizens when they can no longer work.
B) Patriotic people will feel the need to pay more taxes to the government to obtain certain benefits they would not be able to afford.
C) People who want to work should be able to find work without bias and without undue hardship.
D) There are four basic freedoms that are vital to the health of people: speech, worship, freedom from want, and freedom from fear.

23. The author mentions that several aspects of the social economy need to be improved immediately. Which of the following does he <u>not</u> cite as an example in the passage?

A) Expanding retirement benefits
B) Expanding healthcare benefits
C) Expanding draft by the military
D) Expanding labor opportunities

24. In lines 10-25 ("I have ... their applause."), the author makes the claim that raising taxes is an action that will be enthusiastically supported by a patriotic populace. Which of the following would be an effective counterargument to this claim?

A) Americans are uninterested in pursuing freedom of any kind, and the four freedoms listed here are not considered important.
B) The average citizen already feels overburdened by taxes and feels the money is not being well-spent by the government.
C) Individuals will easily assent to the idea of a greater tax burden since it will naturally lead to a more prosperous state.
D) Patriots of all kinds are part of the natural makeup of America, and some will feel that the support of government is something that should be contemplated and debated.

25. Which of the following most precisely describes what the author means in lines 45 when he states, "That is no vision of a distant millennium"?

A) The author believes that these freedoms will no longer be attainable if action is not taken soon.
B) The author believes that, if his policies are enacted, these freedoms will last far into the future.
C) The author believes that these freedoms can only be attained by enacting the policies he has described.
D) The author believes that these freedoms are attainable in the near future.

26. As used in line 49 of the passage, the word "order" most nearly means

A) A command given by a military leader
B) An authoritative decision or direction
C) An arrangement of items in sequence
D) A system of world politics and society

27. As used in line 73 of the passage, the word "end" most nearly means

A) Death
B) Purpose
C) Outcome
D) Conclusion

28. Which selection from the passage best supports the idea that America is constantly evolving toward a better situation?

A) Lines 37-44 ("The fourth ... the world.")
B) Lines 51-55 ("To that new ... without fear.")
C) Lines 56-62 ("Since the beginning ... the ditch.")
D) Lines 65-68 ("This nation ... guidance of God.)

29. Read the following excerpt from an independent commentary on this passage. What idea from the passage is emphasized in this excerpt?

> It highlights the important social issues of the day, the very same issues our nation is struggling with at the moment. What can we do about our elderly? Do class distinctions matter? The fact of the matter is, no one wants to take care of a sickly aging relative, regardless of class. Then again, most of our elderly don't want to live with their offspring, either—rich or poor.

A) The need for a social safety net for the aging populace
B) The need for a lack of social class distinctions
C) The fact that many of the elderly do not want long-term care
D) The idea that people want to live independently

Questions 30-39 are based on the following passage.

The phylum Annelida, named for the Latin word *anellus*, meaning "ring," includes earthworms, leeches, and other similar organisms. In their typical form, these animals exhibit bilateral symmetry, a cylindrical cross section, and an elongate body divided externally into segments (*metameres*) by a series of rings (*annuli*). They are segmented internally as well, with most of the internal organs repeated in series in each segment. This organization is termed *metamerism*. Metameric segmentation is the distinguishing feature of this phylum, and provides it with a degree of evolutionary plasticity in that certain segments can be modified and specialized to perform specific functions. For example, in some species certain of the locomotor *parapodia*, or feet, may be modified for grasping, and some portions of the gut may evolve digestive specializations.

The gut is a straight, muscular tube that functions independently of the muscular activity in the body wall. The Annelida resemble the nematodes, another worm phylum, in possessing a fluid-filled internal cavity separating the gut from the body wall. In both phyla, this cavity is involved in locomotion. However, in the annelids, this space is formed at a much later time during the development of the embryo, and presumably evolved much later as well. This fluid-filled internal space is called a true *coelom*.

The annelid excretory and circulatory systems are well developed, and some members of the phylum have evolved respiratory organs. The nervous system offers a particular example of metameric specialization. It is concentrated anteriorly into enlarged cerebral ganglia connected to a ventral nerve cord that extends posteriorly and is organized into repeating segmental ganglia.

This phylum includes members bearing adaptations required for aquatic (marine or freshwater) or terrestrial habitats. They may be free-living entities or exist as parasites. Among the best known are the earthworm *Lumbricus*, the water leech *Hirudo*, and the marine worm *Nereis*.

Graphic 1

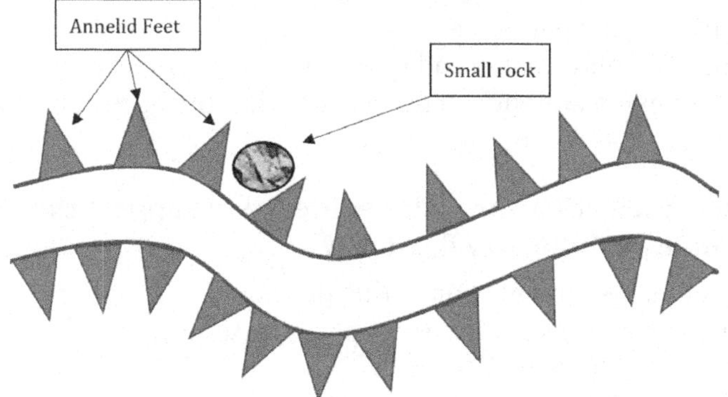

30. What is the purpose of this passage?

A) To describe the annelid nervous system
B) To describe the annelid digestive system
C) To introduce distinctive features of annelid anatomy
D) To define metamerism

31. What is the main difference between the Annelida and all other animal phyla?

A) The Annelida are worms.
B) The Annelida include the leeches.
C) The Annelida are metameric.
D) The Annelida are aquatic.

32. Which of the following is one evolutionary advantage of segmentation?

A) Segmented animals have many feet.
B) Segmented animals have a fluid-filled coelom.
C) Segments can specialize to perform certain functions.
D) Segments can evolve into more advanced forms of life.

33. What is meant by the term *metamerism* used in line 12?

A) Segmentation of the anatomy
B) A series of rings
C) Bilateral symmetry
D) Evolutionary plasticity

34. What is meant by the term *parapodia* used in line 18?

A) Specialization
B) Grasping appendages
C) Locomotion
D) Feet

35. Lines 24-34 discuss annelids and nematodes. Which of the following best describes how the author relates the characteristics of these two phyla?

A) Compare and contrast
B) Parts and whole
C) Cause and effect
D) Relative importance

36. The purpose of the paragraph in lines 45-47 in the passage is to:

A) Give familiar examples of members of the annelid phylum
B) Show that annelids may be parasites
C) Tell the reader that annelids may be adapted to aquatic environments
D) Show that there are many annelids in nature and that they are adapted to a wide variety of habitats

37. Which of the following selections provides evidence to support the statement that metamerism confers some evolutionary flexibility?

A) Line 12-13 ("Metameric segmentation ... this phylum")
B) Lines 17-21 ("in some species ... digestive specializations")
C) Lines 22-24 ("The gut ... body wall")
D) Lines 24-29 ("The Annelida ... in locomotion")

38. Some annelids form features to perform certain functions. Which function does Graphic 1 seem to be illustrating?

A) Annelid feet may be used for locomotion or movement.
B) Annelid feet may be used for climbing.
C) Annelid feet may be able to produce secretions.
D) Annelid feet may be used to grasp things.

39. After the first sentence, which of the following describes the structure of this passage relative to the paragraph content sequence?

A) Body parts; body systems; types, habitats, names; distinctive feature
B) Distinctive feature; body parts; body systems; types, habitats, names
C) Body systems; distinctive feature; types, habitats, names; body parts
D) Types, habitats, names; distinctive feature; body parts; body systems

Questions 40-49 are based on the following passage.

The planet Pluto was discovered in 1930 by an American astronomer named Clyde Tombaugh and was quickly added to our list of planets. Pluto keeps an elliptical orbit with a period of about 248 years where it occasionally crosses the orbit of Neptune. Pluto is even known to have several moons! Since 1978, five moons have been confirmed! Despite all of this, Pluto's status as a planet has been challenged recently, demoting it to a dwarf planet.

In 2006, the International Astronomical Union (IAU) met to establish a definition for planets. Until this meeting, there was surprisingly no formalized definition for a planet, all the while, more and more celestial bodies have been discovered all throughout our solar system. If strict rules weren't applied, any number of would-be planets could be added to our taxonomy.

The IAU created a checklist of needs to qualify an object as a planet. First, the object must have an orbit around the Sun. Many objects get caught in the gravity of the Sun, but very few actually enter a regular orbit.

Second, a planet must have enough mass to assume what is called hydrostatic equilibrium. This simply means that the gravity of the planet is strong enough to form a nearly spherical shape. Lucky for Pluto, it meets the first two conditions!

The third condition is where Pluto falls short: a planet must have "cleared the neighborhood" of its own orbit. The planet's gravity, which is a result of its mass, must be strong enough that it either absorbs other objects that cross its path or will fling them out of the way. Pluto is simply not massive enough to protect itself from the interference of other planets and objects that come into contact with it. The dwarf planet's orbital path also is more irregular than that of other planets, likely because of the gravitational interference of other objects. All eight of the other planets in our solar system seem mostly unaffected by objects and have a very stable orbit. As a result, Pluto has been reclassified as a dwarf planet for the time being.

Even with clear reasoning, there is a huge pushback regarding Pluto's status as a dwarf planet. Many scientists point out that asteroids remain near Earth and Jupiter, indicating that even our own planet has not cleared its neighborhood of other bodies. Just a century ago, the existence of Pluto was not yet confirmed. Now the tug of war between science and sentimentality holds Pluto's fate. Perhaps the advancement of technology will further expand our knowledge of these mid-sized celestial bodies and help us understand this cherished pseudo-planet.

Pluto's Estimated Mass (1931-2006)

Year	Mass (as a multiple of Earth's mass)
1931	1
1948	0.1 or 1/10
1976	0.01 or 1/100
1978	0.0015 or 1/650
2006	0.00218 or 1/459

40. Which of the following best states the purpose of the passage?

A) To entertain the reader with the differences between dwarf-planets and planets, using Pluto as an example
B) To describe the differences between planets and dwarf-planets and produce excitement for future research
C) To persuade the reader that Pluto's reclassification to a dwarf-planet is a good thing and has valid reasoning
D) To inform the reader of Pluto's reclassification to a dwarf-planet and the reasoning behind the decision

41. Which of the following does the passage list as a scientific reason in favor of Pluto being considered a planet?

A) Pluto has cleared its neighborhood.
B) Pluto has a regular orbit around the sun.
C) Pluto has a moon.
D) Pluto has always been a planet.

42. What is a probable definition for "celestial bodies" as found in lines 16-17 of the passage?

A) Large objects in space
B) Meteors and meteorites
C) Unconfirmed planets
D) Dwarf planets with moons

43. What does it mean for an object to have hydrostatic equilibrium as found in lines 27-28?

A) It has equal parts water and air.
B) Its mass in water helps it form into a spherical shape.
C) Its gravity is strong enough to hold a spherical shape.
D) The mass of the planet holds it in a steady shape without changing.

44. As used in line 38, the word "massive" most nearly means

A) Taking up space
B) Having mass
C) Moving quickly
D) Rotating consistently

45. Which of the following is the best stand-in for the word "sentimentality" as used in line 57?

A) Rationalism
B) Empiricism
C) Ethics
D) Nostalgia

46. What stance does the author hold regarding the status of Pluto as a dwarf planet?

A) He disagrees with the status and wants Pluto to be reinstated as a planet because the definition of a planet is inconsistent.
B) He agrees with the status because it is consistent with the IAU's guidelines.
C) He gives neither opinion but desires more information to make a clear determination.
D) He disagrees because Pluto has always been called a planet and should not be changed.

47. Review the chart entitled "Pluto's Estimated Mass (1915-2006)" What is the general trend over time regarding the estimation of Pluto's mass?

A) Pluto's estimated mass largely remained the same
B) Pluto's estimated mass increased over time.
C) Pluto's estimated mass had no real trend over time.
D) Pluto's estimated mass decreased over time.

48. Does the chart support Pluto's reclassification from planet to dwarf planet as its estimated mass has changed?

A) Yes, because a planet must have a large enough mass to clear its neighborhood, and Pluto's mass is estimated much lower than before
B) Yes, because Pluto has retained a spherical shape, even though the estimated mass has changed
C) No, because there is not enough information to support Pluto's reclassification
D) No, because Pluto's estimated mass has increased over time, but it continues to have an unstable orbit

49. Of the following, which would be the most suitable title for this passage?

A) Distinguishing Planets from Moons
B) The IAU's Taxonomy of Celestial Bodies
C) Pluto: Science vs. Sentiment
D) A Planet Once Again

Writing and Language

Questions 1–11 are based on the following passage.

A symbol of industry and perseverance, beavers have figured in literature, cartoons, and art for centuries. They have been valued in past centuries by the wealthy, who prized their fur for hats and coats, and they have been despised by farmers for the destruction of trees and stopping up of waterways. But while beavers are familiar figures, many of their contributions [1] were not as widely known. Their diligent building habits accomplish more than simply piling up sticks and creating ponds. Their dams serve not only as a barricade for the [2] beaver's benefit, but they also filter sediment and pollutants such as nitrogen and phosphorus from the water. Additionally, the dams aid the environment by trapping soil that is eroding from the land [3] upstream; slowing the loss and aiding the growth of crops on these lands.

1.

A) NO CHANGE
B) is
C) are
D) was

2.

A) NO CHANGE
B) beavers'
C) land's
D) their

3.

A) NO CHANGE
B) upstream, which is slowing
C) upstream; which slows
D) upstream, slowing

At one time the beaver population in North America numbered in the [4] ten's or possibly even hundreds of millions, but in the 17th century their numbers were decimated due to the demand for fur. In fact, the fur trade led to a conflict called the Beaver Wars (also known as the French and Iroquois Wars) between 1629 and 1701. Due to the extensive trapping for fur and the more recent use of their glands for perfume and medicine, the US beaver population has [5] declined sharply in the past few centuries.

4.

A) NO CHANGE
B) ten's, or possibly even hundred's
C) tens—or possibly even hundreds
D) tens or possibly even hundreds

5.

A) NO CHANGE
B) declines sharply
C) sharp declined
D) declined in a sharp way

With protective measures in place, beavers are now beginning to make a comeback in the US, but a new population brings its own problems. For example, the building of their dams [6] destroy trees and can hinder use of the water, so there is a question of how to encourage beavers while protecting natural resources and private property. Property owners can use several methods to discourage [7] beavers, wrapping tree trunks in metal mesh, spraying repellant on trees and bushes along the water, and setting traps. The wire mesh prevents the beavers from chewing the bark and thereby killing the trees. The repellant discourages beavers from eating the sprayed foliage because of [8] it's unpleasant taste. Finally, beavers can be trapped and relocated, [9] which encouraging them to settle in a new place.

Despite the aggressive fur trapping and the fact that many view these rodents as pests, beavers have shown resilience by continuing to thrive and adapt as necessary. Their colonies can be found throughout most of North America, as well as areas of South America, Asia, and Europe. [10] However, beavers are still in danger of extinction and need special protection.

[11]

6.

A) NO CHANGE
B) destroys
C) are destroying
D) destroyed

7.

A) NO CHANGE
B) beavers;
C) beavers:
D) beavers

8.

A) NO CHANGE
B) its
C) their
D) theirs

9.

A) NO CHANGE
B) that is encouraging
C) encouraging
D) encourage

10. How should the author modify the closing statement to best summarize the selection?

A) NO CHANGE
B) Sometimes they need to be settled in a new place, but this gives beavers a chance to thrive while keeping property undamaged.
C) All that beavers really want is to live in peace, building their dams.
D) Although beavers may bring challenges, their contributions make them an invaluable environmental asset.

11. The author is considering adding an anecdote about beavers devastating the crop on a small farm. To which paragraph should this be added?

A) the 1st paragraph
B) the 2nd paragraph
C) the 3rd paragraph
D) it should not be added

Questions 12–22 are based on the following passage.

What do wedding invitations, ancient Eastern pottery, and medieval books have in common? Each is likely to contain examples of calligraphy, a style of writing that has been used for [12] millennium in cultures around the world. Calligraphy, literally meaning "beautiful writing," has been used as an expression of history, belief, and beauty for people groups from a variety of religions, values, and socioeconomic levels. Some cultures view it as an artistic form of writing, while others consider it pure art. While these cultures represent a diverse tradition, calligraphy is generally divided into two [13] categories: Eastern and Western.

12.

A) NO CHANGE
B) a millennia
C) millennia
D) more than a millennia

13.

A) NO CHANGE
B) categories.
C) categories;
D) categories-

Eastern calligraphy, in particular, is not merely a writing style but a respected art form—superior to painting—that can be seen in manuscripts, vases, and even decoration on weapons. [14] The roots, in China, of calligraphy can be traced back more than 2,000 years. An elite Chinese education, as far back as the Han dynasty, included training in calligraphy. Several distinct styles developed, as each ancient kingdom had a unique set of characters. However, each style had careful [15] guidelines, such as the order of the brushstrokes when creating each character.

Calligraphy has also played a significant role in the Arab world. Heavily employed in a religious setting, [16] copying manuscripts or creating Islamic art were common uses of calligraphy. Beginning in the late 1900s, [17] calligraphy was used in the Hurufiyya movement to create modern art while seeking to preserve its distinctly Arabic influence.

14.

A) NO CHANGE
B) In China, the roots of calligraphy
C) The roots of calligraphy, in China
D) The roots of, in China, calligraphy

15.

A) NO CHANGE
B) tools
C) history
D) meaning

16.

A) NO CHANGE
B) calligraphy was commonly used in copying manuscripts or creating Islamic art
C) common uses of calligraphy included copying manuscripts or creating Islamic art
D) frequently calligraphy was used to copy manuscripts or create Islamic art

17.

A) NO CHANGE
B) calligraphy was employed in the Hurufiyya movement
C) the Hurufiyya movement invented calligraphy
D) the Hurufiyya movement used calligraphy

Like Islamic calligraphy, Western calligraphy was most commonly used for copying religious manuscripts before the invention of the printing press. [18] In large part this was due to the fact that very few outside of the monasteries were literate. This began to change when Charlemagne rose to power in the late eighth century. He made a great effort to promote scholarship and the literary arts, including contributions to book-copying centers. [19] Charlemagne was never able to learn to write himself.

After the printing press came into use, the creation of hand-copied books naturally declined, [20] so calligraphy remained in practice and continues to this day. In fact, a modern calligraphy movement began in the late [21] 1800s and is still flourishing more than a century later. Some calligraphers continue to use tools very similar to the ones employed centuries ago, while others use technology to create their designs. [22] Although not everyone uses this technology, it proves that calligraphy has moved into the modern world.

18.

A) NO CHANGE
B) Altogether
C) Completely
D) Somewhat

19. Where is the best place for this sentence?

A) NO CHANGE
B) At the beginning of this paragraph, because it gives background for why Charlemagne advocated for writing.
C) In the previous paragraph, as a transition to this one.
D) It should be removed from the selection because the information is not relevant.

20.

A) NO CHANGE
B) however
C) yet
D) because

21.

A) NO CHANGE
B) 1800's
C) 18th century
D) eighteenth century

22. Which of the following sentences would make a good conclusion to the selection?

A) NO CHANGE
B) Calligraphy has lasted for thousands of years in China, truly standing the test of time.
C) Bridging the gap between the written word and art, and between diverse cultures, calligraphy is an enduring tradition.
D) Thanks to the various world religions, the ancient art of calligraphy has been preserved for today's audience.

Questions 23–33 are based on the following passage and supplementary material.

The familiar notes of Joplin's [23] "The Entertainer," for many, bring back memories of chasing the local ice cream truck, wrinkled dollar bills in hand. Choosing from a brightly colored menu and slowly eating drippy ice cream bars was a quintessential part of childhood summers for many. Today these trucks are [24] lesser common than a couple of decades ago, leading some to wonder why ice cream is no longer as popular. However, despite the vanishing ice cream trucks, the consumption of frozen treats remains a [25] depleting business. As society has changed, the method of attracting customers has also adapted.

23.

A) NO CHANGE
B) *The Entertainer*,
C) The Entertainer,
D) the entertainer

24.

A) NO CHANGE
B) less common
C) less uncommon
D) not as uncommon

25.

A) NO CHANGE
B) shaky
C) volatile
D) booming

1.[26] Increasing, health is a concern for Americans, and ice cream consumption has steadily decreased since the turn of the century. *2.* Concerns over fat and sugar content have caused many to blacklist the treat in favor of healthier options. *3.* [27] Whether yogurt is a healthy alternative to ice cream is debatable, particularly as servings can be larger and toppings can add hundreds of sugar-dense calories. *4.* One of these options is frozen yogurt, which has grown into a thriving business in recent decades. *5.* The trucks that cruised neighborhoods at one time [28] are replaced with thousands of tiny shops offering self-serve yogurt and toppings. *6.* Even so, frozen yogurt is providing significant competition to the ice cream industry as consumers eagerly respond to the lower-calorie offering.

26.

A) NO CHANGE
B) Greater
C) Greatly
D) Increasingly

27. Where is the best place for this sentence?

A) NO CHANGE
B) After sentence 4
C) After sentence 5
D) After sentence 6

28.

A) NO CHANGE
B) were
C) have been
D) is

[29] Ice cream remains an overwhelmingly popular treat, both in the US and around the globe. [30] Although ice cream and frozen yogurt sales have stagnated in the US, worldwide consumption of ice cream is on the rise. To meet the demand at home and abroad, the US produces large amounts of ice cream, close to a billion gallons per year. Much of this goes to neighboring nations: the US exports 60,000 metric tons just to Canada, Mexico, and the Caribbean. Since the origin of ice cream can be traced all the way back to 200 B.C. in China, and since China is the most populous nation in the world, it is not surprising that it is also the world's greatest consumer of ice cream, though several nations, including New Zealand, the US, and Australia, consume more per person. [31]

Gallons of Frozen Dessert Sold Annually in the US

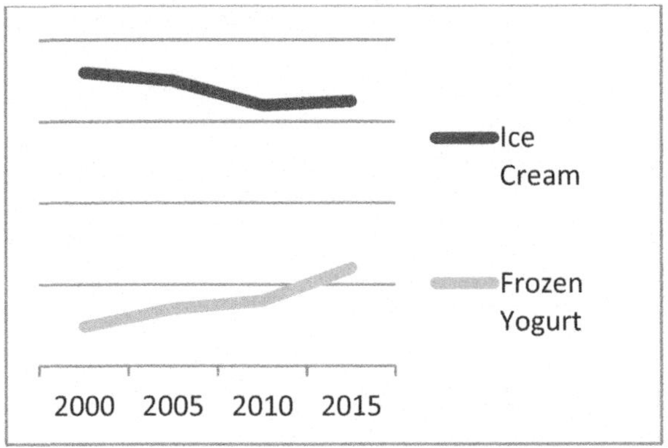

29. How can the author best transition from the previous paragraph?

A) NO CHANGE
B) Because of the popularity of frozen yogurt, ice cream remains
C) Due to this competition, ice cream is no longer
D) Despite the competition, ice cream remains

30. Which of the following statements best uses the information given in the graph?

A) NO CHANGE
B) Even though ice cream sales have dropped slightly in the US since 2000, as frozen yogurt sales climb
C) While frozen yogurt sales have boomed in the last decade
D) Despite declining interest in ice cream over the past several years

31. Which of the following facts would be useful to add to this paragraph?

A) NO CHANGE
B) The amount of ice cream produced per year by Blue Bell
C) The amount of ice cream consumed per year in China
D) The most popular flavor of frozen yogurt

It seems [32] unusual that while frozen yogurt may be the new trend, ice cream is still a beloved American—and global—dessert. And as healthier options continue to arise, the market is projected to keep increasing. So [33] while you may not hear the tinny notes of an ice cream truck in your neighborhood this summer, your options for a cold, sweet treat are only increasing. [33]

32.

A) NO CHANGE
B) unexpected
C) apparent
D) unlikely

33.

A) NO CHANGE
B) whether
C) however
D) unfortunately

Questions 34–44 are based on the following passage.

A young 13th-century mathematician named Leonardo of Pisa is [34] guilty of introducing the Hindu-Arabic numeral system (0, 1, 2 ...) to the Western world. Though he received little recognition in his day, his work had a lasting impact on modern society, permanently changing the way mathematics was [35] viewed, and calculations were performed. Although Leonardo (sometimes known as Leonardo Bonacci or Leonardo Fibonacci) [36] was young, he was very knowledgeable, today he is virtually unknown except for one famous contribution: the Fibonacci sequence. [37] Sadly, the sequence wasn't even his own discovery, as it had been well known for centuries prior to appearing in his book *Liber Abaci* (or *Book of Calculation*).

34.

A) NO CHANGE
B) responsible for
C) the one who was
D) in charge of

35.

A) NO CHANGE
B) viewed;
C) viewed:
D) viewed

36. Which of the following is the best introduction for this sentence?

A) NO CHANGE
B) lived centuries ago, his work endures
C) is famous for many things
D) made numerous other contributions to mathematics

37.

A) NO CHANGE
B) Ironically
C) Disappointingly
D) Tragically

1. The Fibonacci sequence, sometimes called "nature's secret code," is an infinite pattern. *2.* Rather than a simple, linear sequence such as 1, 3, 5, 7..., this sequence is more complex. *3.* Each term is achieved by adding the two previous terms: 1, 1, 2, 3, 5.... *4.* Graphing the numbers creates a steep curve. *5.* [38] <u>This curve is represented in various ways in nature. *6.* It can be seen in the</u> growth pattern of many sunflower seeds, the curve of a shell, and even the whorl of a galaxy. *7.* [39] <u>The Fibonacci sequence is closely related to the Golden Ratio, which also appears in various objects, as well as manmade structures.</u> *8.* [40] <u>Although this sequence only appears in select aspects of nature, it illustrates how nature always follows a pattern.</u>

38. What is the best way to combine the underlined portion?

A) NO CHANGE
B) This curve shows up in almost every part of nature, such as the
C) This curve is represented in a variety of natural forms, including the
D) Fibonacci can be seen in numerous ways in nature, such as the

39. Which sentence best supports the main idea of the paragraph?

A) NO CHANGE
B) Not all sunflowers follow this design; approximately 20% have a different but equally intricate pattern.
C) Although Fibonacci never knew the extent of his discovery, he revolutionized mathematics.
D) Following this design allows plants to optimize their efficiency, fitting the maximum number of seeds into a given space.

40. What is the best location for this sentence?

A) NO CHANGE
B) after sentence 4
C) after sentence 6
D) DELETE, because this sentence does not fit in this paragraph

Although the number sequence has been studied and used in a variety of [41] ways, Fibonacci's introduction of the numeral system is arguably a much greater contribution. Originally this system was developed in India well over 1,000 years ago, and it offers a mathematical system much more [42] challenging to advanced mathematics, such as the algebra that is now the bane of many students. Prior to the Hindu-Arabic system, the Western world relied on Roman numerals and instruments such as the abacus. These are more complicated for calculations, and Roman numerals are also more challenging when writing out long numbers. Fibonacci included decimal places along with the ten digits of the Arabic system. While numbers are written differently in different parts of the world, the general system is accepted worldwide.

When Fibonacci introduced the *modus Indorum* ("method of the Indians," as he called the Hindu-Arabic system), he could not have [43] prophesied that his work would spread around the world. [44] Yet every time you glance at a clock, make a purchase, or count the number of donuts in the box, you should thank Fibonacci for his system. The modern world relies on the contribution of this young, little-known Italian mathematician.

41.

A) NO CHANGE
B) ways:
C) ways;
D) ways

42.

A) NO CHANGE
B) difficult
C) conducive
D) agreeable

43.

A) NO CHANGE
B) understood
C) known
D) foretold

44. Does this sentence fit in the selection?

A) Yes, because the supporting examples are relevant
B) Yes, because it sums up the main idea of the selection
C) No, because the examples are not relevant
D) No, because the tone does not fit with the rest of the selection

Math – No Calculator

Questions 1–13 are multiple choice. Questions 14–17 are grid-in.

1. A taxi ride costs \$4.25 for the first mile and \$0.70 for each mile after the first. Which of the following functions $c(d)$ gives the total cost (in dollars) of traveling d miles ($d \geq 1$)?

A) $c(d) = 3.55 + 0.70(d + 1)$
B) $c(d) = 3.55 + 0.70(d - 1)$
C) $c(d) = 4.25 + 0.70d$
D) $c(d) = 4.25 + 0.70(d - 1)$

2. Which of these expresses the equation $y = 4x - 2$ as x in terms of y?

A) $x = 4y - 2$
B) $x = -4y + 2$
C) $x = \frac{1}{4}y + 2$
D) $x = \frac{1}{4}y + \frac{1}{2}$

3. Which of the following is equivalent to the inequality $2|x + 3| - 9 \geq -1$.

A) $-1 \leq x \leq 7$
B) $-7 \leq x \leq 1$
C) $x \leq -1$ and $x \geq 7$
D) $x \leq -7$ and $x \geq 1$

4. The solution to which of the following systems of inequalities is graphed below?

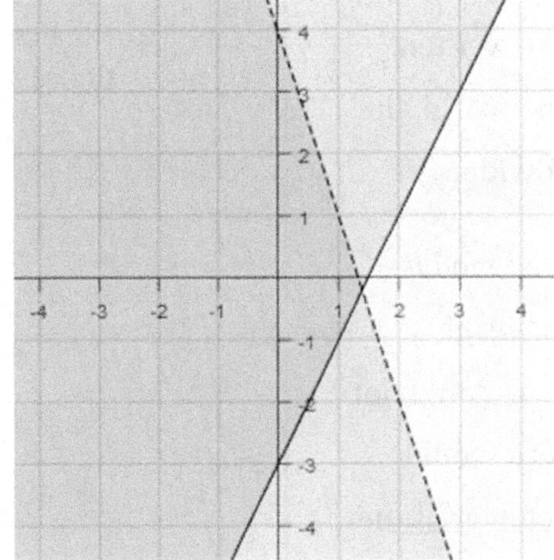

A) $y < -3x + 4$
$4x - 2y \leq 6$
B) $y \geq 2x - 3$
$y < 3x + 4$
C) $x < -3y + 4$
$y + 3 \leq 2x$
D) $y > 4 - 3x$
$y \leq 2x - 3$

5. Which of the following is the correct graph of the system of inequalities below?

$$x - y > 1$$
$$2x + y > 2$$

A) 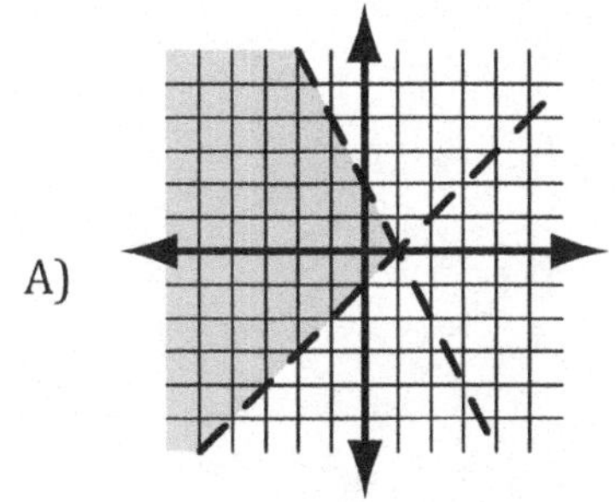

C) 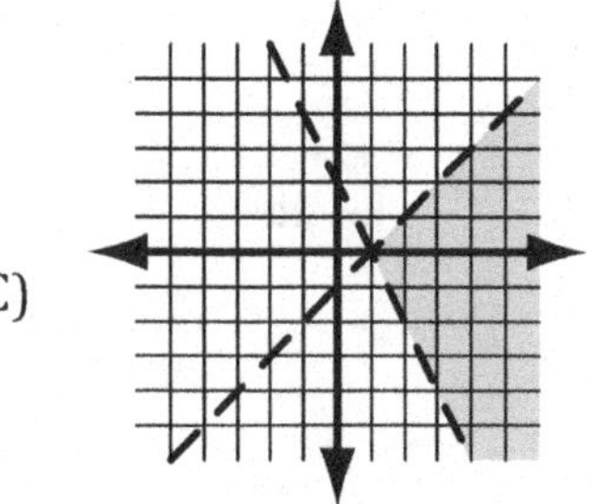

B) 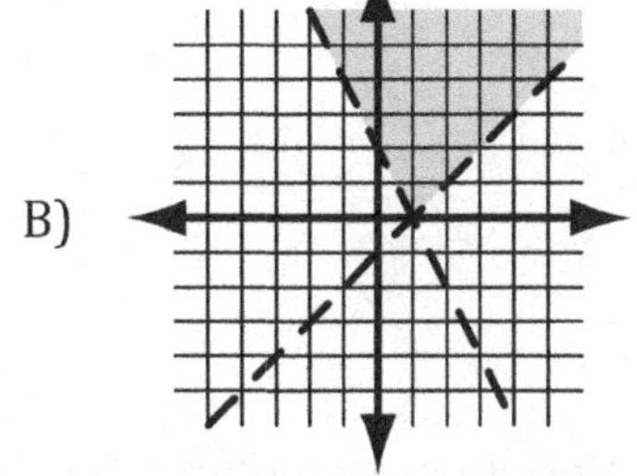

D) 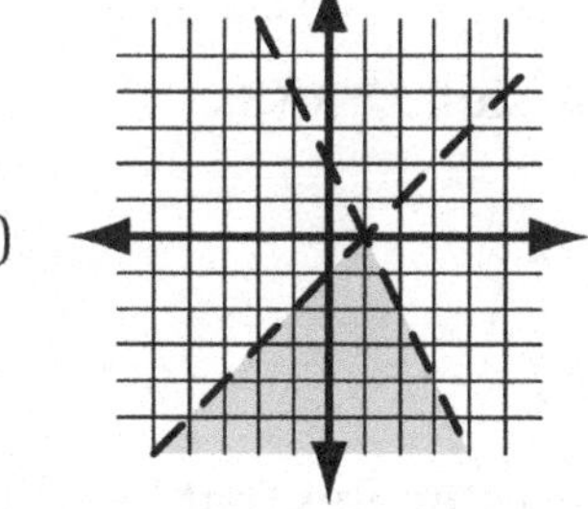

6. Which of the following is equivalent to $3 - 2x < 5$?

A) $x < 1$
B) $x > 1$
C) $x < -1$
D) $x > -1$

7. A certain exam has 30 questions. A student gets 1 point for each question he gets right and loses half a point for a question he answers incorrectly; he neither gains nor loses any points for a question left blank. If *C* is the number of questions a student gets right and *B* is the number of questions he leaves blank, which of the following represents his score on the exam?

A) $C - \frac{1}{2}B$
B) $C - \frac{1}{2}(30 - B)$
C) $C - \frac{1}{2}(30 - B - C)$
D) $(30 - C) - \frac{1}{2}(30 - B)$

8. A building has a number of floors of equal height, as well as a thirty-foot spire on top. If the height of each floor in feet is *h*, and there are *n* floors in the building, which of the following represents the building's total height in feet?

A) $n + h + 30$
B) $nh + 30$
C) $30n + h$
D) $30h + n$

9. If $x + y > 0$ when $x > y$, which of the following cannot be true?

A) $x = 6$ and $y = -1$
B) $x = -3$ and $y = 0$
C) $x = -4$ and $y = -3$
D) $x = 3$ and $y = -3$

10. Simplify the expression $\frac{x^2+2x-24}{5x-20}$.

A) $\frac{x-4}{5}$
B) $\frac{x+6}{5}$
C) $\frac{(x-4)(x+6)}{5(x-4)}$
D) $\frac{(x+4)(x+6)}{5(x-4)}$

11. Simplify the expression $x^6 \times (3x)^2$.

A) $3x^8$
B) $3x^{12}$
C) $9x^8$
D) $9x^{12}$

12. A theater manager estimates that he will sell 600 tickets to a play if he prices tickets at \$10 each. He also estimates that he will sell fifty fewer tickets for every dollar the price is raised or fifty more tickets for every dollar the price is lowered. Write a function $r(x)$ for the estimated revenue if the theater raises the price by x dollars.

A) $r(x) = -50x^2 - 100x + 6000$
B) $r(x) = -50x^2 + 100x + 6000$
C) $r(x) = 50x^2 - 1100x - 6000$
D) $r(x) = 50x^2 + 1100x + 6000$

13. Compare the graphs of $f(x) = 3^x$ and $g(x) = 3^{x+1}$.

A) The graph of g is the graph of f shifted one unit down.
B) The graph of g is the graph of f shifted one unit up.
C) The graph of g is the graph of f shifted one unit to the left.
D) The graph of g is the graph of f shifted one unit to the right.

14. Exponential functions grow by equal factors over equal intervals. By what factor does the exponential function $f(x) = 3 \times 2^x$ grow over every interval whose length is 3?

Grid your answer.

15. A librarian makes 50% more per hour for each hour that he works in excess of 40 hours each week. The linear function $s(h) = 27h + 720$ represents his weekly salary (in dollars) if he works h hours more than 40 hours that week. For example, his weekly salary is $s(10) = 990$ dollars if he works 50 hours in one week (because $10 + 40 = 50$). What is his hourly wage (in dollars) after he has already worked the initial 40 hours in one week?

Grid your answer.

16. Calculate the sixth term $f(6)$ of the sequence defined as:

$$f(n) = \begin{cases} 1 & n = 1, 2 \\ f(n-1) + 2f(n-2) & n > 2 \end{cases}$$

Grid your answer.

17. Consider the function $f(x) = (x - 3)(x^2 - x - 2)$. What is the sum of all values of x for which the graph of the function intersects the x-axis?

Grid your answer.

Math – Calculator

Questions 1–27 are multiple choice. Questions 28–31 are gridded.

1. Solve the following system of equations.

$$y = 3x + 2$$
$$2x + y = 7$$

A) $x = -1, y = 5$
B) $x = -1, y = 9$
C) $x = 1, y = 5$
D) $x = 1, y = 9$

2. The table below lists values for x and $f(x)$.

x	$f(x)$
1	2
2	5
3	10
4	17
5	26

Which of the following equations describes the relationship between x and $f(x)$?

A) $f(x) = x + 1$
B) $f(x) = x^2$
C) $f(x) = (-x)^2$
D) $f(x) = x^2 + 1$

3. Which of the following equations represents the relationship between x and y, shown in the table below?

x	y
-3	-21
-1	-3
0	6
2	24
5	51

A) $y = 9x + 6$
B) $y = 7x$
C) $y = 3x + 18$
D) $y = 12x + 6$

4. The mean test grade on Ms. Juarez's biology final was 86, while the median test grade was 82.5. What could explain the difference between these two values?

A) Most students scored less than 80.
B) Most students scored between 82.5 and 86.
C) Several students had low, outlying scores, pulling the median down.
D) Several students had high, outlying scores, pulling the mean up.

5. If the two lines $2x + y = 0$ and $y = 3$ are plotted on a typical xy-coordinate grid, at which point will they intersect?

A) (-1.5, 3)
B) (1.5, 3)
C) (-1.5, 0)
D) (4, 1)

6. What is the value of $\frac{x^3+2x}{x+3}$ when $x = -1$?

A) $-\frac{3}{2}$
B) $-\frac{2}{3}$
C) $\frac{1}{2}$
D) $\frac{3}{4}$

7. What is the value of $\frac{2x-2}{x-3}$ when $x = -1$?

A) 0
B) 1
C) 2
D) -2

8. Simplify: $4(-3 + 5i) + 6(1 - 3i)$.

A) $18 + 38i$
B) $13 + 18i$
C) $-6 + 2i$
D) $-6 - 2i$

9. An MP3 player is set to play songs at random from the fifteen songs it contains in its memory. Any song can be played at any time, even if it is repeated. There are 5 songs by Band A, 3 songs by Band B, 2 by Band C, and 5 by Band D. If the player has just played two songs in a row by Band D, what is the probability that the next song will also be by Band D?

A) 1 in 5
B) 1 in 3
C) 1 in 9
D) 1 in 27

10. 9.5% of the people in a town voted for a certain proposition in a municipal election. If the town's population is 51,623, about how many people in the town voted for the proposition?

A) 3,000
B) 5,000
C) 7,000
D) 10,000

11. A reporter for a school newspaper surveys the students at the school to ask if they prefer chocolate, vanilla, or strawberry ice cream. Of the students who answer her question, 35% prefer vanilla, and 40% prefer chocolate. What percent of the students she surveyed prefer strawberry?

A) 15%
B) 25%
C) 45%
D) There is not enough information to say.

12. Liz runs a woodworking stand at a community market. She purchases a friend's handmade pens for $15 each to sell along with her own goods. To make a profit, she marks the pens up by 30%. On the last day of the market, she marks down everything by 20%. How much are the pens now?

A) $15.60
B) $15.90
C) $16.64
D) $17.90

13. Mrs. Patterson's classroom has sixteen empty chairs. All the chairs are occupied when every student is present. If $\frac{2}{5}$ of the students are absent, how many students make up her entire class?

A) 16 students
B) 32 students
C) 24 students
D) 40 students

14. The probability that Alisha chooses a philosophy class is 0.30. The probability that she chooses a qualitative methods class, given that she chooses a philosophy class, is 0.40. Finally, the probability she chooses a philosophy class or a qualitative methods class is 0.62. What is the probability she chooses a qualitative methods class?

A) 0.32
B) 0.38
C) 0.44
D) 0.52

Question 15 is based on the following figure (not drawn to scale):

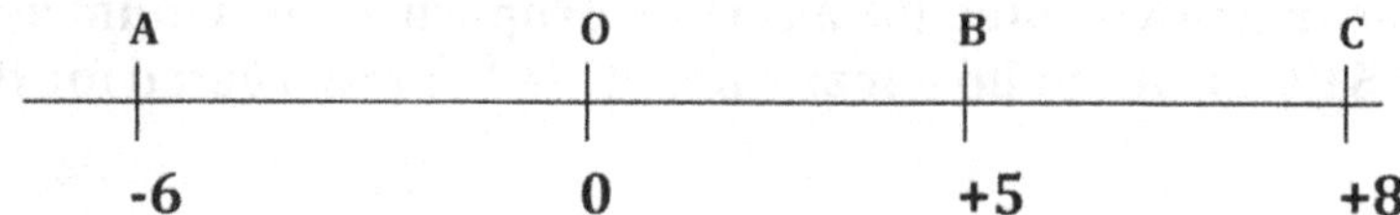

15. In the figure, A, B, and C are points on the number line, where O is the origin. What is the ratio of the distance $\overline{BC}$ to distance $\overline{AB}$?

A) 3:5
B) 8:5
C) 8:11
D) 3:11

16. The numbers of volunteers in different states are shown in the table below. Which of the following statements is true?

Texas	8	17	18	19	20	21	21	21	22	28	29	31	41	45	48
New Mexico	7	11	15	29	30	30	31	33	34	36	37	42	44	44	45

A) The numbers of volunteers in Texas have a greater median and mean.
B) The numbers of volunteers in Texas have a greater median and a smaller mean.
C) The numbers of volunteers in Texas have a smaller median and mean.
D) The numbers of volunteers in Texas have a smaller median and a greater mean.

17. Marcus is purchasing hamburger patties and hot dogs for a community barbecue. He needs a total of 500, and plans to buy at least twice as many hot dogs as hamburgers. Which of the following systems of equations/inequalities represents his purchase, if x represents hamburgers and y represents hot dogs?

A) $x \geq y$
$2x + y = 500$

B) $x \geq 2y$
$x + y = 500$

C) $x \leq 2y$
$2x + 3y = 500$

D) $2x \leq y$
$x + y = 500$

18. Given the table shown below, what is the probability that a student is a Democrat or prefers math?

	History	Science	Math	Total
Democrat	13	30	37	80
Republican	20	38	12	70
Total	33	68	49	150

A) $\frac{129}{150}$
B) $\frac{46}{75}$
C) $\frac{37}{150}$
D) $\frac{37}{80}$

Questions 19 and 20 are based on the following table:

Kyle bats third in the batting order for the Badgers baseball team. The table below shows the number of hits that Kyle had in each of 6 consecutive games played during one week in July.

Day of Week	Number of Hits
Monday	1
Tuesday	2
Wednesday	3
Thursday	1
Friday	1
Saturday	4

19. What is the mode of the numbers in the distribution shown in the table?

A) 1
B) 2
C) 3
D) 4

20. What is the mean of the numbers in the distribution shown in the table?

A) 1
B) 2
C) 3
D) 4

Questions 21 and 22 refer to the following information.

The table below records the amount of sleep that a group of students had the night before a test, the number of students in each group, and the test scores of each group.

	Group 1	Group 2	Group 3
Amount of Sleep	<6.5 hrs	6.5–7.5 hrs	>7.5 hrs
Number of Students	6	4	2
Test Scores	83, 77, 89, 68, 91, 72	82, 88, 77, 90	86, 93

21. What is the probability that a randomly chosen student slept less than 6.5 hours and scored in the 80s?

A) $\frac{1}{4}$
B) $\frac{1}{6}$
C) $\frac{2}{9}$
D) $\frac{5}{12}$

22. Which group has the lowest mean score?

A) Group 1
B) Group 2
C) Group 3
D) multiple groups share the lowest mean

23. Solve the equation $\sqrt{4x-3}+2=x$ for x.

A) $x = 1$
B) $x = 7$
C) $x = -1$ and $x = 7$
D) $x = 1$ and $x = 7$

24. If $f(x)$ is a quadratic function with roots at $x = -4$ and $x = 6$, what is $f(x)$?

A) $f(x) = x^2 - 24$
B) $f(x) = x^2 - 10x + 24$
C) $f(x) = x^2 - 2x - 24$
D) $f(x) = x^2 + 2x - 24$

25. Which of the following represents the sum of $\frac{3}{x+2} + \frac{x}{x^2+10x+16}$?

A) $\frac{3}{x+2}$
B) $\frac{x+6}{x+8}$
C) $\frac{2(x+6)}{(x+2)(x+8)}$
D) $\frac{4(x+6)}{(x+8)(x+2)}$

26. Which of the following represents the product of $(4x^3 - 2x + 4)(x - 8)$?

A) $4x^4 - 32x^3 + 18x - 32$
B) $4x^4 - 32x^3 - 18x^2 - 2x - 12$
C) $4x^4 - 32x^3 - 2x^2 + 20x - 32$
D) $4x^4 - 28x^3 - 2x^2 + 16x - 4$

27. In the figure, *ABCD* is a parallelogram. The angles are m∠$B = (3x)°$ and m∠$C = (4x + 5)°$. Find m∠A.

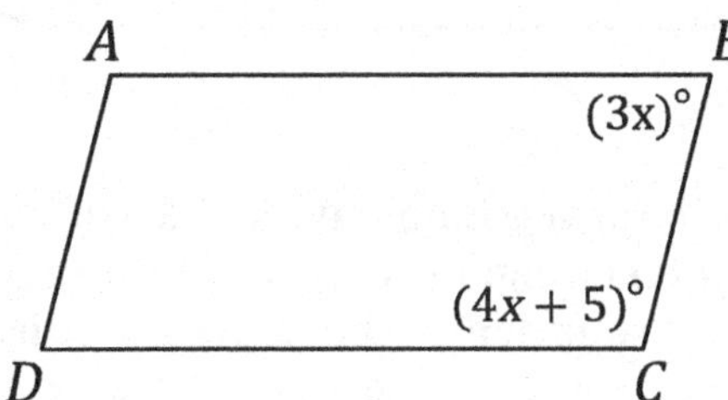

A) m∠A = 95°
B) m∠A = 100°
C) m∠A = 105°
D) m∠A = 110°

28. In the figure, the radius of circle *C* is 8. What is the area of the shaded sector, rounded to the nearest tenth?

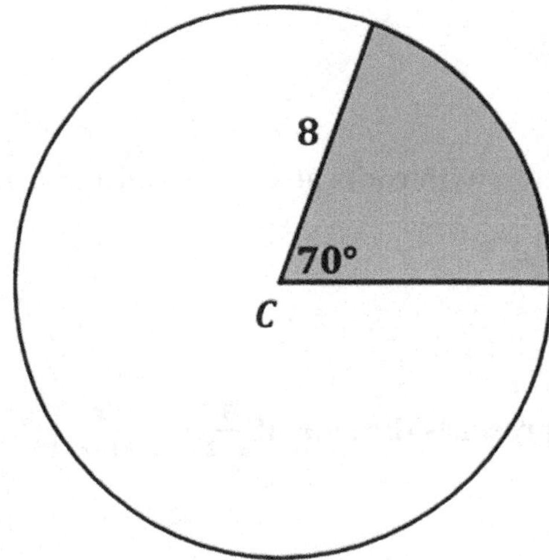

Grid your answer.

29. The figure shows the shape of a large swimming pool in a Las Vegas resort. The pool is a rectangle with semicircles on either end. If the pool is 8 ft deep throughout, what is the volume of the pool in cubic feet, rounded to the nearest whole number?

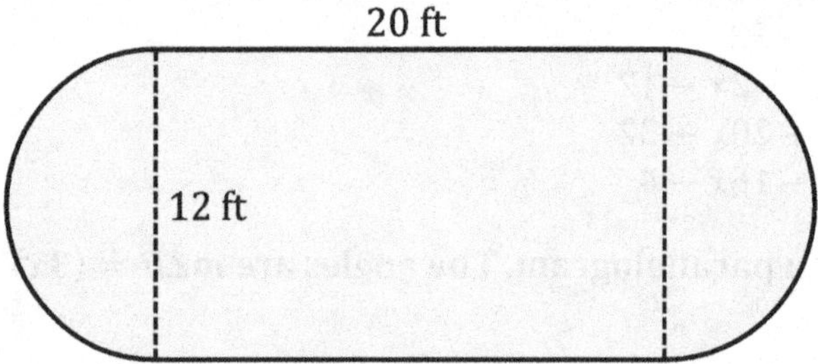

Grid your answer.

30. In the figure, ΔABC is an equilateral triangle with sides of length 10 in. Circle O is inscribed in this triangle, so that it is tangent to ΔABC at three points, the midpoint of each side. What is the radius of circle O rounded to the nearest tenth?

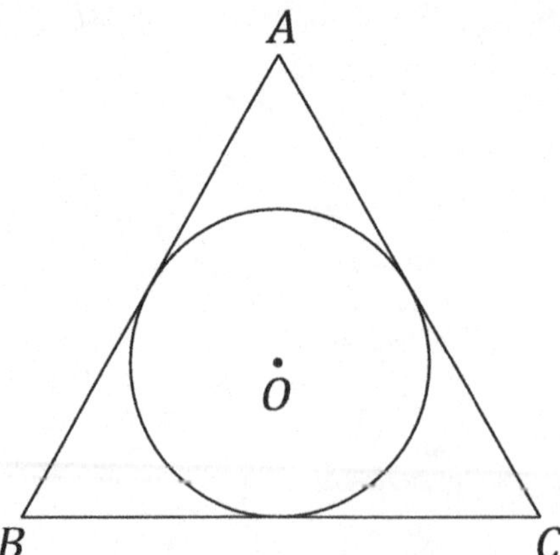

Grid your answer.

31. A seller purchases wholesale merchandise and makes a profit by selling it for more than she paid for it. When she purchases an item, she adds 25% to the price she paid for it, and lists it for sale at that price. If an item does not sell within 6 months, she places it on clearance, and reduces the price by 10%. What is her percentage profit on clearance items, rounded to the nearest tenth of a percent?

Grid your answer.

Answer Key and Explanations

Reading

1. Choice C is the best answer. Choice B is incorrect because Mother did not forbid any presents. Choices A and D give some of the problems presented in the selection, but do not offer a complete summary. Lines 14-17 ("We haven't got ... where the fighting was.") show that Father is not around. Lines 3-8 ("It's so dreadful ... injured sniff") indicate that the girls are poor and hint at being unable to purchase even nice clothes. Each of the sisters makes their displeasure known.

2. Choice C is the best answer. Of the options listed, Choice C is the only one that refers to men suffering in the army. Choice A references a lack of Christmas presents but does not mention the reason for this. Choice B talks about the girls not having their father with them for some indefinite period of time, but that does not by itself imply that there is a war going on. Choice D discusses the limited usefulness of their theoretical monetary contributions.

3. Choice D is the best answer. We know from the very first line in the passage that Christmas is approaching and Jo's comment in lines 14-15 ("We haven't ... long time") indicates that their father is not expected to return home anytime soon. Thus, the most reasonable inference is that he is not likely to return home in time for Christmas. Although the sisters are all concerned about their father's wellbeing, there is nothing to indicate that he is likely to die, as in Choice C. Similarly, we have no indication about his preference for what his daughters do with their money as in Choices A and B.

4. Choice D is the best answer. The other sisters all specify what they want to buy: Amy in lines 41-42 ("I shall ... drawing pencils"), Beth in line 38 ("I planned ... new music"), and Jo in lines 34-35 ("I do ... for myself"). We are given no indication as to what Meg wants.

5. Choice B is the best answer. In the context of the sentence, Amy's sniff indicates that her sense of fairness, vanity, and pride has been offended. While Amy is indeed sympathetic to the sentiments expressed by her sisters as in Choice C, injured would not be a word used to express that. There is nothing in this passage indicating Amy has been physically harmed as in Choice A, or is ill as in Choice D.

6. Choice C is the best answer. *Undine and Sintram* (de la Motte Fouqué, 1855) is a novella based on a fairy tale. The reader who is unfamiliar with this title can deduce it from the context of lines 34-37: after saying "I do want to buy Undine and Sintram for myself," the following sentence reads, "'I've wanted it so long,' said Jo, who was a bookworm." The author would not mention that Jo was a bookworm in this sentence unless the item named were a book.

7. Choice D is the best answer. The presence of a hearth brush and kettle-holder indicate a fireplace. The fact that the fireplace "hears" Beth's sigh when no one else does means that Beth is close to it.

8. Choice A is the best answer. Previously, Beth has said that she plans to spend her dollar on new music (Line 38), so the inference that can be made here is that Beth would like to be practicing music. Drawing (Choice B) is what Amy does. She says she will buy Faber's drawing pencils with her dollar. Housework (Choice C) is what Beth complains makes it difficult for her to practice. Schoolwork (Choice D) is what Amy complains about after Beth's complaint.

9. Choice C is the best answer. As the sisters discuss their situation, it is clear that each one of them faces a particular set of challenges. They all desire things that they do not have, and they are all required to do things they would prefer not to. The passage also indicates that their father is away fighting in a war. Although one of the sisters mentions that there are other girls who have plenty of pretty things, the overarching sense of the passage is that everyone has their own troubles.

10. Choice B is the best answer. In lines 1-4 of passage 1 ("At this second...at the first."), his second inaugural address, Lincoln discusses his first address, describing how the first actions in the coming Civil War were just beginning to take place. The country had suffered much since then as the war got underway and continued throughout his first term as president. This change in the nation inspired the plea for an end to the hostilities that dominates his second inaugural address.

11. Choice C is the best answer. "Peculiar" can mean odd (Choice A) or bizarre (Choice B), but these make no sense in this context. "Peculiar" can also mean specific (Choice C), unique, particular, distinctive, or characteristic, which is the meaning in this case, because in lines 33-36, Lincoln was referring to the specific and unique situation that, "One-eighth of the whole population were colored slaves, not distributed generally over the Union, but localized in the southern part of it," and the specific interest these slaves constituted. Appropriate (Choice D) is another synonym offered by a thesaurus for the second (correct) meaning, but its denotation of suitable or fitting does not make sense in this context as specific, unique, particular, distinctive, etc. does.

12. Choice C is the best answer. Lincoln's Biblical quotation established the subsequent supposition that the war is an example of the woe for causing offenses described in the quotation (just as previously in the same sentence he supposed American slavery was one of the offenses that must needs come). Choice A does not support the supposition that God gave the war as woe; if anything, it supports his contention that despite their basic differences regarding slavery. In lines 28-29, it is said that "both parties deprecated war." Choice B reinforces the parallelism and comparison/contrast established in lines 24-26 ("saving the Union without war/destroy it without war"; "make war rather than let the nation survive/accept war rather than let it perish") and continued in lines 44-50 ("Neither...expected....Neither anticipated....Each looked for....") rather than supporting that war was God's giving both sides woe for offenses. Choice D supports that even though everyone wanted the war to end soon ("Fondly...away", penultimate sentence), if it lasted longer it would be God's will.

13. Choice C is the best answer. Lincoln's final paragraph, lines 84-92 of passage 1 ("With malice toward...with all nations."), issues a plea for "malice toward none, with charity for all." This statement represents an attempt to heal the pain that existed between the North and South during the Civil War. Lincoln wants the United States to reunite and move on from the war as a solid, individual, caring nation.

14. Choice A is the best answer. Lincoln believed that the South was wrong for making war by trying to secede from the Union, and the North was right for trying to maintain the Union by refusing to accept the hostile action. The quote in lines 28-32 ("Both parties ... war came.") shows he believed the actions of the North were more justifiable than those of the South.

15. Choice A is the best answer. In lines 75-83 of passage 1, Lincoln states that "if God wills that it [the war] continue ... until every drop of blood drawn with the lash shall be paid by another drawn with the sword, as was said three thousand years ago, so still it must be said 'the judgments of the Lord are true and righteous altogether.'" This statement indicates Lincoln's believe that the war was a product of God's will.

16. Choice D is the best answer. By using the same syntactic structure in "what we say here" and "what they did here", Lincoln employed parallel structure to reinforce his message contrasting words vs. deeds. Epiphora (Choice A), epistrophe, is repeating the same words/phrases at the *ends* of sentences/clauses. An example in Lincoln's Gettysburg Address is: "that government of the people, by the people, for the people..." in its final sentence. Choice B, Anaphora, is repeating the same words/phrases at the *beginnings* of clauses/sentences, as Dickens did in the opening of *A Tale of Two Cities*: "It was the best of times, it was the worst of times, it was the age of wisdom, it was the age of foolishness..." etc. (he used "it was" 10 times in one sentence). Repetition (Choice C) involves simply repeating the same word/phrase/clause multiple times. Parallelism/parallel structure does not require exact word repetition, but symmetrical sentence/clause structure arranging the same parts of speech in the same word order.

17. Choice B is the best answer. The closest meaning is freedom for all citizens, which would include slaves. Lincoln issued the Emancipation Proclamation over nine months before the Gettysburg Address, but the Civil War was still being fought over the issue of slavery. In lines 22-35 ("It is for us...from the earth."), he called for "us the living" to finish the "unfinished work" of the soldier and "highly resolve that these dead shall not have died in vain" by giving the nation a "new birth of freedom." Without reaffirming the nation's basis of freedom and equality, the nation would "perish from the earth" and the soldiers would have died in vain. The entire paragraph, lines 15-35 ("But, in a larger sense... perish from the earth."), leads up to this meaning. Choice A is wrong because this does not indicate freedom from war: the speech does not say ending the war would bring freedom; but by restoring the nation's original foundations of freedom and equality for which soldiers fought, the dead would not die in vain— not that soldiers should be freed from fighting the war as in Choice C. Slavery violated the foundations of US democracy; hence Choice D makes no sense in this context.

18. Choice A is the best answer. Lincoln was reminding his audience that the nation was formed with the ideas of liberty and equality as foundations—seen symmetrically in the opening and closing sentences—and reasoning that upholding those ideals was the best way to honor the soldiers who fought for that nation. Choice B is not the main idea as he explicitly stated in the third lines 16-17 ("we cannot consecrate - we cannot hallow - this ground") because the soldiers had done so "far beyond our poor power to add or detract." He continues to say their deeds will never be forgotten even though his and others' words would—making Choice C incorrect. Completing soldiers' unfinished work refers not to declaring a cease-fire (Choice D) in particular but to ensuring the nation's democratic government and its founding principles would not "perish from the earth."

19. Choice C is the best answer. In the Second Inaugural Address, Lincoln said in lines 86-87, "...let us strive on to finish the work we are in..." and in the Gettysburg Address, lines 23-25, "...to be dedicated here to the unfinished work which they who fought here have thus far so nobly advanced." He spoke of Choices A, B, and D in the former speech, but not overtly in the latter.

20. Choice D is the best answer. Lincoln delivered his Second Inaugural Address after a time of great hardship for the United States. His plea for the country's resolution of its severe problems must have been an emotional experience for the president, and his voice must have conveyed this emotionality as he read the speech. As a result, reading the transcript could not have quite the same emotional impact as hearing it in person. The tone of the address is not anger (Choice A), but rather the desire for reconciliation and peace. For the same reason, Choice C is also not the best choice since the speaker is not seeking to intimidate those listening. Choice B is not relevant to the different experiences of reading and hearing.

21. Choice A is the best answer. Following the phrase, "I have called for personal sacrifice" in line 10, the author states, "A part of the sacrifice means the payment of more money in taxes" for "a greater portion of this great defense program" in lines 12-16. While he called for taxpayers to support the military, in this passage he did not equate personal sacrifice with serving in the military (Choice B). While he described worldwide arms reduction (Choice C), he did not equate this with personal sacrifice, but with the fourth freedom: freedom from fear. The four freedoms (Choice D) he identified were "essential human freedoms", i.e., things all human beings had rights to, not examples of personal sacrifice.

22. Choice D is the best answer. There are four basic freedoms that are vital to the health of people: speech, worship, freedom from want, and freedom from fear. This speech is typically referred to as the "Four Freedoms" speech. In it, the author articulates the basic freedoms he believes in. These freedoms are the central focus of the speech, since it supports the other ideas that he is focusing on (i.e., social issues). Choice A is a single detail in the speech, Choice B is not articulated, and Choice C is not in the speech.

23. Choice C is the best answer. In this passage, there is no mention of expanding the draft of citizens into military service. As examples of aspects of the social economy needing "immediate improvement," the author cited, "We should bring more citizens under the coverage of old-age pensions...."; "We should widen the opportunities for adequate medical care"; and "We should plan a better system by which persons deserving or needing gainful employment may obtain it."

24. Choice B is the best answer. The argument that needs to be evaluated is that people will be happy to give more money in taxes to the government. It would be safe to raise the counterargument that the general population may already believe they are paying enough in taxes and don't think the government is spending that money wisely. Not everyone will be happy to give more to the government to spend. Choices A and D do not address the question. Choice C agrees with the author's premise.

25. Choice D is the best answer. In stating, "That is no vision of a distant millennium," the author is saying that we do not have to wait hundreds or thousands of years to see the freedoms that he has described become reality. While the author would likely agree with some or all of the statements listed in the other answer choices, none of them reflects the meaning of the statement in question.

26. Choice D is the best answer. After describing the four freedoms he identified, the author states that the vision of a world founded on those freedoms was "attainable in our own time and generation" and that it would be "the very antithesis of the so-called new order of tyranny," referring to the "order" that dictators wanted to impose. He further described the "cooperation of free countries, working together in a friendly, civilized society" as "the world order which we seek." This context establishes that "order" most nearly means a system of world politics and society rather than a military leader's command (Choice A), an authoritative decision or direction (Choice B), or an arrangement in sequence (Choice C).

27. Choice C is the best answer. FDR spoke of freedom, defining it in line 69 as "the supremacy of human rights everywhere." This is the "high concept" he refers to in the following line 72. In this context, the "end" of victory does not mean death, as in Choice A. It does not precisely mean purpose (Choice B), as in the common phrase "a means to an end" (a way of achieving a purpose): he was not saying victory was the only purpose of the concept, but rather that this concept could have no other outcome (Choice C) or result than victory. "End" can also mean conclusion (Choice D), i.e., the termination or finishing of something, which does not fit the meaning in this context quite as precisely as in Choice C because it does not imply cause and effect as "outcome" does.

28. Choice C is the best answer. The sentence found in lines 56-62, "Since the beginning of our American history, we have been engaged in change—in a perpetual peaceful revolution—a revolution which goes on steadily, quietly adjusting itself to changing conditions—without the concentration camp or the quick-lime in the ditch" is the only statement listed here that directly supports the idea that FDR thought that America is constantly moving toward a better way of life.

29. Choice A is the best answer. It emphasizes the need for a social safety net for the aging populace. While the other ideas in Choices B and C are clearly mentioned in the blog, they are not derived from the speech. Choice A is the only one that discusses an idea that shows up in the speech.

30. Choice C is the best answer. The passage describes several distinctive features of annelid anatomy and tells how some of them differ from other worms. Descriptions of the annelid anatomy can be found throughout the passage, whereas the other answer choices are too specific, though they are mentioned.

31. Choice C is the best answer. The text defines metameres as segments, and discusses segmentation as the distinguishing feature of the phylum.

32. Choice C is the best answer. In lines 12-17 ("Metameric segmentation...specific functions."), the text gives the example of feet specializing into grasping organs to illustrate this evolutionary advantage of segmental plasticity. It gives specific examples, but describes the helpfulness of segmentation for performing specialized functions.

33. Choice A is the best answer. The term "metamerism" is defined in lines 9-12 ("They are...termed metamerism.") of the selection as an organization of the anatomy into segments.

34. Choice D is the best answer. The term parapodia is defined in lines 17-21 ("For example...digestive specializations.").

35. Choice A is the best answer. The author compares annelids and nematodes when he describes both as having a fluid-filled internal *coelom* or cavity separating the body wall and gut, and both having this cavity involved in their locomotion. The author also contrasts the two phyla in that annelids develop this cavity much later during both embryonic growth (and presumably evolutionary progress). None of the other answer choices accurately reflect the structure of this paragraph.

36. Choice D is the best answer. Lines 45-47 ("This phylum...terrestrial habitats."), tell us that annelids can live in salt or fresh water and on land, and then gives examples of each in the following sentences. This helps demonstrate that there are many types of annelids and that they live in a variety of habitats. Choices A, B, and C are wrong because they do not represent all of the information presented in these lines. Choice D is the most comprehensive choice.

37. Choice B is the best answer. The author mentions the adaptability of metameres in lines 15-17, noting that "certain segments can be modified and specialized." The author then gives examples of how this is seen in lines 18-21: "certain of the locomotor *parapodia*, or feet, may be modified for grasping, and some portions of the gut may evolve digestive specializations."

38. Choice D is the best answer. The text gives the example of parapodia modified for grasping. The graphic shows a set of Annelid legs that seem to be grabbing a small rock.

39. Choice B is the best answer. After the initial topic sentence, paragraph 1 ("The phylum...digestive specializations.") discuss metameric segmentation as a distinctive feature of annelids. Then, paragraph 2 ("The gut...true coelom") discusses annelid body parts, i.e., the gut, body wall, and coelom, including their functions, development, and differences and similarities of the latter between annelids and nematodes. paragraph 3 ("The annelid...segmental ganglia.") then discusses annelid body systems, including excretory, circulatory, respiratory, and nervous. Finally, paragraph 4 ("This phylum...worm Nereis.") includes annelid habitat adaptations and names three well-known types.

40. Choice D is the best answer. The passage puts Pluto forth as the main topic, but goes into depth about the reclassification and the reasoning behind Pluto's reclassification, primarily in lines 32-41 ("The third...with it."). Choice A is wrong because the passage was not primarily for entertainment and the focus was on Pluto, not primarily distinguishing planets and dwarf-planets. Choice B is wrong because the purpose was not to excite people about future research as much as it was to discuss past research. Choice C is wrong because the passage was not persuasive in tone. The author held a primarily informative stance throughout the passage and did not seem to take a side on the matter.

41. Choice B is the best answer. Lines 21-34 ("The IAU...own orbit") provide the three requirements for an object to be a planet. Choice B does refer to a required quality of a planet, that it has a regular orbit. Pluto does, in fact, have a regular orbit around the sun, though it is not as regular as the 8 true planets. Pluto has not cleared its neighborhood, making Choice A wrong. Pluto has a moon, but this is not considered a requirement for a planet, making Choice C wrong. Finally, some may argue that because Pluto was a planet, it should remain a planet, but this is not a scientific basis of reasoning.

42. Choice A is the best answer. The passage does not give any clarification on what a celestial body is. The passage implies that there are many celestial bodies in our solar system, and that some could have been confirmed as planets. This indicates that some are unconfirmed planets, but also implies that some would not be considered planets or dwarf planets. Meteors and meteorites are not discussed and are too specific of a definition for celestial body. The only definition that fits in the context is Choice A, any object in space.

43. Choice C is the best answer. As described in lines 26-30 ("Second, a planet...spherical shape."), a planet is said to be in hydrostatic equilibrium when its gravity is enough to cause it to form into a nearly spherical shape. Despite the prefix 'hydro-', This principle does not refer to water in any way.

44. Choice B is the best answer. In lines 31-38, the author explains that a planet must have sufficient gravity to clear its neighborhood, further elaborating that this gravity is a result of the planet's mass. Thus, when the author says that Pluto is not massive enough, he is referring specifically to the planet's mass. A planet's size is often related to its mass, but it is the mass and not the size of the planet that provides the gravitational attraction.

45. Choice D is the best answer. Nostalgia is the best stand-in for sentimentality, as sentimentality and nostalgia both refer to an emotional attachment. Choice B, empiricism, and Choice A, rationalism, are both more related to science than to sentiment and emotions. Choice C, ethics, does not fit, as there is no moral dilemma about Pluto's status as a planet.

46. Choice C is the best answer. He gives neither opinion. The author is mainly neutral to this change and only points out what historically has taken place. In lines 58-61 ("Perhaps the...pseudo-planet."), the author does advocate for advancement of technology to help understand these matters further.

47. Choice D is the best answer. Pluto's estimated mass decreased over time, indicating that scientists had likely been largely overestimating Pluto's mass and are getting more precise with time. The estimate for 2006 breaks the trend by increasing the estimated mass, but the chart still shows a recognizable downward trend as a whole.

48. Choice A is the best answer. The passage states in lines 34-38 ("The planet's...of the way.") that a planet's gravity, as a result of its mass, is how it clears its neighborhood. The chart shows a decline in Pluto's estimated mass over time, showing less confidence in Pluto's ability to clear its neighborhood.

49. Choice C is the best answer. Choice A is not correct because the passage does not discuss moons specifically, though it does hint at a major theme of the passage, in that it describes distinguishing planets from other large celestial bodies. Choice B is a good second choice because the majority of the passage includes a description of qualifications of a planet, however, a taxonomy implies discussing many types of bodies. Choice B also does not include Pluto in the topic, which is the primary focus of the passage. Choice D is wrong because Pluto has not been made a planet once again, therefore contradicting the passage. Choice C is correct because the passage as a whole is describing Pluto, giving scientific reasoning for it being changed in status to a dwarf planet. The sentiment aspect comes into play primarily in the final paragraph, lines 49-61 ("Even with clear...pseudo-planet"), as it discusses the major pushback against Pluto's reclassification. That pushback is largely founded in emotion, rather than rationality.

Writing and Language

1. Choice C is the best answer. The sentence is in present tense and the subject (contributions) is plural, so "are" is correct. Answer choice B would be used with a singular subject. Answer choices A and D would be used in a past tense sentence.

2. Choice B is the best answer. The correct answer is beavers', because it refers to multiple animals, not just one (A). The sentence is referring to the benefit of the beavers, not the land (C). Using "their" (D) could refer to the beavers, but would not flow grammatically: "the their benefit."

3. Choice D is the best answer. The correct answer is "upstream, slowing." Using a semicolon (A or C) is not correct because the clause after the semicolon is not an independent clause (a portion that could be a stand-alone sentence). Using "upstream, which is slowing" (B) adds unnecessary verbiage and confuses the subject.

4. Choice D is the best answer. "Tens" and "hundreds" are plural, not possessive, so A and B are incorrect. The clause "or possibly even hundreds" could be set off with commas or dashes, but would need punctuation on both ends, so C is incorrect (and B is also incorrect for this reason). Answer choice D uses the correct plural forms and omits all punctuation for "or possibly even hundreds," which is grammatically correct.

5. Choice A is the best answer. The sentence is grammatically correct as it is written. Answer choice B is incorrect because it uses present tense, rather than referring to an event that began in the past and is ongoing. Answer choice C is incorrect because the verb (declined) needs an adverb (sharply) rather than an adjective (sharp). Answer choice D adds unnecessary verbiage, which can confuse the meaning.

6. Choice B is the best answer. The correct answer is "destroys" because the subject (building) is singular, not plural (A), and the sentence is in present tense. Do not be confused by the direct object "dams," which is plural. Answer choice C is incorrect because the subject is singular. Answer choice D is incorrect because the sentence is in present tense, not past.

7. Choice C is the best answer. A colon is correct here because it can be used to introduce a list. Lists should not be introduced with commas (A) or semicolons (B), nor should punctuation between the clause and the list be absent (D).

8. Choice B is the best answer. The correct answer is "its," which is the possessive form of "it." In contrast, "it's" (A) is incorrect because it refers to the contraction of the words "it is." Using "their" or "theirs" (C and D) is incorrect because the subject (foliage) is singular.

9. Choice C is the best answer. The correct answer is "encouraging," which is a present participle modifying the verbs "trapped" and "relocated." It would be correct to write, "which encourages," but not "which encouraging" (A) or "that is encouraging" (B). Finally, "encourage" (D) is an incorrect form of verb for a participle phrase.

10. Choice D is the best answer. The main point of the selection, as can be seen in the opening paragraph, is that beavers make important contributions to the environment. Choices A and B may be true, but are not the main point and therefore poor choices for summarizing. Answer choice C is a subjective opinion.

11. Choice C is the best answer. The third paragraph mentions the destruction beavers can cause, so it would be the best place for this anecdote.

12. Choice C is the best answer. The word "millennia" is plural, while "millennium" is singular. Thus "a millennia" (B and D) are grammatically incorrect, as is using "millennium" (A) without an article.

13. Choice A is the best answer. A colon is used to define or introduce something, such as a new term or a list. Here the sentence is defining or explaining the two categories, so a colon is correct. A period (B) is incorrect because the part of the sentence after the punctuation ("Eastern and Western") is not a complete sentence. A semicolon (C) cannot be used because it is used to separate two independent clauses, and "Eastern and Western" is not a stand-alone sentence. While a dash could potentially be used here, a hyphen (D) is incorrect because it is only used for joining words (such as "well-being"), rather than joining clauses.

14. Choice B is the best answer. Answer choice B is best because it is the most readable. Answer choices A and D divide the phrase "the roots of calligraphy," which makes comprehension more difficult. Answer choice C is an awkward way of sharing the location.

15. Choice A is the best answer. The sentence is referring to a set of rules or guidelines that govern each style of calligraphy.

16. Choice B is the best answer. As it is written, this sentence has a dangling modifier. The subject of the sentence should be "calligraphy," but answer choices A, C, and D place other words directly after the comma, which makes these words appear to be the subject and leads to confusion.

17. Choice D is the best answer. It is better to begin the clause with "the Hurufiyya movement" to stay in active voice rather than passive voice (so A and B are incorrect). Calligraphy was invented long before the Hurufiyya movement, so answer choice C is incorrect.

18. Choice A is the best answer. The sentence is saying that the main reason calligraphy was mostly used for religious methods is that most of those who could write were in the monasteries, where religious works were copied. So it might not be the only reason (as answer choices B and C state), but it is the main reason (so answer choice D is incorrect).

19. Choice D is the best answer. The detail about Charlemagne is interesting and explains why he may have encouraged scholarship, but is not a helpful supporting detail for this paragraph on Western calligraphy, or for the selection as a whole.

20. Choice C is the best answer. The clause beginning with the underlined word is in contrast to the previous clause, so answer choices A and D are incorrect because they imply agreement. Answer choice B is incorrect because the word "however" needs different punctuation: it would need to be preceded by a semicolon and followed by a comma.

21. Choice A is the best answer. An apostrophe (B) is incorrect because the date is plural, not a contraction or possessive. The eighteenth century refers to the 1700s, more than two centuries ago, so answer choices C and D are incorrect.

22. Choice C is the best answer. Answer choice A is incorrect because it only addresses the idea of modern calligraphy that was introduced in this paragraph, rather than summarizing the whole selection. Answer choice B is incorrect because it focuses on China rather than both Eastern and Western cultures that the selection included. Answer choice D is incorrect because religion is not the only reason calligraphy survived. Answer choice C sums the ideas explored in the selection.

23. Choice A is the best answer. Titles of musical works are enclosed in quotation marks, not italics like a book title (B).

24. Choice B is the best answer. The correct phrase is "less common." The term "lesser" (A) is typically used when comparing two items in quantity or quality. Saying that something is less, or not as, uncommon (C and D) means that it is more common, which does not fit the meaning of the text.

25. Choice D is the best answer. The sentence sets up a contrast in the first half of the sentence, stating that trucks are less common now than in the past. The use of the word "while" alerts us to the contrast, so we can expect that the following information is something that does not fit with declining ice cream trucks. The word that best contrasts with this decline is "booming." Both "depleting" (A) and "shaky" (B) are in line with a declining business and do not fit with "while." The word "volatile" (C) implies both upswings and downswings in business, which does not smoothly contrast with the decline in trucks.

26. Choice D is the best answer. The adverb "increasingly" is the correct opening for this sentence. "Increasing" (A) is an adjective and is not appropriate to open a sentence without the noun it is modifying (although it would be acceptable to write, "Health is an **increasing** concern for Americans"). "Greater" (B) is also an adjective, and "greatly" (C) does not convey the idea that the concern is growing.

27. Choice D is the best answer. The concerns about frozen yogurt's nutrition should be brought up after the subject of frozen yogurt has been introduced, which happens in sentences 4–5. Sentence 6 then answers the nutrition concerns by stating that "even so," frozen yogurt remains popular, so it is a good sentence to follow the underlined statement.

28. Choice C is the best answer. The sentence is written in present tense, so "were" (B) is incorrect. However, it is referring to an action that has already occurred, so "are" (A) and "is" (D) are incorrect. Using the present perfect "have been" is correct.

29. Choice D is the best answer. The previous paragraph closes by stating that frozen yogurt is providing competition to the ice cream industry. Answer choice A does not address this competition. Answer choice B is illogical, stating that ice cream sales are high because of the competition. Answer choice C gives wrong information by stating that ice cream is no longer popular. Only answer choice D provides the correct contrast: that ice cream is still popular even though frozen yogurt is providing competition.

30. Choice B is the best answer. The graph shows that ice cream sales declined slightly in the US between 2000 and 2015, while frozen yogurt sales rose. Answer choice B reflects this. Answer choice A incorrectly states that sales of both ice cream and frozen yogurt have stagnated, implying lack of growth or some decline. Answer choice C leaves out the information on ice cream and fails to mention that the sales are in the US (which is significant since the second part of the sentence refers to worldwide consumption). Answer choice D also fails to mention that the declining sales are in the US, which makes the sentence confusing.

31. Choice C is the best answer. It would be useful to add some extra data to support the points of the selection, so answer choice A is incorrect. The amount of ice cream produced by a single company (B) is not necessarily helpful since no mention is made of specific companies or how many are producing ice cream. Since the paragraph mentions that China consumes the most ice cream in the world, it would be useful to add the amount, so answer choice C is correct. Flavors of frozen yogurt (D) are not relevant to the point of the selection, which focuses on amounts eaten and the competition between frozen yogurt and ice cream.

32. Choice C is the best answer. The sentence draws a conclusion that should be obvious from the previous paragraphs: that ice cream is still popular in the US. This conclusion is not unusual (A), unexpected (B), or unlikely (D). Rather it is very apparent (C).

33. Choice A is the best answer. The role of the underlined word is to set up a contrast, stating that even though ice cream trucks are no longer common, there are many frozen dessert options. The word "while" (A) best fits this. "Whether" (B) implies uncertainty, and "however" (C) and "unfortunately" (D) do not fit grammatically in this sentence.

34. Choice B is the best answer. The point of the sentence is that Leonardo introduced a numeral system to the Western world. It would be confusing to say he was "guilty of" introducing it (A) because it is a positive accomplishment rather than a crime. Answer choice C is incorrect because it uses awkward and weak wording. Answer choice D is incorrect because it was not something he was tasked with. The correct wording is that Leonardo was responsible for introducing the numeral system. This does not mean that he was given the responsibility to do so, but simply that he is known for being the person to do so.

35. Choice D is the best answer. No punctuation is necessary before the conjunction since there are only two items in this list.

36. Choice D is the best answer. The idea of the sentence is that this mathematician is only known for one thing today. Answer choice A makes a point that is likely true, that Leonardo was young but knowledgeable, but this information is not relevant to the main point, nor is it grammatically correct because of the comma splice (the comma after "knowledgeable" joins two independent clauses, which can only be done by a semicolon or period). Answer choice B states that "his work endures," which contradicts the rest of the sentence that states only one thing endures. This choice also has a comma splice issue. Answer choice C also contradicts by stating that Leonardo is famous for many things. Answer choice D correctly points out that although Leonardo made many mathematical contributions, he is known for only one of these today.

37. Choice B is the best answer. It is ironic that the one thing Fibonacci is known for was actually discovered by someone else. Even though he was a brilliant mathematician, very little of his own work is known. While some may consider the news sad, disappointing, or tragic, the tone of the sentence indicates that this is an interesting, almost amusing fact.

38. Choice C is the best answer. As the selection is written (A), it is choppy, as one short sentence follows a previous short sentence. Answer choice B incorrectly states that the sequence appears in almost every part of nature. With only three examples, we cannot assume the series is pervasive. Answer choice D says that Fibonacci, rather than his sequence, can be seen in nature. Only answer choice C smoothly connects the two sentences without changing or adding information.

39. Choice D is the best answer. The main idea of the paragraph can be gathered from the previous sentences: the Fibonacci sequence is a pattern often seen in nature. Answer choice A is incorrect because it introduces a new topic. Answer choice B is incorrect because it adds a contradictory detail with no information to reconcile it to the main point. Answer choice C is incorrect because it makes unfounded assumptions and claims (that Fibonacci didn't know the extent of his discovery and that he revolutionized mathematics, neither of which can be proven). Further, these statements have nothing to do with the main point of this paragraph. Answer choice D is correct because it gives a supporting detail about the topic of the Fibonacci sequence in nature.

40. Choice D is the best answer. The information in the underlined portion is unsupported (the selection offers no evidence that nature always follows a pattern) and is not relevant. Even if nature did always follow a pattern, this information does not support the points about the Fibonacci sequence.

41. Choice A is the best answer. The sentence is introduced with an adverb clause so should be followed by a comma. A colon (B) is incorrect because the following portion of the sentence is not a definition or list. A semicolon (C) is incorrect because the introductory clause is not an independent clause (so it cannot be a stand-alone sentence). Leaving out punctuation entirely (D) would make the sentence confusing, with no discernible pauses.

42. Choice C is the best answer. The idea of the sentence is that the Arabic system makes mathematical calculations more possible. Thus "challenging" (A) or "difficult" (B) would not fit. "Agreeable" (D) is a positive term, but not the correct connotation.

43. Choice C is the best answer. Fibonacci could not have known future events. While prophecy (A) and foretelling (D) are associated with predicting future events, the passage is not suggesting anything related to this kind of prediction (typically associated with religious or mythological prediction). We have no way of knowing whether Fibonacci could have understood the magnitude of the system spreading through the world (B).

44. Choice D is the best answer. The examples are potentially useful, but the sentence is written in a much more casual tone than the rest of the selection. It uses second person ("you"), which does not appear anywhere else, and then directly addresses the reader, urging him or her, illogically (since Fibonacci is not alive), to thank the mathematician.

Math – No Calculator

1. Choice D is correct. The function for the cost of a taxi ride is a combination of a constant function for the first mile and a linear function for the rest of the ride. The constant function is $c_1(d) = 4.25$ since the cost of the first mile is \$4.25. For the linear part, subtract 1 from d to exclude the first mile, and then multiply the result by 0.70 since it costs \$0.70 per mile. The result is $c_2(d) = 0.70(d - 1)$. Finally, write the function for the total cost of the taxi ride by adding the two functions.

$$\begin{aligned} c(d) &= c_1(d) + c_2(d) \\ &= 4.25 + 0.70(d - 1) \end{aligned}$$

Although not necessary for answering the question, note that this function can also be simplified:

$$\begin{aligned} c(d) &= 4.25 + 0.70d - 0.70 \\ &= 3.55 + 0.70d \end{aligned}$$

2. Choice D is correct.

$$\begin{aligned} y &= 4x - 2 \\ y + 2 &= 4x \\ \frac{y+2}{4} &= x \\ \frac{y}{4} + \frac{2}{4} &= x \\ \frac{1}{4}y + \frac{1}{2} &= x \\ x &= \frac{1}{4}y + \frac{1}{2} \end{aligned}$$

3. Choice D is correct. Solve the inequality:

$$\begin{aligned} 2|x + 3| - 9 &\geq -1 \\ 2|x + 3| &\geq 8 \\ |x + 3| &\geq 4 \end{aligned}$$

$$\begin{aligned} x + 3 &\geq 4 \\ x &\geq 1 \end{aligned}$$

$$\begin{aligned} -(x + 3) &\geq 4 \\ x + 3 &\leq -4 \\ x &\leq -7 \end{aligned}$$

4. Choice A is correct. The positively sloped line has a slope of 2 and a y-intercept of -3; the line is solid, and the region above the line is shaded. Therefore, the graph illustrates the solution to the inequality $y \geq 2x - 3$.

The negatively sloped line has a slope of -3 and a y-intercept of 4; the line is dashed, and the region below the line is shaded. Therefore, the graph illustrates the solution to the inequality $y < -3x + 4$.

In choice A, the second inequality when solved for y is equivalent to $y \geq 2x - 3$.

$$\begin{aligned} 4x - 2y &\leq 6 \\ -2y &\leq -4x + 6 \\ y &\geq 2x - 3 \end{aligned}$$

The solution of the system of inequalities is shown by the region where the two sets of shading overlap.

5. Choice C is correct. The four choices all have the two lines that mark the boundaries of the inequalities plotted identically; the only difference is which sides are shaded. It's therefore not necessary to check that the lines are correct; simply determine which of the areas bounded by the lines pertain to the system of inequalities. One way to do that is to pick a point in each region and check whether it satisfies the inequalities. For instance, in the region on the left, we can pick the origin, $(0, 0)$. Since $0 - 0 \ngtr 1$ and $2(0) + 0 \ngtr 2$, this does not satisfy either inequality. From the top region we can choose, for example, the point $(0, 3)$. $0 - 3 \ngtr 1$, so this fails to satisfy the first inequality. From the bottom region we can choose, for instance, $(0, -2)$. $0 - (-2) > 1$, so the first inequality is satisfied, but $2(0) + (-2) \ngtr 2$, so the second is not. Finally, from the rightmost region we can choose, for example, the point $(2, 0)$. $2 - 0 > 1$ and $2(2) + 0 > 2$, so both inequalities are satisfied; this is the only region that should be shaded in.

6. Choice D is correct. To simplify the inequality $3 - 2x < 5$, we can first subtract 3 from both sides:

$$3 - 2x - 3 < 5 - 3$$
$$-2x < 2$$

Now, we can divide both sides of the inequality by -2. When an inequality is multiplied or divided by a negative number, the direction of the sign changes ($<$ becomes $>$, $\leq$ becomes $\geq$, and vice versa). So $-2x < 2$ becomes $\frac{-2x}{-2} > \frac{2}{-2}$, or $x > -1$.

7. Choice C is correct. If the exam has 30 questions, and the student answered C questions correctly and left B questions blank, then the number of questions the student answered incorrectly must be $30 - B - C$. He gets one point for each correct question, or $1 \times C = C$ points, and loses $\frac{1}{2}$ point for each incorrect question, or $\frac{1}{2}(30 - B - C)$ points. Therefore, one way to express his total score is $C - \frac{1}{2}(30 - B - C)$.

8. Choice B is correct. If there are n floors, and each floor has a height of h feet, then to find the total height of the floors, we just multiply the number of floors by the height of each floor: nh. To find the total height of the building, we must also add the height of the spire, 30 feet. So, the building's total height in feet is $nh + 30$.

9. Choice D is correct. First, test each expression to see which satisfies the condition $x > y$. This condition is only met for answer choices A and D, so only these need to be considered further. Test those choices to see which satisfy the inequality $x + y > 0$. It can be seen that this inequality holds for choice A but not for choice D, since $x + y = 3 + (-3) = 3 - 3 = 0$. In this case $x + y$ is not greater than 0.

10. Choice B is correct. To simplify the expression, first factor the numerator and the denominator. To factor the numerator, use trial-and-error to find two numbers whose sum is 2 and whose product is -24, and then put those numbers into the form $(x + \_)(x + \_)$. For the denominator, factor out the common factor, which is 5.

$$\frac{x^2 + 2x - 24}{5x - 20} = \frac{(x + 6)(x - 4)}{5(x - 4)}$$

Now there is a common factor, $(x - 4)$, in both the numerator and the denominator. Therefore, you can further simplify the expression by cancelling it out.

$$\frac{(x+6)(x-4)}{5(x-4)} = \frac{x+6}{5}$$

11. Choice C is correct. To simplify the expression, first simplify the expression with parentheses. To raise $3x$ to the second power, raise both 3 and x to the second power separately.

$$\begin{aligned} x^6 \times (3x)^2 &= x^6 \times 3^2 \times x^2 \\ &= x^6 \times 9x^2 \end{aligned}$$

Next, multiply the two terms. Since they have the same base and are being multiplied together, add the exponents of the like base, x.

$$\begin{aligned} x^6 \times 9x^2 &= 9x^{6+2} \\ &= 9x^8 \end{aligned}$$

12. Choice B is correct. Revenue is the total amount of money the theater makes from ticket sales. In this case, the revenue is the price of each ticket multiplied by the total number of tickets sold. So, to find the estimated revenue, find the price and the number of tickets sold after the price is raised by x dollars. Then multiply the two quantities together. If the price of a ticket starts at \$10, then the price after it is raised by x dollars will be $10 + x$ dollars. In addition, we are told that the theater sells 50 fewer tickets for every dollar the price is raised. Therefore, the total number of tickets that are sold will be $600 - 50x$. Calculate the revenue function $r(x)$ by multiplying the expressions and simplify the result.

$$\begin{aligned} r(x) &= (10 + x)(600 - 50x) \\ &= -50x^2 + 100x + 6000 \end{aligned}$$

13. Choice C is correct. To transform $f(x)$ into $g(x)$, you have to replace x with $x + 1$. This transformation results in a translation, or shift, of the graph. Specifically, for a particular x, $g(x)$ returns the value of the function $f(x)$ one unit further along the x-axis (to the right). This results in shifting the graph one unit to the left.

14. The correct answer is 8. The length of an interval is the difference between its endpoints. For example, the length of the interval [2,4] is 2. To determine how the given function grows over an interval of length 3, determine the value of f at each endpoint of that interval. Since exponential functions grow by equal factors over equal intervals, you can use any interval of length 3, and your answer will apply to all such intervals. For example, you can use the interval [0,3]:

$$\begin{aligned} f(0) &= 3 \times 2^0 \\ &= 3 \times 1 \\ &= 3 \end{aligned}$$

$$\begin{aligned} f(3) &= 3 \times 2^3 \\ &= 3 \times 8 \\ &= 24 \end{aligned}$$

Since $f(0) = 3$ and $f(3) = 24$, the function grows by a factor of $\frac{24}{3} = 8$ over this interval.

15. The correct answer is 27. The linear function $s(h) = 27h + 720$ starts at 720 when $h = 0$ and increases by 27 every time h increases by 1. Therefore, for every hour after 40, the librarian earns \$27.

16. The correct answer is 21. Since the function is defined recursively, you need to calculate all of the first six terms. The first and second terms are already given in the problem as $f(1) = 1$ and

$f(2) = 1$. To calculate the third term, $f(3)$, take the previous term and add two times the term that is two back:

$$f(3) = f(2) + 2f(1) = 1 + 2 = 3$$

The fourth term is similarly calculated:

$$f(4) = f(3) + 2f(2) = 3 + 2 = 5$$

Continuing in this way, you will find that the first six terms of the sequence are 1, 1, 3, 5, 11, 21. Therefore, the sixth term of the sequence is 21.

17. The correct answer is 4: $f(x) = (x - 3)(x^2 - x - 2)$ is a cubic equation written as a product of a linear factor and a quadratic factor, $x - 3$ and $x^2 - x - 2$, respectively. The quadratic expression $x^2 - x - 2$ can be further factored to $(x - 2)(x + 1)$, so $f(x) = (x - 3)(x^2 - x - 2) = (x - 3)(x - 2)(x + 1)$. The graph of the function crosses the x axis at any point at which the value of $f(x) = 0$. To find the x-intercepts, solve $f(x) = 0 = (x - 3)(x - 2)(x + 1)$ using the zero-product property.

$$x - 3 = 0 \qquad x - 2 = 0 \qquad x + 1 = 0$$
$$x = 3 \qquad x = 2 \qquad x = -1$$

Then the sum is $3 + 2 + (-1) = 4$

Math – Calculator

1. Choice C is correct. Notice that the given system has two equations, and each equation has two variables, x and y. Therefore, the solution of the system of equations must have values for each of the two variables. To find the solution, you can use algebraic methods, graphs, tables, or matrices. For the purposes of this explanation, we will use an algebraic method called substitution.

To begin, notice that the first equation already has y isolated on the left side. Therefore, substitute the left side, $3x + 2$, for y into the second equation, and then solve for x.

$$\begin{aligned} 2x + y &= 7 \\ 2x + (3x + 2) &= 7 \\ 5x &= 5 \\ x &= 1 \end{aligned}$$

To find the value of y, substitute 1 for x in the first equation.

$$\begin{aligned} y &= 3(1) + 2 \\ &= 3 + 2 \\ &= 5 \end{aligned}$$

Therefore, the solution of the given system of equations is $x = 1, y = 5$. Check this solution on your own by substituting the values into the second equations to make sure that you get a true equality.

2. Choice D is correct. For each value of x, $f(x) = x^2 + 1$,

$$\begin{aligned} f(1) &= (1)^2 + 1 = (1)(1) + 1 = 1 + 1 = 2 \\ f(2) &= (2)^2 + 1 = (2)(2) + 1 = 4 + 1 = 5 \\ f(3) &= (3)^2 + 1 = (3)(3) + 1 = 9 + 1 = 10 \\ f(4) &= (4)^2 + 1 = (4)(4) + 1 = 16 + 1 = 17 \\ f(5) &= (5)^2 + 1 = (5)(5) + 1 = 25 + 1 = 26 \end{aligned}$$

3. Choice A is correct. The slope (or ratio of the change in y-values per change in corresponding x-values) may first be calculated. Using the points, $(-3, -21)$ and $(-1, -3)$, the slope can be written as $\frac{-3-(-21)}{-1-(-3)}$ or 9. The slope can then be substituted into the slope-intercept form of an equation, or $y = mx + b$, to find the y-intercept. Doing so gives $y = 9x + b$. Substituting the x- and y-values of any ordered pair will reveal the y-intercept. The following may be written: $-21 = 9(-3) + b$; solving for b gives $b = 6$. Thus, the equation that represents the relationship between x and y is $y = 9x + 6$.

4. Choice D is correct. The median is the score in the middle: half of the students scored higher than 82.5 and half scored lower. The mean is the average, which is calculated by adding all the scores together and dividing by the number of students. Since the mean is higher than the median, this means that some of the students scored high, well above the median, which pulls the mean up above the median grade.

5. Choice A is correct. Since the second line, $y = 3$, is horizontal, the intersection must occur at a point where $y = 3$. If $x = -1.5$, the equation describing the line is satisfied: $2 \times (-1.5) + 3 = 0$.

6. Choice A is correct. To evaluate $\frac{x^3+2x}{x+3}$ at $x = -1$, substitute in -1 for x in the expression:

$$\frac{(-1)^3 + 2(-1)}{(-1) + 3} = \frac{(-1) + (-2)}{2} = \frac{-3}{2} = -\frac{3}{2}$$

7. Choice B is correct. To solve this problem, all we need to do is substitute -1 for every x in the expression and then simplify:

$$\frac{2(-1) - 2}{(-1) - 3} = \frac{-2 - 2}{-4} = \frac{-4}{-4} = 1$$

8. Choice C is correct. Start by distributing each coefficient across the parentheses. Next add the complex binomials. Complex numbers have a real part, a, and an imaginary part, b, and are usually written as $a + bi$. When adding imaginary numbers, add the real parts and the imaginary parts separately:

$$4(-3 + 5i) + 6(1 - 3i) = -12 + 20i + 6 - 18i = (-12 + 6) + (20i - 18i) = -6 + 2i$$

9. Choice B is correct. The probability of playing a song by any band is proportional to the number of songs by that band, divided by the total number of songs, or $\frac{5}{15} = \frac{1}{3}$ for Band D. The probability of playing any particular song is not affected by what has been played previously, since the choice is random.

10. Choice B is correct. The number of people who voted for the proposition is 9.5% of 51,623. If we only require an approximation, we can round 9.5% to 10%, and 51,623 to 50,000. Then 9.5% of 51,623 is about 10% of 50,000, or $(0.1)(50{,}000) = 5{,}000$.

11. Choice B is correct. Since all students who answered her survey said they prefer one of the three flavors; the percentages must add up to 100%. Therefore, the percentage of students who prefer strawberry is:

$$100\% - (35\% + 40\%) = 100\% - 75\% = 25\%$$

12. Choice A is correct. Liz ordinarily sells each pen for 30% more than (or 130% of) her cost:

$$\$15.00 \times 1.3 = \$19.50$$

For the last day of market, she takes 20% off (or sells it for 80% of) the ordinary sale price:

$$\$19.50 \times 0.8 = \$15.60$$

The marked down price is \$15.60.

13. Choice D is correct. Since 16 chairs are empty, and this represents $\frac{2}{5}$ of the total enrollment, then the full class must consist of $\frac{5}{2}(16) = 40$ students.

14. Choice C is correct. The problem may be solved by writing $P(p \text{ or } q) = P(p) + P(q) - P(p \text{ and } q)$. The probability for philosophy or qualitative and the probability for philosophy may be substituted giving $0.62 = 0.30 + P(q) - P(p \text{ and } q)$. Next find the probability that she chooses both philosophy and qualitative by using the formula, $P(p \text{ and } q) = P(p) \times P(q|p)$. Substituting the probabilities of 0.30 and 0.40 gives $P(p \text{ and } q) = 0.30 \times 0.40$, or 0.12. Now, the probability of 0.12

may be substituted into the original equation, giving $0.62 = 0.30 + P(q) - 0.12$. Solving for $P(q)$ gives a probability of 0.44. Thus, there is a 0.44 probability that Alisha chooses a qualitative methods class.

15. Choice D is correct. Since the figure represents the number line, the distance from point A to point B will be the difference, $B - A$, which is $5 - (-6) = 11$. The distance from point B to point C will be the difference, $C - B$, which is $8 - 5 = 3$. So, the ratio $\overline{BC} : \overline{AB}$ will be 3:11.

16. Choice C is correct. The median number of volunteers in Texas is 21, with a mean of approximately 25.9. The median number of volunteers in New Mexico is 33, with a mean of approximately 31.2. Thus, the median and mean numbers of volunteers in Texas are smaller.

17. Choice D is correct. If there are at least twice as many hot dogs (y) as hamburgers (x), then necessarily $y \geq 2x$, or $2x \leq y$. And since hot dogs and hamburgers must add up to 500, then $x + y = 500$.

18. Choice B is correct. The probability may be written as $P(A \text{ or } B) = P(A) + P(B) - P(A \text{ and } B) = \frac{80}{150} + \frac{49}{150} - \frac{37}{150}$, which simplifies to $P(A \text{ or } B) = \frac{46}{75}$.

19. Choice A is correct. The mode is the number that appears most often in a set of data. If no item appears most often, then the data set has no mode. In this case, Kyle achieved one hit a total of three times, two hits once, three hits once, and four hits once. One hit occurred the most times, and therefore the mode of the data set is 1.

20. Choice B is correct. The mean, or average, is the sum of the numbers in a data set, divided by the total number of items. This data set contains six items, one for each gameday. The total number of hits that Kyle had during the week is the sum of the numbers in the right-hand column, or 12. This gives mean $= \frac{12}{6} = 2$.

21. Choice B is correct. There are two students who slept less than 6.5 hours and scored in the 80s. We can add the number of students in each group to find the total number who took the test: $6 + 4 + 2 = 12$. So, the probability is 2 out of 12, or $\frac{1}{6}$.

22. Choice A is correct. We calculate the mean of each group by adding the scores and dividing by the number in each group. The mean of the first group is: $\frac{83+77+89+68+91+72}{6} = 80$

The mean of the second group is: $\frac{82+88+77+90}{4} = 84.25$

The mean of the third group is: $\frac{86+93}{2} = 89.5$

23. Choice B is correct. You can solve the equation using graphs, tables, or algebraic methods. For this explanation, we will approach the problem algebraically. To begin, isolate the square-root sign on the left side by subtracting 2 from both sides.

$$\sqrt{4x - 3} + 2 = x$$
$$\sqrt{4x - 3} = x - 2$$

Then square both sides of the equation and simplify the result.

$$\left(\sqrt{4x-3}\right)^2 = (x-2)^2$$
$$4x - 3 = x^2 - 4x + 4$$

Now solve the resulting equation by moving everything to one side and factoring the resulting quadratic equation.

$$x^2 - 8x + 7 = 0$$
$$(x-7)(x-1) = 0$$
$$x = 7 \text{ and } x = 1$$

Therefore, the possible solutions are $x = 1$ and $x = 7$. Unfortunately, whenever you must square both sides of an equation to solve it, you run the risk of finding an incorrect solution. Consequently, we cannot automatically say that the solutions are $x = 1$ and $x = 7$. We need to check these solutions in the original equation. To do this, substitute them into the given equations and make sure that the result is a true statement.

$x = 1$	$x = 7$
$\sqrt{4\times 1 - 3} + 2 = 1$	$\sqrt{4\times 7 - 3} + 2 = 7$
$\sqrt{1} + 2 = 1$	$\sqrt{25} + 2 = 7$
$1 + 2 = 1$	$5 + 2 = 7$
false	*true*

Since only $x = 7$ leads to a true statement, the solution is $x = 7$.

24. Choice C is correct. The roots of a quadratic function $f(x)$ are the values of x where $f(x) = 0$. Quadratic functions may have two real roots, two imaginary roots, or one real double root. A quadratic function written in the form $f(x) = (x-a)(x-b)$ has roots at $x = a$ and $x = b$. Therefore, to find $f(x)$, substitute the given roots for a and b into $f(x) = (x-a)(x-b)$ and simplify.

$$\begin{aligned} f(x) &= (x-a)(x-b) \\ &= \big(x-(-4)\big)(x-6) \\ &= (x+4)(x-6) \\ &= x^2 - 2x - 24 \end{aligned}$$

25. Choice D is correct. The denominator of the second rational expression may be factored as $(x+8)(x+2)$. Thus, the least common denominator of the two rational expressions is $(x+8)(x+2)$. Multiplying the top and bottom of the first fraction by $(x+8)$, we see that $\frac{3}{x+2} = \frac{3\,(x+8)}{(x+2)(x+8)}$. The sum may be written as $\frac{3(x+8)+x}{(x+8)(x+2)}$, which simplifies to $\frac{4x+24}{(x+8)(x+2)}$. Factoring out a 4 in the numerator gives: $\frac{4(x+6)}{(x+8)(x+2)}$.

26. Choice C is correct. Distributing each term in the expression, $x - 8$, across each term in the trinomial, gives:

$$4x^4 - 2x^2 + 4x - 32x^3 + 16x - 32$$

Writing the expression in standard form gives:

$$4x^4 - 32x^3 - 2x^2 + 20x - 32$$

27. Choice C is correct. In a parallelogram, consecutive angles are supplementary; that is, the sum of their measures is 180°. Use this to write an equation and then solve for x.

$$\begin{aligned} m\angle B + m\angle C &= 180° \\ (4x + 5) + (3x) &= 180 \\ 7x + 5 &= 180 \\ 7x &= 175 \\ x &= 25 \end{aligned}$$

Now use this value to find $m\angle B$ and $m\angle C$.

$$\begin{aligned} m\angle B &= 3x \\ &= 3(25) \\ &= 75° \end{aligned} \qquad \begin{aligned} m\angle C &= 4x + 5 \\ &= 4(25) + 5 \\ &= 105° \end{aligned}$$

In a parallelogram, opposite sides are congruent. Thus, $m\angle A = m\angle C = 105°$.

28. The correct answer is 39.1. The area of a circle is given by the formula $A = \pi r^2$, where r is the length of the radius. A sector is a slice of a circle bounded by two radii. Its area is proportional to the angle between the two radii bounding the sector. Thus, the area of a sector with angle θ (in degrees) is given by the formula

$$A = \pi r^2 \times \frac{\theta}{360}$$

Substitute the value of the radius and angle into this formula and simplify. Round the result to the nearest tenth.

$$\begin{aligned} A &= \pi(8)^2 \times \frac{70}{360} \\ &= 64\pi \times \frac{70}{360} \\ &\approx 39.1 \end{aligned}$$

29. The correct answer is 2825. The pool is a prism, so its volume is calculated by using the formula $V = Bh$, where B is the area of the base (i.e., the area of the given shape) and h is the height (i.e., the depth) of the swimming pool. First calculate B by adding the areas of the rectangle and two semicircles.

The area of the rectangle is given by the formula $A = lw$. Thus,

$$\begin{aligned} A_{\text{rectangle}} &= lw \\ &= 20 \text{ ft} \times 12 \text{ ft} \\ &= 240 \text{ ft}^2 \end{aligned}$$

Now notice that the diameter of each semicircle is 12 ft, so their radius is $r = 12 \div 2 = 6$ ft. Put together, the two semicircles form a complete circle, whose area is given by the formula $A = \pi r^2$. Thus, the total area of the semicircles is

$$\begin{aligned} A_{\text{semicircles}} &= \pi r^2 \\ &= \pi \times (6 \text{ ft})^2 \\ &= 36\pi \text{ ft}^2 \\ &\approx 113.10 \text{ ft}^2 \end{aligned}$$

Then add the two areas to find the total area of the swimming pool.

$$\begin{aligned} B &= A_{\text{rectangle}} + A_{\text{semicircles}} \\ &\approx 240 \text{ ft}^2 + 113.10 \text{ ft}^2 \\ &= 353.10 \text{ ft}^2 \end{aligned}$$

Finally, use this value to find the volume of the pool. Recall that its depth is given as 8 ft in the problem.

$$\begin{aligned} V &= Bh \\ &\approx 353.10 \text{ ft}^2 \times 8 \text{ ft} \\ &\approx 2825 \text{ ft}^3 \end{aligned}$$

30. The correct answer is 2.9. The first step is to draw into the diagram what we are told or can deduce. The circle intercepts the triangle at the midpoints of its sides, so draw a radius that meets the midpoint of AB (marked D below). Next, draw a line from A to the center, noting that this line bisects $\angle BAC$; thus, $m\angle DAO = \frac{1}{2} \times 60° = 30°$. Since D is the midpoint of AB, we know that $AD = \frac{1}{2}(AB) = 5$.

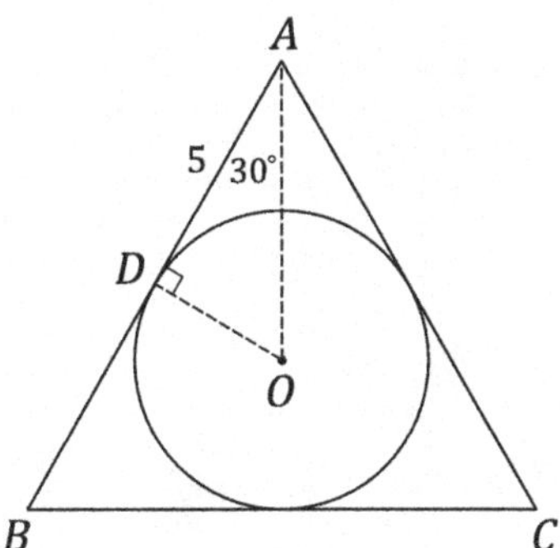

Now we can see that ΔADO is a 30-60-90 triangle. In a 30-60-90 triangle, the ratio of the lengths of the sides is $1:\sqrt{3}:2$. In this triangle, 5 corresponds to $\sqrt{3}$ and the radius r corresponds to 1. Use a proportion to calculate r:

$$\begin{aligned} \frac{1}{\sqrt{3}} &= \frac{r}{5} \\ r\sqrt{3} &= 5 \\ r &= \frac{5}{\sqrt{3}} \approx 2.9 \end{aligned}$$

31. The correct answer is 12.5. Suppose the seller purchases an item for \$100. She then adds 25% to the price she paid for it and lists it for sale at regular price:

$$\text{Regular} = \$100 + 25\% \times \$100 = \$100 + \$25 = \$125$$

If that \$125 item does not sell in 6 months, it is placed on clearance and marked down by 10%:

$$\text{Clearance} = \$125 - 10\% \times \$125 = \$125 - \$12.50 = \$112.50$$

Calculate her profit on the clearance as a percentage of what she paid for it:

$$\text{Profit} = \frac{\text{price sold for} - \text{price paid for}}{\text{price paid for}}$$

$$\text{Profit} = \frac{112.5-100}{100} = \frac{12.5}{100} = 12.5\%.$$

PSAT Practice Test #2

Reading

Questions 1–9 are based on the following passage.

This passage is adapted from Stephen Crane, The Open Boat, *originally published in 1898. After a shipwreck, four survivors are in a lifeboat, seeking land.*

The injured captain, lying in the bow, was at this time buried in that profound dejection and indifference which comes, temporarily at least, to even the bravest and most enduring when, willy nilly, the firm fails, the army loses, the ship goes down. The mind of the master of a vessel is rooted deep in the timbers of her, though he commanded for a day or a decade, and this captain had on him the stern impression of a scene in the greys of dawn of seven turned faces, and later a stump of a top-mast with a white ball on it that slashed to and fro at the waves, went low and lower, and down. Thereafter there was something strange in his voice. Although steady, it was deep with mourning, and of a quality beyond oration or tears.

"Keep 'er a little more south, Billie," said he.

"'A little more south,' sir," said the oiler in the stern.

A seat in this boat was not unlike a seat upon a bucking bronco, and, by the same token, a bronco is not much smaller. The craft pranced and reared, and plunged like an animal. As each wave came, and she rose for it, she seemed like a horse making at a fence outrageously high. The manner of her scramble over these walls of water is a mystic thing, and, moreover, at the top of them were ordinarily these problems in white water, the foam racing down from the summit of each wave, requiring a new leap, and a leap from the air. Then, after scornfully bumping a crest, she would slide, and race, and splash down a long incline, and arrive bobbing and nodding in front of the next menace.

In the wan light, the faces of the men must have been grey. Their eyes must have glinted in strange ways as they gazed steadily astern. Viewed from a balcony, the whole thing would doubtlessly have been weirdly picturesque. But the men in the boat had no time to see it, and if they had had leisure there were other things to occupy their minds. The sun swung steadily up the sky, and they knew it was broad day because the colour of the sea changed from slate to emerald-green, streaked with amber lights, and the foam was like tumbling snow. The process of the breaking day was unknown to them. They were aware only of this effect upon the colour of the waves that rolled toward them.

In disjointed sentences the cook and the correspondent argued as to the difference between a life-saving station and a house of refuge. The cook had said: "There's a house of refuge just north of the Mosquito Inlet Light, and as soon as they see us, they'll come off in their boat and pick us up."

"As soon as who see us?" said the correspondent.

"The crew," said the cook.

"Houses of refuge don't have crews," said the correspondent. "As I understand them, they are only places where clothes and grub are stored for the benefit of shipwrecked people. They don't carry crews."

"Oh, yes, they do," said the cook.

"No, they don't," said the correspondent.

"Well, we're not there yet, anyhow," said the oiler, in the stern.

"Well," said the cook, "perhaps it's not a house of refuge that I'm thinking of as being near Mosquito Inlet Light. Perhaps it's a life-saving station."

"We're not there yet," said the oiler, in the stern.

1. Which choice gives the best summary of the problems presented in this passage?

A) A man is injured and the others are arguing.
B) Several men are stranded in a small lifeboat with an injured captain.
C) There is a disagreement about life-saving stations vs. houses of refuge.
D) Multiple people are sailing on a sea with a storm in the early morning.

2. Which of the following selections provides the best evidence that the men were working very hard?

A) Lines 18–19 ("'Keep 'er ... said he")
B) Lines 22–24 ("A seat ... much smaller")
C) Lines 43–46 ("But the ... their minds")
D) Lines 55–58 ("'In disjointed ... of refuge")

3. Based on what is stated in the passage, what do you know to be true about the captain?

A) He is greatly upset at the loss of his ship.
B) He has been captain of his ship for at least a decade.
C) He is usually the one rowing, but cannot because of his injury.
D) His voice was damaged in the accident.

4. Which of the men does NOT join in the discussion about a house of refuge?

A) The oiler
B) The cook
C) The correspondent
D) The captain

5. As used in line 27, the word "making" most nearly means

A) Creating
B) Preparing for
C) Heading toward
D) Fleeing

6. Which of the following illustrations is used to describe the small boat?

A) An army losing
B) A firm failing
C) A horse running
D) Snow tumbling

7. Which of the following literary devices is used in lines 24–28 ("The craft ... outrageously high.")?

A) Metaphor
B) Simile
C) Alliteration
D) Foreshadowing

8. When the author states that the captain has been "injured" in line 1, this most likely refers to what kind of injury, based on context?

A) Emotional
B) Physical
C) Mental
D) None of the above

9. Which of the following sentences best describes the theme of this passage?

A) In an emergency, no one is better than others and all must work together to survive.
B) It is important to have a plan for emergencies so one does not find oneself in a situation with no escape.
C) No one should be in a small boat when weather is uncertain.
D) It is dangerous to argue in perilous times rather than working to save each other.

Questions 10–20 are based on the following two passages.

Both passages are adapted from addresses given by Dwight D. Eisenhower. The first is his Order of the Day *given on D-Day (June 6, 1944) and the second is his* Farewell Address *(January 17, 1961).*

Passage 1

Soldiers, Sailors, and Airmen of the Allied Expeditionary Force:

You are about to embark upon the Great Crusade, toward which we have striven these many months.

The eyes of the world are upon you. The hopes and prayers of liberty-loving people everywhere march with you.

In company with our brave Allies and brothers-in-arms on other Fronts you will bring about the destruction of the German war machine, the elimination of Nazi tyranny over oppressed peoples of Europe, and security for ourselves in a free world.

Your task will not be an easy one. Your enemy is well trained, well equipped, and battle-hardened. He will fight savagely.

But this is the year 1944. Much has happened since the Nazi triumphs of 1940–41. The United Nations have inflicted upon the Germans great defeats, in open battle, man-to-man. Our air offensive has seriously reduced their strength in the air and their capacity to wage war on the ground. Our Home Fronts have given us an overwhelming superiority in weapons and munitions of war, and placed at our disposal great reserves of trained fighting men. The tide has turned. The free men of the world are marching together to victory.

I have full confidence in your courage, devotion to duty, and skill in battle. We will accept nothing less than full victory.

Passage 2

We now stand ten years past the midpoint of a century that has witnessed four major wars among great nations. Three of these involved our own country. Despite these holocausts America is today the strongest, the most influential and most productive nation in the world. Understandably proud of this pre-eminence, we yet realize that America's leadership and prestige depend, not merely upon our unmatched material progress, riches and military strength, but on how we use our power in the interests of world peace and human betterment.

Throughout America's adventure in free government, our basic purposes have been to keep the peace; to foster progress in human achievement, and to enhance liberty, dignity and integrity among people and among nations. To strive for less would be unworthy of a free and religious people. Any failure traceable to arrogance, or our lack of comprehension or readiness to sacrifice would inflict upon us grievous hurt both at home and abroad.

Progress toward these noble goals is persistently threatened by the conflict now engulfing the world. It commands our whole attention, absorbs our very beings. We face a hostile ideology—global in scope, atheistic in character, ruthless in purpose, and insidious in method. Unhappily the danger it poses promises to be of indefinite duration. To meet it successfully, there is called for, not so much the emotional and transitory sacrifices of crisis, but rather those which enable us to carry forward steadily, surely, and without complaint the burdens of a prolonged and complex struggle—with liberty at stake. Only thus shall we remain, despite every provocation, on our charted course toward permanent peace and human betterment.

Crises there will continue to be. In meeting them, whether foreign or domestic, great or small, there is a recurring temptation to feel that some spectacular and costly action could become the miraculous solution to all current difficulties. A huge increase in newer elements of our defense; development of unrealistic programs to cure every ill in agriculture; a dramatic expansion in basic and applied research—these and many other possibilities, each possibly promising in itself, may be suggested as the only way to the road we wish to travel. But each proposal must be weighed in the light of a broader consideration: the need to maintain balance.

As we peer into society's future, we—you and I, and our government—must avoid the impulse to live only for today, plundering, for our own ease and convenience, the precious resources of tomorrow. We cannot mortgage the material assets of our grandchildren without risking the loss also of their political and spiritual heritage. We want democracy to survive for all generations to come, not to become the insolvent phantom of tomorrow.

Down the long lane of the history yet to be written America knows that this world of ours, ever growing smaller, must avoid becoming a community of dreadful fear and hate, and be, instead, a proud confederation of mutual trust and respect.

Such a confederation must be one of equals. The weakest must come to the conference table with the same confidence as do we, protected as we are by our moral, economic, and military strength. That table, though scarred by many past frustrations, cannot be abandoned for the certain agony of the battlefield.

Happily, I can say that war has been avoided. Steady progress toward our ultimate goal has been made. But, so much remains to be done. As a private citizen, I shall never cease to do what little I can to help the world advance along that road.

10. Which of the following comes closest to summarizing the main idea of Passage 1?

A) We are fighting this battle to save America's future.
B) We are fighting this battle because we have superior weapons and training.
C) We are fighting this battle in the effort to gain or preserve liberty throughout the world.
D) We are fighting this battle because victory is now possible and we must join with our allies.

11. What is the purpose of lines 15–17 of Passage 1 ("Your task ... fight savagely")?

A) He is making sure that the soldiers are taking their task seriously.
B) He is reminding the soldiers that they are more than capable of defeating the enemy so they will not be afraid.
C) He is cautioning the soldiers to be careful and not to rush into battle heedlessly.
D) He is raising a problem to show in the following lines that the soldiers are strong enough to meet it.

12. How could the tone of each passage be described?

A) Motivating in Passage 1 and reflective in Passage 2
B) Inspiring in Passage 1 and warning in Passage 2
C) Forceful in Passage 1 and nostalgic in Passage 2
D) Wistful in Passage 1 and rousing in Passage 2

13. In both passages, Eisenhower calls upon listeners to fight to save __________.

A) Human progress and dignity
B) Liberty
C) Peace
D) The American Dream

14. Which sentence from Passage 2 supports the idea that the author believed that it was important to conserve environmental resources?

A) Lines 8–14 ("Understandably proud ... human betterment")
B) Line 43 ("Crises there ... to be")
C) Lines 58–62 ("As we ... of tomorrow")
D) Lines 68–73 ("Down the ... and respect")

15. In line 5 of Passage 2, the word "holocausts" most nearly means

A) Persecution of religious minorities
B) Battles
C) Periods of great destruction and death
D) Imprisonments in concentration camps

16. In lines 70–73 of Passage 2, the author urges that we "must avoid becoming a community of dreadful fear and hate, and be, instead, a proud confederation of mutual trust and respect." Which rhetorical device does the author use?

A) Alliteration
B) Symbolism
C) Repetition
D) Parallelism

17. In line 76 of Passage 2, the author uses the term "conference table" ________________?

A) Literally
B) Figuratively
C) Both literally and figuratively
D) Neither literally nor figuratively

18. Why does the author mention "four major wars" in lines 2–3 of Passage 2?

A) To show that every generation has major conflicts to deal with
B) To give background for the claim that the US is a powerful and successful nation
C) To warn that the US is quick to join wars
D) To prove that the war is always won by the side the US joins

19. What kind of enemy does the author of Passage 2 imply that the nation is facing in the "conflict" mentioned in line 27?

A) Worldviews that conflicted with American ideals
B) German troops
C) Threats of communism
D) The Cold War

20. How would the experience of reading Passage 1, a transcript of a speech, most likely differ from seeing and hearing the address delivered in person?

A) The author likely was fearful while delivering his address, and this fear is lost in its transcription.
B) The author would likely have increased the emotion in his address with his voice.
C) The author had an impressively loud voice that intimidated his audience.
D) The author's original address was much longer than the version that was later transcribed.

Questions 21–29 are based on the following passage.

This passage is adapted from John Quincy Adams' An Address...Celebrating the Declaration of Independence, *1821.*

The interest, which in this paper has survived the occasion upon which it was issued; the interest which is of every age and every clime; the interest which quickens with the lapse of years, spreads as it grows old, and brightens as it recedes, is in the principles which it proclaims. It was the first solemn declaration by a nation of the only legitimate foundation of civil government. It was the corner stone of a new fabric, destined to cover the surface of the globe. It demolished at a stroke the lawfulness of all governments founded upon conquest. It swept away all the rubbish of accumulated centuries of servitude. It announced in practical form to the world the transcendent truth of the unalienable sovereignty of the people. It proved that the social compact was no figment of the imagination; but a real, solid, and sacred bond of the social union. From the day of this declaration, the people of North America were no longer the fragment of a distant empire, imploring justice and mercy from an inexorable master in another hemisphere. They were no longer children appealing in vain to the sympathies of a heartless mother; no longer subjects leaning upon the shattered columns of royal promises, and invoking the faith of parchment to secure their rights. They were a nation, asserting as of right, and maintaining by war, its own existence. A nation was born in a day.

How many ages hence
Shall this their lofty scene be acted o'er
In states unborn, and accents yet
unknown?*

It will be acted o'er, fellow-citizens, but it can never be repeated. It stands, and must forever stand alone, a beacon on the summit of the mountain, to which all the inhabitants of the earth may turn their eyes for a genial and saving light, till time shall be lost in eternity, and this globe itself dissolve, nor leave a wreck behind. It stands forever, a light of admonition to the rulers of men; a light of salvation and redemption to the oppressed. So long as this planet shall be inhabited by human beings, so long as man shall be of social nature, so long as government shall be necessary to the great moral purposes of society, and so long as it shall be abused to the purposes of oppression, so long shall this declaration hold out to the sovereign and to the subject the extent and the boundaries of their respective rights and duties; founded in the laws of nature and of nature's God. Five and forty years have passed away since this Declaration was issued by our fathers; and here are we, fellow-citizens, assembled in the full enjoyment of its fruits, to bless the Author of our being for the bounties of his providence, in casting our lot in this favored land; to remember with effusions of gratitude the sages who put forth, and the heroes who bled for the establishment of this Declaration; and, by the communion of soul in the re-perusal and hearing of this instrument, to renew the genuine Holy Alliance of its principles, to recognize them as eternal truths, and to pledge ourselves and bind our posterity to a faithful and undeviating adherence to them.

*Shakespeare, *Julius Caesar*

21. What does the author mean by humanity's "social nature" mentioned in line 50?

A) Desire to celebrate together
B) Need for entertainment
C) Tendency to live in community
D) Strong desire for justice

22. Which of the following describes a major theme of the passage?

A) The Declaration of Independence is a document with lasting use.
B) The US is the first of a new kind of world government.
C) The newly-formed US government is evolving to meet the needs of its citizens.
D) The US will never again serve another nation.

23. The author mentions several accomplishments of the Declaration of Independence. Which of the following does he <u>not</u> cite in the passage?

A) Doing away with servitude
B) Proving that the social compact was real
C) Showing that governments founded on conquest were unlawful
D) Paving the way for France to likewise declare independence

24. In lines 25–27 ("children appealing in vain to the sympathies of a heartless mother"), the author uses what literary device?

A) Personification
B) Alliteration
C) Symbolism
D) Allusion

25. What is the author referring to when he speaks of "this paper" in line 1?

A) The Declaration of Independence
B) The Constitution
C) The newspaper
D) The paper on which his speech was written

26. As used in line 4 of the passage, the word "quickens" most nearly means

A) To move more rapidly
B) To be enlivened
C) To speak in a rushed voice
D) To wane

27. As used in line 10 of the passage, the word "fabric" most nearly means

A) Materialism
B) Clothlike
C) System
D) Flag

28. Which selection from the passage best supports the idea that the US deserved freedom from England?

A) Lines 57–73 ("Five and ... to them.")
B) Lines 39–45 ("It stands ... wreck behind.")
C) Lines 34–37 ("How many ... yet unknown?")
D) Lines 30–32 ("They were ... own existence.")

29. What is a possible purpose of the author in including the quote from Shakespeare's *Julius Caesar*?

A) To sound highly educated
B) To give a poetic illustration of his point that the Declaration would be long remembered
C) To show that the US was founded on ancient Roman ideals of law and order
D) To show that the US was a vast land with many states that had not even been formed yet

Questions 30–39 are based on the following passage.

Plankton, the tiny plants and animals that provide food for many ocean dwellers from small fish to the blue whale, make up not only one of the largest collections of organisms but also one of the most diverse. The word "plankton" is derived from the Greek *planktos*, meaning "errant," and describes their habit of drifting with the ocean currents, as these organisms often cannot move independently but are carried along by water movement.

Several of these organisms are known as holoplankton. These organisms, such as algae, spend their lives as plankton. Meroplankton, on the other hand, are only plankton for part of their life cycles and then can become benthic (living on the sea floor) or nektic (able to swim). Typically, meroplankton spend their larval stages as plankton before they reach full maturity.

Plankton are generally sorted into six different categories, called trophic level groups. These groups include the phytoplankton, plants that must stay near the water's surface so they can be exposed to sunlight and perform photosynthesis. Other groups include viruses, bacteria, and fungi, as well as small animals that eat other forms of plankton. Finally, the mixotrophs are both producers and consumers, depending on current needs. For example, on sunny days they may grow by photosynthesis, while at other times they eat smaller plankton for nutrients.

Along with providing food for much of the ocean life, plankton also play a vital role in oxygen production. Phytoplankton release oxygen during photosynthesis, producing approximately half of the earth's oxygen. They also balance the levels of carbon dioxide and oxygen in the atmosphere. Additionally, they contribute to the carbon cycle, helping to store carbon in rocks and sediment rather than releasing it into the atmosphere.

The abundance of plankton in a body of water (they are found not only in the ocean, but also in smaller bodies such as lakes and even ponds) varies according to season and weather, largely depending on light and availability of nutrients. Though largely invisible to the naked eye, they play a vital role in the survival of the earth's life cycle.

Graphic 1

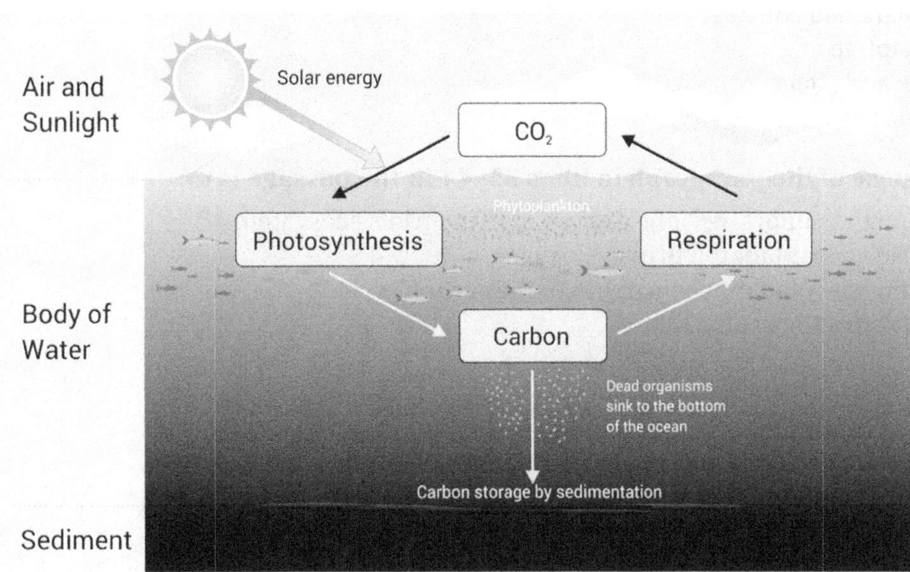

30. What is the primary purpose of this passage?

A) To describe the trophic level groups of plankton
B) To describe the types and functions of plankton
C) To describe the role of plankton in oxygen production
D) To describe the plankton life cycle

31. The main difference between the holoplankton and meroplankton is that:

A) Holoplankton are plankton for their entire lives, while meroplankton are only plankton for part of their lives.
B) Holoplankton are only plankton for part of their lives, while meroplankton are plankton for their entire lives.
C) Holoplankton are plants and meroplankton are animals.
D) Holoplankton live on the sea floor and meroplankton are able to swim.

32. Mixotrophs are different from the other plankton because they can:

A) Be viruses, bacteria, or fungi
B) Live only part of their lives as plankton
C) Adapt to either use photosynthesis or feed on other plankton
D) Produce oxygen

33. What is meant by the term "phytoplankton" used in line 37?

A) The trophic level groups
B) A group of plankton composed of plants
C) A group of plankton that avoids light
D) A group of plankton that can swim independently

34. What is meant by the term "trophic level groups" used in lines 22–23?

A) Plankton that use photosynthesis
B) Plankton that live in tropical regions
C) Viruses, bacteria, and fungi
D) Different classifications for plankton

35. This passage can best be described as ______________________.

A) Compare and contrast
B) Descriptive
C) Cause and effect
D) Persuasive

36. The purpose of the paragraph in lines 35–44 in the passage is to:

A) Explain the importance of plankton to the world's ecosystem
B) Describe how plankton produce oxygen
C) Explain how plankton contribute to the carbon cycle
D) List various types of plankton

37. Which of the following selections provides evidence to support the statement that the population of plankton is affected by storms?

A) Lines 5–11 ("The word ... water movement")
B) Lines 31–34 ("For example ... for nutrients")
C) Lines 37–39 ("Phytoplankton release ... earth's oxygen")
D) Lines 45–50 ("The abundance ... of nutrients")

38. Which of the following does Graphic 1 most likely depict?

A) The life cycle of meroplankton
B) The carbon cycle
C) The movement of plankton on sea currents
D) The distribution of plankton in various ocean levels

39. Which of the following describes the general structure of this passage?

A) Introduction, types of plankton, roles of plankton, conclusion
B) Definition of term, distinctions between plankton, oxygen production, conclusion
C) Importance of plankton, roles of plankton, trophic levels, conclusion
D) Introduction, importance of plankton, types of plankton, conclusion

Questions 40–49 are based on the following passage.

There are three main categories of rock: igneous, metamorphic, and sedimentary. Igneous rocks are formed as molten magma or lava cools and hardens. Metamorphic rock is created as existing rocks undergo immense pressure, heat, or chemical effects. Sedimentary rocks are formed from accumulation and cementation of particles, or when minerals that have dissolved in water are precipitated. Sedimentary rocks may appear to be the most abundant because they are the most common rocks exposed on the Earth's surface, but igneous and metamorphic rock make up the majority of the entire crust of the earth.

Sedimentary rocks are known for depositing in layers. These strata can often be seen in canyons or cliff sides, long stripes or waves. This kind of rock varies from tiny grains of sand to giant boulders to silt.

Sedimentary rocks can be classified into three main categories: clastic, chemical, and organic. Clastic rocks are made of smaller rocks and minerals, called *clasts*, that are displaced by natural forces such as wind, water, or mud and eventually deposited. Through compaction and erosion, the rocks are formed. Clastic rock includes clay, sand, and gravel.

While clastic sedimentary rock is made from solids that have been moved by the elements, chemical sedimentary rock is formed from particles that have been dissolved in liquid and then reprecipitated. The most common type of chemical rock is limestone (certain types), but iron ore, flint, and rock salt are other examples.

Organic sedimentary rocks are created as organic materials, plant and animal debris, are accumulated and eventually form rock due to pressure and heat. As organic material decomposes, it first becomes peat. When peat is covered with earth this increases the pressure and temperature, and the peat becomes lignite. With even greater pressure and temperature, the lignite can become coal. Most types of limestone are also organic rock.

Sedimentary rock, while less abundant than the other types, is more useful for certain applications, such as dating and study of ancient geography. The rock record can be used to show past boundaries and yield clues about past life in fossils. The way layers are deposited can also give information about past occurrences such as floods and earthquakes. While nothing may seem more common or meaningless than a tiny chunk of gravel, it is in reality a chunk of history, preserving a miniature record of geological events.

Earth's Surface		Total Earth Crust	
Sedimentary	75%	Sedimentary	5%
Igneous	15%	Igneous	90%
Metamorphic	10%	Metamorphic	5%

40. Which of the following best states the purpose of the passage?

A) To entertain the reader with the differences between types of rock, using sedimentary rock as an example
B) To describe the differences between various sedimentary rocks and explain how they are formed
C) To persuade the reader that sedimentary rocks are vital to the earth's existence
D) To inform the reader of how sedimentary rocks are formed and why they are the majority of the surface rock

41. Limestone is which of the following types of sedimentary rock?

A) Clastic
B) Chemical
C) Organic
D) Both chemical and organic

42. What is a probable definition for "reprecipitated" as found in line 34 of the passage?

A) Brought back to a solid
B) Mixed with a liquid solution to form a new liquid solution
C) Turned from a liquid into a vapor
D) Evaporated into the atmosphere

43. Which of the following accurately represents the progression of organic material into rock?

A) Lignite, coal, limestone
B) Peat, lignite, coal
C) Peat, coal, limestone
D) Lignite, peat, limestone

44. As used in line 32, the word "elements" most nearly means:

A) The 118 chemical elements of the periodic table
B) Chemical agents that can break down rock
C) Weather events such as rain and wind
D) Rudimentary particles of rock

45. Which of the following is the best stand-in for the word "strata" as used in line 17?

A) Bands
B) Rocks
C) Mountains
D) Igneous rocks

46. What stance does the author seem to hold regarding sedimentary rock?

A) It is important because it helps us understand the past.
B) It is insignificant because it is such a small percentage of the total rock on Earth.
C) It is vital that people understand it so that it can be preserved.
D) It is unfairly given less attention than the other types of rock.

47. Based on the table, what can be concluded about the different types of rock?

A) Sedimentary rock is the most common rock both at the surface and overall.
B) Metamorphic rock is the most common rock overall, but not the most common at the surface.
C) Igneous rock is the most common rock both at the surface and overall.
D) Igneous rock is the most common rock overall, but not the most common at the surface.

48. Does the table support the passage's statement on rock proportions in lines 10–15?

A) Yes, because there is less metamorphic rock than the other kinds both at the surface and throughout the crust.
B) Yes, because sedimentary rock is most populous at the surface but igneous rock is most populous in the crust as a whole.
C) No, because there is not enough information in the passage to match up with the table.
D) No, because the amount of igneous rock in the table is higher than the amount mentioned in the passage.

49. Of the following, which would be the most suitable title for this passage?

A) Three Categories of Rock
B) Sedimentary, Igneous, or Metamorphic: What's the Difference?
C) Varieties of Sedimentary Rock
D) The Geological Value of Sedimentary Rock

Writing and Language

Questions 1–11 are based on the following passage.

While best known for pulling Santa's sleigh every Christmas on his mythical trip to every child's home, reindeer (or caribou as they are typically called in North America) have played an important role in human history. For many people groups in Arctic or subarctic regions, their way of life has depended on reindeer. In Finland, Norway, and other Scandinavian countries, the reindeer serve multiple purposes. They are milked, their meat is a staple part of the diet, their fur is sold or used for clothing, and even [1] <u>its</u> antlers can be powdered for a nutritional supplement. Reindeer were also traditionally used for transportation (and in some regions are still used to pull sleds). Some people groups travel with herds of wild caribou, following their grazing route and depending on the herds of [2] <u>reindeers'</u> for food and shelter. Caribou are so integral to their life that not only the people's physical needs [3] <u>and also</u> their entertainment is centered around the animals, such as games, toys, and songs.

1.

A) NO CHANGE
B) it's
C) their
D) his

2.

A) NO CHANGE
B) reindeer's
C) reindeers
D) reindeer

3.

A) NO CHANGE
B) but also
C) but moreover
D) and even

Life dependent on caribou is a nomadic life. Caribou can travel for [4] hundred's or even thousand's of miles each year as they seek new pasture, as well as traveling to give birth. Through the winter, animals roam to find food. In the spring, females travel to remote areas to calve, [5] having then chosen locations such as islands for the safety of their newborn calves. Although newborn caribou weigh less than fifteen pounds, on average, they begin to walk immediately, and within 24 hours of birth, they are [6] faster than an adult human. Thus, they can keep up with the herd immediately, which increases safety.

As [7] beforely mentioned, caribou weigh less than fifteen pounds at birth, but may be up to 400 pounds at maturity. Despite their bulk they can run at 50 mph for short distances and can maintain a pace of 20 mph for long periods of time. They can also swim quickly across lakes and rushing rivers. Their thick coats protect them against the brutally cold temperatures.

4.

A) NO CHANGE
B) hundred's, or even thousand's
C) hundreds, or even thousands
D) hundreds or even thousands

5.

A) NO CHANGE
B) chose
C) have chosen
D) choosing

6.

A) NO CHANGE
B) more fast
C) as fast
D) even more fast

7.

A) NO CHANGE
B) mentioned priorly
C) previously mentioned
D) mentioned preceding this statement

In the cold climate where they live, very little vegetation grows. During the coldest months little can be [8] found: grasslike plants, small shrubs, and lichen. This lichen is called "reindeer moss" since they are the only animals in the world that can ingest it due to a particular stomach enzyme that only reindeer have. They roam the frozen tundra, [9] which using their powerful sense of smell to locate anything edible beneath the snow and digging to uncover it.

Through the harsh conditions, caribou continue to thrive, migrating annually. Some subspecies have become endangered, but as a whole, the species is still populous. Despite wolves and bears, and the constant threat of starvation, they remain. [10] However, their role has changed over the years.

[11]

8.

A) NO CHANGE
B) found, grasslike
C) found; grasslike
D) found. Grasslike

9.

A) NO CHANGE
B) that is using
C) using
D) use

10. How should the author modify the closing statement to best summarize the selection?

A) NO CHANGE
B) While they may not fly around the world to deliver Christmas gifts, reindeer play an important role in their ecosystem and in many human societies.
C) Reindeer should be protected against the constant encroachment of man on their feeding and calving grounds.
D) Although reindeer may bring challenges, their contributions make them an invaluable environmental asset.

11. The author is considering adding a detail about caribou's hooves, which are scoop-shaped to enable digging. To which paragraph should this be added?

A) The 2nd paragraph
B) The 3rd paragraph
C) The 4th paragraph
D) It should not be added

Questions 12–22 are based on the following passage.

In lists of familiar instruments, oboes rarely appear near the top. While most people would easily recognize a piano or violin, many would not be able to identify an oboe, much less to identify it by sound. Yet it is an instrument that has been used for [12] millennium. The predecessors of today's oboes were popular among shepherds. And in ancient Greece, the famous aulos was a version of the oboe as well.

The oboe is a woodwind instrument, along with instruments [13] such as: the flute, clarinet, and saxophone. Many of these instruments are reed pipes, meaning that a reed is fixed in the mouthpiece. When air is blown into the mouthpiece, the reed causes vibration, which produces a distinctive musical note. [14] The oboe differs from many other reed pipes because of its double reed. This double reed is exposed, meaning it is placed directly in the player's lips rather than being covered by a mouthpiece.

12.

A) NO CHANGE
B) a millennia
C) millennia
D) more than a millennia

13.

A) NO CHANGE
B) such as
C) such as;
D) such as—

14.

A) NO CHANGE
B) The oboe differs, because of its double reed, from many other reed pipes.
C) Differing, from many other reed pipes, the oboe has a double reed.
D) From many other reed pipes, the oboe is different because of its double reed.

In concert performances, the oboe is used to tune the rest of the instruments. Its unique, penetrating sound is easily distinguished from the other instruments, making it easy to follow. And it has a steady pitch, more so than most instruments, making it more [15] undependable for tuning.

An oboe's pitch depends on many factors such as humidity and temperature, but also on how the reed is made. Experienced oboists often make their own reeds. Customizing them to their specific needs and preferences, [16] the reeds are carefully suited for each individual musician. Reeds are often made from a cane called *Arundo donax*, also known as giant reed or elephant grass. For centuries, [17] this cane has been used by artisans to create not only oboes but also other woodwind instruments. Professional oboists often have special [18] tools; making and then adjusting their reeds as needed.

15.

A) NO CHANGE
B) erratic
C) reliable
D) challenging

16.

A) NO CHANGE
B) the reeds are suitable for each musician's needs
C) each reed is carefully suited for an individual musician
D) the musicians carefully design their own reeds

17.

A) NO CHANGE
B) this cane has been harvested by artisans
C) artisans have eschewed this cane
D) artisans have used this cane

18.

A) NO CHANGE
B) tools, making
C) tools: making
D) tools. Making

There are several members of the oboe family, some with lower pitches such as the bass oboe and some with higher pitches like the piccolo oboe. [19] However, the treble and soprano oboes are the most commonly played. The player controls the notes by pressing keys to cover the tone holes. An oboe usually has 23 or 24 tone holes, which are smaller than in many other woodwind instruments. This small size causes the distinctive tone oboes are known for.

Oboes are used in a variety of musical styles, from classical to folk to jazz. Composers such as Bach, Handel, and Haydn composed pieces specifically designed for the oboe. Oboes are often used in film scores, adding to a somber or meaningful scene.

The oboe is unlikely to ever become one of the world's most popular instruments, [20] so it has endured and continues to contribute to the musical scene. From its first orchestral appearance nearly 400 years ago in the [21] 1600's to its varied uses today, it has made its mark. [22] From its haunting notes with only sheep as an audience to its performance in today's largest concert, the oboe creates a unique listening experience.

19. Where is the best place for this sentence?

A) NO CHANGE
B) At the beginning of this paragraph, because it gives background the information on playing.
C) In the previous paragraph, as a transition to this one.
D) It should be removed from the selection because the information is not relevant.

20.

A) NO CHANGE
B) however
C) yet
D) because

21.

A) NO CHANGE
B) 1600s
C) 16th century
D) sixteenth century

22. Which of the following sentences would make a good conclusion to the selection?

A) NO CHANGE
B) Although the oboe has been used for so many years, it has slowly dwindled in popularity and may eventually become unknown.
C) The oboe is slowly winning the hearts of listeners, becoming recognizable and beloved throughout the world.
D) Due to the challenges both of perfecting the double reed and learning to play this difficult instrument, it is sadly unlikely that it will ever take its rightful place as one of the world's most loved instruments.

Questions 23–33 are based on the following passage and supplementary material.

While portrayals of ancient humans typically depict them in coverings made of animal skin, woven fabric was actually a very early invention. Although [23] "The Flintstones" popularized the caveman look of skins, woven flax fibers have been discovered that date back thousands of years. The ancient art of weaving is [24] less unknown today, as machines have largely replaced the handwork of past millennia.

In today's textile industry, materials are sourced from four main types: three natural and one artificial. Natural sources include animals, plants, and minerals. Artificial or synthetic sources, such as polyester, are unique to the last two centuries and have slowly been [25] reducing their portion of the textile market, offering new options to the traditional fabrics.

23.

A) NO CHANGE
B) The Flintstones,
C) *The Flintstones*
D) the flintstones

24.

A) NO CHANGE
B) lesser known
C) less known
D) not as unknown

25.

A) NO CHANGE
B) increasing
C) minimizing
D) eliminating

There is an [26] increasingly demand for inexpensive fabrics for mass production. Traditionally, most people had a small wardrobe and did not replace their clothing often. [27] Today's production is highly wasteful and destructive to the environment, and changes need to be made. Today the average person purchases multiple pieces of clothing every year and landfills are full of discarded items that [28] have went out of style or are too poor in quality to last more than a few months. Fashion trends tend to be fleeting, so new clothing is often worn for a short time before replacing. Thus, there is demand for cheaper materials, and less overall concern with durability.

[29] Despite this trend, many high-quality fabrics are still produced today. Many of these come from natural sources, such as animal fibers and cotton. One of the most prized materials throughout history has been wool. Wool comes primarily from sheep but can also include the hair of alpacas, camels, and goats, among other animals. Wool was a [30] plausible export for many countries in medieval times, but since the 1960s, the value of and demand for wool has dropped significantly due to the development of synthetic fibers.

26.

A) NO CHANGE
B) increasing
C) greatly
D) greater

27. Where is the best place for this sentence?

A) NO CHANGE
B) After sentence 4
C) After sentence 5
D) Remove from the selection because it does not fit.

28.

A) NO CHANGE
B) had went
C) gone
D) have gone

29. How can the author best transition from the previous paragraph?

A) NO CHANGE
B) In accordance with this demand
C) To keep up with higher production
D) In spite of the traditional small wardrobe

30.

A) NO CHANGE
B) innovative
C) primary
D) extensive

Another natural material that has stood the test of time is silk. [31] Despite wool, it has an animal source, but instead of being made from animal hair, it is made from a protein fiber spun by silkworms. The process of harvesting silkworm cocoons, unwinding the thread, and weaving it into fabric has been used for thousands of years. The earliest known example was in China, and China is still the world's top producer by far.

[32] As production of wool and silk continue to grow, they are still in demand throughout the world. Although made more efficient by technological advances, much of the original knowledge from past civilizations is still used. Along with other natural fibers, as well as the more modern synthetic materials, textiles continue to be an important part of human culture, not only to keep people clothed and warm but also to express personality, belief, and values. [33]

Annual Production of Materials in Metric Tons

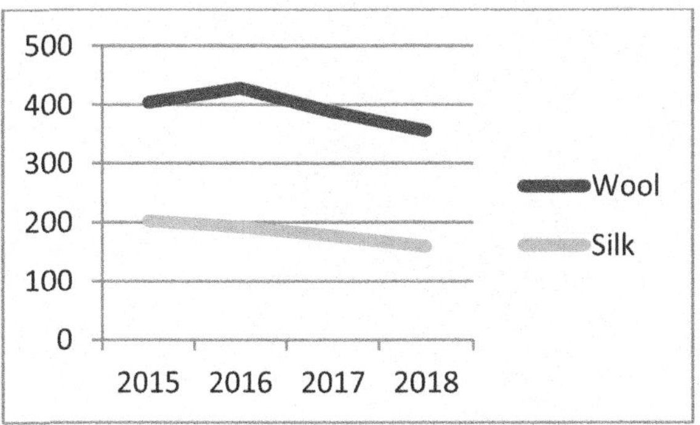

31.

A) NO CHANGE
B) Like
C) In contrast to
D) However

32. Which of the following statements best uses the information given in the graph?

A) NO CHANGE
B) Although production of wool and silk have declined in recent years
C) Despite declining prices on both wool and silk in the past decade
D) Although wool production has dropped as silk remains steady

33. Which of the following facts would be useful to add to the final paragraph?

A) NO CHANGE
B) How wool is harvested and prepared for weaving
C) How synthetic materials are derived
D) How many new silk factories opened in the last decade

Questions 34–44 are based on the following passage.

Scientific Classification, also known as taxonomy, is [34] a methodology of classifying every living being. This provides a [35] way, to organize all animals, plants, and other living things into a database that can be used for comparing and understanding how various parts of the ecosystem fit together.

There are seven levels of classification, beginning with Kingdom, which separates beings into basic categories like plants or animals, and ending with Species, the most specific category, such as a human being or a particular type of mushroom. The animal kingdom, [36] including over one million species, is the largest of the kingdoms. Classification of these animals [37] were determined by their eating and reproductive habits, their breathing and moving, and their embryonic development. Animals range from organisms so small they are invisible to the naked eye to the blue whale, but the one thing all have in common is that they have multiple cells.

34.

A) NO CHANGE
B) a system
C) an organization
D) a procession

35.

A) NO CHANGE
B) way;
C) way:
D) way

36. Which of the following phrases best fits in the sentence?

A) NO CHANGE
B) which includes humans
C) one of either five or six kingdoms, depending on whom you ask
D) the most important of all the kingdoms

37.

A) NO CHANGE
B) is
C) are
D) have been

The second most populous kingdom is Kingdom Plantae, or plants, with over 250,000 species. These include the familiar trees, bushes, and flowers, but also certain types of algae and moss. Like animals, plants are multicellular. They have cell walls made of cellulose. [38] Plants utilize photosynthesis for food. By depending on the sun. This is called being autotrophic. [39] A side effect of photosynthesis is the production of oxygen, benefiting the earth's ecosystems.

The other kingdoms are Fungi, Protista, and Monera (which is often divided into separate kingdoms of Eubacteria and Archaebacteria). Within each of the kingdoms, the classification can be further broken into the following levels: Phylum, Class, Order, Family, Genus, Species. [40] Each different classification level is a taxon. An organism is known by [41] it's last two divisions, genus and species. This is called its binomial nomenclature. Each taxon creates more and more distinctions, from the broadest distinction of Kingdom, such as all animals, to the narrowest distinction of Species, such as *Harmonia axyridis*, or a ladybug.

38. What is the best way to combine the underlined portion?

A) NO CHANGE
B) Depending on the sun, plants utilize photosynthesis for food, this is called being autotrophic.
C) Plants are autotrophic, meaning that they depend on the sun, utilizing photosynthesis for food.
D) Plants depend on the sun to utilize photosynthesis for food, called being autotrophic.

39. What is the best location for this sentence?

A) NO CHANGE
B) after sentence 3
C) after sentence 4
D) DELETE, because this sentence does not fit in this paragraph

40. Does this sentence fit in the selection?

A) Yes, because it sums up the main idea of the selection.
B) Yes, because it provides a definition for a word that is used later.
C) No, because it is an extraneous details that is not relevant to this paragraph.
D) No, because the tone does not fit with the rest of the selection.

41.

A) NO CHANGE
B) its
C) their
D) theirs

This binomial nomenclature gives a universal identification for each species, aiding scientists and anyone studying or researching a particular organism. This name not only identifies the exact species of an organism in the second word, but also its biological relatives in the first [42] word, this is similar to a person's last name.

The scientific classification system has been developed and adapted over the past few centuries, with [43] contributions from many major scientists such as Carl Linnaeus and Charles Darwin. In fact, long before today's system was in place, Aristotle created a system, first dividing organisms into plants and animals and then further classifying by attributes such as whether an animal was a vertebrate, laid eggs, etc. [44] Some animals, like the platypus, are more challenging to classify. Humans have long sought to understand their world better, organizing and comparing the various beings in our ecosystem. While we still have much to discover, and not everyone agrees on how organisms fit together, taxonomy has greatly helped us to know and care for the ecosystems.

42.

A) NO CHANGE
B) word
C) word.
D) word;

43.

A) NO CHANGE
B) opinions about
C) research for
D) questions from

44. Which sentence best supports the main idea of the paragraph?

A) NO CHANGE
B) Today, some scientists propose three domains instead of six kingdoms: Bacteria, Archaea, and Eucarya.
C) At the same time that taxonomy was developed, medical knowledge advanced, perhaps aided by the new discoveries of bacteria and other microscopic organisms.
D) The broad classification into plants or animals remained until comparatively recently, when the microscope aided in discovering new organisms and differentiating between cell types.

Math – No Calculator

Questions 1–13 are multiple choice. Questions 14–17 are grid-in.

1. A hotel room costs \$85 for one guest and \$15 for each additional guest. Which of the following functions $m(n)$ gives the total cost (in dollars) for n guests ($n \geq 1$)?

A) $m(n) = 85 + 15n$
B) $m(n) = 85 + 15(n - 1)$
C) $m(n) = 15 + 85n$
D) $m(n) = 15 + 85(n - 1)$

2. Which of these expresses the equation $y = -2x + 3$ as x in terms of y?

A) $x = 2y - \frac{3}{2}$
B) $x = -2y - 3$
C) $x = -\frac{1}{2}y + \frac{3}{2}$
D) $x = \frac{1}{2}y - \frac{3}{2}$

3. Which of the following is equivalent to the inequality $\frac{1}{2}|x - 3| - 4 \geq 6$?

A) $-2 \leq x \leq 8$
B) $-17 \leq x \leq 23$
C) $x \leq -17$ or $x \geq 23$
D) $x \leq -2$ or $x \geq 8$

4. The solution to which of the following systems of inequalities is graphed below?

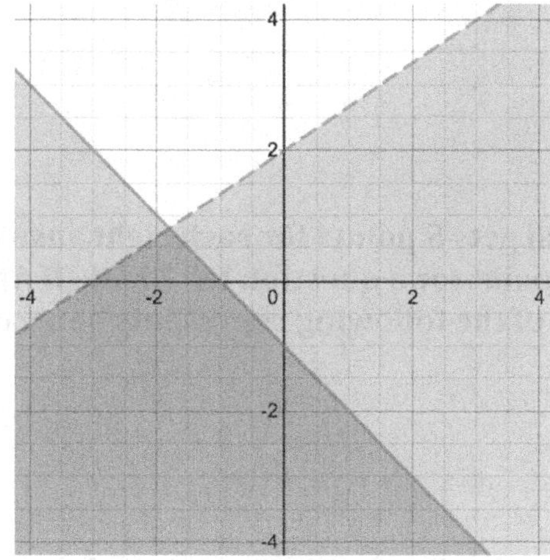

A) $y \leq -x - 1$
$3y - 2x < 6$
B) $y \geq -x - 1$
$y < x + 2$
C) $x < -y + 1$
$y + 3 \leq 2x$
D) $y > 1 - x$
$y \leq 2x + 2$

5. Which of the following is the correct graph of the system of inequalities below?

$$x - 2y > -1$$
$$x + y < 2$$

A) 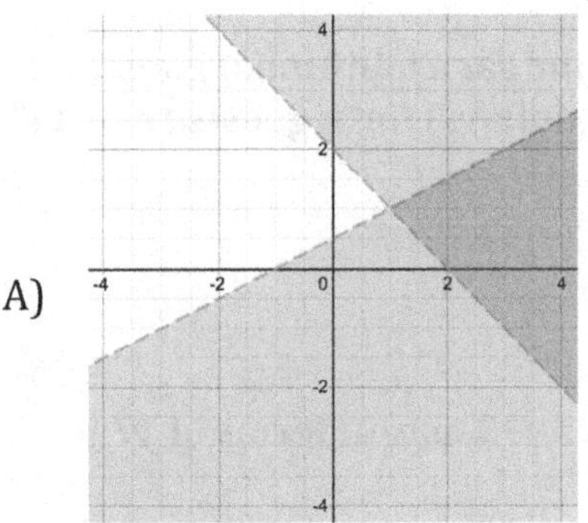

C) 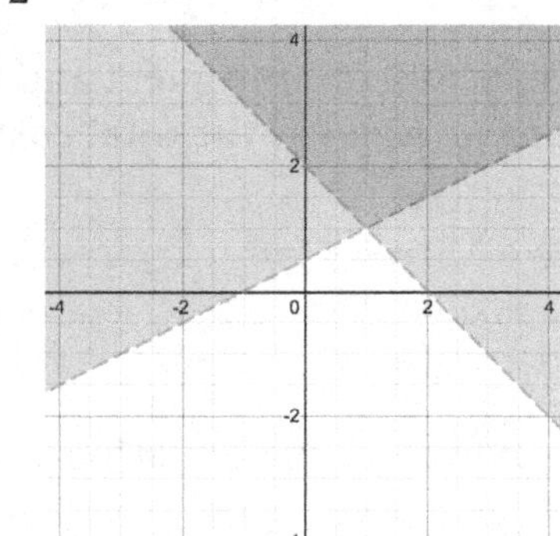

B) 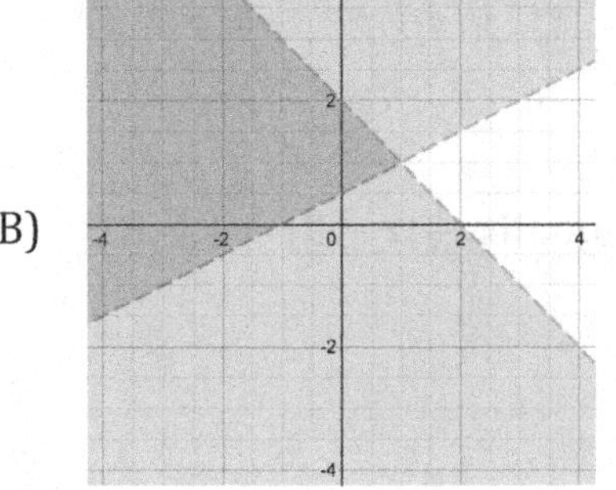

D) 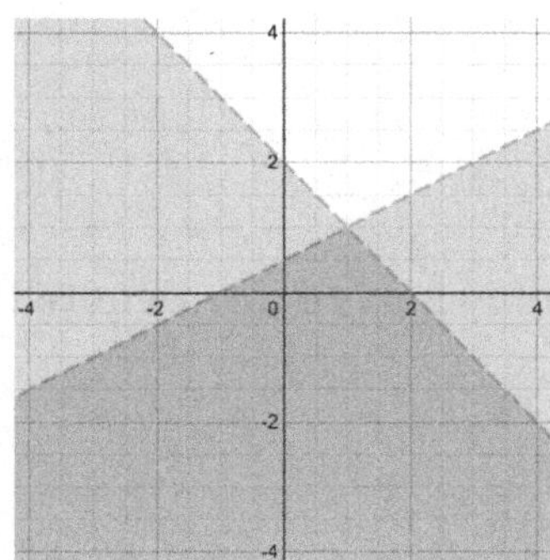

6. Which of the following is equivalent to $2 - \frac{1}{2}x < 1$?

A) $x < 2$
B) $x > 2$
C) $x < -2$
D) $x > -2$

7. A quiz has 10 questions. Andi gets 5 points for each right answer, loses 2 points for each incorrect answer, and loses 1 point for a question left blank. If Andi gets x questions right and y questions wrong, which of the following represents her score on the quiz?

A) $5x - 2y - 1$
B) $4x - 3y - 10$
C) $5x - 2y$
D) $6x - y - 10$

8. Chad is filling out a rental application for an apartment. It has a monthly rate of x plus a one-time deposit of y and an application fee of z. How much will he pay for his first year?

A) $12x + y + z$
B) $x + y + z$
C) $12x + y - z$
D) $x + y - z$

9. If $x - y < 2$, which of the following cannot be true?

A) $x = 6$ and $y = 10$
B) $x = -3$ and $y = -4$
C) $x = 5$ and $y = -8$
D) $x = -3$ and $y = 3$

10. Simplify the expression $\frac{x^2-3x-18}{4x+12}$.

A) $\frac{x+3}{4}$
B) $\frac{(x-6)(x-3)}{4(x+3)}$
C) $\frac{x-6}{4}$
D) $\frac{(x-3)(x+6)}{4(x+3)}$

11. Simplify the expression $x^3 \times (16x)^{\frac{1}{2}}$.

A) $8x^{\frac{7}{2}}$
B) $4x^{\frac{7}{2}}$
C) $8x^{\frac{3}{2}}$
D) $4x^{\frac{3}{2}}$

12. A jeweler sells a certain type of necklace for \$50. She estimates that she can sell 200 necklaces for this price and that she will sell 10 fewer necklaces for every dollar the price is raised and 10 more necklaces for every dollar the price is lowered. Write a function $r(x)$ for the estimated revenue if she raises the price by x dollars.

A) $r(x) = -10x^2 - 300x + 10{,}000$
B) $r(x) = 10x^2 + 300x + 10{,}000$
C) $r(x) = -10x^2 + 300x + 10{,}000$
D) $r(x) = 10x^2 - 300x + 10{,}000$

13. Compare the graphs of $f(x) = 5^x - 2$ and $g(x) = 5^x$.

A) The graph of g is the graph of f shifted two units down.
B) The graph of g is the graph of f shifted two units up.
C) The graph of g is the graph of f shifted two units to the left.
D) The graph of g is the graph of f shifted two units to the right.

14. Exponential functions grow by equal factors over equal intervals. By what factor does the exponential function $f(x) = \frac{4^x}{2}$ grow over every interval whose length is 5?

Grid your answer.

15. A company charges a 30% additional fee for any labor over 100 hours in a given week. The weekly invoice on a job can be represented by the linear function $c(h) = 117h + 9{,}000$, where c is cost and h is hours over 100. For example, if 120 hours are needed one week, the cost will be $c(20) = \$11{,}340$ for 20 hours over 100. What is the hourly rate in dollars for labor over 100 hours?

Grid your answer.

16. Calculate the fifth term $f(5)$ of the sequence defined as:

$$f(n) = \begin{cases} 1 & n = 1 \\ 0 & n = 2 \\ f(n-1) - f(n-2) & n > 2 \end{cases}$$

Grid your answer.

17. Consider the function $f(x) = (x+3)(x^2 - 5x + 4)$. What is the sum of all values of x for which the graph of the function intersects the x-axis?

Grid your answer.

Math – Calculator

Questions 1–27 are multiple choice. Questions 28–31 are gridded.

1. Solve the following system of equations.

$$y = -x + 1$$
$$-3x + y = -3$$

A) $x = 0, y = 1$
B) $x = -1, y = 3$
C) $x = -1, y = 2$
D) $x = 1, y = 0$

2. The table below lists values for x and $f(x)$.

x	$f(x)$
1	0.5
2	2
3	4.5
4	8
5	12.5

Which of the following equations describes the relationship between x and $f(x)$?

A) $f(x) = x^2 - 1$
B) $f(x) = \frac{1}{2}x^2$
C) $f(x) = (-x)^2$
D) $f(x) = x^2 + 1$

3. Which of the following equations represents the relationship between x and y, shown in the table below?

x	y
-2	-14
-1	-8
0	-2
2	10
4	22

A) $y = 6x - 2$
B) $y = 7x$
C) $y = 3x + 18$
D) $y = 12x + 6$

4. The median house value in a town was \$260,000, while the mean value was \$240,000. What could explain the difference between these values?

A) Most house values were above \$260,000.
B) Most house values were between \$240,000 and \$260,000.
C) Several houses had low, outlying values, pulling the mean down.
D) Several houses had high, outlying values, pulling the median up.

5. If the two lines $2y - x = 2$ and $y = 2$ are plotted on a typical xy-coordinate grid, at which point will they intersect?

A) (2,2)
B) (1,2)
C) (2,0)
D) (−1,1)

6. What is the value of $\frac{x^2-6x}{2(x+1)}$ when $x = -2$?

A) 4
B) $-\frac{1}{2}$
C) -8
D) -2

7. What is the value of $\frac{2x+3}{x-1}$ when $x = \frac{1}{2}$?

A) $-\frac{1}{2}$
B) -2
C) -4
D) -8

8. Simplify: $-2(2 + 6i) - 4(2 - 3i)$.

A) $-12 - 24i$
B) -12
C) $4 - 24i$
D) $4 + 12i$

9. Five families go on a camping trip together. Family B (the Browns) has 4 members, Family E (the Emersons) has 3 members, Family G (the Garcias) has 4 members, Family M (the Morenos) has 2 members, and Family W (the Williamses) has 6 members. Four people are randomly selected to prep dinner. Two are from Family W and one is from Family B. What is the probability that the fourth person will also be from Family W?

A) 1 in 2
B) 1 in 4
C) 1 in 5
D) 1 in 8

10. If 71.5% of customers reported in a survey that they were satisfied with their service, and 13,787 responded to the survey, approximately how many did not report that they were satisfied?

A) 4,000
B) 5,000
C) 7,000
D) 10,000

11. A bagel stand offers three types of bagels: plain, blueberry, and cinnamon raisin. If 25% of the bagels purchased on Monday were cinnamon raisin and 40% were blueberry, what percent of the bagels purchased were plain?

A) 25%
B) 35%
C) 45%
D) There is not enough information to say.

12. Marc runs an online business, selling handmade watchbands. He charges for the cost of supplies and shipping, plus a markup of 35% to make a profit. Before Christmas, he has a sale, marking his prices down by 20%. What is the sale price on a watchband if Marc's production and shipping cost was $20?

A) $16.00
B) $19.90
C) $21.60
D) $27.00

13. Twenty-four committee members showed up to a scheduled meeting. If this was only $\frac{3}{8}$ of the entire committee, how many committee members are there?

A) 64
B) 40
C) 18
D) 9

14. The probability that Ella orders a hamburger is 0.4. The probability that she orders French fries, given that she orders a hamburger, is 0.6. Finally, the probability that she orders a hamburger or French fries is 0.72. What is the probability she orders French fries?

A) 0.36
B) 0.44
C) 0.52
D) 0.56

Question 15 is based on the following figure (not drawn to scale):

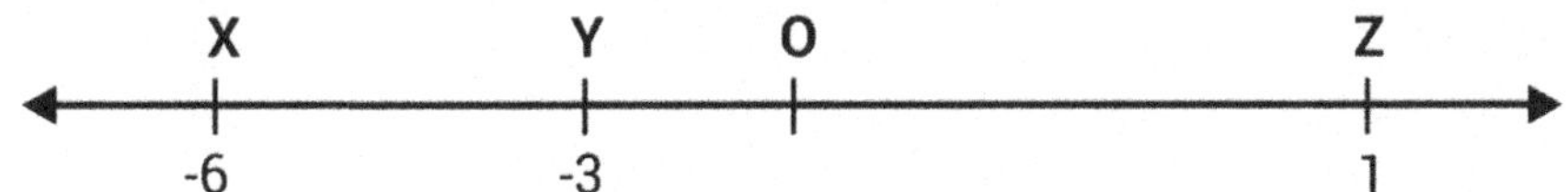

15. In the figure, X, Y, and Z are points on the number line, where O is the origin. What is the ratio of the distance $\overline{YZ}$ to distance $\overline{XY}$?

A) 3:4
B) 4:7
C) 7:4
D) 4:3

16. Professor Chen recorded how many students turned in extra credit assignments each week of the semester in two different classes, as shown in the table below. Which of the following statements is true?

Physics I	1	3	3	5	6	8	4	7	4	8	9	9	12	12	18
Physics II	4	3	5	5	3	7	4	8	6	9	9	10	8	11	17

A) The median is greater in Physics I and the mean is greater in Physics II.
B) The mode is greater in Physics I and the median is greater in Physics II.
C) The range is greater in Physics I and the mean is equal in Physics I and II.
D) The mean and median are both greater in Physics II.

17. Ava is baking cupcakes and brownies for a party. She needs to make at least 150 altogether, and only needs half as many cupcakes as brownies. If x represents cupcakes and y represents brownies, which of the following systems of equations and inequalities represents her baking?

A) $x = \frac{1}{2}y$
$x + y \geq 150$

B) $x = 2y$
$x + y \leq 150$

C) $x = \frac{1}{2}y$
$\frac{1}{2}x + y \geq 150$

D) $2x = y$
$x + \frac{1}{2}y \leq 150$

18. Given the table shown below, what is the probability that a student is a sophomore or prefers French?

	Spanish	**French**	**German**	**Total**
Sophomore	43	27	20	90
Junior	48	38	24	110
Total	91	65	44	200

A) $\frac{27}{200}$
B) $\frac{16}{25}$
C) $\frac{31}{40}$
D) $\frac{13}{40}$

Questions 19 and 20 are based on the following table:

Isabella goes for a jog each morning. The table below shows the number of miles she jogged on six consecutive days.

Day of Week	Miles
Monday	2
Tuesday	2
Wednesday	3
Thursday	3
Friday	2
Saturday	6

19. What is the mode of the numbers in the distribution shown in the table?

A) 1
B) 2
C) 3
D) 4

20. What is the mean of the numbers in the distribution shown in the table?

A) 1
B) 2
C) 3
D) 4

Questions 21 and 22 refer to the following information.

The table below records the number of books each student reads per month (on average), the number of students in each group, and the reading scores of each group in an assessment.

	Group 1	Group 2	Group 3
Number of Books	<3 books	3–7 books	>7 books
Number of Students	4	10	6
Test Scores	83, 77, 79, 69	82, 88, 77, 90, 92, 86, 88, 89, 94, 93	86, 93, 98, 89, 99, 97

21. What is the probability that a randomly chosen student read more than 7 books and scored in the 80s?

A) $\frac{3}{5}$
B) $\frac{3}{10}$
C) $\frac{2}{9}$
D) $\frac{1}{10}$

22. Which group has the lowest median score?

A) Group 1
B) Group 2
C) Group 3
D) More than one group shares the lowest median

23. Solve the equation $1 - \sqrt{3 - 3x} = x$ for x.

A) $x = 1$
B) $x = -2$
C) $x = -1$ and $x = 2$
D) $x = 1$ and $x = -2$

24. If $f(x)$ is a quadratic function with roots at $x = 3$ and $x = -7$, what is $f(x)$?

A) $f(x) = x^2 - 21$
B) $f(x) = x^2 + 4x - 21$
C) $f(x) = x^2 - 4x + 21$
D) $f(x) = x^2 + 4x + 21$

25. Which of the following represents the sum of $\frac{4}{x-4} - \frac{2x}{x^2-3x-4}$?

A) $\frac{2}{x-4}$
B) $\frac{2(x-2)}{(x-4)(x+1)}$
C) $\frac{2(x+2)}{(x-4)(x+1)}$
D) $\frac{2(x-2)}{(x+1)}$

26. Which of the following represents the product of $(3x^3 - x^2 - 6)(x - 5)$?

A) $3x^4 - 16x^3 + 5x^2 - 6x + 30$
B) $3x^4 - 15x^3 - 5x^2 - 6x - 30$
C) $3x^4 - 5x^3 + 5x^2 + 6x - 30$
D) $3x^4 + 16x^3 - 5x^2 + 6x + 30$

27. In the figure, *ABCD* is a parallelogram. The angles are $m\angle A = (5x)°$ and $m\angle B = (2x - 9)°$. Find $m\angle C$.

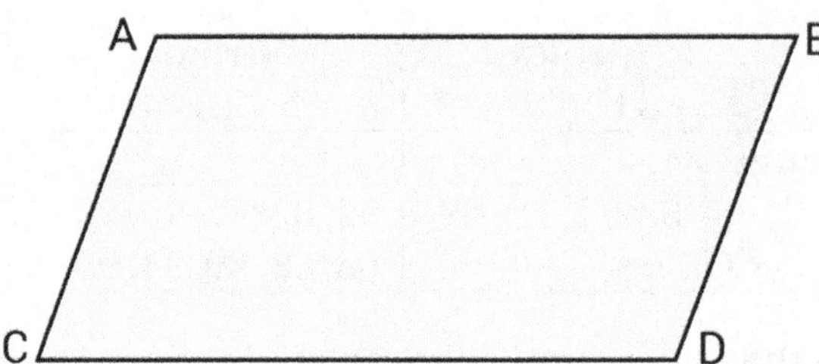

A) $m\angle C = 135°$
B) $m\angle C = 54°$
C) $m\angle C = 45°$
D) $m\angle C = 27°$

28. In the figure, the radius of circle *X* is 4. What is the area of the shaded sector, rounded to the nearest tenth?

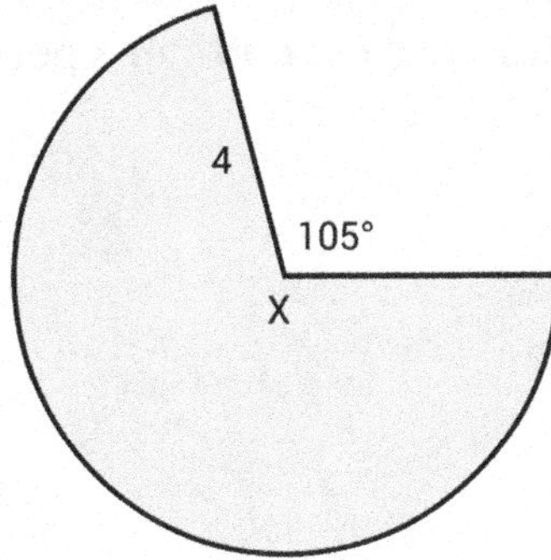

Grid your answer.

29. A cylindrical tank is $\frac{3}{4}$ of the way filled with water. If the radius of the tank is 42 inches and the height is 24 inches, how many gallons of water are in the tank (there are 231 cubic inches in a gallon)? Round to the nearest whole number.

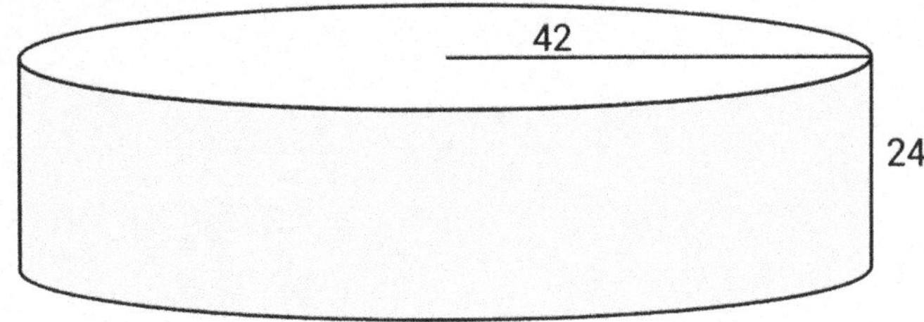

Grid your answer.

30. In the figure, ΔABC is an equilateral triangle with sides of length 12 cm. Circle O is inscribed in this triangle, so that it is tangent to ΔABC at three points, the midpoint of each side. What is the circumference of circle O rounded to the nearest tenth?

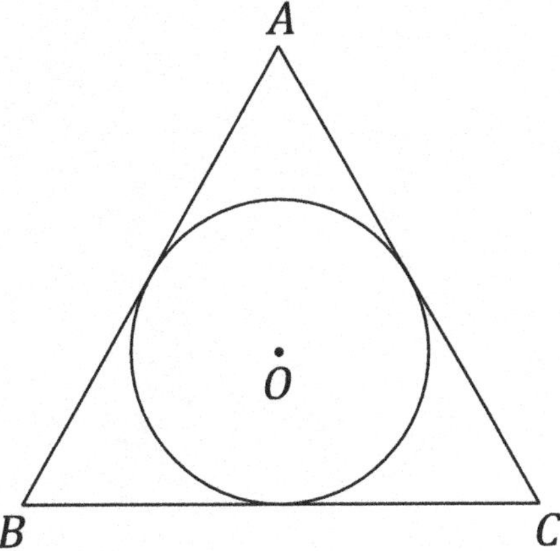

Grid your answer.

31. Gillian purchases a selection of rugs at wholesale prices and adds 30% to the wholesale price to sell at her shop. Some time later, she realizes that she has several rugs left and decides to drop the price by 15% to clear inventory. What percentage profit will she make on the remaining rugs, rounded to the nearest tenth of a percent?

Grid your answer.

Answer Key and Explanations

Reading

1. Choice B is the best answer. Choices A, C, and D all contain truth but do not do a good job of summarizing all the problems. Lines 22–24 indicate that the boat is small. We learn in the very first words that the captain is injured and can infer that the men are stranded from their discussion of being rescued.

2. Choice C is the best answer. The paragraph in lines 38–54 describes how the sun was rising but the men did not notice because they were so focused on keeping the boat afloat that they "had no time to see it" (lines 43–44). The captain's directive to Billie (A) notes that at least one person was actively steering the boat but does not give evidence of the hard work. The description of the boat tossing on the waves (B) explains why the men had to work so hard, but does not show that they were. In lines 55–58 (D), it could possibly be extrapolated that they were speaking in "disjointed sentences" because of the effort they were expending on maneuvering the boat, but this is not certain.

3. Choice A is the best answer. The first paragraph describes the captain's distress over his lost ship as he lies in the lifeboat, describing its sinking ("a stump ... and down," lines 11–14). It mentions that this distress comes whether "he commanded for a day or a decade" (lines 8–9) but does not specify his actual time as a captain (B). There is no indication that he would be rowing if he were not injured (C). Line 7 describes his voice as "strange" and "deep with mourning," but this is due to emotions and not physical damage.

4. Choice D is the best answer. The other men all join the discussion. The cook and correspondent argue about what they will find at a house of refuge, while the oiler reminds them that "we're not there yet" (lines 72, 78). Only the captain is silent during this exchange.

5. Choice C is the best answer. The sentence describes the boat moving like a horse heading toward a fence. It does not use the literal meaning of "creating" (A), nor does it indicate preparation (B) or fleeing (D).

6. Choice C is the best answer. Choices A and B (lines 5–6) are descriptive of the original ship that sank. Choice D (line 50) describes the water. Only choice C (lines 22–37) describes the small boat that is currently stranded on rough water.

7. Choice B is the best answer. A simile compares two things with "like" or "as." These two sentences say that the boat is "like an animal" and "like a horse." A metaphor (A) directly compares two things, such as "the boat was a horse." Alliteration (C) uses multiple words with the same consonant. Foreshadowing (D) hints at future events.

8. Choice B is the best answer. The captain is described as lying in the boat and directing others, which can be inferred to mean that he is physically injured and unable to help maneuver the boat. The first paragraph also contains a description of the emotional effect of the shipwreck on the captain, as his mind was "rooted deep in the timbers of her" (lines 7–8) and his voice was "deep with mourning" (line 16), but it is unlikely that the author is referring to this when he describes "the injured captain, lying in the bow."

9. Choice A is the best answer. The passage shows that the men in the boat (a captain, an oiler, a cook, and a passenger correspondent) must all work to get the boat to land. In an emergency, status, wealth, and power are irrelevant. There is no mention of having or needing an emergency plan (B), and while the small boat is not ideal it was necessary due to the larger ship's wreck (C). Arguing instead of working together (D) is doubtless unwise but the passage does not show that this resulted in danger.

10. Choice C is the best answer. In lines 9–14 of passage 1 ("In company...free world"), Eisenhower lists the goals of the "Great Crusade": to free people from oppression and establish security throughout the world.

11. Choice D is the best answer. Lines 15–17 are a sobering reminder of what the American soldiers will face on the battlefield. Eisenhower shares these details to show that the job is a difficult one, adding emphasis to his later remarks that the soldiers are capable of meeting this challenge.

12. Choice A is the best answer. Passage 1 is a motivating speech to soldiers about to embark on a dangerous and difficult mission. Eisenhower gives a rousing, inspiring speech to motivate them. Passage 2 is a last address to the nation. Eisenhower reflects on his time in office and looks to the future, encouraging his fellow citizens to be a "proud confederation of mutual trust and respect" (lines 72–73) rather than a "community of dreadful fear and hate" (lines 71–72). While there are moments of warning (B) and nostalgia (C) in Passage 2, these are not the overall theme. Choice D is incorrect because Passage 1 is action-oriented rather than wistful.

13. Choice B is the best answer. In lines 6–8 of Passage 1, Eisenhower states that "the hopes and prayers of liberty-loving people everywhere march with you," implying that the battle was for liberty. In line 39 of Passage 2, Eisenhower urges the nation to make sacrifices in an ideological battle "with liberty at stake." Human progress and dignity (A), as well as peace (C) are mentioned in Passage 2 but not Passage 1. Eisenhower addresses Americans, but his concern in both passages is worldwide, not just for the American Dream (D).

14. Choice C is the best answer. In lines 60–62, Eisenhower cautions the nation against living "only for today, plundering ... the precious resources of tomorrow." He warned the audience that this "plundering" would not only damage the future economy but could undermine the entire ideology of the nation. Choice A urges Americans to use power wisely but does not directly allude to environmental resources. Choice B simply states that there will always be crises, and again does not directly mention environmental resources. Choice D refers to the need to become "a proud confederation of mutual trust and respect" rather than a nation that conserves resources.

15. Choice C is the best answer. While the Holocaust of World War II is best known for its persecution of Jews in concentration camps, the term "holocaust" means mass destruction or death, often during war. Eisenhower is using the literal meaning here rather than the familiar connotation.

16. Choice D is the best answer. By using the same syntactic structure in "community of dreadful fear and hate" and "confederation of mutual trust and respect" ("noun" of "adjective" "noun" and "noun"), Eisenhower employed parallel structure to reinforce his message contrasting potential futures. Alliteration (Choice A) is repeating the same consonant sounds, such as "a caring and conscientious community." Choice B, symbolism, involves using an object as a representation of an idea, such as "may the dove of peace flourish in our nation." Repetition (Choice C) involves simply repeating the same word/phrase/clause multiple times. Parallelism/parallel structure does not require exact word repetition, but symmetrical sentence/clause structure arranging the same parts of speech in the same word order.

17. Choice B is the best answer. Eisenhower is discussing a worldwide "confederation ... of equals" (lines 74–75), who can bring up their concerns without fear. Clearly all nations of the world could not meet at a literal table, but are still able to figuratively "come to the conference table" and be heard.

18. Choice B is the best answer. Eisenhower was reminding his audience that the US had been through many difficult and dangerous times to add weight to his statement in lines 4–7: "Despite these holocausts America is today the strongest, the most influential and most productive nation in the world." Since he only references the last 60 years, with no mention of how the conflicts were spaced out, it is unlikely that Eisenhower is pointing out that each generation has conflicts (A). There is also no support for the idea that the US is quick to join wars (C), especially considering that the US was only involved in three of the four wars mentioned. There is no mention of the outcome of the wars (D) except that the US came through them strongly.

19. Choice A is the best answer. Line 30 describes a "hostile ideology" that threatens America's progress. The threat of German troops (B) was over; this was the danger in Passage 1. Communism (C) was a concern at various times in history, most noticeably in the McCarthy era of the early 1950s, but this passage (from 1961) does not clearly indicate communism. The Cold War (D) was in effect during the time this speech was given but again is not clearly identified as the "conflict" in this passage.

20. Choice B is the best answer. Eisenhower's D-Day speech was delivered in a very tense time for the world and particularly for the military audience he was addressing. But Eisenhower gave a stirring address, urging the soldiers to courageous action. If he felt fear, it is unlikely that he showed this as he spoke since it would counteract his message, so Choice A is incorrect. Eisenhower did not have an impressively loud voice and the goal of the speech was inspiration, not intimidation, so Choice C is incorrect. Eisenhower's address was short and to the point, as a long speech is not typically used to rally troops and inspire action, so Choice D is incorrect. But one aspect of a speech that cannot easily transmit through written word is the speaker's vocal emotion, so Choice B is correct.

21. Choice C is the best answer. Adams is stating that the Declaration of Independence will last "forever" (line 45), as long as humanity exists and continues to hold the basic needs and values of humans. People's social nature can be inferred to mean their tendency to congregate together, depending on each other for emotional and other needs. While this may include celebration (A) or entertainment (B), this is not Adams' focus. While today many think of "social" and "justice" together (D), this also falls outside of Adams' main meaning.

22. Choice A is the best answer. The theme of this address, celebrating the Declaration of Independence, points out that it is useful in "every age and every clime" (lines 3–4), and repeats similar sentiments throughout. Adams does imply that the US government is a new kind that will spread, but does not state that it is the first, nor that it will become a world government (B). There is no mention of the government evolving to meet new needs (C). While there is discussion of freedom from servitude, Adams never clearly states (particularly as a passage theme) that the US will never again serve another nation.

23. Choice D is the best answer. While the Declaration of Independence was used as a model for France's own declaration several years later, Adams does not mention this. The other three choices are all found in lines 11–17.

24. Choice A is the best answer. Adams likens the young nation of the US to children and the nation of England to their mother. This is a device known as personification, applying human characteristics to something that is not human. Alliteration (B) uses multiple words with the same consonant. Symbolism (C) involves using an object as a representation of an idea. Allusion (D) is referring to something without clearly stating it.

25. Choice A is the best answer. The title of this selection, as stated at the beginning, is *An Address...Celebrating the Declaration of Independence*. Adams' entire speech is in reference to this document.

26. Choice B is the best answer. The word "quicken" means to be enlivened or made more rapid. Here Adams is not speaking about moving (A) or speaking (C) quickly, but that interest will grow and spread. Waning (D) is the opposite of the correct meaning.

27. Choice C is the best answer. Adams is discussing a "new fabric" that he hopes will spread throughout the world, replacing old, corrupt forms of government with "the unalienable sovereignty of the people." This is not literal cloth (B) or the cloth of a flag (D), nor does it refer to materialism (A).

28. Choice D is the best answer. The sentence found in lines 30–32, "They were a nation, asserting as of right, and maintaining by war, its own existence," is the only statement listed here that directly supports the idea that the US had a right to be its own sovereign nation.

29. Choice B is the best answer. This quote illustrates Adams' point that the Declaration of Independence would be long remembered, in future generations and in places not yet established. It is unlikely that Adams was trying to sound educated (A) as the language differs very little from his normal style of speaking, and as including quotes was a common rhetorical device in this time period. Adams was not drawing a parallel between the US government and ancient Rome (since the play is about a political assassination) (C). Although the quote mentions "states unborn" (line 36), the point was not the size of the US (D) but rather the longevity of the Declaration's message.

30. Choice B is the best answer. The main purpose of the passage is to discuss the various kinds of organisms that compose plankton and to show the role they play in the earth's ecosystem. Trophic levels (A) are mentioned but are only part of the main focus. Oxygen production (C) is an important point but again is only part of the main focus. The life cycle of plankton (D) is never clearly described.

31. Choice A is the best answer. As seen in lines 12–17, holoplankton are plankton for their whole lives, while meroplankton spend only part of their lives as plankton. Choice B transposes these options. Although algae is listed as a type of holoplankton, there is no indication that all holoplankton are plants and all meroplankton are animals (C). The descriptions in choice D are of benthic and nektic plankton, both of which are types of meroplankton.

32. Choice C is the best answer. In lines 29–34 ("Finally, the...for nutrients"), the text gives the example of mixotrophs using photosynthesis to survive on some days, while feeding on other plankton at other times. Viruses, bacteria, and fungi (A) are other trophic level groups, separate from mixotrophs. Meroplankton, not mixotrophs, live only part of their lives as plankton (B). The passage states that phytoplankton produce oxygen (D).

33. Choice B is the best answer. The term "phytoplankton" is defined in lines 24–26 ("plants that ... perform photosynthesis"). Choice A is too broad, including all trophic level groups instead of just one. Phytoplankton need light rather than avoiding it (C). Since phytoplankton are plants, it is illogical that they could swim independently (D).

34. Choice D is the best answer. The term "trophic level groups" is defined in lines 21–23 ("Plankton are ... level groups") as six different categories for classifying plankton. These groups include plankton that use photosynthesis (A) and viruses, bacteria, and fungi (C) but are not limited to those organisms. Tropical regions (B), while sounding similar to "trophic," are not mentioned in the passage.

35. Choice B is the best answer. The author is describing various types of plankton and the roles they play. There is very little comparison and contrast (A) aside from the description of holoplankton and meroplankton. There is also not much of cause and effect (C), aside from the mention of plankton's role in oxygen production and carbon storage. The author is not attempting to persuade readers to any particular action (D).

36. Choice A is the best answer. Lines 35–44 describe the contributions that plankton make to the world's ecosystem. Choices B and C are wrong because they do not represent all of the information presented in these lines. Choice D is referring to the paragraph in lines 21–34.

37. Choice D is the best answer. Lines 45–50 state that the amount of plankton is dependent on weather, so we can infer that the population is affected by storms. Choice A describes how plankton are moved by water. Choice B does mention "sunny days," so this could refer to weather, but describes how plankton adapt to survive in different types of weather, rather than the population changing. Choice C makes no mention of weather or population.

38. Choice B is the best answer. Lines 40–43 describe the role of plankton in the carbon cycle, helping to store carbon in rocks and sediment. The graphic shows a cycle from carbon dioxide to photosynthesis to carbon to respiration and finally back to carbon dioxide, with some carbon settling to the sediment.

39. Choice A is the best answer. The first paragraph introduces the concept of plankton, giving a brief explanation. The next two paragraphs discuss various types of plankton. The fourth paragraph discusses plankton's roles in oxygen production and carbon storage, and the final paragraph wraps up the discussion.

40. Choice B is the best answer. The passage is informative, not entertaining (A) or persuasive (C). It simply explains several types of sedimentary rock and describes how they are formed. Choice D is incorrect because there is no explanation of why sedimentary rock is the majority of the rock at the surface.

41. Choice D is the best answer. As seen in lines 35–36 and 47, certain types of limestone are chemical and other types are organic.

42. Choice A is the best answer. The passage is explaining how chemical rocks are formed. Only choice A makes sense for forming rock. The other choices describe forming liquid (B), gas (C), and evaporating entirely (D).

43. Choice B is the best answer. As described in lines 41–46 ("As organic ... become coal"), organic material first becomes peat, then lignite, and then coal. Limestone is mentioned as another type of organic rock but is not part of this progression.

44. Choice C is the best answer. Lines 30–32 are describing particles that have been moved by forces of nature, such as wind, rain, and mud, similar to the description in lines 23–26.

45. Choice A is the best answer. From the previous sentence, we know that *strata* refers to the layers of rock. A fitting synonym would be *bands*. The sentence is not merely referring to rocks in general (B), or mountains, even though it mentions cliff sides (C). It is referring to sedimentary rock, not igneous (D).

46. Choice A is the best answer. The author mentions in the last paragraph that the rock record is useful to help understand past events. Answer choice B gives the opposite opinion. Answer choice C is incorrect because there is no call to action for the reader to act to preserve the rock. Answer choice D is incorrect because there is no evidence in the passage that sedimentary rock receives an "unfair" amount of attention.

47. Choice D is the best answer. We can see on the left side of the chart that igneous rock is not the most populous rock at the surface, but on the right side we note that it is the most populous rock overall.

48. Choice B is the best answer. The passage states in lines 10–15 ("Sedimentary rocks ... the earth") that sedimentary rocks are most abundant at the surface, but igneous rock is more populous in the crust as a whole. These two points are reflected in the information in the table. Choice A gives information from the table that is not discussed in the passage. Choice C is incorrect because the passage does have enough information to match the table (not every statistic must be discussed for the table to support the passage). Choice D is incorrect because a specific amount of any rock is not mentioned in the passage.

49. Choice C is the best answer. The passage opens by mentioning the three types of rock, but after the first few sentences the focus is on sedimentary. The others are only mentioned to introduce the main subject of sedimentary rock. Thus, choices A and B are not good titles because they imply that all three types of rock are discussed equally. Choice D is not suitable because the majority of the passage merely describes the different varieties of sedimentary rock and how they are formed. Only the last paragraph briefly touches on the geological value it provides, so this is not the main focus of the passage and should not be the title.

Writing and Language

1. Choice C is the best answer. The sentence is using plural terms for each of the other items in the list, so "their" is correct. "Its" (A) is singular and "it's" (B) is possessive. "His" (D) is also singular.

2. Choice D is the best answer. The correct answer is "reindeer," because this is the plural form. The possessive form (A, B) is not appropriate in this sentence (and choice A is not even a correct possessive), and "reindeers" (C) is not the correct plural form.

3. Choice B is the best answer. The correct answer is "but also." The corresponding phrase for "not only" is "but also." Using "and" (A, D) does not go with the contrast set up by "not only." "But moreover" (C) is unwieldy and impractical.

4. Choice D is the best answer. "Hundreds" and "thousands" are plural, not possessive, so A and B are incorrect. The clause "or even thousands" could be set off with commas or dashes, but would need punctuation on both ends, so C is incorrect (and B is also incorrect for this reason). Answer choice D uses the correct plural forms and omits all punctuation for "or even thousands," which is grammatically correct.

5. Choice D is the best answer. The sentence is written in present tense, so answer choice D is the clearest and best fit. Answer choice A is present perfect, which can be used but in this case is awkward and unnecessarily wordy. Answer choice B is past tense. Answer choice C is another form of present perfect but does not fit grammatically in the sentence.

6. Choice A is the best answer. The correct answer is "faster" because this correctly uses the comparative adjective. Answer choice B is incorrect because the correct superlative form is "faster." Answer choice C does not grammatically fit because the following word would need to be "as," not "than." Answer choice D is unnecessarily wordy and again uses the incorrect superlative form.

7. Choice C is the best answer. The correct answer is "previously mentioned," which uses an adverb properly. "Beforely" (A) and "priorly" (B) are not words, and the wording in choice D is convoluted and lengthy.

8. Choice A is the best answer. A colon is correct here because it can be used to introduce a list. Lists should not be introduced with commas (B) or semicolons (C). Creating a new sentence (D) is incorrect because the subsequent list is a fragment on its own.

9. Choice C is the best answer. The correct answer is "using," which is a present participle modifying the verb "roam." "Which using" (A) or "that is using" (B) do not fit grammatically. Finally, "use" (D) is an incorrect form of verb for a participle phrase.

10. Choice B is the best answer. The main point of the selection, as can be seen in the opening paragraph, is that caribou make important contributions to the world and have been particularly instrumental to human society. Choice B states this, while also referring back to the opening statement about Christmas. Choice A is vague, since there is no description of how their role has changed. Choice C may be true, at least for the endangered subspecies, but it is not the main point of the passage, so it should not be used to summarize. Choice D could be a good summation if the challenges brought by reindeer had been mentioned in the passage.

11. Choice C is the best answer. The fourth paragraph mentions caribou digging through the snow to find food, so this would be the best place to mention their hooves.

12. Choice C is the best answer. The word "millennia" is plural, while "millennium" is singular. Thus "a millennia" (B and D) are grammatically incorrect, as is using "millennium" (A) without an article.

13. Choice B is the best answer. A colon is used to define or introduce something, such as a new term or a list, but is only used after an independent clause (a clause that can be a stand-alone sentence). Here the first part of the sentence is not an independent clause, so a colon (A) is inappropriate. A semicolon (C) is incorrect for the same reason, since it is used to join independent clauses. Likewise, a dash (D) cannot be used in this way except after an independent clause. No punctuation is necessary in this sentence.

14. Choice A is the best answer. Answer choice A is best because it is the most readable. The other choices rearrange the wording in a way that makes it more difficult to decipher the meaning.

15. Choice C is the best answer. The sentence is explaining that oboes are used for tuning because of their steady pitch. The only logical choice is that they are reliable for tuning. The other three choices all have a negative connotation, which would not fit here.

16. Choice D is the best answer. As it is written, this sentence has a dangling modifier. The subject of the sentence should be "musicians," but answer choices A, B, and C place other words directly after the comma, which makes these words appear to be the subject and leads to confusion.

17. Choice D is the best answer. It is better to begin the clause with "artisans" to stay in active voice rather than passive voice (so A and B are incorrect). Choice C is incorrect because "eschewed" is the opposite of the correct meaning.

18. Choice B is the best answer. The part of the sentence after the punctuation is a dependent clause, so a semicolon (A) and period (B) are both inappropriate since this part cannot be a standalone sentence. Also, this part is not a definition or an explanation of the first part, nor is it a list, so a colon (C) is inappropriate.

19. Choice A is the best answer. This sentence fits well in its current position, adding detail to the broader opening sentence rather than becoming the opening sentence (B). It would not fit in a different paragraph (C), and it is relevant to the passage so it should not be removed (D).

20. Choice C is the best answer. The clause beginning with the underlined word is in contrast to the previous clause, so answer choices A and D are incorrect because they imply agreement. Answer choice B is incorrect because the word "however" needs different punctuation; it would need to be preceded by a semicolon and followed by a comma.

21. Choice B is the best answer. An apostrophe (A) is incorrect because the date is plural, not a contraction or possessive. The sixteenth century refers to the 1500s, more than 400 years ago, so answer choices C and D are incorrect.

22. Choice A is the best answer. Answer choice A does the best job of bringing the passage to a conclusion. It refers back to the shepherds from the first paragraph, mentions the oboe's modern use, and ends with the common theme of the oboe's unique sound. Answer choices B and C make unsupported, opposite claims (that the oboe is either disappearing from common knowledge entirely or that it is becoming more popular). Answer choice D makes a statement that could possibly fit in the passage (although it is an opinion) but does not summarize or go along with the main themes of the passage.

23. Choice C is the best answer. Titles of television shows or movies are italicized. If the sentence referenced a specific episode, it would be in quotation marks (A).

24. Choice C is the best answer. The correct phrase is "less known." The term "lesser" (B) is typically used when comparing two items in quantity or quality. Saying that something is less, or not as, unknown (A and D) means that it is more known, which does not fit the meaning of the text.

25. Choice B is the best answer. From the context of the sentence we can see that artificial materials are becoming more popular, so "increasing" is the best choice. Choices A and C convey the opposite, while "eliminating" (D) implies that artificial fabrics are no longer used at all.

26. Choice B is the best answer. The adjective "increasing" is the correct opening for this sentence. "Increasingly" (A) is an adverb and is not appropriate to modify this noun. "Greatly" (C) is also an adverb, and both "greatly" and "greater" (C) are grammatically incorrect because the article is "an" rather than "a."

27. Choice D is the best answer. This sentence, unlike the rest of the selection, gives a strong opinion rather than simply sharing facts. This makes it unfitting for the passage.

28. Choice D is the best answer. The sentence is written in present tense, so the present perfect "have gone" is correct. "Have went" (A) is grammatically incorrect, as is "had went" (B), which is also past perfect, so neither would fit in this sentence. "Gone" (C) does not fit grammatically in this sentence structure (it would need to be "have gone").

29. Choice A is the best answer. The previous paragraph closes by mentioning a demand for cheaper materials. This paragraph gives a contrasting description of higher-quality fabric. So the transition needs to show this contrast. Answer choices B and C use transition words that agree rather than contrast ("In accordance with...to keep up with"). Answer choice D provides a contrast but is not contrasting the trend toward cheaper materials. The small wardrobe is mentioned earlier in the paragraph and is not in contrast with the subsequent paragraph.

30. Choice C is the best answer. The sentence shows that wool was at one time a major part of commerce, although that has now changed. The best word to convey this is "primary." "Plausible" (A) does not fit because it means *believable* or *reasonable*, and this sentence is sharing a fact, not an opinion or theory that is uncertain. "Innovative" (B) and "extensive" (D) are both possibilities as far as meaning goes, but since both start with a vowel they cannot come after the article "a."

31. Choice B is the best answer. The role of the underlined word is to set up a comparison, stating that just as wool has an animal source, so does silk. The word "like" (B) best fits this. "Despite" (B) and "in contrast to" (C) show contrast instead of comparison, and "however" (D) does not fit grammatically in this sentence.

32. Choice B is the best answer. The graph shows a decline in both wool and silk, so choices A and D are incorrect. From the graph's title we know this is referring to production, not prices, so answer choice C is incorrect.

33. Choice A is the best answer. As this is the concluding paragraph, any information needs to either be transitional from the previous paragraph, to refer back to main themes for closure, or to expound on the main idea. Answer choices B, C, and D all give specific details on a single textile, which are not relevant for the closing paragraph. Answer choice D is the closest, because silk production is (very briefly) discussed in accordance with the chart, but it is still best to keep the paragraph on the broad topic of textiles in general.

34. Choice B is the best answer. The sentence is saying that taxonomy is a way, or system, of classification. We could also call it a method, but methodology (A) is the reasoning or theory behind a method. We could say it is an organizational system, but an organization (C) refers to a business or association. We could call it a process, but a procession (D) refers to a group of people moving together in one direction, like a parade.

35. Choice D is the best answer. No punctuation is necessary. A comma (A) is not needed to separate the clauses. A semicolon (B) is inappropriate because the part of the sentence after this is not an independent clause. A colon (C) is not appropriate because the following part of the sentence is not a list or definition.

36. Choice A is the best answer. The idea of the sentence can be gathered from the clauses before and after the underlined portion: "The animal kingdom … is the largest of the kingdoms." Thus, the detail about the number of species in the kingdom is the most relevant. That this kingdom includes humans (B) is not relevant to this point, nor is the argument over how many kingdoms there are in total (C). Answer choice D is an opinion and does not provide any supporting details, so it does not fit in this sentence or anywhere in the passage.

37. Choice B is the best answer. Although the noun "animals" is plural, it is not the subject of the sentence. "Classification" is the true subject, and since it is singular, the only possible answer choice that agrees with it is "is." Choices A, C, and D are all plural.

38. Choice C is the best answer. As the selection is written (A), it is choppy, with three short sentences (one of which is a fragment). Choice B is a comma splice, as the second comma connects two independent clauses (it should be a semicolon or period). Choice D is succinct, but the second clause is not clear. It sounds like "food" is "called being autotrophic," or possibly that photosynthesis and autotrophic are synonyms. Choice C is clear and succinct.

39. Choice A is the best answer. The information in the underlined portion is relevant because it shares a significant detail about Kingdom Plantae that connects to other information in the paragraph. The best place is its current location, after photosynthesis has already been introduced.

40. Choice B is the best answer. Later in the paragraph, reference is made to taxons. Without the definition in this sentence, the reader might not understand.

41. Choice B is the best answer. The correct answer is "its," which is the possessive form of "it." In contrast, "it's" (A) is incorrect because it refers to the contraction of the words "it is." Using "their" or "theirs" (C and D) is incorrect because the subject (organism) is singular.

42. Choice D is the best answer. The punctuation separates two independent clauses, so a comma cannot be used (A). A semicolon or period is necessary. The period in choice C is incorrect because the change does not include capitalizing "this." Omitting the punctuation (B) gives a run-on sentence.

43. Choice A is the best answer. The wording that makes the most sense is "contributions from," implying that these scientists aided in developing the classification system. "Opinions from" could also work, but "opinions about" (B) means opinions about the scientists rather than the classification, which does not make sense. Likewise, "research for" (C) implies that research is being done FOR the scientists rather than by them. Finally, "questions from" (D) is vague, not clearly explaining the scientists' role.

44. Choice D is the best answer. The main idea of the paragraph is that taxonomy has been the work of a long period of time. This appears in the first sentence, and the second sentence gives a supporting historical detail. The best answer choice is D because it builds on this idea, giving another detail about the history of taxonomy. Answer choice A gives a detail about a specific classification issue but does not make any mention of taxonomy's history. Answer choice B gives a somewhat relevant detail about different opinions in taxonomy but doesn't support the main idea. This sentence would be more appropriate in a different paragraph. Answer choice C gives a statement on a completely unrelated topic, loosely tying it in with taxonomy, but it does not support the main idea.

Math – No Calculator

1. Choice B is correct. The function for the cost of a hotel room is a combination of a constant function for the first guest and a linear function for the remaining guests. The constant function is $m_1(n) = 85$ since the cost of the first guest is \$85. For the linear part, subtract 1 from n to exclude the first guest, and then multiply the result by 15 since it costs \$15 per additional guest. The result is $m_2(n) = 15(n - 1)$. Finally, write the function for the total cost of the hotel room by adding the two functions.

$$\begin{aligned} m(n) &= m_1(n) + m_2(n) \\ &= 85 + 15(n - 1) \end{aligned}$$

Although not necessary for answering the question, note that this function can also be simplified:

$$m(n) = 85 + 15n - 15 = 70 + 15n$$

2. Choice C is correct. Solve the equation for x:

$$\begin{aligned} y &= -2x + 3 \\ y - 3 &= -2x \\ \frac{y-3}{-2} &= x \\ \frac{y}{-2} - \frac{3}{-2} &= x \\ -\frac{1}{2}y + \frac{3}{2} &= x \\ x &= -\frac{1}{2}y + \frac{3}{2} \end{aligned}$$

3. Choice C is correct. Solve the inequality:

$$\begin{aligned} \frac{1}{2}|x-3| - 4 &\geq 6 \\ \frac{1}{2}|x-3| &\geq 10 \\ |x-3| &\geq 20 \end{aligned}$$

$$\begin{aligned} x - 3 &\geq 20 \\ x &\geq 23 \end{aligned}$$

$$\begin{aligned} -(x - 3) &\geq 20 \\ x - 3 &\leq -20 \\ x &\leq -17 \end{aligned}$$

Thus $x \leq -17$ or $x \geq 23$.

4. Choice A is correct. The positively sloped line has a slope of $\frac{2}{3}$ and a y-intercept of 2; the line is dashed, and the region below the line is shaded. Therefore, the graph illustrates the solution to the inequality $y < \frac{2}{3}x + 2$. The negatively sloped line has a slope of –1 and a y-intercept of –1; the line is solid, and the region below the line is shaded. Therefore, the graph illustrates the solution to the inequality $y \leq -x - 1$.

In choice A, the second inequality when solved for y is equivalent to $y < \frac{2}{3}x + 2$:

$$\begin{aligned} 3y - 2x &< 6 \\ 3y &< 2x + 6 \\ y &< \frac{2}{3}x + 2 \end{aligned}$$

5. Choice D is correct. The four choices all have the two lines that mark the boundaries of the inequalities plotted identically; the only difference is which sides are shaded. It's therefore not necessary to check that the lines are correct; simply determine which of the areas bounded by the lines pertain to the system of inequalities.

One way to do that is to pick a point in each region and check whether it satisfies the inequalities. For instance, we can pick the origin, (0,0). Since $0 - 2(0) > -1$ and $0 + 0 < 2$, this point satisfies both equations. The only graph with (0,0) in the darkest shaded region is D.

6. Choice B is correct. To simplify the inequality $2 - \frac{1}{2}x < 1$, we can first subtract 2 from both sides:

$$\begin{aligned} 2 - \frac{1}{2}x - 2 &< 1 - 2 \\ -\frac{1}{2}x &< -1 \end{aligned}$$

Now, we can divide both sides of the inequality by $-\frac{1}{2}$. When an inequality is multiplied or divided by a negative number, it flips ($<$ becomes $>$, $\leq$ becomes $\geq$, and vice versa). So $-\frac{1}{2}x < -1$ becomes $\frac{1}{2}x > 1$. We then multiply both sides by 2 to yield $x > 2$.

7. Choice D is correct. If the quiz has 10 questions, and Andi answered x questions correctly and y questions incorrectly, then she must have left $10 - x - y$ questions blank. She gets 5 points for each right answer, or $5(x) = 5x$ points total. She loses 2 points for each incorrect answer, or $2(y) = 2y$ points total. She loses 1 point for each blank answer, or $1(10 - x - y) = 10 - x - y$ points total. So, her total score can be expressed as $5x - 2y - (10 - x - y) = 6x - y - 10$.

8. Choice A is correct. There are twelve months in a year, and Chad will be paying x for each of those months, or $12x$ in total. He will pay the deposit and application fee once each. So, the total cost is $12x + y + z$.

9. Choice C is correct. Test each answer choice to see which satisfies the inequality. For answer choice A, $6 - 10 = -4$, which is less than 2. For answer choice B, $-3 - (-4) = 1$, which is less than 2. For answer choice C, $5 - (-8) = 13$, which is NOT less than 2. For answer choice D, $-3 - 3 = -6$, which is less than 2. Thus, only the values in answer choice C fail to satisfy the inequality.

10. Choice C is correct. To simplify the expression, first factor the numerator and the denominator. To factor the numerator, find two numbers whose sum is –3 and whose product is –18, and then put those numbers into the form $(x + \_)(x + \_)$. For the denominator, factor out the common factor, which is 4:

$$\frac{x^2 - 3x - 18}{4x + 12} = \frac{(x+3)(x-6)}{4(x+3)}$$

Now there is a common factor, $(x + 3)$, in both the numerator and the denominator. Therefore, you can further simplify the expression by cancelling it out:

$$\frac{(x+3)(x-6)}{4(x+3)} = \frac{x-6}{4}$$

11. Choice B is correct. To simplify the expression, first simplify the expression with parentheses. To raise $16x$ to the $\frac{1}{2}$ power, raise both 16 and x to the $\frac{1}{2}$ power separately.

$$x^3 \times (16x)^{\frac{1}{2}} = x^3 \times 16^{\frac{1}{2}} \times x^{\frac{1}{2}}$$

To raise something to the $\frac{1}{2}$ power is the same as taking the square root, so $16^{\frac{1}{2}} = 4$. We then combine like terms by adding exponents:

$$x^3 x^{\frac{1}{2}} = x^{\frac{6}{2}} x^{\frac{1}{2}} = x^{\frac{7}{2}}$$

Finally, we rewrite the equation as $4x^{\frac{7}{2}}$.

12. Choice A is correct. Revenue is the total amount of money the jeweler makes from necklace sales. In this case, the revenue is the price of each necklace multiplied by the total number of necklaces sold. So, to find the estimated revenue, find the price and the number of necklaces sold after the price is raised by x dollars. Then multiply the two quantities together. If the price of a necklace starts at \$50, then the price after it is raised by x dollars will be $50 + x$ dollars. In addition, we are told that the jeweler sells 10 fewer necklaces for every dollar the price is raised. Therefore, the total number of necklaces that are sold will be $200 - 10x$. Calculate the revenue function $r(x)$ by multiplying the expressions and simplify the result:

$$\begin{aligned} r(x) &= (50 + x)(200 - 10x) \\ &= -10x^2 - 300x + 10{,}000 \end{aligned}$$

13. Choice B is correct. To transform $f(x)$ into $g(x)$, you have to add 2. This transformation results in a translation, or shift, of the graph. The x-value is not affected, so the translation is vertical, along the y-axis. Adding 2 to transform $f(x)$ into $g(x)$ moves the graph up two units.

14. The correct answer is 1024. The length of an interval is the difference between its endpoints. For example, the length of the interval [2,4] is 2. To determine how the given function grows over an interval of length 5, determine the value of f at each endpoint of that interval. Since exponential functions grow by equal factors over equal intervals, you can use any interval of length 5, and your answer will apply to all such intervals. For example, you can use the interval [0,5]:

$$f(0) = \frac{4^0}{2} = \frac{1}{2}$$

$$f(5) = \frac{4^5}{2} = \frac{1{,}024}{2} = 512$$

Since $f(0) = \frac{1}{2}$ and $f(5) = 512$, the function grows by a factor of $512 \div \frac{1}{2} = 1{,}024$ over this interval.

15. The correct answer is 117. Note that the linear function $c(h) = 117h + 9{,}000$ starts at 9,000 when $h = 0$ and increases by 117 every time h increases by 1. Therefore, for every hour after 100, the company charges $117.

16. The correct answer is 0. Since the function is defined recursively, you need to calculate all of the first five terms. The first and second terms are already given in the problem as $f(1) = 1$ and $f(2) = 0$. To calculate the third term, $f(3)$, take the previous term and subtract the term that is two back:

$$f(3) = f(2) - f(1) = 0 - 1 = -1$$

The fourth term is similarly calculated:

$$f(4) = f(3) - f(2) = -1 - 0 = -1$$

And the fifth term is:

$$f(5) = f(4) - f(3) = -1 - (-1) = 0$$

17. The correct answer is 2. The function $f(x) = (x + 3)(x^2 - 5x + 4)$ is a cubic equation written as a product of a linear factor and a quadratic factor, $x + 3$ and $x^2 - 5x + 4$, respectively. The quadratic expression $x^2 - 5x + 4$ can be further factored to $(x - 4)(x - 1)$, so $f(x) = (x + 3)(x^2 - 5x + 4) = (x + 3)(x - 4)(x - 1)$. The graph of the function crosses the x-axis at any point at which the value of $f(x) = 0$. To find the x-intercepts, solve $f(x) = 0 = (x + 3)(x - 4)(x - 1)$ using the zero-product property:

$x + 3 = 0$	$x - 4 = 0$	$x - 1 = 0$
$x = -3$	$x = 4$	$x = 1$

Then, the sum is $-3 + 4 + 1 = 2$.

Math – Calculator

1. Choice D is correct. Notice that the given system has two equations, and each equation has two variables, x and y. Therefore, the solution of the system of equations must have values for each of the two variables. To find the solution, you can use algebraic methods, graphs, tables, or matrices. For the purposes of this explanation, we will use an algebraic method called substitution.

To begin, notice that the first equation already has y isolated on the left side. Therefore, substitute the right side, $-x + 1$, for y into the second equation, and then solve for x:

$$\begin{aligned} -3x + y &= -3 \\ -3x + (-x + 1) &= -3 \\ -4x &= -4 \\ x &= 1 \end{aligned}$$

To find the value of y, substitute 1 for x in the first equation:

$$\begin{aligned} y &= -(1) + 1 \\ &= -1 + 1 \\ &= 0 \end{aligned}$$

2. Choice B is correct. For each value of x, $f(x) = \frac{1}{2}x^2$:

$$\begin{aligned} f(1) &= \frac{1}{2}(1)^2 = \frac{1}{2}(1)(1) = \frac{1}{2} = 0.5 \\ f(2) &= \frac{1}{2}(2)^2 = \frac{1}{2}(2)(2) = \frac{4}{2} = 2 \\ f(3) &= \frac{1}{2}(3)^2 = \frac{1}{2}(3)(3) = \frac{9}{2} = 4.5 \\ f(4) &= \frac{1}{2}(4)^2 = \frac{1}{2}(4)(4) = \frac{16}{2} = 8 \\ f(5) &= \frac{1}{2}(5)^2 = \frac{1}{2}(5)(5) = \frac{25}{2} = 12.5 \end{aligned}$$

3. Choice A is correct. The slope (or ratio of the change in y-values per change in corresponding x-values) may first be calculated. Using the points, $(0, -2)$ and $(2,10)$, the slope can be written as $\frac{10-(-2)}{2-0}$ or 6. The slope can then be substituted into the slope-intercept form of a linear equation, or $y = mx + b$, to find the y-intercept. Doing so gives $y = 6x + b$. Substituting the x- and y-values of any ordered pair will reveal the y-intercept. The following may be written: $-2 = 6(0) + b$; solving for b gives $b = -2$. Thus, the equation that represents the relationship between x and y is $y = 6x - 2$.

4. Choice C is correct. The median is the score in the middle: half of the houses are priced above $260,000 and half are priced below. The mean is the average, which is calculated by adding all the values together and dividing by the number of houses. Since the mean is lower than the median, this means that some of the houses have low values, well below the median, which pulls the mean down below the median value.

5. Choice A is correct. Since the second line, $y = 2$, is horizontal, the intersection must occur at a point where $y = 2$. We can use this value in the first equation, substituting 2 for y, to solve for x:

$$\begin{aligned} 2(2) - x &= 2 \\ -x &= -2 \\ x &= 2 \end{aligned}$$

So, the point of intersection is (2,2).

6. Choice C is correct. To evaluate $\frac{x^2-6x}{2(x+1)}$ at $x = -2$, substitute in -2 for x in the expression:

$$\begin{aligned} \frac{(-2)^2 - 6(-2)}{2(-2+1)} &= \frac{4 - (-12)}{2(-1)} \\ &= \frac{16}{-2} \\ &= -8 \end{aligned}$$

7. Choice D is correct. To solve, we simply substitute $\frac{1}{2}$ for every x in the expression and simplify:

$$\begin{aligned} \frac{2\left(\frac{1}{2}\right) + 3}{\frac{1}{2} - 1} &= \frac{1+3}{-\frac{1}{2}} \\ &= \frac{4}{-\frac{1}{2}} \\ &= \frac{4}{1} \times \frac{(-2)}{1} \\ &= -8 \end{aligned}$$

8. Choice B is correct. Start by distributing each coefficient across the parentheses. Next add the complex binomials. Complex numbers have a real part, a, and an imaginary part, b, and are usually written as $a + bi$. When adding imaginary numbers, add the real parts and the imaginary parts separately:

$$\begin{aligned} -2(2 + 6i) - 4(2 - 3i) &= -4 - 12i - 8 - (-12i) \\ &= (-4 - 8) + (-12i + 12i) \\ &= -12 \end{aligned}$$

9. Choice B is correct. The probability of selecting a person from any particular family is proportional to the number of people in that family, divided by the total number of people. We add the number from each family to find the total number: $4 + 3 + 4 + 2 + 6 = 19$. Since three have already been selected, there are 16 people left to choose from. Four of these are from Family W, so the probability of choosing one of them is $\frac{4}{16}$, or $\frac{1}{4}$.

10. Choice A is correct. The number of people who reported that they were satisfied is 71.5% of 13,787. If we require only an approximation, we can round 71.5% to 70%, and 13,787 to 14,000. We can calculate 70% of 14,000: $(0.7)(14{,}000) = 9{,}800$, which is approximately 10,000. So, if approximately 10,000 out of 14,000 customers reported satisfaction, then approximately $14{,}000 - 10{,}000 = 4{,}000$ customers did not report satisfaction.

11. Choice B is correct. Since only these three flavors of bagels were available, the percentages must add up to 100. Therefore, the percentage of purchases of plain bagels is:

$$100\% - (25\% + 40\%) = 100\% - 65\% = 35\%$$

12. Choice C is correct. Marc ordinarily sells this watchband for 35% more than (or 135% of) his cost:

$$\$20.00 \times 1.35 = \$27.00$$

For the sale, he takes 20% off (or sells it for 80% of) the regular price:

$$\$27.00 \times 0.8 = \$21.60$$

Thus, the marked down price is $21.60.

13. Choice A is correct. If 24 is $\frac{3}{8}$ of the whole committee, then the committee must consist of $\frac{8}{3}(24) = 64$ members.

14. Choice D is correct. To find the probability of the union of two events, use the equation $P(h \text{ or } f) = P(h) + P(f) - P(h \text{ and } f)$. The probability for hamburgers or French fries and the probability for hamburgers may be substituted giving $0.72 = 0.40 + P(f) - P(h \text{ and } f)$. Next, find the probability that she chooses both a hamburger and French fries by using the formula, $P(h \text{ and } f) = P(h) \times P(f|h)$. Substituting the probabilities of 0.4 and 0.6 gives $P(h \text{ and } f) = 0.4 \times 0.6$, or 0.24. Now, the probability of 0.24 may be substituted into the original equation, giving $0.72 = 0.4 + P(h) - 0.24$. Solving for $P(f)$ gives a probability of 0.56. Thus, there is a 0.56 probability that Ella orders French fries.

15. Choice D is correct. Since the figure represents the number line, the distance from point Y to point Z is the difference $\text{Z} - \text{Y}$, which is $1 - (-3) = 4$. The distance from point X to point Y is the difference $\text{Y} - \text{X}$, which is $-3 - (-6) = 3$. So, the ratio $\overline{\text{YZ}} : \overline{\text{XY}}$ is 4:3.

16. Choice C is correct. We can reorder the numbers in each class to discover the median, mean, mode, and range for each:

Physics I: 1, 3, 3, 4, 4, 5, 6, 7, 8, 8, 9, 9, 12, 12, 18

Physics II: 3, 3, 4, 4, 5, 5, 6, 7, 8, 8, 9, 9, 10, 11, 17

Since the median is in 3 of the four answer choices, it will provide the most information in addressing the question. Let's start there. To find the median, we take the number in the middle when in chronological order. Since there are 15 numbers in each category, this will be the 8th number, which is 7 for both Physics I and Physics II. So, the medians are also equal. At this point we can rule out every option except for choice C. For completeness, here are the other measures:

To find the mean, we add the numbers in each category and divide by the total:

$$\text{Physics I: } \frac{109}{15} \approx 7.3$$

$$\text{Physics II: } \frac{109}{15} \approx 7.3$$

Thus, we see that the means are equal.

To find the mode, we look for the number most often repeated in each series. In Physics I, the numbers 3, 4, 8, 9, and 12 are each repeated twice. In Physics II, the numbers 3, 4, 5, 8, and 9 are each repeated twice. So, we cannot compare modes.

To find the range, we subtract the smallest number in each category from the largest:

$$\text{Physics I:} 18 - 1 = 17$$

$$\text{Physics II:} 17 - 3 = 14$$

So, the range in Physics I is greater than the range in Physics II.

17. Choice A is correct. If there are half as many cupcakes (x) as brownies (y), then we can write this as $x = \frac{1}{2}y$ (or alternatively as $2x = y$). Since the sum of cupcakes and brownies is at least 150, we can write this as $x + y \geq 150$.

18. Choice B is correct. To find the probability of the union of two events, use the equation $P(S \text{ or } F) = P(S) + P(F) - P(S \text{ and } F) = \frac{90}{200} + \frac{65}{200} - \frac{27}{200}$, which simplifies to $P(S \text{ or } F) = \frac{128}{200} = \frac{16}{25}$.

19. Choice B is correct. The mode is the number that appears most often in a set of data. If no item appears most often, then the data set has no mode. In this case, Isabella ran 2 miles three times, 3 miles twice, and 6 miles once. Since she ran 2 miles most often, the mode is 2.

20. Choice C is correct. The mean, or average, is the sum of the numbers in a data set, divided by the total number of items. This data set contains six items. The total number of miles that Isabella jogged is the sum of the numbers in the right-hand column, or 18. This gives a mean of $\frac{18}{6} = 3$.

21. Choice D is correct. There are two students who read more than 7 books and scored in the 80s. We can add the number of students in each group to find the total number of students who took the test: $4 + 10 + 6 = 20$. So, the probability is 2 out of 20, or $\frac{1}{10}$.

22. Choice A is correct. We calculate the median of each group by writing the scores in order from least to greatest and then finding the value in the middle:

Group 1: 69, 77, 79, 83, so the mean is halfway between 77 and 79, or 78.

Group 2: 77, 82, 86, 88, 88, 89, 90, 92, 93, 94, so the mean is halfway between 88 and 89, or 88.5.

Group 3: 86, 89, 93, 97, 98, 99, so the mean is halfway between 93 and 97, or 95.

Thus, Group 1 has the lowest median.

23. Choice D is correct. To begin, isolate the square root sign on the left side by subtracting 1 from both sides and then making each side negative:

$$\begin{aligned} 1 - \sqrt{3 - 3x} &= x \\ -\sqrt{3 - 3x} &= x - 1 \\ \sqrt{3 - 3x} &= -x + 1 \end{aligned}$$

Then square both sides of the equation and simplify the result:

$$\left(\sqrt{3-3x}\right)^2 = (-x+1)^2$$
$$3-3x = x^2-2x+1$$

Now solve the resulting equation by moving everything to one side and factoring the resulting quadratic equation:

$$x^2+x-2=0$$
$$(x+2)(x-1)=0$$
$$x=-2, x=1$$

Therefore, the possible solutions are $x = -2$ and $x = 1$. Unfortunately, whenever you must square both sides of an equation to solve it, you run the risk of finding an incorrect solution. Consequently, we cannot automatically say that the solutions are $x = -2$ and $x = 1$. We need to check these solutions in the original equation. To do this, substitute them into the given equations and make sure the result is a true statement:

$$x=-2$$
$$1-\sqrt{3-3(-2)}=-2$$
$$1-\sqrt{9}=-2$$
$$1-3=-2$$
true

$$x=1$$
$$1-\sqrt{3-3(1)}=1$$
$$1-\sqrt{0}=1$$
$$1=1$$
true

Since both choices lead to a true statement, the solution is $x = -2, x = 1$.

24. Choice B is correct. The roots of a quadratic function $f(x)$ are the values of x where $f(x) = 0$. Quadratic functions may have two real roots, two imaginary roots, or one real double root. A quadratic function written in the form $f(x) = (x-a)(x-b)$ has roots at $x = a$ and $x = b$. Therefore, to find $f(x)$, substitute the given roots for a and b into $f(x) = (x-a)(x-b)$ and simplify:

$$\begin{aligned} f(x) &= (x-a)(x-b) \\ &= (x-3)(x-(-7)) \\ &= (x-3)(x+7) \\ &= x^2+4x-21 \end{aligned}$$

25. Choice C is correct. The denominator of the second rational expression may be factored as $(x-4)(x+1)$. Since the first expression has a denominator of $(x-4)$, the least common denominator of the two rational expressions is $(x-4)(x+1)$. Multiplying the top and bottom of the first expression by $(x+1)$, we see that $\frac{4}{x-4} = \frac{4\,(x+1)}{(x-4)(x+1)}$. The sum may be written as $\frac{4(x+1)-2x}{(x-4)(x+1)}$, which simplifies to $\frac{2x+4}{(x-4)(x+1)}$. Factoring out a 2 in the numerator gives: $\frac{2(x+2)}{(x-4)(x+1)}$.

26. Choice A is correct. Distributing each term in the expression, $x-5$, across each term in the trinomial, gives:

$$3x^4-x^3-6x-15x^3+5x^2+30$$

Writing the expression in standard form gives:

$$3x^4 - 16x^3 + 5x^2 - 6x + 30$$

27. Choice C is correct. In a parallelogram, consecutive angles are supplementary; that is, the sum of their measures is 180°. Use this to write an equation and then solve for x.

$$\begin{aligned} m\angle A + m\angle B &= 180° \\ (5x) + (2x - 9) &= 180 \\ 7x - 9 &= 180 \\ 7x &= 189 \\ x &= 27 \end{aligned}$$

Now use this value to find $m\angle A$ and $m\angle B$.

$$\begin{aligned} m\angle A &= 5x \\ &= 5(27) \\ &= 135° \end{aligned} \qquad \begin{aligned} m\angle B &= 2x - 9 \\ &= 2(27) - 9 \\ &= 45° \end{aligned}$$

In a parallelogram, opposite angles are congruent. Thus, $m\angle B = m\angle C = 45°$.

28. The correct answer is 35.6. The area of a circle is given by the formula $A = \pi r^2$, where r is the length of the radius. A sector is a slice of a circle bounded by two radii. Its area is proportional to the angle between the two radii bounding the sector. Thus, the area of a sector with angle θ (in degrees) is given by the formula:

$$A = \pi r^2 \times \frac{\theta}{360}$$

We first must find the angle for the sector. If 105° is the angle outside the shaded sector, and the interior angles of a circle add up to 360°, then the angle for the shaded sector is $360 - 105 = 255°$. Substitute the value of the radius and angle into this formula and simplify. Round the result to the nearest tenth.

$$\begin{aligned} A &= \pi(4)^2 \times \frac{255}{360} \\ &= 16\pi \times \frac{255}{360} \\ &\approx 35.6 \end{aligned}$$

29. The correct answer is 431 or 432. The tank is a cylinder, so its volume is calculated by using the formula $V = \pi r^2 h$, where r is the radius of the tank and h is the height. Since the tank is only $\frac{3}{4}$ of the way full, we can write the volume as: $V = \frac{3}{4}\pi r^2 h$. Using 42 for the radius and 24 for the height, we can calculate the volume of water in cubic inches:

$$V = \frac{3}{4}\pi(42)^2(24) \approx 99{,}751.85 \text{ in}^3$$

Now we convert cubic inches to gallons. As given in the problem, there are 231 cubic inches in a gallon. So, we can use unit conversions:

$$\frac{99{,}751.85 \text{ in}^3}{1} \times \frac{1 \text{ gal}}{231 \text{ in}^3} \approx 431.826 \text{ gal}$$

Rounding to the nearest whole number gives 432 gallons. Truncating would give 431 gallons

30. The correct answer is 21.7 or 21.8. The first step is to draw into the diagram what we are told or can deduce. The circle intercepts the triangle at the midpoints of its sides, so draw a radius that meets the midpoint of AB (marked D below). Next, draw a line from A to the center, noting that this line bisects $\angle BAC$; thus, $m\angle DAO = \frac{1}{2} \times 60° = 30°$. Since D is the midpoint of AB, we know that $AD = \frac{1}{2}(AB) = 6$.

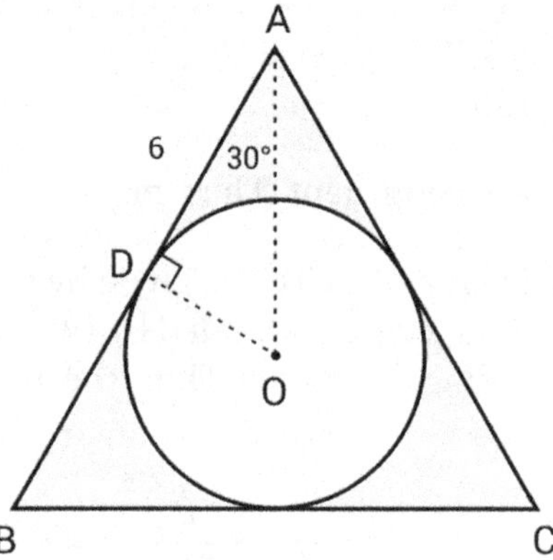

Now we can see that ΔADO is a 30-60-90 triangle. In a 30-60-90 triangle, the ratio of the lengths of the sides is $1{:}\sqrt{3}{:}\,2$. In this triangle, 6 corresponds to $\sqrt{3}$ and the radius r corresponds to 1. Use a proportion to calculate r:

$$\frac{1}{\sqrt{3}} = \frac{r}{6}$$
$$r\sqrt{3} = 6$$
$$r = \frac{6}{\sqrt{3}} \approx 3.464$$

Now we can find the circumference using the formula $C = 2\pi r$:

$$C = 2\pi(3.464) \approx 21.77$$

Rounding to the nearest tenth, this gives a circumference of 21.8 cm or truncating gives 21.7 cm.

31. The correct answer is 10.5. Suppose Gillian purchases a rug for \$100. She then adds 30% to the price she paid for it and lists it for sale at regular price:

$$\text{Regular} = \$100 + (30\% \times \$100) = \$100 + \$30 = \$130$$

She later marks the remaining rugs down by 15%:

$$\text{Clearance} = \$130 - (15\% \times \$130) = \$130 - \$19.5 = \$110.5$$

Calculate her profit on the discounted rugs as a percentage of what she paid for it:

$$\text{Profit} = \frac{\text{price sold for} - \text{price paid for}}{\text{price paid for}}$$

$$\text{Profit} = \frac{110.5 - 100}{100} = \frac{10.5}{100} = 10.5\%$$

How to Overcome Test Anxiety

Just the thought of taking a test is enough to make most people a little nervous. A test is an important event that can have a long-term impact on your future, so it's important to take it seriously and it's natural to feel anxious about performing well. But just because anxiety is normal, that doesn't mean that it's helpful in test taking, or that you should simply accept it as part of your life. Anxiety can have a variety of effects. These effects can be mild, like making you feel slightly nervous, or severe, like blocking your ability to focus or remember even a simple detail.

If you experience test anxiety—whether severe or mild—it's important to know how to beat it. To discover this, first you need to understand what causes test anxiety.

Causes of Test Anxiety

While we often think of anxiety as an uncontrollable emotional state, it can actually be caused by simple, practical things. One of the most common causes of test anxiety is that a person does not feel adequately prepared for their test. This feeling can be the result of many different issues such as poor study habits or lack of organization, but the most common culprit is time management. Starting to study too late, failing to organize your study time to cover all of the material, or being distracted while you study will mean that you're not well prepared for the test. This may lead to cramming the night before, which will cause you to be physically and mentally exhausted for the test. Poor time management also contributes to feelings of stress, fear, and hopelessness as you realize you are not well prepared but don't know what to do about it.

Other times, test anxiety is not related to your preparation for the test but comes from unresolved fear. This may be a past failure on a test, or poor performance on tests in general. It may come from comparing yourself to others who seem to be performing better or from the stress of living up to expectations. Anxiety may be driven by fears of the future—how failure on this test would affect your educational and career goals. These fears are often completely irrational, but they can still negatively impact your test performance.

Elements of Test Anxiety

As mentioned earlier, test anxiety is considered to be an emotional state, but it has physical and mental components as well. Sometimes you may not even realize that you are suffering from test anxiety until you notice the physical symptoms. These can include trembling hands, rapid heartbeat, sweating, nausea, and tense muscles. Extreme anxiety may lead to fainting or vomiting. Obviously, any of these symptoms can have a negative impact on testing. It is important to recognize them as soon as they begin to occur so that you can address the problem before it damages your performance.

The mental components of test anxiety include trouble focusing and inability to remember learned information. During a test, your mind is on high alert, which can help you recall information and stay focused for an extended period of time. However, anxiety interferes with your mind's natural processes, causing you to blank out, even on the questions you know well. The strain of testing during anxiety makes it difficult to stay focused, especially on a test that may take several hours. Extreme anxiety can take a huge mental toll, making it difficult not only to recall test information but even to understand the test questions or pull your thoughts together.

Effects of Test Anxiety

Test anxiety is like a disease—if left untreated, it will get progressively worse. Anxiety leads to poor performance, and this reinforces the feelings of fear and failure, which in turn lead to poor performances on subsequent tests. It can grow from a mild nervousness to a crippling condition. If allowed to progress, test anxiety can have a big impact on your schooling, and consequently on your future.

Test anxiety can spread to other parts of your life. Anxiety on tests can become anxiety in any stressful situation, and blanking on a test can turn into panicking in a job situation. But fortunately, you don't have to let anxiety rule your testing and determine your grades. There are a number of relatively simple steps you can take to move past anxiety and function normally on a test and in the rest of life.

Physical Steps for Beating Test Anxiety

While test anxiety is a serious problem, the good news is that it can be overcome. It doesn't have to control your ability to think and remember information. While it may take time, you can begin taking steps today to beat anxiety.

Just as your first hint that you may be struggling with anxiety comes from the physical symptoms, the first step to treating it is also physical. Rest is crucial for having a clear, strong mind. If you are tired, it is much easier to give in to anxiety. But if you establish good sleep habits, your body and mind will be ready to perform optimally, without the strain of exhaustion. Additionally, sleeping well helps you to retain information better, so you're more likely to recall the answers when you see the test questions.

Getting good sleep means more than going to bed on time. It's important to allow your brain time to relax. Take study breaks from time to time so it doesn't get overworked, and don't study right before bed. Take time to rest your mind before trying to rest your body, or you may find it difficult to fall asleep.

Along with sleep, other aspects of physical health are important in preparing for a test. Good nutrition is vital for good brain function. Sugary foods and drinks may give a burst of energy but this burst is followed by a crash, both physically and emotionally. Instead, fuel your body with protein and vitamin-rich foods.

Also, drink plenty of water. Dehydration can lead to headaches and exhaustion, especially if your brain is already under stress from the rigors of the test. Particularly if your test is a long one, drink water during the breaks. And if possible, take an energy-boosting snack to eat between sections.

Along with sleep and diet, a third important part of physical health is exercise. Maintaining a steady workout schedule is helpful, but even taking 5-minute study breaks to walk can help get your blood pumping faster and clear your head. Exercise also releases endorphins, which contribute to a positive feeling and can help combat test anxiety.

When you nurture your physical health, you are also contributing to your mental health. If your body is healthy, your mind is much more likely to be healthy as well. So take time to rest, nourish your body with healthy food and water, and get moving as much as possible. Taking these physical steps will make you stronger and more able to take the mental steps necessary to overcome test anxiety.

Mental Steps for Beating Test Anxiety

Working on the mental side of test anxiety can be more challenging, but as with the physical side, there are clear steps you can take to overcome it. As mentioned earlier, test anxiety often stems from lack of preparation, so the obvious solution is to prepare for the test. Effective studying may be the most important weapon you have for beating test anxiety, but you can and should employ several other mental tools to combat fear.

First, boost your confidence by reminding yourself of past success—tests or projects that you aced. If you're putting as much effort into preparing for this test as you did for those, there's no reason you should expect to fail here. Work hard to prepare; then trust your preparation.

Second, surround yourself with encouraging people. It can be helpful to find a study group, but be sure that the people you're around will encourage a positive attitude. If you spend time with others who are anxious or cynical, this will only contribute to your own anxiety. Look for others who are motivated to study hard from a desire to succeed, not from a fear of failure.

Third, reward yourself. A test is physically and mentally tiring, even without anxiety, and it can be helpful to have something to look forward to. Plan an activity following the test, regardless of the outcome, such as going to a movie or getting ice cream.

When you are taking the test, if you find yourself beginning to feel anxious, remind yourself that you know the material. Visualize successfully completing the test. Then take a few deep, relaxing breaths and return to it. Work through the questions carefully but with confidence, knowing that you are capable of succeeding.

Developing a healthy mental approach to test taking will also aid in other areas of life. Test anxiety affects more than just the actual test—it can be damaging to your mental health and even contribute to depression. It's important to beat test anxiety before it becomes a problem for more than testing.

Study Strategy

Being prepared for the test is necessary to combat anxiety, but what does being prepared look like? You may study for hours on end and still not feel prepared. What you need is a strategy for test prep. The next few pages outline our recommended steps to help you plan out and conquer the challenge of preparation.

Step 1: Scope Out the Test

Learn everything you can about the format (multiple choice, essay, etc.) and what will be on the test. Gather any study materials, course outlines, or sample exams that may be available. Not only will this help you to prepare, but knowing what to expect can help to alleviate test anxiety.

Step 2: Map Out the Material

Look through the textbook or study guide and make note of how many chapters or sections it has. Then divide these over the time you have. For example, if a book has 15 chapters and you have five days to study, you need to cover three chapters each day. Even better, if you have the time, leave an extra day at the end for overall review after you have gone through the material in depth.

If time is limited, you may need to prioritize the material. Look through it and make note of which sections you think you already have a good grasp on, and which need review. While you are studying, skim quickly through the familiar sections and take more time on the challenging parts.

Write out your plan so you don't get lost as you go. Having a written plan also helps you feel more in control of the study, so anxiety is less likely to arise from feeling overwhelmed at the amount to cover.

STEP 3: GATHER YOUR TOOLS

Decide what study method works best for you. Do you prefer to highlight in the book as you study and then go back over the highlighted portions? Or do you type out notes of the important information? Or is it helpful to make flashcards that you can carry with you? Assemble the pens, index cards, highlighters, post-it notes, and any other materials you may need so you won't be distracted by getting up to find things while you study.

If you're having a hard time retaining the information or organizing your notes, experiment with different methods. For example, try color-coding by subject with colored pens, highlighters, or post-it notes. If you learn better by hearing, try recording yourself reading your notes so you can listen while in the car, working out, or simply sitting at your desk. Ask a friend to quiz you from your flashcards, or try teaching someone the material to solidify it in your mind.

STEP 4: CREATE YOUR ENVIRONMENT

It's important to avoid distractions while you study. This includes both the obvious distractions like visitors and the subtle distractions like an uncomfortable chair (or a too-comfortable couch that makes you want to fall asleep). Set up the best study environment possible: good lighting and a comfortable work area. If background music helps you focus, you may want to turn it on, but otherwise keep the room quiet. If you are using a computer to take notes, be sure you don't have any other windows open, especially applications like social media, games, or anything else that could distract you. Silence your phone and turn off notifications. Be sure to keep water close by so you stay hydrated while you study (but avoid unhealthy drinks and snacks).

Also, take into account the best time of day to study. Are you freshest first thing in the morning? Try to set aside some time then to work through the material. Is your mind clearer in the afternoon or evening? Schedule your study session then. Another method is to study at the same time of day that you will take the test, so that your brain gets used to working on the material at that time and will be ready to focus at test time.

STEP 5: STUDY!

Once you have done all the study preparation, it's time to settle into the actual studying. Sit down, take a few moments to settle your mind so you can focus, and begin to follow your study plan. Don't give in to distractions or let yourself procrastinate. This is your time to prepare so you'll be ready to fearlessly approach the test. Make the most of the time and stay focused.

Of course, you don't want to burn out. If you study too long you may find that you're not retaining the information very well. Take regular study breaks. For example, taking five minutes out of every hour to walk briskly, breathing deeply and swinging your arms, can help your mind stay fresh.

As you get to the end of each chapter or section, it's a good idea to do a quick review. Remind yourself of what you learned and work on any difficult parts. When you feel that you've mastered the material, move on to the next part. At the end of your study session, briefly skim through your notes again.

But while review is helpful, cramming last minute is NOT. If at all possible, work ahead so that you won't need to fit all your study into the last day. Cramming overloads your brain with more information than it can process and retain, and your tired mind may struggle to recall even previously learned information when it is overwhelmed with last-minute study. Also, the urgent nature of cramming and the stress placed on your brain contribute to anxiety. You'll be more likely to go to the test feeling unprepared and having trouble thinking clearly.

So don't cram, and don't stay up late before the test, even just to review your notes at a leisurely pace. Your brain needs rest more than it needs to go over the information again. In fact, plan to finish your studies by noon or early afternoon the day before the test. Give your brain the rest of the day to relax or focus on other things, and get a good night's sleep. Then you will be fresh for the test and better able to recall what you've studied.

Step 6: Take a Practice Test

Many courses offer sample tests, either online or in the study materials. This is an excellent resource to check whether you have mastered the material, as well as to prepare for the test format and environment.

Check the test format ahead of time: the number of questions, the type (multiple choice, free response, etc.), and the time limit. Then create a plan for working through them. For example, if you have 30 minutes to take a 60-question test, your limit is 30 seconds per question. Spend less time on the questions you know well so that you can take more time on the difficult ones.

If you have time to take several practice tests, take the first one open book, with no time limit. Work through the questions at your own pace and make sure you fully understand them. Gradually work up to taking a test under test conditions: sit at a desk with all study materials put away and set a timer. Pace yourself to make sure you finish the test with time to spare and go back to check your answers if you have time.

After each test, check your answers. On the questions you missed, be sure you understand why you missed them. Did you misread the question (tests can use tricky wording)? Did you forget the information? Or was it something you hadn't learned? Go back and study any shaky areas that the practice tests reveal.

Taking these tests not only helps with your grade, but also aids in combating test anxiety. If you're already used to the test conditions, you're less likely to worry about it, and working through tests until you're scoring well gives you a confidence boost. Go through the practice tests until you feel comfortable, and then you can go into the test knowing that you're ready for it.

Test Tips

On test day, you should be confident, knowing that you've prepared well and are ready to answer the questions. But aside from preparation, there are several test day strategies you can employ to maximize your performance.

First, as stated before, get a good night's sleep the night before the test (and for several nights before that, if possible). Go into the test with a fresh, alert mind rather than staying up late to study.

Try not to change too much about your normal routine on the day of the test. It's important to eat a nutritious breakfast, but if you normally don't eat breakfast at all, consider eating just a protein bar. If you're a coffee drinker, go ahead and have your normal coffee. Just make sure you time it so that the caffeine doesn't wear off right in the middle of your test. Avoid sugary beverages, and drink enough water to stay hydrated but not so much that you need a restroom break 10 minutes into the test. If your test isn't first thing in the morning, consider going for a walk or doing a light workout before the test to get your blood flowing.

Allow yourself enough time to get ready, and leave for the test with plenty of time to spare so you won't have the anxiety of scrambling to arrive in time. Another reason to be early is to select a good seat. It's helpful to sit away from doors and windows, which can be distracting. Find a good seat, get out your supplies, and settle your mind before the test begins.

When the test begins, start by going over the instructions carefully, even if you already know what to expect. Make sure you avoid any careless mistakes by following the directions.

Then begin working through the questions, pacing yourself as you've practiced. If you're not sure on an answer, don't spend too much time on it, and don't let it shake your confidence. Either skip it and come back later, or eliminate as many wrong answers as possible and guess among the remaining ones. Don't dwell on these questions as you continue—put them out of your mind and focus on what lies ahead.

Be sure to read all of the answer choices, even if you're sure the first one is the right answer. Sometimes you'll find a better one if you keep reading. But don't second-guess yourself if you do immediately know the answer. Your gut instinct is usually right. Don't let test anxiety rob you of the information you know.

If you have time at the end of the test (and if the test format allows), go back and review your answers. Be cautious about changing any, since your first instinct tends to be correct, but make sure you didn't misread any of the questions or accidentally mark the wrong answer choice. Look over any you skipped and make an educated guess.

At the end, leave the test feeling confident. You've done your best, so don't waste time worrying about your performance or wishing you could change anything. Instead, celebrate the successful completion of this test. And finally, use this test to learn how to deal with anxiety even better next time.

Review Video: Test Anxiety
Visit mometrix.com/academy and enter code: 100340

Important Qualification

Not all anxiety is created equal. If your test anxiety is causing major issues in your life beyond the classroom or testing center, or if you are experiencing troubling physical symptoms related to your anxiety, it may be a sign of a serious physiological or psychological condition. If this sounds like your situation, we strongly encourage you to seek professional help.

How to Overcome Your Fear of Math

The word *math* is enough to strike fear into most hearts. How many of us have memories of sitting through confusing lectures, wrestling over mind-numbing homework, or taking tests that still seem incomprehensible even after hours of study? Years after graduation, many still shudder at these memories.

The fact is, math is not just a classroom subject. It has real-world implications that you face every day, whether you realize it or not. This may be balancing your monthly budget, deciding how many supplies to buy for a project, or simply splitting a meal check with friends. The idea of daily confrontations with math can be so paralyzing that some develop a condition known as *math anxiety*.

But you do NOT need to be paralyzed by this anxiety! In fact, while you may have thought all your life that you're not good at math, or that your brain isn't wired to understand it, the truth is that you may have been conditioned to think this way. From your earliest school days, the way you were taught affected the way you viewed different subjects. And the way math has been taught has changed.

Several decades ago, there was a shift in American math classrooms. The focus changed from traditional problem-solving to a conceptual view of topics, de-emphasizing the importance of learning the basics and building on them. The solid foundation necessary for math progression and confidence was undermined. Math became more of a vague concept than a concrete idea. Today, it is common to think of math, not as a straightforward system, but as a mysterious, complicated method that can't be fully understood unless you're a genius.

This is why you may still have nightmares about being called on to answer a difficult problem in front of the class. Math anxiety is a very real, though unnecessary, fear.

Math anxiety may begin with a single class period. Let's say you missed a day in 6th grade math and never quite understood the concept that was taught while you were gone. Since math is cumulative, with each new concept building on past ones, this could very well affect the rest of your math career. Without that one day's knowledge, it will be difficult to understand any other concepts that link to it. Rather than realizing that you're just missing one key piece, you may begin to believe that you're simply not capable of understanding math.

This belief can change the way you approach other classes, career options, and everyday life experiences, if you become anxious at the thought that math might be required. A student who loves science may choose a different path of study upon realizing that multiple math classes will be required for a degree. An aspiring medical student may hesitate at the thought of going through the necessary math classes. For some this anxiety escalates into a more extreme state known as *math phobia*.

Math anxiety is challenging to address because it is rooted deeply and may come from a variety of causes: an embarrassing moment in class, a teacher who did not explain concepts well and contributed to a shaky foundation, or a failed test that contributed to the belief of math failure.

These causes add up over time, encouraged by society's popular view that math is hard and unpleasant. Eventually a person comes to firmly believe that he or she is simply bad at math. This belief makes it difficult to grasp new concepts or even remember old ones. Homework and test grades begin to slip, which only confirms the belief. The poor performance is not due to lack of ability but is caused by math anxiety.

Math anxiety is an emotional issue, not a lack of intelligence. But when it becomes deeply rooted, it can become more than just an emotional problem. Physical symptoms appear. Blood pressure may rise and heartbeat may quicken at the sight of a math problem – or even the thought of math! This fear leads to a mental block. When someone with math anxiety is asked to perform a calculation, even a basic problem can seem overwhelming and impossible. The emotional and physical response to the thought of math prevents the brain from working through it logically.

The more this happens, the more a person's confidence drops, and the more math anxiety is generated. This vicious cycle must be broken!

The first step in breaking the cycle is to go back to very beginning and make sure you really understand the basics of how math works and why it works. It is not enough to memorize rules for multiplication and division. If you don't know WHY these rules work, your foundation will be shaky and you will be at risk of developing a phobia. Understanding mathematical concepts not only promotes confidence and security, but allows you to build on this understanding for new concepts. Additionally, you can solve unfamiliar problems using familiar concepts and processes.

Why is it that students in other countries regularly outperform American students in math? The answer likely boils down to a couple of things: the foundation of mathematical conceptual understanding and societal perception. While students in the US are not expected to *like* or *get* math, in many other nations, students are expected not only to understand math but also to excel at it.

Changing the American view of math that leads to math anxiety is a monumental task. It requires changing the training of teachers nationwide, from kindergarten through high school, so that they learn to teach the *why* behind math and to combat the wrong math views that students may develop. It also involves changing the stigma associated with math, so that it is no longer viewed as unpleasant and incomprehensible. While these are necessary changes, they are challenging and will take time. But in the meantime, math anxiety is not irreversible—it can be faced and defeated, one person at a time.

False Beliefs

One reason math anxiety has taken such hold is that several false beliefs have been created and shared until they became widely accepted. Some of these unhelpful beliefs include the following:

There is only one way to solve a math problem. In the same way that you can choose from different driving routes and still arrive at the same house, you can solve a math problem using different methods and still find the correct answer. A person who understands the reasoning behind math calculations may be able to look at an unfamiliar concept and find the right answer, just by applying logic to the knowledge they already have. This approach may be different than what is taught in the classroom, but it is still valid. Unfortunately, even many teachers view math as a subject where the best course of action is to memorize the rule or process for each problem rather than as a place for students to exercise logic and creativity in finding a solution.

Many people don't have a mind for math. A person who has struggled due to poor teaching or math anxiety may falsely believe that he or she doesn't have the mental capacity to grasp mathematical concepts. Most of the time, this is false. Many people find that when they are relieved of their math anxiety, they have more than enough brainpower to understand math.

Men are naturally better at math than women. Even though research has shown this to be false, many young women still avoid math careers and classes because of their belief that their math abilities are inferior. Many girls have come to believe that math is a male skill and have given up trying to understand or enjoy it.

Counting aids are bad. Something like counting on your fingers or drawing out a problem to visualize it may be frowned on as childish or a crutch, but these devices can help you get a tangible understanding of a problem or a concept.

Sadly, many students buy into these ideologies at an early age. A young girl who enjoys math class may be conditioned to think that she doesn't actually have the brain for it because math is for boys, and may turn her energies to other pursuits, permanently closing the door on a wide range of opportunities. A child who finds the right answer but doesn't follow the teacher's method may believe that he is doing it wrong and isn't good at math. A student who never had a problem with math before may have a poor teacher and become confused, yet believe that the problem is because she doesn't have a mathematical mind.

Students who have bought into these erroneous beliefs quickly begin to add their own anxieties, adapting them to their own personal situations:

I'll never use this in real life. A huge number of people wrongly believe that math is irrelevant outside the classroom. By adopting this mindset, they are handicapping themselves for a life in a mathematical world, as well as limiting their career choices. When they are inevitably faced with real-world math, they are conditioning themselves to respond with anxiety.

I'm not quick enough. While timed tests and quizzes, or even simply comparing yourself with other students in the class, can lead to this belief, speed is not an indicator of skill level. A person can work very slowly yet understand at a deep level.

If I can understand it, it's too easy. People with a low view of their own abilities tend to think that if they are able to grasp a concept, it must be simple. They cannot accept the idea that they are capable of understanding math. This belief will make it harder to learn, no matter how intelligent they are.

I just can't learn this. An overwhelming number of people think this, from young children to adults, and much of the time it is simply not true. But this mindset can turn into a self-fulfilling prophecy that keeps you from exercising and growing your math ability.

The good news is, each of these myths can be debunked. For most people, they are based on emotion and psychology, NOT on actual ability! It will take time, effort, and the desire to change, but change is possible. Even if you have spent years thinking that you don't have the capability to understand math, it is not too late to uncover your true ability and find relief from the anxiety that surrounds math.

Math Strategies

It is important to have a plan of attack to combat math anxiety. There are many useful strategies for pinpointing the fears or myths and eradicating them:

Go back to the basics. For most people, math anxiety stems from a poor foundation. You may think that you have a complete understanding of addition and subtraction, or even decimals and percentages, but make absolutely sure. Learning math is different from learning other subjects. For example, when you learn history, you study various time periods and places and events. It may be important to memorize dates or find out about the lives of famous people. When you move from US history to world history, there will be some overlap, but a large amount of the information will be new. Mathematical concepts, on the other hand, are very closely linked and highly dependent on each other. It's like climbing a ladder – if a rung is missing from your understanding, it may be difficult or impossible for you to climb any higher, no matter how hard you try. So go back and make sure your math foundation is strong. This may mean taking a remedial math course, going to a tutor to work through the shaky concepts, or just going through your old homework to make sure you really understand it.

Speak the language. Math has a large vocabulary of terms and phrases unique to working problems. Sometimes these are completely new terms, and sometimes they are common words, but are used differently in a math setting. If you can't speak the language, it will be very difficult to get a thorough understanding of the concepts. It's common for students to think that they don't understand math when they simply don't understand the vocabulary. The good news is that this is fairly easy to fix. Brushing up on any terms you aren't quite sure of can help bring the rest of the concepts into focus.

Check your anxiety level. When you think about math, do you feel nervous or uncomfortable? Do you struggle with feelings of inadequacy, even on concepts that you know you've already learned? It's important to understand your specific math anxieties, and what triggers them. When you catch yourself falling back on a false belief, mentally replace it with the truth. Don't let yourself believe that you can't learn, or that struggling with a concept means you'll never understand it. Instead, remind yourself of how much you've already learned and dwell on that past success. Visualize grasping the new concept, linking it to your old knowledge, and moving on to the next challenge. Also, learn how to manage anxiety when it arises. There are many techniques for coping with the irrational fears that rise to the surface when you enter the math classroom. This may include controlled breathing, replacing negative thoughts with positive ones, or visualizing success. Anxiety interferes with your ability to concentrate and absorb information, which in turn contributes to greater anxiety. If you can learn how to regain control of your thinking, you will be better able to pay attention, make progress, and succeed!

Don't go it alone. Like any deeply ingrained belief, math anxiety is not easy to eradicate. And there is no need for you to wrestle through it on your own. It will take time, and many people find that speaking with a counselor or psychiatrist helps. They can help you develop strategies for responding to anxiety and overcoming old ideas. Additionally, it can be very helpful to take a short course or seek out a math tutor to help you find and fix the missing rungs on your ladder and make sure that you're ready to progress to the next level. You can also find a number of math aids online: courses that will teach you mental devices for figuring out problems, how to get the most out of your math classes, etc.

Check your math attitude. No matter how much you want to learn and overcome your anxiety, you'll have trouble if you still have a negative attitude toward math. If you think it's too hard, or just have general feelings of dread about math, it will be hard to learn and to break through the anxiety. Work on cultivating a positive math attitude. Remind yourself that math is not just a hurdle to be cleared, but a valuable asset. When you view math with a positive attitude, you'll be much more likely to understand and even enjoy it. This is something you must do for yourself. You may find it helpful to visit with a counselor. Your tutor, friends, and family may cheer you on in your endeavors. But your greatest asset is yourself. You are inside your own mind – tell yourself what you need to hear. Relive past victories. Remind yourself that you are capable of understanding math. Root out any false beliefs that linger and replace them with positive truths. Even if it doesn't feel true at first, it will begin to affect your thinking and pave the way for a positive, anxiety-free mindset.

Aside from these general strategies, there are a number of specific practical things you can do to begin your journey toward overcoming math anxiety. Something as simple as learning a new note-taking strategy can change the way you approach math and give you more confidence and understanding. New study techniques can also make a huge difference.

Math anxiety leads to bad habits. If it causes you to be afraid of answering a question in class, you may gravitate toward the back row. You may be embarrassed to ask for help. And you may procrastinate on assignments, which leads to rushing through them at the last moment when it's too late to get a better understanding. It's important to identify your negative behaviors and replace them with positive ones:

Prepare ahead of time. Read the lesson before you go to class. Being exposed to the topics that will be covered in class ahead of time, even if you don't understand them perfectly, is extremely helpful in increasing what you retain from the lecture. Do your homework and, if you're still shaky, go over some extra problems. The key to a solid understanding of math is practice.

Sit front and center. When you can easily see and hear, you'll understand more, and you'll avoid the distractions of other students if no one is in front of you. Plus, you're more likely to be sitting with students who are positive and engaged, rather than others with math anxiety. Let their positive math attitude rub off on you.

Ask questions in class and out. If you don't understand something, just ask. If you need a more in-depth explanation, the teacher may need to work with you outside of class, but often it's a simple concept you don't quite understand, and a single question may clear it up. If you wait, you may not be able to follow the rest of the day's lesson. For extra help, most professors have office hours outside of class when you can go over concepts one-on-one to clear up any uncertainties. Additionally, there may be a *math lab* or study session you can attend for homework help. Take advantage of this.

Review. Even if you feel that you've fully mastered a concept, review it periodically to reinforce it. Going over an old lesson has several benefits: solidifying your understanding, giving you a confidence boost, and even giving some new insights into material that you're currently learning! Don't let yourself get rusty. That can lead to problems with learning later concepts.

Teaching Tips

While the math student's mindset is the most crucial to overcoming math anxiety, it is also important for others to adjust their math attitudes. Teachers and parents have an enormous influence on how students relate to math. They can either contribute to math confidence or math anxiety.

As a parent or teacher, it is very important to convey a positive math attitude. Retelling horror stories of your own bad experience with math will contribute to a new generation of math anxiety. Even if you don't share your experiences, others will be able to sense your fears and may begin to believe them.

Even a careless comment can have a big impact, so watch for phrases like *He's not good at math* or *I never liked math*. You are a crucial role model, and your children or students will unconsciously adopt your mindset. Give them a positive example to follow. Rather than teaching them to fear the math world before they even know it, teach them about all its potential and excitement.

Work to present math as an integral, beautiful, and understandable part of life. Encourage creativity in solving problems. Watch for false beliefs and dispel them. Cross the lines between subjects: integrate history, English, and music with math. Show students how math is used every day, and how the entire world is based on mathematical principles, from the pull of gravity to the shape of seashells. Instead of letting students see math as a necessary evil, direct them to view it as an imaginative, beautiful art form – an art form that they are capable of mastering and using.

Don't give too narrow a view of math. It is more than just numbers. Yes, working problems and learning formulas is a large part of classroom math. But don't let the teaching stop there. Teach students about the everyday implications of math. Show them how nature works according to the laws of mathematics, and take them outside to make discoveries of their own. Expose them to math-related careers by inviting visiting speakers, asking students to do research and presentations, and learning students' interests and aptitudes on a personal level.

Demonstrate the importance of math. Many people see math as nothing more than a required stepping stone to their degree, a nuisance with no real usefulness. Teach students that algebra is used every day in managing their bank accounts, in following recipes, and in scheduling the day's events. Show them how learning to do geometric proofs helps them to develop logical thinking, an invaluable life skill. Let them see that math surrounds them and is integrally linked to their daily lives: that weather predictions are based on math, that math was used to design cars and other machines, etc. Most of all, give them the tools to use math to enrich their lives.

Make math as tangible as possible. Use visual aids and objects that can be touched. It is much easier to grasp a concept when you can hold it in your hands and manipulate it, rather than just listening to the lecture. Encourage math outside of the classroom. The real world is full of measuring, counting, and calculating, so let students participate in this. Keep your eyes open for numbers and patterns to discuss. Talk about how scores are calculated in sports games and how far apart plants are placed in a garden row for maximum growth. Build the mindset that math is a normal and interesting part of daily life.

Finally, find math resources that help to build a positive math attitude. There are a number of books that show math as fascinating and exciting while teaching important concepts, for example: *The Math Curse; A Wrinkle in Time; The Phantom Tollbooth;* and *Fractals, Googols and Other Mathematical Tales*. You can also find a number of online resources: math puzzles and games, videos that show math in nature, and communities of math enthusiasts. On a local level, students can compete in a variety of math competitions with other schools or join a math club.

The student who experiences math as exciting and interesting is unlikely to suffer from math anxiety. Going through life without this handicap is an immense advantage and opens many doors that others have closed through their fear.

Self-Check

Whether you suffer from math anxiety or not, chances are that you have been exposed to some of the false beliefs mentioned above. Now is the time to check yourself for any errors you may have accepted. Do you think you're not wired for math? Or that you don't need to understand it since you're not planning on a math career? Do you think math is just too difficult for the average person?

Find the errors you've taken to heart and replace them with positive thinking. Are you capable of learning math? Yes! Can you control your anxiety? Yes! These errors will resurface from time to time, so be watchful. Don't let others with math anxiety influence you or sway your confidence. If you're having trouble with a concept, find help. Don't let it discourage you!

Create a plan of attack for defeating math anxiety and sharpening your skills. Do some research and decide if it would help you to take a class, get a tutor, or find some online resources to fine-tune your knowledge. Make the effort to get good nutrition, hydration, and sleep so that you are operating at full capacity. Remind yourself daily that you are skilled and that anxiety does not control you. Your mind is capable of so much more than you know. Give it the tools it needs to grow and thrive.

Tell Us Your Story

We at Mometrix would like to extend our heartfelt thanks to you for letting us be a part of your journey. It is an honor to serve people from all walks of life, people like you, who are committed to building the best future they can for themselves.

We know that each person's situation is unique. But we also know that, whether you are a young student or a mother of four, you care about working to make your own life and the lives of those around you better.

That's why we want to hear your story.

We want to know why you're taking this test. We want to know about the trials you've gone through to get here. And we want to know about the successes you've experienced after taking and passing your test.

In addition to your story, which can be an inspiration both to us and to others, we value your feedback. We want to know both what you loved about our book and what you think we can improve on.

The team at Mometrix would be absolutely thrilled to hear from you! So please, send us an email at tellusyourstory@mometrix.com or visit us at mometrix.com/tellusyourstory.php and let's stay in touch.

Additional Bonus Material

Due to our efforts to try to keep this book to a manageable length, we've created a link that will give you access to all of your additional bonus material:

mometrix.com/bonus948/psat

Made in the USA
Las Vegas, NV
02 September 2023